GLOBAL SECURITY IN THE TWENTY-FIRST CENTURY

GLOBAL SECURITY IN THE TWENTY-FIRST CENTURY

The Quest for Power and the Search for Peace

Second Edition

Sean Kay

ROWMAN & LITTLEFIELD PUBLISHERS, INC.

Lanham • Boulder • New York • Toronto • Plymouth, UK

Published by Rowman & Littlefield Publishers, Inc.
A wholly owned subsidiary of The Rowman & Littlefield Publishing Group, Inc.
4501 Forbes Boulevard, Suite 200, Lanham, Maryland 20706
http://www.rowmanlittlefield.com

Estover Road, Plymouth PL6 7PY, United Kingdom

British Library Cataloguing in Publication Information Available

Library of Congress Cataloging-in-Publication Data

Kay, Sean, 1967-
  Global security in the twenty-first century : the quest for power and the search for peace / Sean Kay. — 2nd ed.
    p. cm.
  Includes bibliographical references and index.
  ISBN 978-1-4422-0613-7 (cloth : alk. paper) — ISBN 978-1-4422-0614-4 (pbk. : alk. paper) — ISBN 978-1-4422-0615-1 (electronic)
  1. Security, International. 2. Peace. I. Title.

JZ5588.K39 2011
355'.033—dc22

2011010697

Printed in the United States of America

Contents

Preface

IN THE FIVE YEARS SINCE THE FIRST EDITION OF *Global Security in the Twenty-First Century*, the world has witnessed dramatic changes. We have seen a war between Russia and Georgia, concerns about proliferation of nuclear weapons in Iran and North Korea, continued questions related to the rise of China, and the challenges that confront America—now under the leadership of President Barack Obama—and its relative position in the world. We have seen the ongoing demands of asymmetric conflict and terrorism, a global economic collapse, threats to human security—including the H1N1 fears that gripped much of the world—and growing concerns about energy and the environment. We have also experienced extraordinary popular people's movements for democracy in the Arab world from Tunisia and Egypt to Bahrain, Yemen, Libya, and the death of Osama bin Laden. In Libya, we witnessed the deployment of military power against the civilian population and a military intervention by a coalition of like-minded states, including the United States, France, Italy, and Great Britain, to secure humanitarian efforts there. We also witnessed massive disasters due to acts of nature in the form of earthquakes in China, Haiti, New Zealand, and Japan and historic floods in Pakistan and Australia. In the case of Japan, the release of radiation from nuclear power plants raised new doubts about the safety of nuclear energy. For many people across the globe, we have entered a period largely defined by uncertainty and even fear, and yet, we also see extraordinary reminders of the power of humanity and the potential for progress. This second edition places these challenges in the conceptual frameworks of how we think about global security and the quest for power and the search for peace. It builds on and updates the data on the major global security trends in 2011 and continues to frame these challenges with a forward-looking question of how they create opportunity for those who wish to channel the quest for power into the positive search for peace. A new final chapter continues the emphasis on education and global security and prompts thinking as to how students, educators, and practitioners can themselves take an active role in making a difference in the twenty-first century global security setting.

In the first edition of *Global Security*, I had a chance to thank many people I was indebted to over a couple of decades of work. They know who they are, and they know I remain very appreciative. I would like to thank especially Susan McEachern and her team at Rowman & Littlefield for their outstanding support—especially Alden Perkins, Carrie Broadwell-Tkach, and Jen Kelland. I am always grateful to Pam Laucher, my administrative assistant at Ohio Wesleyan University, without whom I simply could not do much of anything, and also to Rebekah Smith for her outstanding research assistance on this edition. Also at Ohio Wesleyan, David Robbins and Chuck Stinemetz have provided essential support for my scholarly work and teaching. Initial research on the material on education and global security was done while working as a visiting fellow at the Hoover Institute at Stanford University, where I am very grateful to David Brady, Michael McFaul, John Abizaid, Kori Schake, and Scott Sagan. I am particularly grateful to colleagues at the Mershon Center for International Security Studies at The Ohio State University for the opportunities to engage with the program there—especially Richard Hermann, Jennifer Mitzen, John Mueller, and Alexander Wendt. Finally, I would again say thank you to my lovely wife, Anna-Marie, and our three children, Cria, Siobhan, and Alana: you are the eyes of the world, and our future is in your very capable hands. Throughout my career, my parents have been my bedrock foundation of support, and my gratitude is boundless. This book is dedicated to them: David and Jennifer Kay.

Sean Kay
Delaware, Ohio, May 2011

1

The Dynamics of Global Security

SECURITY IS THE ABSENCE OF A THREAT to the stability of the international system, to countries, or to individuals. This is a fairly utopian state of affairs reflecting an ideal setting—but it is a core goal that states and people desire in a quest for power and a search for peace. Until the late twentieth century, security thinking emphasized the nation-state and competition for power in the international system. In the twenty-first century, this traditional focus on the nation-state and power remains central. However, major transformations within the international system demand a broader understanding of the sources of both security and insecurity. The quest for power and the search for peace have become global as great power interests coexist uneasily with risks of major regional conflict. Technology and trade, asymmetric threats such as genocide and terrorism, issues affecting human security, and environmental and energy concerns pose a multitude of new challenges. This book examines the evolving global dimensions of security, surveys the major conceptual frameworks for understanding the quest for power and the search for peace, and provides detailed assessments of major security challenges at the dawn of the twenty-first century. The book concludes with an assessment of the relationship between conceptual frameworks and policy practice to make the quest for power and the search for peace one and the same.

The Globalization of Security

Terrorist attacks on the United States on September 11, 2001, introduced many Americans to a new sense of danger. The nature of the attacks was particularly

In spring 2010, the United States confronted the worst environmental crisis in its history with a massive oil disaster in the Gulf of Mexico, illustrating the major vulnerabilities that modern states face in both energy and environmental security. Source: U.S. Coast Guard.

troubling because they illustrated three new elements of global security. First, the nation-state as a protective barrier to ward off threats was no longer as strong as many people had presumed. Second, modern technology that people rely on for global access—in this case, the airplane—was the weapon. Third, the attackers were linked through a network of global relationships stretching from the United States to Europe and the Middle East, commencing in Afghanistan. This attack represented a new kind of war in which the pathways of globalization were the means of channeling power. Nearly ten years later, another major event exposed further dilemmas inherent in global security—a massive earthquake, tsunami, and nuclear crisis in Japan. The combination of natural disaster met straight on with modern threats posited by radiation and the demand for energy in the international system. Indeed, just one year earlier, the United States experienced the greatest environmental disaster in its history with a major oil spill in the Gulf of Mexico. At the core of these crises rests a new kind of security dilemma in a globalized environment of challenge and opportunity. The expanded opportunity for power to serve both conflict and peace, or danger versus progress, embodies perhaps the most fundamental challenge for international relations in the twenty-first century. Will globalization provide new capacities for war, threats, and danger? Or will globalization facilitate new and innovative paths to peace?

Globalization's central component is interdependence, which is accelerated by advanced technology, trade, political relationships, transboundary communication, and the movement of people, goods, and services. Interdependence also implies interconnectedness; it is difficult for any state to be completely isolated from events occurring elsewhere in the world.[1] This process includes an enormous reduction of transportation costs and accelerated communication while breaking down artificial barriers to the flows of goods, services, capital, knowledge, and people across borders.[2] Globalization allows new forms of interactions that alter the nature of power in the international system and globalize security in four ways. First, major countries in the international system continue to reflect the relative distribution of global power. The United States, Russia, China, and the European Union reflect a hierarchy of military capabilities in the international system. Second, the expansion of trade, travel, communications, and other manifestations of the integrated global economy create new channels for exercising power outside the nation-state. Third, globalization can rapidly turn local problems into major international challenges that impact regional and global security. Fourth, the processes of globalization increase the complexity and reach of international anarchy, creating fear in some cases and stimulating demands for creative problem solving in others. Because there is no global government, globalization remains an unregulated phenomenon. Illustrating this dilemma, by 2011 it had become very clear that the most significant challenge to global change, stability, and security was not a military, but rather an economic, problem.

International security experts have been pointing to the rise of global security challenges for some time. In 1952, Arnold Wolfers introduced debate over the larger meaning of national security beyond the defense of territory.[3] In 1977, Lester Brown introduced global assessments of environmental and energy challenges, arguing that national security included these dimensions as well as military issues.[4] In 1983, Barry Buzan framed the meaning of security as including military, social, economic, political, and environmental dimensions.[5] In 2000, Graham Allison identified the security consequences of globalization as technology that helps with military targeting of weapons, advances in technologies of weapons of mass destruction, the erosion of the dominant role of the nation-state, "CNNization" that allows citizens to watch wars in their living rooms, global networks in communication and trade, global networks that create incentives among elites to coordinate policy to create predictability, and the prominent role of nonstate actors in impacting international outcomes. Crucially, globalization heightens new security priorities such as the illegal drug trade, terrorism, disease, smuggling, and organized crime.[6]

Globalization dynamics have had a major effect on the security dilemma. The traditional security dilemma focused analytical attention on the degree to which an effort by one state to increase its security might be perceived as a threat by another state. Globalization forces a more expansive understanding of the security dilemma because of the number of issues with security implications. For example, China would see globalization as a tool for increasing its national economic power, which reflects a relative increase in its people's security. As China's economic strength expands, the standard of living for its citizens will grow. Subsequently, China's energy consumption will increase dramatically with local, regional, and global effects on the environment. Meanwhile, as China integrates into the global economic system, its leadership faces a significant dilemma. Global information flows can lead to increasing pressure on China's communist leadership to democratize or risk popular unrest and internal instability. Globalization also exposes historically isolated China to a range of transboundary phenomena such as diseases like HIV/AIDS. Thus, for a country like China, the dynamics of global security provide both challenges and opportunities.

The New Distribution of Power

Globalization has altered the meaning of power and the means through which it is channeled. Traditionally, power grew from military capabilities, economic strength, natural resources, and the capacity to transform these assets into influence. In this context, applied power is the ability to get someone to do something that they otherwise would not do.[7] Though its manifestations are transforming, power remains a constant. As David Baldwin writes, "Economic security, environmental security, identity security, social security, and military security are different forms of security, not fundamentally different concepts. . . . Voting power, military power, economic power, and persuasive power are different forms of the same social phenomenon, i.e. power."[8] Thus, globalization is both a product and a tool of power in the international system. As Stanley Hoffmann notes, globalization is a "sum of techniques (audio and videocassettes, the Internet, instantaneous communications) that are at the disposal of states or private actors."[9] Now we can add to that Facebook, Twitter, and a wide range of social networking websites and applications. During Iran's popular Green Revolution in summer 2009, democracy protestors in that country got much of the information out to the world via Twitter. Likewise, in Egypt in 2011, Facebook was an important initial organizing tool for pro-democracy protest movements. Ironically, government efforts to shut it down backfired as the online protest community simply moved out into the streets en mass. Also in Egypt, cable news networks like Al Jazeera were vital to circumventing the propaganda efforts of state-run television. In this sense, globalization dynamics and their continued advancement through technological innovations are neither cause nor effect but rather means by which the key determining factor—power—is exercised. There are five particularly important kinds of power in the early decades of the twenty-first century: state power; soft power; asymmetric power; the power of information, intellect, and creativity; and the power of nature.

The Nation-State

The first major form of power reflects the classic function of the nation-state. State power derives from the tradition of sovereignty in international relations. Sovereignty implies that states have the sole authority over what happens within their own borders. States have both a right to sovereignty and a duty to respect the sovereignty of other states. Sovereignty has often been threatened as state interests clash, leading to wars. Historically, states have sought to marshal the resources necessary either to provide for their defense or to project state power. States with insufficient power have often fallen victim to external aggression or had to make bargains with other states to garner protection. State power is thus generally measured in terms of hard military capabilities, natural resources, population, and economic capacity.

States remain the primary actors in the global security environment. However, the means of exercising and measuring state power are undergoing significant change. Globalization can erode state authority as interdependence breaks down national barriers. However, globalization can also be an important tool for enhancing state power. For example, during the 1990s, in considering war-fighting options against the United States, the Chinese military studied a range of new kinds of attacks to achieve victory. These included terrorism, drug trafficking, environmental degradation, and computer-virus propagation. When China faced possible conflict with the United States over Taiwan in 1996, military strategists indicated that "[their forces] would not be sufficient. . . . So we realized that China needs a new strategy to right the balance of power."[10] These planners saw complexity in warfare as a neutralizing factor against American conventional military dominance. Any war between China and the United States would thus be guided in Beijing as "unrestricted war," which takes "nonmilitary forms and military forms and creates a war on many fronts."[11]

The complexity of globalization can also show significant limits on the exercise of state power. When Yugoslavia began threatening Kosovar Albanians with ethnic cleansing in 1999, the members of the North Atlantic Treaty

Organization (NATO) went to war against Yugoslavia. The war raised significant sovereignty questions because Kosovo was a territorial region within Yugoslavia. Moreover, the states in NATO were deeply divided over how to wage the war. Knowing this, Yugoslavia sought to influence NATO's consensus-based decision-making procedures by swaying public sentiment against the war, hoping to break the coalition of allied states—backed diplomatically by a friendly government in Russia. Yugoslavia had no hope of defeating the allied countries of North America and Western Europe that make up NATO. So, rather than fight conventionally, Yugoslavia sought to deter an attack by pointing its military not at NATO but at the ethnic Albanians whom NATO was trying to save. When NATO went to war in March 1999, Yugoslavia carried out its threat, forcing eight hundred thousand ethnic Albanians to flee Kosovo. Unable to reach agreement on a ground invasion, NATO went to war only with airpower—which was insufficient to achieve the objective of a quick victory and a negotiated settlement. Yugoslavia thus adopted a strategy of waiting out the NATO air campaign and hoping that the alliance would divide. Yet, a key element of globalization unraveled this Yugoslav strategy. Televised images of mass deportations of ethnic Albanians, reminiscent of World War II's Holocaust, hardened European public opinion against Yugoslavia and bolstered NATO's resolve to win the war.[12] In 2008, Kosovo declared its independence, backed by most of Europe and the United States. Then, in 2008, Moscow used their support for Kosovar sovereignty to justify its invasion of the Republic of Georgia to support Russian-friendly minorities there. In 2011, NATO yet again confronted deep internal divisions about the launch of an air war inside Libya. Within days of the war's beginning, key allies like Turkey were blocking action; France insisted that NATO should not run the operation; Italy said if NATO did not, it would block access to its air bases; Germany refused to participate at all; and the United States believed it could hand over the war to its NATO allies in a matter of days, without having achieved agreement on that in advance. Although these early differences were reconciled, the basic tensions of operating in the coalition remained. Meanwhile, attacks by Libyan troops on rebels continued, underneath the allied provision of a no-fly zone.

The Kosovo War and the 2011 initial engagements in Libya demonstrated the limits of conventional military force as a tool of state power. The combined capabilities of some of the most powerful countries in the world took three months to defeat Yugoslavia—a backward and isolated country at the time. This weakness stemmed not from a lack of military capability but rather from political division over waging war as an alliance for a humanitarian cause. Technology also showed significant limitations in the battlefield. America had become so militarily advanced that keeping communications with allied countries secret was problematic. American military advancement had its own vulnerabilities and limitations. American stealth-bomber technology makes airplanes very hard to detect on radar; however, Yugoslav forces shot down one of these planes when it was flying slowly with the moon backlighting it. The United States had the best geospatial mapping capability in the world; yet, the people working the technology had not updated the maps of Belgrade—leading American airplanes to bomb the Chinese embassy. The technology, in that case, had great precision, but the people working it made serious errors. American airplanes were prepared to target antiaircraft batteries—but the Yugoslav forces opted not to fire them and risk exposing their locations; this decision forced American airplanes to fly above fifteen thousand feet, limiting their accuracy and leading to inadvertent civilian deaths among those NATO was trying to save. Thus, a new tension was emerging—and could be seen playing out in Iraq, Afghanistan, and Libya—over the relative benefits of multilateralism in providing legitimacy for military operations versus the relative effectiveness and costs associated with it.

Ultimately, technology is not a substitute for sound state strategy. As Edward Luttwak writes, "New technologies are only relevant insofar as their potential is exploited, which in turn is only possible if resources are denied to old structures and old activities—perhaps to the point of extinction—in order to supply resources for new structures and new activities."[13] This reality became clear when the United States had to balance the relative benefits of using drone aircraft to bomb terrorist targets in Pakistan. At one level, these provided an effective means to hit specific targets without risk to U.S. troops. However, they often killed innocent civilians and thus provoked anti-American responses among peoples whose support was essential to military success. Moreover, when a drone killed a terrorist leader, that tactical success became moot when another terrorist simply replaced the target. In effect, using technology to kill terrorists risks simultaneously creating more of them.

By 2011, the global economic situation had begun to reshape how states could exert power in the international system. The United States had spent over $1 trillion on wars in Iraq and Afghanistan and was spending $708 billion per year on defense at a time when many observers considered the biggest threat to America's relative position in the world to be its $14 trillion national debt. Meanwhile, Washington had struggled for the better part of the spring and summer of 2010 to stop a massive oil leak in the Gulf of Mexico, suggesting that economic ambitions were now outpacing the rapid shift in relative power in the world. During deliberations over whether to increase American troop levels in Afghanistan in November 2009, U.S. President Barack Obama told his senior staff, "Our entire national policy can't just be focused on terrorism." He then noted that the world's 6 billion people have a vast range and diversity of concerns, and we must also focus on our own economy because it's the foundation of our strength in the world. "We can't lose sight of that, and we have too much in recent years."[14] Yet, he opted to surge an additional thirty thousand troops into Afghanistan. By 2011, critics were suggesting that the mission was not showing substantial benefits but rather considerable distraction from other, higher-priority national security concerns, and a majority of the American public had turned against the war.

As Robert Pape has shown, the United States' relative economic position has been in rapid decline in the early twenty-first century, while China's economic capacity has grown consistently.[15] Pape uses comparative economic data to show that America's share of gross world product reflects one of the largest declines in modern history, surpassed only by the collapse of the Soviet Union. The United States might be forced to retrench and reorient its strategic objectives to better reflect the emerging distribution of power.[16] New American vulnerabilities became clear even before the 2008 economic collapse. According to former U.S. Treasury secretary Hank Paulson, when Russia invaded Georgia earlier in 2008, he was informed that a high-level Russian overture was made to co-opt China in a plan to simultaneously sell holdings in Fannie Mae and Freddie Mac (large U.S. government holdings). This move would have forced the United States to spend massive amounts of government treasuries to shore up these domestic holdings.[17] China rejected this purported Russian overture. However, by 2010, a new attitude had taken hold in China. In response to an American announcement of $6.4 billion in arms sales to Taiwan, China said that it would cease military-to-military partnership cooperation with the United States and impose economic penalties on related American companies. China accused the United States of being "rude" and "arrogant" and using "Cold War thinking" in selling these weapons to Taiwan. A leading daily newspaper with close ties to the governing Chinese Communist Party opined, "It's time the US was made to feel the heat for the continuing arms sales to Taiwan. . . . It would be folly to underestimate the Chinese unity over the Taiwan question. . . . Punishing companies that sell weapons to Taiwan is a move that would be supported by most Chinese."[18]

Soft Power

Globalization places a high value on the ability of states to work within the realm of soft power. "Soft power" refers to the overall attractiveness of a state to others and its ability to accomplish goals without resorting to the threat or use of force. Soft-power gains are made not by imposing one's will on others but by setting examples with one's actions that others might want to emulate.

Key tools to soft power are credibility in relation to commitments, economic and educational capacity, and an ability to build effective multilateral coalitions for negotiating the networks of global security. States making these kinds of adjustments are likely to emerge as winners in conditions in which the exercise of effective soft power is necessary. Measuring soft power focuses attention on issues such as effective diplomacy and education, for example, because a strong understanding of and attention to the culture, traditions, and security concerns of others is essential to effective persuasion.[19]

In a global security dynamic that emphasizes soft power, economic capacity can become a crucial measurement of power. The traditional emphasis in studying globalization has been on the worldwide interconnectedness of economic activity. This economic interdependence creates both opportunity and vulnerability among nation-states. How well states adjust to emerging economic trends can be crucial to their capacity for soft-power influence in international relations. China, for example, wields growing economic influence over the United States because it has been purchasing American treasury bonds, which Washington sold in order to finance its debt. China gained from this by promoting a strong dollar, which helped it to export goods to the United States. However, if China and other Asian countries seek other currencies or commodities to invest in, the subsequent withdrawal of resources from the American economy could have a devastating impact on U.S. power. Ultimately, soft economic power can also translate into hard military power. The relative rise in economic capacity of countries like China and India thus serves as a fundamental challenge to American economic dominance in the twenty-first century.[20] At the same time, economic crisis can also serve to incentivize countries to pool resources and look for ways to cooperate with and complement each other in promoting common international security objectives.

The effective exercise of soft power can create conundrums for states with significant advantages in hard military power. A country with substantial military capabilities might find that, in wartime, it is more efficient to fight alone or with coalitions of the willing rather than to adhere to the cumbersome decision-making procedures of international organizations. By "going it alone," a state will not have other countries shaping its war-fighting plans and strategies. On the other hand, without the diplomatic approval of the international community, a military intervention can lack legitimacy and set dangerous precedents for the future. More immediately, while independent war fighting might be more efficient, a state also will find itself alone in the aftermath of victory (or defeat), paying virtually all the human and economic costs. Significantly, without allies to share the burden of winning the peace after a war, a state might find that fighting a war in the first place was not worth it. If isolated in costly unilateral military operations, a state can deplete both its hard and soft power.

Debates over the exercise of hard military power and effective use of soft power surrounded the American decision to invade Iraq in 2003. Soft power did play into some of America's strategy toward Iraq through fall 2002. The United States initially challenged the United Nations to enforce its own requirements for Iraqi disarmament. This effort eventually gained a new resolution that led to UN weapons inspectors returning to Iraq in fall 2002. The effort to build a case at the United Nations reflected a desire to shape international and domestic opinion in favor of American policy toward Iraq. This approach appeared to work when Iraq agreed to readmit weapons inspectors. Nevertheless, during the winter, the Americans continued to build up their hard-power capabilities in the Persian Gulf, thus signaling limits to their willingness to apply soft-power tactics. Meanwhile, the United States sought to build an international coalition that would support the use of force. A coalition was achieved, though it was largely political, with few additional countries supplying troops. The United States, by March 2003, had opted not to allow another round of weapons inspections, which would have gained additional diplomatic support. Though that diplomatic support could have translated into more cost sharing and additional troops to assist the U.S. long-term occupation in Iraq, the United States invaded without it and consequently paid the high price of waging war largely alone. The United States also took a significant hit to its reputation when, after invading, little evidence to support its prewar intelligence claims on Iraqi weapons of mass destruction was discovered. By 2010, this decision looked to be one of the most self-defeating military decisions in history—even just in economic terms. The UN weapons inspectors, who worked up through March 2003, only cost $80 million; the U.S. military invasion and occupation of Iraq had cost nearly $1 trillion by 2011.

Countries that opposed the American invasion of Iraq were able to gain short-term concessions or raise the costs to the United States of its action by exercising their own soft-power options. Germany, France, and Russia successfully insisted on the return of UN weapons inspectors to Iraq during fall 2002. Turkey refused to give basing access to American troops, thus forcing the United States to fight only a one-front war through Kuwait. With no invasion from the north, it became much harder to move troops into key locations in Iraq. American offers of up to $30 billion in direct money and loan credits were not sufficient to persuade Turkey to support Washington's Iraq invasion. Tiny Belgium used procedures in NATO to halt a separate Turkish request for collective defense in the event of an Iraqi attack on Turkey following an American invasion. The Belgian view appeared to be that the best way to prevent an attack on Turkey was not to have a war in the first place. Authorizing defense of Turkey, the Belgians argued, only made a war more likely. The UN weapons inspectors also played an important role by putting information into the public debate, which bolstered the diplomatic initiatives of those countries that opposed the war. Ultimately, however, the limits of soft power were exposed when the United States rejected additional inspections, and the invasion of Iraq went forward.

Asymmetric Power

How much hard or soft power a state possesses is no longer an absolute measure of security. Through channels of global trade, transportation, technology, and communication, actors with very little power can do serious damage to the national interests and security of powerful countries. Power is diffused so that the asymmetric exercise of influence is possible. There are rarely symmetries of power—when everyone in a security dynamic has equal power. Military, economic, and political differences skew the balance of forces among international actors. However, conflicting parties can apply tactics that are asymmetric in nature, or outside the legitimate realm of power projection; in other words, they can "not fight fair." While such activity is not new, the acceleration of globalization provides a range of means for nonstate actors to apply asymmetric power and increase its effects.

Asymmetric tactics are used to overcome conventional military superiority with violence that humanity generally considers unacceptable. States and societies do not have the luxury of assuming chivalry in their enemies. This challenge surfaced in a contemporary environment after, in late 1992, the United States deployed troops on a humanitarian mission to feed victims of famine in Somalia. Local political dynamics eventually led to conflict between American troops and Somali warlords. Somali irregular militias used asymmetric tactics to kill eighteen American soldiers in October 1993. These Somalis then took the bodies of American soldiers, abused them, and paraded them, stripped of clothing, on worldwide television. The American response was to withdraw from Somalia. The killing and barbaric desecration of these American soldiers were sufficient to send the United States, the world's most advanced military superpower, into retreat. The lesson: attack the United States by inflicting casualties and creating shock and horror through the networks of global communication. In fact, given the United States' overwhelming conventional military power, the likelihood of anyone fighting it conventionally seemed remote.

Deceased al Qaeda terrorist leader Osama bin Laden has said that he and his movement drew inspiration from the presumed weakness of the United

States following the Somalia debacle. Subsequently, a gathering storm of terrorist threat culminated in the 2001 al Qaeda attacks on the World Trade Center and the Pentagon in the United States. If their objective was to prompt a retrenchment of American power and increase recruitment to the al Qaeda cause, the attacks failed miserably. America's global engagement expanded dramatically after the September 11 attacks, and the terrorists, who claimed to act on behalf of Islam, were widely condemned throughout the Muslim world. However, these spectacularly horrifying incidents were portrayed repeatedly on global television and seared into the memories of people around the world. The problem for powerful states is that conventional power has little application to deterring or fighting against such asymmetric tactics.

The increasing appeal of asymmetric tactics as a tool of warfare is due in part to globalization networks that facilitate the proliferation of technology that can allow for devastating asymmetric attacks. Weapons of mass destruction in the hands of terrorists, for example, could prove particularly dangerous. Also, governments in some parts of the world might pursue limited nuclear weapons capabilities to have just enough power to raise the costs to any country that might attack. North Korea, for example, could not defeat the United States conventionally. But the United States might have to think very hard about attacking North Korea if the cost of war could be losing Seattle or San Francisco to nuclear explosions. Considering the nexus of weapons of mass destruction, organized crime, and terrorism, the need to understand and reduce asymmetric threats to global security is pressing, but the will to invest resources in this area is challenged, especially given global economic uncertainty, which thus exacerbates the emerging dilemmas of global security.

Meanwhile, as weak states pose the risk of causing regional problems that can become global crises, they can consume considerable time and energy among great powers. For example, Fareed Zakaria observes about Iran, "The GDP of Iran is 1/68 that of the United States, its military spending 1/110 that of the Pentagon. If this is 1938 . . . then Iran is Romania, not Germany. North Korea is even more bankrupt and dysfunctional. Its chief threat—the one that keeps the Chinese government awake at night—is that it will implode, flooding the region with refugees—that's power?"[21] Iran posed a threat not necessarily because it might attack its neighbors but because its obtaining nuclear weapons could set off a nuclear chain reaction in the region. Certainly, Israeli fears could also rise; thus, Israel could launch an attack and set off a regional war. As likely, nuclear weapons would spread relatively quickly to Egypt, Saudi Arabia, Syria, and Turkey. A Saudi diplomat was asked how to respond to a nuclear Iran and answered, "With another nuclear weapon."[22] Given their extensive energy interests in the Persian Gulf region, the United States and other great powers simply could not ignore the dangers of a nuclear

Iran—even if taken as a direct measure of power, the country was really not a threat in conventional terms.

The Power of Information, Intellect, and Creativity

The new dimensions of power in the twenty-first century level the playing field of international security in ways that nation-states can find difficult to constrain or adapt to. Popular movements and the ideas advocated through proliferating media networks place public demands on states as well as international institutions to react to security problems in ways that they might otherwise not. The powerless (as measured in traditional terms) can become powerful as control over information and access to knowledge become central to agenda setting.[23] This new access to power has been reflected in major international social movements that demand significant international change. For example, during the 1990s nongovernmental organizations successfully lobbied the World Bank to alter its loan policy in the underdeveloped world so that development projects would first be given an environmental impact assessment. Public international interest groups advocating for the environment, human rights, and labor standards took to the streets with major demonstrations at the 1999 World Trade Organization (WTO) meetings in Seattle. While the legal mandate of the WTO was limited to trade issues, these protestors forced the WTO member states to acknowledge the relationships between free trade and human rights, or free trade and the environment. In summer 2005, millions of people around the world united for simultaneous "Live 8" concerts by popular musicians to put pressure on the leaders of the leading industrial nations—the Group of Eight, or G8—to respond to their agenda of assistance and debt relief in Africa. Dramatically, starting with Tunisia in January 2011, popular movements rapidly collapsed authoritarian governments there and then in Egypt, followed by major movements for popular change in Bahrain, Iran, Yemen, and Libya—with pressure for political change emerging at the grassroots and general levels even in places like Syria and Saudi Arabia.

The diffusion of power into the hands of activist citizens around the world means that states must account for both domestic and global public opinion. As interdependence unites national economies, changes in public attitudes ranging from purchasing choices to opinions on war and peace can have a significant impact on global security. Should international consumers opt, for example, to boycott American-made goods, stop sending students to American universities, or start buying environmentally friendly products for purchases like cars, the American economy would be seriously damaged. America confronts a unique dilemma because its productive economy is the engine that drives many of the processes of globalization. Yet, if globalization is seen as a primarily American phenomenon, then the United States will also be blamed for associated problems—even if that blame is not merited.

Illustrating America's dilemma, a 2002 opinion survey by the Pew Global Attitudes Project showed that 50 percent of the public in Britain and 54 percent of that in Canada—America's two closest allies in the world—saw the expansion of American customs and values as a negative phenomenon.[24] Such public attitudes can make it very difficult for governments to pursue pro-American policies if they fear retribution at election time for supporting initiatives from Washington. By 2010, however, Pew surveys showed that favorable attitudes toward America had rebounded, largely reflecting a more positive view of the global leadership of President Barack Obama. On the other hand, there was no clear correlation between those favorable attitudes and the ability to persuade other countries to go along with major American national security priorities in terms of the war in Afghanistan, sanctions on Iran, or economic relations with China. Moreover, despite major efforts by Barack Obama and his secretary of state, Hillary Clinton, to reach out to the Muslim world in steady public diplomacy, America's favorable ratings in key Muslim countries actually fell in 2010. Egypt, Pakistan, and Turkey were all tied with the lowest favorability ratings toward the United States in the Muslim world—at 17 percent. These were also three of the largest recipients of American foreign aid. Interestingly, ratings favorable to America in Indonesia (the country with the world's largest Muslim population and where Barack Obama lived as a child) stood at 59 percent—an increase from 37 percent in 2008.[25] America is not alone, though, in facing a backlash, due to its large global role, that risks its soft power. China's growing economic investments have also contributed to public protest. For example, China's state-owned corporation Minimetals proposed buying Noranda, Canada's largest mining company. This effort prompted protests among Canada's miners, who worried about what Chinese ownership would mean for their job security. In the shoe-producing town of Elche, Spain, five hundred demonstrators set Chinese warehouses on fire to protest cheap Chinese shoes while demanding that Spain restrict Chinese imports.[26]

Television and the Internet provide instant global images and communication that allow the rapid transmission of ideas across borders. The results can give real meaning to the idea that one person can change the world. For example, the 1997 Nobel Peace Prize was awarded to Jody Williams, an activist from Vermont who grew concerned about landmines, organized activists across borders, put her fax machine to work, and, through tireless effort, successfully promoted an international treaty that banned landmines, causing a direct increase in human security worldwide. During the summer 2009 popular democracy movement in Iran, the powerful image of a young girl named Neda Agha-Soltan dying after being shot by representatives of her own government gained global sympathy for the Iranian dissidents. Demonstrating how these popular movements can create complexities, however, the international community had to be careful not to take sides. First, they risked alienating the Iranian government and derailing prospects for negotiating the termination of Iran's nuclear weapons program. Second, they also risked feeding into the nationalist narrative that democracy protestors are simply tools of the West, justifying a crackdown. Still, such images of action, peace, and resistance have over time become iconic statements of power in the global system. From Mohandas K. Gandhi marching, to Irish Catholic prisoners on a hunger strike in Northern Ireland, to the fall of the Berlin Wall, to a man in China, armed with nothing but two shopping bags, standing up to a tank, to the release from prison of Nelson Mandela in South Africa and from house arrest of Aung San Suu Kyi in Myanmar—all these images can inspire people into action in the hope of building a more peaceful world. The power of that hope was made clear in the early 2011 collapse of the authoritarian rule of Hosni Mubarak, who had controlled Egypt, often brutally, for over thirty years but was pressured out by the sustained engagement of peaceful demonstrators in the streets.

Of course, these channels of communication and action can be used for good and ill and by the strong and the weak. By forcing serious security challenges onto the public agenda, we can ask hard questions and, perhaps, achieve serious solutions. For example, in the twenty-first century, will a child lucky enough to be born in a developed country have security whereas one born in an underdeveloped country will not? Can the world be at peace when millions of children die every year from preventable and curable diseases; when 1 in 6 people worldwide do not get the basic level of water they need to live, 2.5 billion (including 1 billion children) lack basic sanitation facilities, and 2.7 billion people survive on less than $2 per day; when a child dies of extreme poverty every five seconds? Do the wealthy countries of the world, like the United States, want to live within a national gated community, keeping the dangerous outside world at bay? Is such a policy option even possible anymore? And, if it is not, then what proactive engagement is necessary for resolving problems before they become unmanageable crises? Only when these hard questions are asked can solutions begin to be found.

The Power of Nature

Power must also be considered in terms of humanity's natural environment. "Don't mess with mother nature" is an oft-repeated phrase. The natural world has a way of balancing itself. Yet, our planet has never before witnessed the kind of activity that humans have engaged in during the past one hundred years. Human behavior is having significant environmental impact ranging from climate change to the destruction of forests and the diminishing avail- ability of freshwater. Catastrophic natural disasters—such as the December 2004 tsunamic event in South Asia; Hurricane Katrina, which devastated much of the American Gulf Coast in August 2005; the October 2005 earthquake in Pakistan; the 2008 earthquake in China; the 2010 earthquake in Haiti and floods in Pakistan and Australia; and the 2011 earthquakes in New Zealand and Japan—can cause their own security problems for states and their people. The catastrophe in Japan was especially acute as a resulting crisis at its nuclear plants caused a global reassessment of the viability of nuclear power and its relative safety—a dilemma as nuclear power had been increasingly viewed as one of the best and cleanest alternatives to the carbon-based energy consump- tion that had accelerated global climate change. The global demand for energy is growing exponentially with the rise of modern industrial powers such as China and India. In this sense, the question of environmental security entails more than just achieving sustainable development or protecting endangered species. The central issue is whether humanity's own behavior is decreasing its own security in relation to the environment. In 2010, the most powerful nation in the world, the United States, let its economic ambitions for energy outpace its own capacity to stop a massive oil leak in the Gulf of Mexico. The power of nature is forcing a redefinition of the search for peace to include the need to live in harmony with the environment.

Overview of the Book

This text examines the conceptual and policy implications of global security. Chapter 2 surveys the role of realism in explaining power and security rela- tionships and shows how realism has been adapted in order to understand new security challenges. Chapter 3 views the search for peace through the frameworks of liberalism and new security paradigms, including constructiv- ism, transnational civil society, pacifism and peace movements, postmodern- ism, feminism and gender, and revolutionary approaches to security. Chapter 4 reviews the distribution of power in the international system with detailed study of the grand strategies and military capabilities of the United States, Russia, China, and the European Union. Chapter 5 considers the strategic consequences of major regional flash points: India and Pakistan, the Korean Peninsula, China and Taiwan, the Persian Gulf and the Middle East, and Eurasia. Chapter 6 outlines the security implications of technology and trade, including revolutions in military affairs, the role of information and security, the military use of space, the business of security, security privatization, and the relationship between international sanctions and security. Chapter 7 examines asymmetric conflict with a focus on genocide and ethnic cleansing, as well as terrorism and insurgency. Chapter 8 surveys challenges to human security with an emphasis on human rights and democracy, population and demographic change, food and health, and the human costs of war. Chapter 9 focuses on the meaning of environmental and energy security and assesses the security implications of global warming, deforestation and land use, water security, energy scarcity and safety, and the role of nuclear energy. Chapter 10 concludes with a reexamination of the major conceptual frameworks in light of these global security trends. The conclusion reviews the relationship between theory and practice in global security outcomes and provides a perspective on education and global security. It also provides perspective on how individuals might engage to make their own positive difference advancing the use of power in the ongoing search for peace.

Suggested Reading

Bacevich, Andrew. *The Limits of Power: The End of American Exceptionalism.* New York: Metropolitan Books, 2008.

Bhagwati, Jagdish. *In Defense of Globalization.* Oxford: Oxford University Press, 2004.

Brown, Michael, Steven E. Miller, Owen R. Cote Jr., and Sean M. Lynn-Jones, eds. *New Global Dangers: Changing Dimensions of International Security.* Cambridge, MA: MIT Press, 2004.

Buzan, Barry. *People, States, and Fear: An Agenda for International Security Studies in the Post–Cold War Era.* 2nd ed. New York: Lynne Rienner, 1991.

Clark, Ian. *Globalization and International Relations Theory.* Oxford: Oxford University Press, 1999.

Keohane, Robert O., and Joseph S. Nye. *Power and Interdependence.* 3rd ed. New York: Longman, 2001.

Kugler, Richard L., and Ellen L. Frost, eds. *The Global Century: Globalization and National Security.* Washington, DC: National Defense University Press, 2001.

Morgenthau, Hans J. *Politics among Nations: The Struggle for Power and Peace.* New York: Knopf, 1985.

Stiglitz, Joseph. *Making Globalization Work.* New York: W. W. Norton, 2007.

Zakaria, Fareed. *The Post-American World.* New York: W. W. Norton, 2009.

Illustrating the extent of and challenges to global power in the twenty-first century, an American CH-47 Chinook comes in for a landing to pick up soldiers following an air-assault mission to the Daymirdad District Center in Wardak Province, Afghanistan, January 9, 2011. Source: U.S. Army photo by Sgt. Sean P. Casey.

2

The Quest for Power

THE DOMINANT APPROACH TO UNDERSTANDING the role power plays in global security has been realism. Realism reflects a set of assumptions about the way security relationships are ordered in the context of the general distribution of power. In the realist paradigm, the nation-state is traditionally the central actor in the international system, and the quest for power is the key means to advancing security. Realists see international actors making cost-benefit assumptions to advance the national interest as defined in terms of power. Realists conclude that the key objective of states is survival, and power is the means to that end. States will thus calculate their interests in terms of power and the international situation that they face. Realists see the international system as reflecting a condition of anarchy where the nation-state is the highest source of legitimate political authority. Consequently, a state must rely on itself for safety. Realists generalize that all states are the same in their pursuit of national interests and that moral aspects of domestic laws and government are not relevant to determining international outcomes. Realists note, however, that there are various levels of power distribution among nation-states and that power must be understood in terms of both absolute and relative capabilities. Realists assume that states will ask not only "Who will gain?" in a competitive situation but also "Who will gain more?" Increasingly, realism has been adapted to move beyond the primary focus of the nation-state to apply its assumptions to the new dynamics of international security. Realists are generally pessimistic about human nature. Thus, while people might see themselves as peaceful, the same cannot be safely assumed about others. Humankind is power maximizing, selfish, evil, and even sinful.[1]

This chapter examines the core propositions of traditional realist approaches to international security. It then illustrates how elements of realism have been adapted to explain the globalized flows of power in the twenty-first century.

The Traditions of Realism

The central assumptions of realism date to the work of the ancient Greek historian Thucydides. Through the Melian Dialogue, Thucydides illustrated that, when it comes to international security, the strong do what they can, and the weak do what they must. Italian political philosopher Niccolò Machiavelli used his study *The Prince* to illustrate national interest in security and survival. As Machiavelli writes, "A man striving in every way to be good will meet his ruin among the great number who are not good. Hence it is necessary for a prince, if he wishes to remain in power, to learn how not to be good and to use his knowledge or refrain from using it as he may need." In Machiavelli's view, a leader should "care nothing for the accusation of cruelty so long as he keeps his subjects united and loyal; by making a very few examples he can be more truly merciful than those who through too much tender-heartedness allow disorders to arise whence come killings and rapine."[2] Thomas Hobbes advanced the concept of power and anarchy. In *Leviathan*, Hobbes asserts, "Man has a perpetual and restless desire for power."[3] He notes that when two individuals desire the same thing—which in reality both together cannot enjoy—then they will become enemies. Over time, they will endeavor to destroy or subdue one another. Thus, political actors have only themselves to rely on, for there is no government over the governments. In the anarchic world, incentives for war are built into the international system as men seek to become first "masters of other men's persons, wives, children and cattle." Hobbes separated the interests of survival from the moral imperatives of humankind, writing, "To this war of every man, against every man, this also is consequent; that nothing can be unjust. The notions of right and wrong, justice and injustice have there no place. Where there is no common power, there is no law: where no law, no injustice." To Hobbes, "covenants without the sword are but words and of no strength to secure man at all."

In the twentieth century, Hans J. Morgenthau characterized international politics as a struggle for power. He stressed both the physical and psychological dimensions of power, which he saw as the ability to control the minds and actions of others. Morgenthau believed that people seek the most power they can attain. The amount of power needed for security derives from the conditions a state faces; thus, states might pursue power to maintain a status quo (defensive), wage an imperial expansion (offensive), or gain prestige.[4] George

Kennan critiqued efforts to create a moralistic and legalistic international order. Instead, states should set the best example at home so that other states will gravitate toward those values rather than recoil at having values foisted upon them. Kennan was also a firm believer in the defensive use of power to offset an enemy, as evidenced by his policy of containment toward the Soviet Union.[5] Henry Kissinger evaluated the advantages of the balance of power for stability in international relations through detailed assessment of the strategies of great powers during the nineteenth century.[6] Kennan and Kissinger applied realism while serving in the U.S. government—Kennan as the author of the containment policy and Kissinger as the author of the doctrine of détente with the Soviet Union and China.

In the 1970s, some realists assessed how the structure of the international system shapes state behavior. Kenneth N. Waltz presented the structure of the international system as constant. He concluded that the system would only truly change if there were alterations in its organizing principles or capabilities. As a finite amount of power exists in the international system, states will compete to gain access in order to advance self-help. To Waltz, the more states are exposed to vulnerabilities created by interdependence, the more likely they will come into conflict. Conflict is less likely when fewer interested actors compete for power.[7] Robert Gilpin focused attention on the relative distribution of power and systemic change. Territorial, political, and economic expansion will likely occur until the marginal costs of further change are equal to or greater than the marginal benefits. As states rise in terms of power and become overly invested in expansive military engagements, they can risk underinvesting in their domestic economic strength. Expansionistic foreign and military policies will promote reactions, such as external balancing forces, which limit the power of a rising state. Alternatively, they might lead to internal economic decline, forcing a retrenchment. Gilpin noted that when one actor's power is rising and another's is declining, the international system is most likely to promote a transformational war.[8]

Realists have also been concerned with why and how power is exerted within the international system. Robert J. Art identified four kinds of military power. Defensive use of force is the deployment of military power to do two things: ward off an attack or minimize danger in the event of an attack. Deterrent use of force entails the deployment of military power in order to prevent an adversary from doing some undesirable thing that he might otherwise be tempted to do by threatening him with unacceptable punishment if he does it. In compellant use of force, military power is deployed either to stop an adversary from doing something that he has already undertaken or to get him to do something that he has not yet undertaken. Finally, swaggering is the deployment of military power for purposes other than defense, deterrence, or compulsion, usually with peaceful exercises or demonstrations of military capability.[9] The relative distribution of power is also a key determinant of how much security a state needs. At the core of concern over potential conflict lies the traditional concept of the security dilemma.

The Security Dilemma and Incentives for War

While two or more states in the international system might not want conflict with each other, the nature of the system can force them to assume the worst, creating a security dilemma. Latent power, such as economic or technological gains in one state that can be transformed into military capabilities, can cause a state to increase its defensive capacity. This defensive action can be perceived as threatening to other states. As John Herz writes, "Since none can ever feel entirely secure in such a world of competing units, power competition ensues, and the vicious circle of security and power accumulation is on."[10] There is danger in the belief that an increase in military strength always leads to an increase in security.[11] Robert Jervis places the relationship between offensive and defensive strategy within the context of the security dilemma. When offensive strategy has the advantage, one country's armed forces will find it easier to destroy those of another and to take the latter's territory rather than defend its own. When defensive strategy has the advantage, it is easier to protect and hold than it is to move forward and destroy an adversary. Jervis notes that the security dilemma is most dangerous when the only good route to security for a state is perceived to be expansion. States that might prefer to maintain the status quo still might feel they have little choice but to prepare for an offensive strategy to ensure their safety. Even small gains made by another state can result in real or perceived vulnerabilities for another. As Jervis notes, a state might choose offensive weapons even if it prefers the status quo because (1) if the offensive strategy has a great advantage over the defensive, protection through defensive forces will be too expensive; (2) status quo states may need offensive weapons to regain territory lost in the opening stages of any war that might occur; and (3) a state might feel that it must be prepared to take the offensive either because the other side will make peace only if it loses territory or because the state has commitments to attack if the other makes war on a third party.[12]

Stephen Van Evera demonstrates several factors that create incentives for offensive doctrines: opportunistic expansionism appears easier; expansionism for defensive purposes or to resist expansion is attractive; rewards for moving first are higher; windows of opportunity for an enemy are larger if one is on the defensive; states tend (when conquest is easy) to adopt more dangerous diplomatic tactics that are more likely to cause war; states with offensive advantages will negotiate less when they can have their way with military power; states will become more secretive to protect their offensive edge; states will race harder and faster to develop arms when the offensive strategy dominates; and, finally, conquest becomes still easier as offensive dominance becomes self-reinforcing.[13] Van Evera concludes that "the prime threat to the security of modern great powers is . . . themselves. Their greatest menace lies in their own tendency to exaggerate the dangers they face, and to respond with counterproductive belligerence."[14]

The security dilemma is especially intense in a condition where nuclear weapons are involved. If two adversarial parties have only a handful of nuclear weapons between them, one state might risk launching a first-strike attack against the other to eliminate the latter's capability to retaliate. Conversely, a state that feels its retaliatory capability is threatened might opt to launch its weapons arsenal first—a "use it, or lose it" scenario. During the Cold War, the development by both adversaries of a full-scale "second-strike" capability ameliorated this element of the security dilemma. Had the Soviet Union launched a surprise attack against the United States, the United States still could have retaliated because enough of its nuclear capability would have survived. For the United States, this meant developing a mix of nuclear capabilities via a triad including long-range intercontinental ballistic missiles (ICBM), mobile submarine-launched missiles, and heavy bombers ready to launch on a moment's notice. The Soviet Union had similar capabilities, using mobile land forces via an extensive train system and submarines, long-range bombers, and ICBMs. As a result, neither side could risk launching a surprise nuclear attack because doing so would mean mutual suicide—or as it was called, MAD: mutual assured destruction.

Seeking to further ameliorate the security dilemma, the United States and the Soviet Union agreed in 1972 to ban the development and deployment of missile-defense systems with the Anti-Ballistic Missile (ABM) treaty. The intent was to ensure that neither side might develop the capacity to eliminate the other's retaliatory capability and thereby create incentives for one or the other to launch a first-strike attack. If one side, for example, had a missile-defense system able to shoot down incoming missiles, the other side would be extremely vulnerable because its retaliatory counterstrike would be insufficient to dissuade the former from starting a war. The missile-defense dynamic reemerged during the 1980s with the Strategic Defense Initiative—derisively referred to as "Star Wars" by skeptics—proposed by the United States. By the 1990s, the United States opted initially to develop a limited system. By 2004, the United States had withdrawn from the ABM treaty and begun deployment of a ballistic missile-defense system. This new defensive system illustrates the dynamics behind the security dilemma. If the United States could shoot down a couple dozen incoming missiles from North Korea, that same capability would affect China, which in 2004 had two dozen hardened-silo intercontinental ballistic missiles. If China felt that its limited nuclear deterrent was marginalized, it might build more missiles and make them mobile. This in turn would raise alarm in India, which might build more missiles and thus exacerbate fears in its long-time adversary Pakistan. Meanwhile, the United States might build a larger missile defense, alarming Russia. Indeed, concurrent plans by the United States to deploy a radar array in the Czech Republic and missile interceptors in Poland raised considerable alarm in Russia. However, President Barack Obama scrapped this deployment in 2009. His administration preferred a more regionally focused theater missile-defense system arrayed toward Iran. In fall 2010, the United States had successfully persuaded Russia to cooperate in building that system.

Misperception, Coercion, and Credibility

Threats can be real or perceived. For example, Poland still perceived Russia as a threat to its security after the Cold War—which drove Poland to seek security guarantees through the North Atlantic Treaty Organization (NATO) in the 1990s and subsequently made it amenable to missile-defense systems, as well as associated support troops, in its territory. Russia did not pose a significant conventional military threat, but Poland's historical experiences living under brutal totalitarian governments controlled by Moscow shaped how it viewed Russia. Poland would continually pressure its NATO allies for harder guarantees of its security. After Russia invaded the Republic of Georgia in 2008, the Polish prime minister said, "Poland and the Poles do not want to be in alliances in which assistance comes at some point later—it is no good when assistance comes to dead people."[15]

Conversely, many Russians saw NATO as a Cold War alliance led by its recent military adversaries, the United States and Germany; thus, many Russians perceived its expansion as a threat. NATO leaders' agreement in spring 2008 that Ukraine and Georgia would eventually become NATO members set off alarm bells in Russia relative to its own security. Several months later, Russia was at war in Georgia over disagreements about minority Russian populations there. Ironically, in 2010, Ukraine announced that it no longer sought NATO membership but preferred to remain neutral. The loser here was the United States in that, in previous years, it could have likely made a deal with Russia over Ukraine in exchange for Russian help on isolating the Iranian nuclear program. Washington refused this arrangement, driven by its perception of its own power and reputation and the sense that it did not have to make such bargains. The crucial variable at play in all of these dynamics was the perception, not the actuality, of threat—but the outcomes were real nonetheless.

National leaders do not always have perfect, or even near-perfect, information; thus, they often rely on existing perceptions when making cost-benefit analyses. Additionally, states might impose their own standards of expected behavior on others by determining how they would behave in a given situation rather than understanding how another actor might define its own interests. When two or more states look at a single phenomenon, one might see a threat while others see nothing of consequence. Both reactions carry risks. Assuming a threat when there is none can create a self-fulfilling prophecy. Alternatively, seeing no threat when one looms can be catastrophic.

The personal characteristics of decision makers also impact how a particular state will perceive international events and thus shape policies. Existing or learned perceptions shape views of reality—even if those assumptions or learned patterns of cognition are wrong. Cognitive and psychological factors can exacerbate the security dilemma. Stress can lead decision makers to respond with intellectual rigidity that restricts their ability to cope with complexity. Also, when decision time is short, the ability to examine a broad range of possibilities can be limited.[16] Domestic inputs also influence perceptions of threats. Bureaucratic interests can skew a full airing of factors pertaining to the national interest, or important information might be ignored in bureaucracies to satisfy cognitive worldviews of decision makers. Also, major changes in political culture affect how states perceive the international environment. Such internal changes also affect how others view them. For example, Germany and Japan in 2011 were not the same war-prone states that they were in the first half of the twentieth century. Nevertheless, other states might view these countries as potential threats based on both their latent power capabilities and their historical patterns of behavior.

Realists also see states using their power capabilities, including military force, as a tool of coercion. Coercion can involve the threat of force designed to convince another actor or state to do something it otherwise would not do. Coercion can take benign forms, like persuasion, or it can take more aggressive forms, like intimidation and blackmail. Coercion might manifest as naked aggression to make strategic or tactical gains in an offensive campaign. However, coercion can also be a tool, as in using the threat of force to back up diplomacy in order to avoid conflict. Alexander George notes that, in such a setting, decision makers must choose (1) what to demand of the opponent, (2) whether and how to create a sense of urgency for compliance, (3) whether to threaten punishment for noncompliance and what kind, and (4) whether to rely solely on the threat of punishment or also to offer positive inducements to secure acceptance.[17] Two operational dilemmas, however, are associated with a solely diplomatic approach to coercion. First, it is hard to know how much threat is necessary to persuade an opponent to comply. Must a country mobilize army divisions, deploy aircraft carriers around the world, or put nuclear forces on alert? Or can small, limited air strikes send the necessary messages? Second, coercive diplomacy may only work if a state is prepared to actually use force. This creates a variation on the security dilemma in that, once having threatened force, a state might be compelled to use it to defend its credibility—even if the conflict is of relatively little national interest.

A credibility dilemma can pose two distinct problems for decision makers. First, the target of coercion might not believe that a threat is serious and thus refuse to comply. Second, other major powers will be watching to see if a state conducting a coercive strategy will maintain the credibility of its diplomatic rhetoric. A state might thus find itself engaged in wars in the name of prestige and credibility rather than immediate vital interests. For example, in March 1998, U.S. Secretary of State Madeleine K. Albright declared, "We are not going to stand by and watch the Serbian authorities do in Kosovo what they can no longer get away with doing in Bosnia."[18] In August 1998, Secretary Albright expressed her "strong view that the ongoing Serbian offensive and the unacceptable actions that have taken place in the context of that offensive only increase the chances of there being military action by NATO."[19] After a year of having American threats of military force ignored on the ground, the United States led its NATO allies into a war. A crisis with, at best, marginal vital interest emerged as a major challenge to American prestige and credibility, prompting the United States and its allies to launch an offensive war. As British prime minister Tony Blair said to the House of Commons at the onset of war, "To walk away now would destroy NATO's credibility."[20] After the war, President Bill Clinton exacerbated the dilemma by declaring, "Whether you live in Africa or Central Europe, or any other place, if somebody comes after innocent civilians and tries to kill them en masse because of their race, their ethnic background or their religion, and it's within our power to stop it, we will stop it."[21]

Offensive Realism

The quest for material power can lead to aggressive, expansionist policy agendas, reflected historically in terms of colonial empire and hegemonic spheres of influence. John J. Mearsheimer assesses these tendencies via the concept of offensive realism. He demonstrates that great powers are concerned mostly with survival, which can only be ensured by attaining the maximum amount of military power and strategic influence. Mearsheimer sees the anarchical nature of the international system as requiring great powers to increase their capabilities at the expense of rivals and to take advantage of situations in which the benefits outweigh the costs.[22] Mearsheimer concludes that an ideal state of affairs for any great power is to dominate the entire world. However, as that is impossible, states seek to become regional hegemonic powers to assert the maximum degree of control and influence. As great powers attain this status, they inevitably run into other powers with similar geostrategic interests, and conflict can result. This, Mearsheimer concludes, is the tragedy of great power politics: states would likely prefer to sustain a status quo via defensive mechanisms, but the structure of the international system forces them into offensive postures that can provoke conflict as states seek domination through war.

The sources of conflict, according to offensive realism, come from the great powers' attempts to achieve four basic objectives: regional hegemony (which includes offensive action and actions designed to prevent other powers from infringing on that regional domination), maximization of wealth, dominance of power with large land armies, and nuclear superiority over rivals.[23] Strategies for attaining these objectives include war and blackmail. States might also pursue bloodletting, which ensnares other powers in intractable conflicts, forces them to drain resources, and thus saps their strength. Mearsheimer finds evidence to support the case for offensive realism by looking at the historical examples of Japan, Germany, the Soviet Union, and Italy during the late 1800s through 1945. In these cases, evidence shows that each sought as much domination in the international system as it could get. When poor choices were made, overstretch occurred, or defensive coalitions forced a retrenchment.

Mearsheimer also notes that, even during the Cold War period of mutual assured destruction, the United States and the Soviet Union did not willingly accept the status quo. Instead, each sought, through arms races, to gain some form of nuclear advantage over the other. Mearsheimer observes that the United States would have been able to absorb a first strike by the Soviet Union and still retaliate with a level of destruction that would kill about 30 percent of the Soviet Union's population and destroy about 70 percent of its industry. Using effective targeting of the two hundred largest Soviet cities, this task could have been accomplished with a mix of nuclear weapons resulting in the equivalent of about four hundred one-megaton bombs. However, not satisfied with this minimal level of deterrence, Washington's military plans far exceeded this estimate. In 1976, even after a period of détente and arms-control treaties with the Soviets, U.S. military planning listed twenty-five thousand potential targets in the USSR for nuclear attack. By 1983, this listing contained fifty thousand potential targets.[24] While both sides did seek such advantages, the structure of mutual assured destruction was nevertheless a barrier to war.

The Realist Path to Security

Realists believe that the quest for security is best understood as a product of the distribution and exercise of power. War might be prevented if a powerful state is relatively satisfied with the status quo and acts with restraint. Alternatively, several powers might share a common interest in an existing status quo and adjust their relations as necessary to maintain equilibrium. States might also find themselves engaged with each other in a manner that reinforces a stable international system, as during the Cold War. They can also capitulate in the face of a threat in order to avoid war or may choose balancing or bandwagoning strategies to preserve their sovereignty. Balancing can be done unilaterally, by increasing capabilities to create equilibrium, or by gathering enough capabilities to make any attack too costly to contemplate. Balancing also can include forming mutual defense agreements between two or more states. States might also bandwagon toward the state that is a threat or dominates a region.[25] In bandwagoning, smaller states align with the source of danger by cutting a deal with a more powerful state to ensure survival or even share the gains of conquest.[26] Balancing and bandwagoning can contribute to a stable balance of power, which is the primary source of security among states according to most realist analysis. In an ideal balance-of-power system, defensive military postures would dominant, and there would be no power seeking to alter the status quo.

Deterrence

Often seen as the most effective way to marshal the use of power to prevent war, deterrence is a psychological relationship in a conflict situation in which one side convinces the other not to attack because of the threat of a damaging response. As Gordon A. Craig and Alexander L. George put it, deterrence is an "effort by one actor to persuade an opponent not to take action of some kind against his interests by convincing the opponent that the costs and risk of doing so will outweigh what he hopes to gain thereby."[27] Craig and George stress that the key elements of deterrence rest on the assumption that an opponent is rational. States will weigh their interests and thus convey a commitment to defend those interests backed by threats that must be credible and sufficiently potent in the eyes of an opponent. Such threats must demonstrate will and resolution; thus, adequate capabilities must exist to make such will credible.[28] Deterrence is built into a stable balance-of-power relationship. If adversaries have an equal amount of military capability, neither side will want to engage in direct conflict because the costs of war will outweigh any potential gains. When each side in a conflict has the ability to punish the other in the face of aggression, war is not likely.

Deterrence works at two levels: conventional and nuclear. Conventional land deterrence is central to controlling territory and has historically been the most important measure of the balance of power. Naval power and, in the twentieth century, airpower are critical tools of power projection, but land capabilities are key to stability even in a situation where nuclear deterrence is also important. Even under the nuclear umbrella of the Cold War, the United States and the Soviet Union both invested in massive ground troop deployments in Europe and Asia. Conventional deterrence is also important because not all wars involving nuclear powers will include the use of nuclear weapons.[29] States possessing nuclear weapons must be prepared to engage in land warfare as insurance against preemptive attack. Conventional deterrence is also important because the level of destruction that nonnuclear weapons can wreak remains very high. As the conventional balance of power reached a stalemate during World War I, for example, hundreds of thousands of soldiers still died in months-long battles.

Nuclear weapons play a unique political and operational role in modern deterrence. As Robert Jervis notes, nuclear weapons have several political effects. First, the devastation of an all-out war would be unimaginably enormous. Second, both sides in a conflict would be exposed to this devastation—making both major losers. Third, this devastation would occur extremely quickly, and even the smallest of skirmishes could lead to a very dangerous escalation.[30] Nuclear deterrence theory has a built-in assumption of extreme risk. Should the theory ever be proven wrong, the consequences would be devastating. Deterrence posits that a state will not instigate conflict because the assumed benefits of aggression are not worth the associated costs. Also built into the theory is the assumption that, as during the Cold War, geographic separation will provide some warning time before a local conflict escalates into nuclear war. The theory leaves unanswered the question of how much capability is needed to attain effective deterrence at either the conventional or the nuclear level. Alternatively, how little deterrence a state has can also raise questions about the possibility of waging war. War would thus still be likely even if nuclear weapons were present—and their use might be more likely when too few nuclear weapons were present. The theory also raises unanswered questions about the threshold at which a state will risk introduction of nuclear weapons into a conflict. The United States would use its nuclear deterrent to defend its own territory, but would it risk its territory to protect allies? War is more likely, as Mearsheimer observes, when states underestimate the relative power of an opposing state or coalition because they exaggerate their own capabilities or the number of allies they can count on to fight on their side.[31]

The Cuban Missile Crisis illustrates both the effects and dangers of deterrence. By the mid-1950s, the United States had established military and economic advantages over the Soviet Union. In 1962, the Soviet Union embarked on a coercive strategy to project its deterrent capacity, and perhaps also to increase its negotiating leverage on European issues, by deploying nuclear-capable missile systems and associated warheads ninety miles off the U.S. East Coast in Cuba. The Soviet Union did not necessarily need to engage in this action in Cuba at that time; it could instead have granted political guarantees to Fidel Castro with potentially the same effect of deterring an American attack on the island nation. However, by 1962, the health of the Soviet system was in question. Some 4 million East Berliners had fled into West Berlin, prompting the Soviet Union to order construction of the Berlin Wall. The Soviets faced a credibility dilemma in Cuba. If Moscow failed to support its newfound ally in Castro, its other allies around the world might question the legitimacy of the Soviet commitment to their defense. Prestige, strategy, and survival considerations combined to provoke the Soviet Union to pursue an offensive strategy as a reflection of its perceived security needs. These weapons and missiles were basically useless as defensive weapons. Moscow gambled that its actions would yield an outcome favorable to Soviet objectives—successful deterrence and a possible negotiation.

U.S. aerial intelligence discovered the presence of missile-delivery systems in Cuba in September 1962. The Americans did not know at the time that nuclear warheads were in Cuba. However, missiles and their launching systems were visibly in place. The United States ruled out an invasion of Cuba to remove the missiles as too risky. Thus, Soviet deterrence limited American options. In a televised address on October 22, 1962, President John F. Kennedy informed the American public of the missiles' presence and declared a precise deterrent posture, stating that the United States would consider any attack from Cuba as an attack on America by the Soviet Union. He also declared that the United States would impose a naval "quarantine" to isolate Cuba from any further shipments of weapons. The American ambassador to the United Nations went before the Security Council and presented the evidence of the Soviet missiles in Cuba to the world.

The United States did not have good information about the USSR's intentions. For example, had a coup in Moscow precipitated the crisis? How would the Soviets respond to the American deterrent posture, especially regarding naval action on international waters? At what point might the Soviets back down? At what point might they challenge Kennedy on the credibility of his deterrent threat? Likewise, the Soviet Union could not know for sure whether the United States was prepared to engage in global thermonuclear war. In the end, the Cuban Missile Crisis was resolved through a combination of deterrence and diplomacy. If Moscow withdrew the missiles from Cuba under UN inspection, Washington promised not to invade Cuba. Washington also agreed to remove nuclear missiles it had based in Turkey. Both sides had stared into the abyss of nuclear annihilation, and both had reacted as deterrence theory would predict. War was avoided through the exercise of diplomacy backed with the threat of credible military force. Nonetheless, this extremely dangerous test of deterrence led both sides to recognize a need for peaceful coexistence. The structure of nuclear deterrence would be sustained but with increased controls, such as a hotline between Washington and Moscow and nuclear arms-control treaties designed to prevent future crises.[32]

Another Cold War example of deterrence involved intermediate-range nuclear forces (INFs) deployed in Europe by the Soviet Union and the United States. During the 1970s, détente gradually failed as Soviet economic stagnation and decline prompted Moscow to challenge the international system with offensive strategies. The USSR developed and deployed the SS-20, an intermediate-range missile to be launched from within the Soviet Union and aimed at Western European targets. A two-stage land-mobile missile, the SS-20 had a range of between forty-four hundred and five thousand kilometers. The deployment was intended to undermine the credibility of the American commitment to Western Europe and, perhaps, to coerce the Europeans into negotiations with Moscow. The Soviet deployment upset the existing balance of power by giving Moscow an advantage in first-strike capabilities against Western Europe. The United States responded with a "dual-track" approach: diplomacy backed by the threat of military power. The United States and its NATO allies declared that the Soviets could either withdraw their forces, or the United States would deploy a deterrent force to restore the balance of power. The Soviets did not respond affirmatively, and in December 1979, the United States announced its decision to deploy 108 Pershing II and 464 ground-launched cruise missiles in Western Europe targeting the Soviet Union. The United States offered not to deploy if the Soviets withdrew their INFs, but Moscow rejected this proposal and insisted on bringing British and French nuclear systems into the equation. Efforts to negotiate failed, and the United States deployed its missiles, restoring the balance of nuclear power in Europe. By 1987, however, the Soviet Union was in deep retrenchment under the policies of its new leader, Mikhail Gorbachev, and a first order of business was to negotiate the INF treaty with the United States, entirely eliminating this class of nuclear weapons.

Deterrence is inherently dangerous because it must be credible to succeed. In 1939, both France and Britain made a deterrence-based pledge to defend

Poland if it were attacked by Germany. But that promise was worth no more than the paper it was written on. Germany did not respect the threat because the British and the French provided no guarantees to back it up. They deployed no advance forces to signal the consequences of action. Similarly, in 1990, the United States failed to send an adequate deterrent message to Iraq about the consequences of any invasion of Kuwait. When, in the days before the invasion, Saddam Hussein met with the U.S. ambassador to Iraq, he asked her about America's position on ongoing Iraqi-Kuwaiti oil and territorial disputes. Her official instructions were that the United States took no position on such inter-Arab issues. Hussein took this as a yellow, if not a green, light to invade Kuwait and gambled that the United States was not willing to defend the country. After the invasion, the United States did deploy three hundred thousand troops to Saudi Arabia, which successfully deterred further Iraqi aggression.

Alliances and Concerts

An alliance is a grouping of two or more actors intended to accomplish a particular objective. Alliances can facilitate expansion and aggression, or they can be defensive measures formed in response to a threat. Alliances are an important means to security for smaller states, which can join forces to attain a balance of power against a threat that one state acting alone cannot accomplish. Alliances can thus be necessary for effective deterrence. However, the commitments that alliances entail can also lead to war. Often short-term relationships established during wartime, alliances typically do not last beyond the threat that initiated them. Once entered into, permanent alliances can present significant management problems because smaller states might not contribute equally to providing the collective safety benefits that larger states guarantee. If a threat becomes too overriding or an alliance is not based on credible commitments, states might seek neutrality, negotiate a deal with the adversary, or pursue alternative means to their own defense.

The modern state system originated from an alliance formed as a key provision of the Peace of Westphalia, which ended the Thirty Years War in 1648. The treaty allowed that it was "free perpetually to each of the states of the Empire, to make Alliances with strangers for their preservation and safety; Provided nevertheless such Alliances be not against the Emperor, and the Empire; nor against the Public Peace of this Treaty."[33] The next several hundred years reflected patterns of shifting alliances as a means of averting or winning war. Alliances were not seen as permanent, and notions like "The enemy of my enemy is my friend" and "Today's friend is tomorrow's enemy" were common. At core, up to World War I, the basic premise held that alliances should shift depending on the balance of power. Fluctuating alliance commitments during the nineteenth century were seen as useful to maintaining the general health of the international system. In particular, states made alliances to ensure that no single power became strong enough to overturn the status quo.

Two significant alliances emerged in the early nineteenth century that reflected variations on the balance of power as a means toward peace. The first, the Quadruple Alliance between Britain, Prussia, Russia, and the Austro-Hungarian Empire, was formed in response to Napoleonic France's rise in power and waging of expansionistic war. Embedded within the Quadruple Alliance, a strategic arrangement born of necessity to defeat France, was another, the Holy Alliance, comprising the three monarchic eastern powers of Prussia, Russia, and the Austro-Hungarian Empire. The objective of the Holy Alliance was both to prevent the system from being overturned and to prevent the revolutionary ideas of France from disrupting their domestic rule. By the late 1800s, the international system had witnessed a return to shifting alliances, which eventually became a major cause of World War I, when states mobilized their militaries to show support for alliance commitments, prompting fear among potential enemies. Alliance commitments also served to undermine the general peace after World War I as the international community sought to build the League of Nations. Rather than putting faith in such international commitments to alleviate its security fears, France built a system of alliances designed to encircle Germany. As a result, however, this sense of external threat became a justification for the rise of German nationalism, which would impel Germany to pursue an aggressive expansionist agenda, leading to World War II.

During the Cold War, the United States led a global network of defensive alliances to contain the Soviet Union. In Europe, the United States worked with its allies to establish NATO, which signaled in advance to the Soviet Union that an attack on any member of the organization would be considered an attack on all its members. In Asia, the United States used a combination of multilateral and bilateral frameworks. In the ANZUS Treaty, the United States established security pacts with Australia and New Zealand. Though it was never as fully developed, the Southeast Asia Treaty Organization, or SEATO, paralleled the NATO concept and included the United States, Australia, France, Britain, New Zealand, Pakistan, the Philippines, and Thailand. Unable to maintain cohesion during the Vietnam War, this alliance was disbanded in 1977. Meanwhile, the United States had bilateral alliances with Japan and South Korea. Washington promised to defend Taiwan if it were attacked, unless Taiwan's own actions provoked that attack.

The promise of collective defense creates a public good—a benefit that, once provided, all recipients utilize whether they contribute to defraying the costs of service provision or not. A nation with a greater demand than others for a public good will place a higher value on its provision. That state may provide a disproportionate level of the collective good, while the smaller members of an alliance tend to supply only suboptimal amounts. A small country that views defense costs as a burden could withdraw from (or not contribute to) an alliance but still receive defense benefits.[34] A comparison of relative defense expenditures as a percentage of gross national product (GNP) among major alliance members demonstrated disproportionate cost sharing in NATO.[35] In 1953, the United States spent 14.7 percent of its GNP on defense, while France and Britain spent around 11 percent; in the Federal Republic of Germany, the spending was less than 5 percent. As the U.S. level fell over time, so too did those of the European allies. By 1970, the American percentage had leveled off, while European contributions continued to decline. By 1980, the U.S. figure had fallen to 5.5 percent, whereas only Britain's percentage had risen. At the height of the 1980s Cold War tensions, U.S. defense spending rose to 6.5 percent while European spending remained unchanged. Over time, European contributions to the collective defense hovered just above or below 3 percent of GNP on average. While the United States was a global power with significant out-of-area responsibilities, such as the Korean and Vietnam wars, even adjusting for the non-NATO portion of national defense expenditures, a comparison shows a significantly disproportionate defense burden. As one study demonstrated, the United States, with 48 percent of the aggregated NATO GDP, provided 66 percent of NATO defense costs when Vietnam was excluded from the assessment. To attain equity, the United States would have to have spent $1.1 trillion less on defense between 1961 and 1988.[36]

The basic trade-off within NATO was that the United States gained significant influence over European defense priorities, while the Europeans gained by saving on defense spending, allowing them to invest in socioeconomic priorities. While this exchange worked for both sides, the ebbs and flows of the Cold War would nevertheless affect the alliance. Non-European conflicts, especially the Vietnam War, would strain allies that took divergent views on the war. Most significantly, the nuclear equation raised doubts about the credibility of America's commitment to defend its European allies. To France, the answer was clearly no—America could not be relied on. In 1966, France thus withdrew from the military-planning component of NATO. Nevertheless, for all of the associated costs and management difficulties, NATO remained cohesive throughout the Cold War and ultimately emerged as the victor without ever having to fire a shot. The credibility of the deterrent value of America's defensive grand strategy embodied in its alliance system was thus key to preventing World War III.

An alternative to alliances is the more collective concept of great power systems management. During the 1800s, the international system witnessed the rise of five relatively equal powers that dominated the international system. The form was referred to as a "concert" of powers, which saw individual states acting on their interests in harmony with other states. This multipolar order began with the Quadruple Alliance but expanded in 1815 to include the defeated France after the Napoleonic Wars. During this period, states increased their communication with each other and incorporated other states' interests into calculations of their own concerns. The general health of the system was deemed good, and thus a preference for the status quo was ingrained in the cultures of the participating powers. War was considered a legitimate tool of statecraft, but the major powers generally coordinated their efforts to manage change. States also negotiated for mutual gain as it might be worth sacrificing momentary benefits for longer-term payoffs. Institutional mechanisms of communication were created to facilitate this approach to systems management via conference diplomacy.[37] The goal was, as Lord Castlereagh of Britain put it, "to adopt an open and direct mode of intercourse in the conduct of business and to repress on all sides, as much as possible, the spirit of local intrigue in which diplomatic policy is so falsely considered to consist and which so frequently creates the very evil which it is intended to avert."[38]

The nineteenth-century balance-of-power management model could not be sustained as the harmony of interests eventually diverged, culminating in World War I. However, the basic idea of great power systems management was enshrined in the architecture of the League of Nations, which created a council for the major powers to act as an executive body to manage international security. After World War II, this model survived in the UN Security Council with its five permanent members, the United States, Britain, France, Russia, and China, remaining the core managers of global power into the twenty-first century. Less formal means of concert management have helped states to prevent conflict or negotiate its end. The Group of Eight (G8), a forum of the world's eight leading industrial powers, has coordinated economic priorities and helped to resolve disputes among its members as well as other industrialized nations. In the 1990s, the leading European powers created the Contact Group to sponsor negotiations to end war in the former Yugoslavia. This model is attractive to many realists, who see it resulting in international cooperation rather than anarchy while affirming the basic argument that the causal factor in that outcome is the relative distribution of power. This model was expanded when the G8 was enlarged into the G20 to engage a broader set of common national economic interests in 1999; it became a primary forum for coordinating national and international economic interests after the global recession that began in 2008.

Hegemonic Stability and Offshore Balancing

Hegemonic stability implies that peace is the by-product of great power dominance over a region. A particular region might be highly unstable, but a dominant major power will maintain order based on its own interest. In this context, France and Germany reconciled their historic security dilemma after World War II due to the presence of American power in Western Europe. France felt secure that it could rely on a lasting peace because Germany had been divided, and American troops were on West Germany's soil. Hegemonic stability theory is consistent with the argument that the bipolar distribution of power during the Cold War prevented major war. In the words of Kenneth N. Waltz, "Although we would prefer that East Europeans freely choose their governors, we may nevertheless understand that the Soviet Union's managing a traditionally volatile part of the world has its good points."[39] The benefit of regional hegemony is that wars are unlikely when one country has dominance over a region. This condition exists when an embedded great power will not tolerate instability within its region for fear of outside interference. Efforts by an outside power to exert influence within a major regional power's area of interest is likely to provoke hard balancing behavior by the local hegemon—as during the Cuban Missile Crisis.

The overall benefit of hegemonic stability is the absence of regional war. The downside is that smaller states can be subjugated to the will of the larger power. This condition puts pressure on regional great powers to exercise dominance in a manner acceptable to the smaller states that receive benefits from the collective good of stability. The United States appeared to understand this dilemma during the Cold War as it chose a form of hegemony that fostered multilateralism over total dominance. The United States did not exploit its smaller allies but engaged them in a system of regional security management. The United States also permitted France's choice to depart from NATO's military-planning organization in 1966. Conversely, when the Hungarians and Czechoslovaks pursued policies divergent from those of the Soviet Union during the Cold War, Moscow intervened with force. Thus, hegemonic power can create management problems, especially given states' efforts to escape the influence of the dominant power. Hegemonic stability is nevertheless often beneficial if previously aggressive states are pacified as a result—as were Germany and Japan after World War II.[40] Of course, the quality of that stability depends greatly on the nature of the hegemon and how power is exercised.

An alternative approach to exercising regional power is offshore balancing. When a state pursues this strategy, its presence is constantly felt, but it leaves no direct footprint on the ground. An offshore balancer—like Britain in the nineteenth century and the United States before the world wars—must act with a careful mix of power and restraint.[41] An offshore balancer holds its power in reserve and only intervenes when it is necessary to shift the balance of power or to restore order to a region. The end result can be military intervention and armed conflict. However, the careful exercise of the right amount of power by an outside actor at precisely the right moment can just as likely prevent war. Offshore balancing can be practiced by large and small powers. The ultimate effect is for external actors to gain power while retaining the capacity to shift alignments based on how they perceive their interests. Such powers are in an especially strong position to shape security outcomes because they often hold the key to consolidating, or opposing, whatever trends in regional security might be emerging.

Realism Revised

Realism remains central to explaining global security because most of its bedrock assumptions remain valid. States continue to be the primary actors in the international system, and they assess their security requirements in terms of power. New threats such as terrorism and weapons proliferation confirm the growing role of anarchy in international relations but also prompt citizens to look to their governments for protection. In this context, the caution and pessimism inherent in realism continue to have merit. Additionally, real or potential conflicts among states persist. Realists rightly demonstrate that the relative distribution of power in the international system is still in a competitive flux in the twenty-first century. Great powers, grand strategy, and national competition continue as the United States dominates, but other powers—including Russia, China, India, the EU, and regional powers like Japan and Brazil—contend for influence. The twenty-first-century security transformation also challenges some core elements of realism. A conceptual framework that defined national and international security strictly in state and military terms would not be dealing with the "reality" of international security in this century. Moreover, the ways actors respond to challenges might take new forms. Balancing behavior still exists, but it might not necessarily have the traditional contours realists predict. Asymmetric power also raises significant questions about the function of deterrence. Additionally, the traditional realist, in overemphasizing self-help, risks failing to recognize that states might choose to define their interests in cooperative terms. Indeed, a purely realist-driven security strategy might lead states to assert power in ways that can create significant costs under conditions of global interdependence.

Global Security

Realists do not ignore the impact of globalization on security. Rather, they find that power remains the dominant factor affecting systems structure and state behavior. Michael Mastanduno notes that there are at least three major realist approaches to explaining the emerging international system. First, realists who focus on international competition, not only actual military conflict, provide a geoeconomic framework for assessing global security. In this context, the lessening of military conflict among great powers does not mean that competitive forces are eliminated. Rather, they "evolve into different areas [with] the competition for markets, raw materials, high value-added employment, and the mastery of advanced technology all becoming a surrogate for traditional military competition."[42] Such competition will likely continue until a state opts for a more aggressive strategy to turn the distribution of power in the international system to its advantage and thus spark more traditional security competition. This approach suggests that great powers will mobilize for international economic competition; states will therefore be sensitive to their position relative to other states vis-à-vis economic gain; and powerful states will likely organize relations with their neighbors in order to enhance their relative positions in the global system, thus leading to new alliance structures. A second realist model sees the international system returning to a multipolar structure. A third model, unipolarity, views the international system as dominated by American primacy. Globalization thus takes on a predominantly American character. America would thus have to adopt a specific strategy of preponderance to ensure that no other major regional power could rise to the level of peer competitor.[43]

In 1990, at a moment of general optimism about the prospects for peace with the end of the Cold War, John J. Mearsheimer laid out a realist scenario for a new era defined by a return to anarchy, dangerous multipolarity, and the resulting instability. The international system would likely see major crises in areas of the world that had been stable during the Cold War. Mearsheimer argued that the United States could not sustain global primacy and that it would eventually withdraw from areas such as Germany, where it had placed high priority during the Cold War. The end result would be a multipolar system in which power imbalances and relative power competition would dominate, and more actors would seek nuclear weapons. Mearsheimer predicted a rise in nationalism prompting states not benefiting from the status quo to seek a more aggressive foreign policy. Meanwhile, areas with close ethnic and national integration would experience intense conflict. Mearsheimer looked to Europe and saw several possible scenarios based on realist assumptions. Europe might emerge with no nuclear weapons—which would be the most dangerous outcome, as it would in effect return Europe to the state of affairs that existed between the world wars. Alternatively, a "current-ownership" scenario—where existing nuclear states retained weapons (Britain, France, and Russia) and nonnuclear states remained nuclear-free (e.g., Germany)—might persist in Central Europe. Such a scenario seemed unlikely as eventually Germany would grow insecure if relying on conventional weapons in the absence of a permanent American security guarantee (which Germany might or might not want to sustain). The final scenario followed the logic that Germany would develop nuclear weapons. If likely, such an outcome would hopefully be well managed by those powers currently in possession of nuclear weapons.[44]

A strong counterargument to Mearsheimer's assumptions, especially about Europe, was that international institutions would constrain states by promoting rules and norms of acceptable international behavior and thereby facilitate cooperation toward peace. Mearsheimer addressed this assumption by critiquing the role of international institutions and their promotion of what he referred to as a "false promise of security." Institutions such as the European Union or NATO are seen in this realist perspective as dependent on the distribution of power in the international system—not as having independent effects on state behavior. This realist view cautions that there is a risk that a state would put hopes in an international institution for security. As Mearsheimer writes, "Another state may be reliably benign, but it is impossible to be certain of that judgment because intentions are impossible to divine with 100 percent certainty."[45] Institutions might matter, but only as tools of state strategy.

Kenneth N. Waltz used realist assumptions to predict an emerging multipolarity in the international system based on the eventual rise of Germany (or Europe collectively), Japan, and China. Waltz saw nuclear weapons capability as remaining central to the structure of the international system—and he believed that Germany and Japan would inevitably aspire to attain it: "Pride knows no nationality. How long can Japan and Germany live alongside other nuclear states while denying themselves similar capabilities? Conflicts and crises are certain to make them aware of the disadvantages of being without the military instruments that other powers command. Japanese and German nuclear inhibitions arising from World War II will not last indefinitely; one might expect them to expire as generational memories fade."[46]

Christopher Layne offers a similar analysis, noting that the international system will move toward multipolarity because (1) unipolar systems contain the seeds of their own demise in that the hegemonic power's dominance creates an environment conducive to the emergence of new great powers, and (2) the entry of new great powers into the international system erodes the hegemon's relative power and, ultimately, its preeminence.[47] In addition,

Peter Liberman contests the assertions that modernization inhibits war and that conquest does not pay. Liberman notes that modernization makes nations easy to coerce. Modernization allows tyrants to monopolize coercive resources more easily; rapid communication and mobility allow conquerors to use their coercive resources efficiently. Moreover, modern societies' wealth provides vulnerability to coercion, as wealth can be held hostage for compliance.[48]

To the extent that globalization reflects accelerated interdependence, neorealism has considerable ground on which to expand the assumption that interdependence breeds conflict. As Waltz wrote in 1979, interdependence raises a core problem as self-help implies that "states that feel insecure must ask how the gain will be divided. They are compelled to ask not 'Will both of us gain?' but 'Who will gain more?'"[49] This situation is heightened in a condition of interdependence for, as Waltz writes, "States that are heavily dependent or closely interdependent worry about securing that which they depend on. The high interdependence of states means that the states in question experience, or are subject to, the common vulnerability that high interdependence entails."[50] Waltz notes that rather than overcoming inequality, globalization has reinforced disparity in the international system, which is still dominated not by economic integration but rather by the continued role of the state. Waltz uses data to show that, as a percentage of GNP, the world in 2000 was only about as interdependent as it was in 1910 if measured by trade and capital flows. Significantly, Waltz notes that the core of the global system remains power—and that the phenomenon of globalization reflects the dominance of American power in the international system.[51]

While acknowledging that new security challenges have emerged, John Mearsheimer concludes that they do not pose a sufficient threat to alter the basic dynamics of power among the states in the international system. Dangers such as HIV/AIDS, environmental degradation, unbounded population growth, and global warming are, Mearsheimer writes, a cause for concern, but "there is little evidence that any of them is serious enough to threaten the survival of a great power."[52] Also, as Randall Schweller has shown, actors in international politics can find themselves having to compete over positional goods in a climate of social scarcity. Positional goods are either scarce in some imposed sense or subject to congestion and crowding through more extensive use. Scarcities include both physical scarcity, for instance, in terms of raw materials, and social scarcity, which has to do with pride of place and the quest for goods that maintain a certain standard of living. Such scarcity can result from, for example, "the increased demand for oil due to the emergence of newly industrialized states; or, more generally, the destruction of the global commons due to over-utilization of dwindling resources for the dumping of industrial waste products into common water supplies."[53] Given these conditions of high interdependence and mutual vulnerability, economic growth and social mobility can be a direct cause of competition and conflict.

Primacy and the New Balancing

From a structural perspective, globalization reflects an outward push of American dominance in the international system. As Waltz posits, "What appears to us as globalization appears to much of the world, no doubt to most of the world, very simply as Americanization. In other words, the world is no longer bipolar. It's now unipolar. There is one great power and one only. This condition has not existed since Rome. That is, no country has dominated the relevant part of the globe since Rome, to the extent that we do. And of course Rome's realm was a part of the world. Our realm is the entire globe."[54] The frustration that some states and cultures feel at being on the receiving end of creeping globalization might subsequently work against this trend toward interdependence. As such, American unipolarity might be seen as a threat against which to balance. Alternatively, the unipolar moment is heralded as a positive force that spreads peace and harmony in international politics because of the unique role that the United States plays as a benign hegemon and as a stabilizing force in world politics. Journalist Charles Krauthammer introduced the concept of a unipolar moment into the international security lexicon in 1990 when he argued, "The true geopolitical structure of the post–Cold War world . . . [is] a single pole of world power that consists of the United States at the apex of the industrial West. Perhaps it is more accurate to say the United States and behind it the West."[55] Krauthammer has since argued against multipolarity and asserted that realists should not "want to forfeit unipolarity for the familiarity of traditional multipolarity" as "multipolarity is inherently fluid and unpredictable."[56] Krauthammer advocates a "new unilateralism" that is "clear in its determination to self-consciously and confidently deploy American power in pursuit of global ends."[57]

American primacy might be seen as healthy for the international system because, were it not there, the system could collapse into traditional patterns of international competition. As Michael Mastanduno has shown, the United States has, since the end of the Cold War, pursued a grand strategy designed to sustain American primacy.[58] These dynamics are likely to persist because, as Stephen Brooks and William Wolforth assert, there are virtually no major constraints on the exercise of American power.[59] Yet, America's rise to power has been based on norms of both restraint and multilateralism—historically making its power less threatening to other states.[60] States will compete for primacy because its value lies in the ability not only to win wars but also to achieve a state's goals without military force. Samuel Huntington holds that "primacy is thus an alternative to war. . . . A state such as the United States that has achieved international primacy has every reason to attempt to maintain that primacy through peaceful means so as to preclude the need of having to fight a war to maintain it."[61]

Huntington argues that, while primacy is an important component of world order, the international system at the dawn of the twenty-first century was, in fact, not unipolar. Unipolarity would mean that there was one superpower, no significant major powers, and many minor powers. Huntington sees the distribution of power at that time as having been "uni-multipolar" with one superpower and several major powers. This situation creates a dilemma for both the United States and other major powers as Washington often acts as if it were a unipolar power, provoking resentment and a desire for change among other significant states. Huntington asserts that a brief unipolar moment at the end of the Cold War had passed by the end of the century. These conditions create a serious problem for the United States because, as he writes, "on issue after issue, the United States has found itself increasingly alone, with one or a few partners, opposing most of the rest of the world's states and peoples."[62] Huntington notes that the United States had been increasingly viewed internationally—well before the 2003 invasion of Iraq—as a "rogue superpower." Responses to American primacy at the international level could include the formation of an antihegemonic coalition involving several major powers. Huntington observes that this has yet to occur, however, because it is too early and also because many states benefit from America's world position. He notes that "the international relations theory that predicts balancing under the current circumstances is a theory developed in the context of the European Westphalian system established in 1648."[63] Instead, Huntington sees global politics as "multicivilizational," so that balancing might occur in ways that not only cross the traditional boundaries of nation-states but also include cultural cleavages that might prevent states from forming antibalancing coalitions (e.g., between Russia and China).

States and nonstate actors have new tools provided by globalization that impact the means of pursuing balancing strategies. Steven Walt notes that in some cases, states might bandwagon toward the United States out of fear of American power or a desire to reap rewards for cooperation. States might also engage in regional balancing to make it more difficult for Washington to exert influence in a particular region; this may be done directly or indirectly, simply by frustrating the use of American power. States and their associated nonstate advocates might penetrate into the American political system. As an open democracy, the United States is particularly vulnerable to this new form of balancing. A variety of actors can gain access to internal political processes—via direct lobbying or through expatriates or citizens of their country—to influence U.S. foreign policy. States might align with the United States to influence and constrain American policy by acting as part of American-led coalitions. They might use international institutions and international public opinion to constrain the exertion of American power. Other options include passive resistance where international actors effectually ignore the United States. States also might blackmail the United States—for example, by attaining weapons of mass destruction. Additionally, states and other international actors might incorporate asymmetric tools such as terrorism. Finally, large popular movements might seek to delegitimize the United States in an effort to win hearts and minds across borders.[64]

An emerging tool for states wishing to redistribute power in the modern international system is "soft-power balancing." "Soft power" has been described primarily by neoliberal scholars drawing from the traditions of idealism. However, on the role of soft power there is a convergence of analysis between realists and contemporary liberals who see soft power as essential to the legitimacy of the United States as a sole superpower in the international system. To sustain that legitimacy, the United States has historically used calculated policy mechanisms and choices to avoid soft-power balancing by both allies and enemies. A country's relative soft power is derived from its ability to attract others through the unique appeal and attractiveness of its values and system by co-opting rather than coercing people. To Joseph S. Nye, soft power "rests on the ability to set the political agenda in a way that shapes the preferences of others."[65] Nye shows that "the universality of a country's culture and its ability to establish a set of favorable rules and institutions that govern areas of international activity are critical sources of power."[66] Though realists maintain that hard military and economic power are still the predominant variables shaping international security, soft power is increasingly seen as an important component of contemporary grand strategy, especially for balancing options. This is an ironic development because the mechanisms through which the United States rose to power—multilateral institutions such as the United Nations, NATO, and global economic institutions—are now the tools by which other states can conduct soft-power balancing.

Robert A. Pape has detailed the dynamics of soft-power balancing and noted that the unilateral tendencies of the United States at the turn of the century have provoked balancing behavior—but of a nonmilitary nature. Pape explains the lack of hard balancing against the United States as based initially on its "unparalleled reputation for non-aggressive intentions."[67] Pape argues that, in fact, major powers are in the early stages of creating balancing mechanisms against the United States and that if the United States continues to pursue an aggressive unilateralist tendency, such forces will intensify. He notes that in addition to the historical fear of a possible attack by a larger power, states also worry about the "possibility that one major power will rise to the position of a global hegemon." In such a case, "a state could do many harmful acts, from re-writing the rules of international conduct to its long-term advantage to exploiting world economic resources for relative gain, to imposing imperial rule on second ranked powers, and, potentially, to conquer[ing] any state in the system."[68] To Pape, soft-power balancing behavior includes "actions that do not directly challenge unipolar leader's military preponderance, but that do delay, complicate, and increase the costs of using that extraordinary power. Nonmilitary tools, such as international institutions, economic statecraft, and strict interpretations of neutrality, can have a real, if indirect, effect on the military prospects of a superior state. More important, soft balancing can also establish a basis of cooperation for more forceful, hard balancing measures in the future."[69]

Pape notes that traditional realists should not dismiss soft balancing because there do exist concrete options that can constrain and frustrate the exercise of primacy. Such policy options include territorial denial of staging areas or air and naval transit, economic strengthening via regional trade blocs and other restrictive trade actions, entangling diplomacy via the use of rules and procedures in important international organizations, and the signaling capacity of states to coordinate expectations of mutual balancing behavior. While soft balancing might not stop the United States from making near-term gains, it can impose real military and economic costs on its, or any other large state's, exertion of power.

Alliances, Dissuasion, and Strategic Partnerships

Modern realism is challenged to explain the role of deterrence and alliances in the context of new global security threats. Realists do assert that deterrence remains effective against states in the traditional sense. Also, some realists posit that the demands of emerging threats like nuclear proliferation are logical and, in fact, will produce peace. Realists also view the role of alliances in the contemporary environment with some skepticism. Alliances are possible as a response to new security threats, but to be effective, they must be organized around a common threat perception and an agreed response. Realists do recognize, however, that new forms of cooperation at the strategic level are possible among great and medium powers as shifts in global power place a high premium on temporary alignments such as strategic partnerships and coalitions of the willing.

Realists have struggled with the survival of NATO after the Cold War. Realist theory of alliances generally predicts that, in the absence of a threat, alliances will collapse. Some analysts suggest that NATO might have been sustained as a reserve "insurance" policy to hedge against a hypothetical new Russian threat. However, few would have predicted NATO's expansion to include new members in Central and Eastern Europe or that it would wage an offensive war against Yugoslavia in 1999, fight in Afghanistan, or intervene in Libya in 2011. As a pillar of American dominance in Europe, NATO has served as a tool for Washington to manage the rise of the European Union as a security alternative and to constrain both Germany and Russia as peer competitors. Nevertheless, by 2010, the United States was looking to save money by reviewing and possibly reducing European deployments, and NATO was struggling with its new role in the war in Afghanistan and showed serious fractures very early in the humanitarian intervention in Libya in 2011. While NATO's survival seemed assured, the relevance of its survival was increasingly questionable.

Many pro-NATO advocates and bureaucratic interests advocated a change for NATO to meet new threats. However, identifying a common threat is not the same as aligning shared means to meet it. On September 12, 2001, after the terrorist attacks by al Qaeda on New York and Washington, DC, the NATO allies declared them an "Article 5" matter, meaning they constituted an attack on all NATO members. However, when the United States went to retaliate, it circumvented NATO and excluded all the allies except for Britain. Rajan Menon notes that alliances like NATO might be useful for the promotion of values and democracy—but there is no reason why a military alliance per se is necessary to accomplish this objective.[70] As Bruno Tertrais observes, the assertion by U.S. President George Bush that in the war on terrorism countries were "either with us or against us" harkened to a broad coalition of those on the inside of a grand coalition of as many as 136 countries aligned to fight terrorism.[71] Nevertheless, if "alignment" replaces formal "alliances," and if "temporary and bilateral" replaces "permanent and multilateral," then such relationships carry risk over time. States that align with a major power might find themselves attacked by terrorists for their affiliation. Large powers might put undue pressure on supporting states to engage in actions that are either counter to their own national interests or unsustainable in terms of domestic public support.

Variations on realism also address the challenges to the traditional notion of deterrence and its application to nonconventional threats. Richard Kugler offers "dissuasion" as a complement to traditional deterrence. Dissuasion entails an effort by a state to convince a country or coalition to refrain from courses of action that would menace the state being dissuaded's interests and goals or otherwise endanger world peace.[72] Dissuasion implies an international relationship that is not confrontational but could become so if not carefully handled. Dissuasion is intended to discourage an adversary from engaging in foreign policies and military behaviors that could produce political confrontation, military competition, and war. At a tactical level, sufficient defensive measures for homeland security can persuade terrorist groups that the risk of detection and failure is not worth the expenditure of scarce resources. Dissuasion can send a signal from one country to another (e.g., from the United States to China) that it is not worth considering a military buildup that might in the future rival another power as that buildup will be met with true military capabilities. If, however, dissuasion is "pursued in heavy-handed ways, it can be counterproductive, it can help intensify regional polarization and militarization, motivate countries to pursue asymmetric strategies aimed at negating U.S. strengths, alienate allies, and trigger the formation of coalitions against the United States."[73]

Another emerging concept consistent with realism is the strategic partnership. States use strategic partnerships to enhance or justify close relationships with others who seek mutual gains.[74] The concept is purposefully vague and has been applied to a variety of international security relationships. For offensive realism, a strategic partnership can be a tool used by a powerful state or group of states to maximize political, economic, and military dominance in the international system. Consistent with defensive realism, strategic partnerships can reflect balancing behavior as states use them to constrain other powers. Strategic partnerships are sometimes part of a grand scheme for systemic change, but diplomats may also use them as a rhetorical device to navigate the rough edges of shifting global politics. The term can also connote a contemporary spin on traditional balance-of-power politics. Or it may constitute window dressing to justify bilateral alliances arising out of pragmatic necessity.

A survey of strategic partnerships shows that the term has been used in five specific kinds of state-to-state relationships. First, the United States and Turkey used the term to describe their bilateral relationship during the 1990s. Turkey, in turn, also set out to build its own strategic partnership with Israel. In this case, the term was used to bolster the relationship between traditional allies (United States and Turkey) and to signal a desire for a new relationship (Turkey and Israel). However, if the term could be used to define a relationship between hard military allies, what did this do to the overall concept of alliance? Second, the term was used to project reassurance—for example, the United States built a strategic partnership with Romania after that country was initially excluded from NATO membership in 1997. Meanwhile, the United States also offered a third form of strategic partnership to Russia as a means of engaging Moscow as a tool to manage Russia's great power decline.

But if Romania and Turkey had the same relationship with the US as Russia, what did that mean? The term was applied, fourth, by the United States to its relationship with China as a justification for engagement with a potential adversary. In a fifth example, Russia and China developed their own strategic partnership, explicitly intending to promote their cooperation as a tool for complicating American primacy.

Asymmetric Threats, Ethnic Conflict, and Identity Realism

Realism has shown adaptability in scholarly applications of traditional concepts to new threats such as terrorism and ethnic conflict. Additionally, the notion that states are all, in effect, "the same" has been adjusted to better reflect the relationship between a state "identity" and variations in how states define their interests. Core concepts of realism, including rational actor models and balance-of-power stability, still apply to these cases. These new security threats do challenge the traditional realist focus on the primacy of the nation-state. However, the fact that security challenges exist beyond the nation-state does not necessarily mean that other core assumptions that drive realist thinking are outdated.

Assessing the asymmetric threat of terrorism, Robert Pape surveyed suicide terrorist attacks from 1980 through 2001. The data shows that, rather than being driven solely by "crazy" fanatics, they have a strategic, and rational, logic.[75] Religion is a relevant factor, but mainly as a recruitment tool. Pape's evidence points to four fundamental conclusions about suicide terrorism: suicide terrorism is strategic, designed to coerce modern democracies to make concessions; suicide terrorism is rising in number of incidents because terrorists are learning that it pays; in spite of some gains, more ambitious suicide terrorist campaigns are not going to achieve major gains; and, finally, the most promising way to contain suicide terrorism is to reduce terrorists' confidence in their ability to carry out such attacks on the target society.[76] These conclusions are supported by three key findings: (1) timing—nearly all suicide attacks occur in organized, coherent campaigns, not as isolated or randomly timed incidents; (2) nationalist goals—suicide terrorists' campaigns are directed at gaining control of what the terrorists see as their national homeland territory, specifically at ejecting foreign forces from that territory; and (3) target selection—all suicide terrorist campaigns in the last two decades have been aimed at democracies, which make more suitable targets from the terrorists' point of view.[77] Pape also shows that terrorists are not likely to achieve overly ambitious goals. Overly dramatic attacks can backfire for terrorist groups as such acts will not likely impact the interests of states with significant wealth or security issues at stake.

Ethnic conflict, because it can occur within states as well as transcend state borders, is an important challenge for realist approaches to contemporary security. Nevertheless, application of realist assumptions to this growing security challenge has helped to better explain the origins of, and possible solutions to, ethnic conflict. For example, Chaim Kaufmann notes that, in ethnic wars, the extreme forces and passions that drive ethnic identities to the point of war are unlikely to yield to appeals to cease fire and negotiate a settlement. Intermingled population settlement patterns can thus create a new variation on the security dilemma that serves to intensify violence, motivate ethnic cleansing, and prevent de-escalation unless warring parties are separated. Kaufmann shows that stable resolutions of ethnic conflict can only occur when opposing groups are separated into defensible enclaves. As a result, the international community should abandon idealistic hopes of restoring multiethnic states and integrating populations and instead facilitate and protect population movements to create national homelands. The only other alternative is to let the warring parties battle it out via ethnic cleansing until one side emerges victorious.[78]

Another variation on realism, "identity realism," combines realist assumptions with the study of culture. This approach seeks to explain how states come to perceive their interests and why they might not always behave in ways that traditional realism would predict. Alastair Iain Johnston argues that the balance-of-power and balance-of-threat aspects of neorealism do not adequately explain contemporary Chinese security choices. Realist focus on the offensive desire to expand power and compete for primacy does help to describe some of China's behavior. However, it fails to provide a complete explanation because China does not appear to be especially unsatisfied with the status quo of American primacy and indeed is making some important gains from political and economic cooperation with the United States. Johnston concludes that Chinese security policy is best explained by "identity realism"—which explains why status is as important to Chinese leaders as security—and that the major threats to China are those that serve to constrain the achievement of higher status.[79] Identity realism suggests that if there is an increase in the intensity of identity or efforts to intensify identification, one can expect to see more competitive behavior directed at external forces.[80] Such an approach, Johnston maintains, helps to address a shortcoming in more traditional realist assessments of state strategies because it accounts for variations in the intensity of strategic choices and in the responses of different groups to similar changes in relative capabilities.[81] In this context, self-help is shaped by internal identity formation, which then devalues external forces, turning them into threats to the legitimacy of a group's concept of itself inside the nation-state.

Clash of Civilizations

A "clash-of-civilizations" approach blends realist assessments of interdependence with the impact of culture to explain the sources of conflict. The idea of cultural conflict is not new in international security. However, the idea of a clash of civilizations posits that international security trends increasingly reflect a repositioning of global conflict away from states and toward alignment among civilizational kinship. Samuel Huntington advanced this position in 1993 with his assessment of the rise of civilizations and impending conflict along new fault lines that transcend the traditional nation-state.[82] Huntington assumes that neither ideological nor economic incentives but cultural factors will drive international relations in the twenty-first century.

A civilization is defined as the broadest level of community with which individuals affiliate. Huntington identified eight major world civilizations: Western, Confucian, Japanese, Islamic, Hindu, Slavic-Orthodox, Latin American, and possibly African. He offered six reasons for a pending clash of civilizations. First, the kinds of differences that emerge between civilizational groups are real and basic. Such identities are the most difficult for people to abandon. Second, the interactions between different civilizations are increasing. This enhances people's consciousness of their own identity, heightening awareness of differences from and animosities toward others. Third, economic modernization and subsequent social change separates people from their basic identity and weakens nation-states as a source of identification. This source has been replaced by religion, which often manifests in the form of fundamentalist movements designed to advance and protect the boundaries of civilizations. Fourth, civilization consciousness is enhanced by the "dual role of the West"—which is at the peak of its power—but also prompts a backlash against it. Fifth, cultural identification is less mutable, thus less easily compromised and resolved, than political or economic differences. Finally, economic regionalism is growing along cultural lines, which will further enhance the global dynamics of civilizational conflict.

Huntington points to regional fault lines in the world where civilizations meet and conflict is likely. As civilizations transcend traditional state boundaries, groups or nations are likely to rally around the states that most closely approximate their civilizational interests. Huntington notes that the "West" faces a particularly difficult challenge because other civilizations have a common cause in challenging the dominant civilization. Facing likely conflict, civilizations have three possible reactions: (1) to isolate themselves to avoid penetration by the West; (2) to bandwagon and join with the West; and (3) to balance the West by developing economic and military capabilities and forging alliances with other non-Western societies. States torn internally by competing civilizational preferences are likely to experience a particularly high amount of stress in this kind of conflict.

Huntington asserts that he was not endorsing a clash. Rather, he sought to set forth a descriptive hypothesis as to what the future might hold. Nevertheless, traditional realists might resist the temptation to move beyond the interest of states, noting also that there have been a number of state-to-state and civil conflicts within the civilizations identified by Huntington—for example, between Iran and Iraq in the 1980s. By 2005 most Iraqis killed in Iraq were dying as a result of attacks undertaken by their countrymen. Subsequently, Huntington's approach has been criticized for assuming cohesion within civilizations that are in fact quite diverse and in some cases divided— for example, among Shiite and Sunni Muslims. Furthermore, if strictly applied as policy, Huntington's assumptions might generate self-fulfilling prophecies. For example, if one looks at Russia and assumes that certain civilizational traits will lead Moscow toward conquest and authoritarianism, expanding NATO as an anti-Russian alliance would seem important. Russia's authoritarian and expansionist past, however, does not determine its future. Indeed, expansion of NATO would risk creating a self-fulfilling prophecy, exacerbating the clash of civilizations should Russia abandon the West in favor of its own perceived security needs. Nonetheless, Huntington's analysis, while controversial, was among the most important conceptual arguments and significant modifications of the realist paradigm at the onset of the twenty-first century.

Economic Realism

Economic realism is a state-centric approach to political economy that focuses on the state's role in maximizing economic power to attain power objectives. To economic realists, the purpose of the state is to develop economic strengths and protect against vulnerabilities to advance the national interest. Economic realists view the international economic system as competitive and economic relationships as based on zero-sum gains in which there are always winners and losers. States might thus work within the emerging global security dynamics to use their economic power via the channels of globalization to expand their wealth. In this sense, globalization is a power tool used by states seeking to consolidate and expand their relative international positions. Alternatively, economic realists might see a particular economic order as providing stability to the world economy and thus justifying hegemony as preventing future conflict. Or economic realism could also have a defensive component in which states seek to adjust domestic economic policy to resist the encroachment of global challenges to sovereignty.

As Richard Rosecrance has shown, the modern trading system was embedded in world politics on the basis of the strength of the alliance arrangements pursued during the Cold War.[83] This system reflected the dominant preferences exercised by the primacy of the United States in close keeping with its security objectives. As Barry Buzan shows, three specific paths can lead to the extension of the relationship between economic strategy and security. The first is a direct argument: when the threat of war is high, an entire economy is geared toward enhancing military strength. The second extends military logic but adds to it, by analogy, other areas in which the legitimate responsibilities of governments can be defined in national security terms. For example, when economic threats have the highest profile in many citizens' view, a conflation of social and national security logic can be highly appealing for political actors. In the third path, states might attack the nature of global free market logic and the dangers of surrendering economic control to outside forces.[84] Investment in military capabilities can significantly increase the power of a state and thus create a perception of threat for other states. Consistent with the security dilemma, this can in turn lead them to adapt their strategies. Alternatively, an overinvestment in military capabilities can create overstretch and force a state to retrench and reform—or even lead to collapse. The end of the Cold War reflected key aspects of this dynamic as the United States significantly increased its economic investment in the military, forcing the Soviet Union either to match it or negotiate. Meanwhile, the costs of the external occupation of Eastern Europe also domestically drained the economic power of the Soviet Union.

Within the global security environment, it is possible that economic warfare will serve as a surrogate for traditional means of conflict. States might employ international sanctions on enemy states to induce change or punish behavior. States might, alternatively, offer economic rewards to those states that do cooperate with strategic objectives. Ethan Kapstein offers eight specific ways in which economic warfare can be employed: embargo, or a prohibition on exports to the enemy and its allies; boycott, or a prohibition on buying goods from the enemy and its allies; blacklisting of domestic or third-country firms that trade with the enemy; strategic purchasing, or the buying of defense-related commodities on world markets; dumping, or the sale of stockpiled goods at lower prices; impounding, confiscating, or nationalizing enemy-owned assets; strategic bombing, sabotage, or other military operations against enemy economic targets; and propaganda, or the deliberate use of economic misinformation to create panic, hoarding, and confusion in enemy territory.[85] Kapstein also notes the impact of the de-escalation from warfare or conflict as states have a high incentive to switch "from guns to butter." Such moves can be destabilizing because loss of demand for military goods and services can redirect the resource base for military capabilities. While military conversion can yield an economic gain, it can also lead states to be underprepared should new threats emerge on the horizon. Attaining the right balance between guns and butter remains one of the most significant challenges confronting states as they pursue their national interests.

Economic realists see a strong role for the state within the domestic economy in mounting a defensive response to external forces—such as the market pressures of economic globalization. State creation of protective barriers can include the imposition of tariffs on foreign imported goods and services; nontariff barriers such as health and safety regulations and other standards; pricing limits to restrain trade; technological restrictions; and the dumping of surplus goods into foreign markets at lower-than-competitive prices. States might also pursue protectionist policies to give infant industries an advantage via direct investment. The historical track record of such actions has not been good. However, they are realist-based responses to the perceived threat of globalization given the role of the state and its desire to sustain or maximize power.

The structural role of power distribution can also help explain the increased role in international relations played by multinational corporations. As Robert Gilpin has shown, the 1980s and 1990s saw an extraordinary expansion of corporate power in the developed parts of the world combined with an increasing concentration of power among media, entertainment, and telecommunications firms.[86] Such a development presents a challenge both to the traditional dominance of nation-states and also to the ability of less developed states and their firms to expand their economic capabilities. The result can be a tendency to pursue protectionist policies or to regulate multinational firms. However, if too many states pursued such a policy, the results would be costly for the global economy. Gilpin's analysis of international political economy strikes a balance, concluding that "although for many, globalization is a threat, it is also part of the solution to underdevelopment."[87] Gilpin's approach reflects pragmatism in economic realism, which historically often viewed underdeveloped economies as being of value only to the extent that wealthy states could exploit their resources.

A central question for realists is whether the economic interdependence that drives globalization increases the likelihood of war. Realists have generally answered this question by noting that much of the same competitive logic of security competition can apply to economic models because relative power shifts are also important factors in assessing the security needs of states. As John Mearsheimer writes, "Once relative gains considerations are factored into the equation, it becomes impossible to maintain the neat dividing line between economic and military issues, mainly because military might is significantly dependent on economic might. . . . The relative size of a state's economy has profound consequences for its standing in the international balance of military power."[88] Realists see the interdependence of economic ties as creating vulnerability and thus providing incentives for states to deny an enemy any economic advantage. Additionally, great powers are going to conflict with each other as they seek ever-expanding access to resources as a means of growing their economies. In sum, there is no reason, in the realist view, to assume that economic interdependence and globalization inherently create peace.

Realists As Optimists

Robert Gilpin notes that realists maintain a particular worldview grounded in core propositions, but that does not necessarily mean that they like it:

Although realists recognize the central role of the state, security, and power in international affairs, they do not necessarily approve of this situation. The teacher who first introduced me to realism as an analytic perspective, Professor George Little of the University of Vermont, was a Quaker pacifist; yet, when I was an undergraduate, Little once chided me for my naïve and unrealistic views on a particular development in international politics. Martin Wight, the author of one of the most important tracts on realism in this century, *Power Politics* (1986), was also a Christian pacifist. Even Hans Morgenthau in his influential *Politics Among Nations*, having Adolf Hitler in mind, condemned "universal nationalism," that is, imperialistic behavior, as immoral. One of his basic messages was that states should try to respect the interests of other states.[89]

Indeed, a variety of factors related to perceptions of self-interest can modify many of the impulses that realists worry about. Dale C. Copeland has shown that expectations of future trade gains can lead states to avoid risks that would sever the benefits of future trade. "When expectations for trade are positive, leaders expect to realize the benefits of trade into the future and therefore have less reason for war now; trade will indeed 'constrain.' . . . If, however, leaders are pessimistic about future trade, fearing to be cut off from vital goods or believing that current restrictions will not be relaxed, then the negative expected value of peace may make war the rational strategic choice."[90] In that sense, the political economy of the global security environment can lead states to forgo conflict in expectation of future strategic gains. Charles Glaser uses realist concepts to show how states will work to organize their military-policy options during peacetime to coordinate policies designed to avoid arms races. Glaser proposes the use of "contingent realism," which asserts that cooperative policies are an important type of self-help in that "states seeking security should see benefits in cooperative policies that can communicate be-nign motives." Thus, states will have a self-help motive in promoting policies that emphasize nonthreatening military capabilities and signal their benign intentions via arms control, unilateral defense, and unilateral restraint (the later two implying the unilateral decision to prioritize defensive capabilities). Glaser concludes, "Instead of a strong propensity toward security competi-tion, we find that states' choices between cooperation and competition are highly conditional, with no general preference for competition."[91]

Summary

Historically, realism has been the dominant approach to understanding the quest for power in international security. A long tradition in the form of anarchy, interest, power, and war provides strong evidence of the salience of realist traditions. Realism's primary focus on power continues to give it considerable relevance to global security because, while its manifestations have expanded, power remains central to understanding security behavior. Realism has proven to be a flexible and adaptive approach to the emerging security environment. Perhaps the most important legacy of realism is that it can serve as a methodological tool with which to test and challenge ongoing efforts in the more idealistic search for peace. Realism can serve as a means through which to test alternative approaches; first challenging them with the hard critiques made available by the traditions of realism will only make them more attainable. As E. H. Carr surmised, human nature seeks to build a better world, but if not challenged by realism, such approaches risk crashing on the rocks of reality.[92]

Suggested Reading

Brown, Michael, Sean Lynn-Jones, and Steven E. Miller, eds. *Contemporary Realism and International Security.* Cambridge, MA: MIT Press, 1995.

Carr, E. H. *The Twenty Years' Crisis: 1919–1939.* London: Perennial, 1964.

Craig, Gordon A., and Alexander L. George. *Force and Statecraft: Diplomatic Problems of Our Time.* 3rd ed. Oxford: Oxford University Press, 1995.

Donnelly, Jack. *Realism and International Relations.* Cambridge: Cambridge Univer-sity Press, 2000.

Gilpin, Robert. *Global Political Economy: Understanding the International Economic Order.* Princeton, NJ: Princeton University Press, 2001.

Huntington, Samuel P. *The Clash of Civilizations and the Remaking of World Order.* New York: Simon and Schuster, 1998.

Kapstein, Ethan B., and Michael Mastanduno, eds. *Unipolar Politics: Realism and State Strategies after the Cold War.* New York: Columbia University Press, 1999.

Keohane, Robert O., ed. *Neorealism and Its Critics.* New York: Columbia University Press, 1985.

Mearsheimer, John J. *The Tragedy of Great Power Politics.* New York: W. W. Norton, 2003.

Nye, Joseph S. *Soft Power: The Means to Success in World Politics.* New York: Public Affairs, 2004.

Opposition supporters wave roses during an antigovernment protest advancing calls for democratization in Tunisia on January 26, 2011. Source: Reuters/Khaled Abdullah.

3

The Search for Peace

THE COUNTERPOINT TO REALISM IS IDEALISM, which asserts that human nature is inherently good and that power in its many forms can be used to achieve positive outcomes in the search for peace. While reflecting popular sentiment, traditional manifestations of idealism have shown significant limits in terms of guaranteeing peace. Broadly, idealism is made problematic by the basic question of whose ideals should dominate. Functionally, the approach has often generated counterproductive results. The idea, for example, that diplomatic accommodation promotes peace was shattered at the beginning of World War II when Germany broke various international commitments. The effort to build a hierarchical security governance system based on collective security in the League of Nations, in which all states in a community identify and punish an aggressor, failed to prevent World War II. International law has fared better as governments have broadly accepted some general rules regarding international conflicts, such as the Geneva Conventions, which govern the conduct of war, define war crimes, and protect prisoners of war and civilians in conflict. Arms control and disarmament have also had success in terms of limiting or reducing armaments as a path to peace. Some general moral rules, such as human rights, have been recognized as universal norms. Despite inherent dilemmas, idealism remains an international constant as states and citizens work to build a world that is both secure and peaceful. This chapter surveys contemporary idealist frameworks associated with liberalism and examines modern approaches to security studies, including social theory, civil-society theory, pacifism, postmodernism, gender studies, and revolutionary approaches to international change.

Liberalism

Liberalism is grounded primarily in idealism and seeks to identify the conditions under which a more peaceful international society is attainable. As Michael Doyle notes, "The peaceful intent and restraint that liberalism does manifest in limited aspects of its foreign affairs announces the possibility of a world peace this side of the grave or of world conquest. . . . It has strengthened the prospects for a world peace established by the steady expansion of a separate peace among liberal societies."[1] Doyle focuses analytical attention on the moral commitment to three sets of rights: (1) freedom from arbitrary authority; (2) rights necessary to protect and promote the capacity for freedom, which include social and economic rights such as equal opportunity in education and rights to health care and employment; and (3) democratic participation or representation.[2] Some liberals fault realists for being intellectually incapable of adequately explaining the "reality" of the new international system. Seyom Brown, for example, asserts that the "narrowly focused 'realist' lens fails to illuminate many of the momentous developments occurring within, above, and across the jurisdictions of the nation-states that are creating dangerous incongruities in world politics and society."[3] Brown argues that realism has become largely irrelevant to policy analysis because of its failure to comprehend some of the world's most serious predicaments. He challenges the meaning of "interests," which should evolve from "national" to "world" levels, including (1) survival of the human species, (2) reduction in the amount of killing and other extremely brutal treatment of human beings, (3) provision of conditions for healthy subsistence to all people, (4) protection of citizens' rights, (5) preservation of cultural diversity, (6) preservation of the planet's basic natural ecologies and environment, and (7) enhancement of accountability.[4]

Stephen Krasner summarizes liberal theory as having three core assumptions. First, there are many different kinds of actors, including state-owned enterprises, multinational corporations, public international organizations, nongovernmental organizations, private foundations, and terrorists, as well as states. Second, these actors are all rational and calculating, but they pursue different objectives: corporate executives want profits or sales; the rulers of states want security and higher levels of well-being for their populations; environmental groups want to preserve the ecosphere. Furthermore, various actors have different power capabilities in different areas; specific actors influence outcomes in some arenas but not in others. Third, international relations, especially regarding international political economy, offer opportunities for everyone to gain at the same time. Actors are more concerned with their absolute well-being than with their relative position vis-à-vis others.[5] Andrew Moravcsik asserts that liberalism is at least as methodologically sound as realist traditions and argues that liberalism, like realism, focuses on the primacy of societal actors. Liberalism also assumes that states represent a subset of domestic society and that via these interests a state establishes preferences in world politics. Furthermore, liberals believe that the situation of interdependence is a key determinant of state behavior.[6] Robert O. Keohane identifies three kinds of modern liberalism: republican liberalism, commercial liberalism, and regulatory liberalism. Republican liberalism views democratic republics as more peaceful than dictatorships, thereby placing domestic systems as a key determinant of state behavior. Commercial liberalism focuses on the natural harmony of interests that lead to cooperation derived from trade and mutual dependency. Regulatory liberalism stresses the role that the establishment of international rules can play in facilitating peace.[7]

Contemporary liberalism offers no procedural guarantees of peace—a departure from more utopian forms of collective security or international law. Liberalism does offer a basic belief that peace is possible, but inducements and facilitation might be necessary. Keohane notes that liberalism may reduce the likelihood of the use of force. However, the opposite is possible as moral causes have motivated wars, such as with U.S. intervention in Vietnam. Keohane points, as reasons for intervention, to the desire to protect American direct foreign investment in underdeveloped countries, the need to protect access to raw materials that fuel economic power such as oil in the Persian Gulf, and a drive to punish those who use asymmetric power to threaten the liberal state—such as terrorists who seek to disrupt the freedom of movement of goods and services or citizens' travel.[8]

One of the more ambitious statements of contemporary liberalism was made by Francis Fukuyama, who argued in 1989 that the world had witnessed the "end of history." Fukuyama argued that the end of the Cold War meant the triumph not only of the West but of the Western idea of liberalism. Moving away from Marxism and nationalism, Fukuyama saw Western liberal democracy as representing the final form of human government. He asserted that the end of history would be a difficult time: "The struggle for recognition, the willingness to risk one's life for a purely abstract goal, the worldwide ideological struggle that called forth daring, courage, imagination, and idealism, will be replaced by economic calculation, the endless solving of technical problems, environmental concerns, and the satisfaction of sophisticated consumer demand."[9] Nonetheless, new dominant patterns in the international system would overcome the kinds of traditional behavior patterns that had brought nations into conflict. A decade later, however, Fukuyama retreated significantly from this position after witnessing ten years of rising nationalism and ongoing conflict around the world.[10]

Neoliberal Institutionalism

As a theory of international relations, neoliberalism was first explained by Robert Keohane and Joseph Nye in 1974. Neoliberal institutionalism explains the conditions that complex interdependence presents to states and posits that anarchy creates an interest among states to achieve cooperation. The focus on the role of the state, anarchy in the international system, and the advancement of the national interest is consistent with realist traditions. However, unlike realists, neoliberals are optimistic that cooperation and mutual gains are possible. Neoliberals seek to show how informal international institutions and formal international organizations can facilitate such cooperation—leading to a higher prospect of creating a more peaceful world. Neoliberal institutionalism focuses analytical attention on the study of international regimes and the norms, principles, rules, and decision-making procedures that they embody through formal or informal processes.[11] Neoliberal theory places international institutions and their embodiment in international organizations at the core of state-driven efforts to facilitate cooperation. So long as the benefits of cooperation outpace the costs, states will sacrifice short-term interests for long-term mutual gains.[12] The fact that states invest prestige and resources in international institutions is seen as important evidence of the demand for formalized multilateral cooperation. Neoliberal institutionalism does not, however, assert that all institutions will matter at all times. Also, the theory does not suggest that institutions act independently of the distribution of power among states. Moreover, neoliberal scholarship does not intrinsically assume successful outcomes of cooperation. As Keohane writes, "Neoliberal approaches can backfire as policy prescriptions."[13]

The neoliberal approach to international institutions traditionally focused analytical attention on economic and environmental cooperation, where the dangers of defection from cooperation are low, rather than classical security cooperation, where the dangers of defection are high.[14] Nevertheless, in a global security environment, neoliberals have advanced important arguments about the relationship between international institutions and security. International institutions—through established headquarters, staff, planning, rules, and procedures—are thought to help states manage coordination and collaboration problems of collective action and make cooperation on security provision easier to achieve. Such interaction, proximity, and transparency are thought to foster reassurance and trust, thereby reducing the sense of vulnerability and fear that results from international anarchy. As Keohane and Nye demonstrate, security institutions can aid the exercise of influence, constrain bargaining strategies, balance or replace other institutions, signal governments' intentions by providing others with information and making policies more predictable, specify obligations, and impact both the interests and preferences of states.[15]

Contemporary liberalism also emphasizes the role of institutions—reflecting and advancing principles and norms of community standards, working in conjunction with information sharing, rules, and decision-making procedures—as mechanisms for lowering the transaction costs of multilateral enforcement strategies against states that violate global or regional community standards of acceptable state behavior. Neoliberal theory posits that states share an interest in establishing principles and norms to facilitate cooperation and provide clarity from international anarchy. Principles and rules of institutions help states to address the uncertainty of the future and to avoid establishing counterproductive precedents.[16] From this interaction, institutions are thought to, as Charles Kupchan notes, raise the costs of defection and define what constitutes it, while at the same time advancing interstate socialization by promoting the concept of an international community.[17] In this sense, security institutions can become important promoters of community values and also tools for channeling enforcement against violators of community principles and norms.

Some neoliberal scholars note that the theory has insufficiently accounted for the content of principles, norms, and institutional activity.[18] Judith Goldstein and Robert Keohane assess the role of ideas in shaping interests in terms of worldviews, principles, and causal beliefs. Goldstein and Keohane write that, as regards ideas embedded in institutions, "once a policy choice leads to the creation of reinforcing organizational and normative structures, that policy idea can affect the incentives of political entrepreneurs long after the interests of its initial proponents have changed."[19] There are limits, however, to the power of ideas and institutions in a world governed by interest-maximizing states. For example, as Keohane notes, just because democracies come together to cooperate does not by necessity mean that they will work together to export democracy. He writes, "Democracies may act to stop starvation or extreme abuses of human rights, as in Somalia, but they are unlikely to sacrifice significant welfare for the sake of democracy—especially when people realize how hard it is to create democracy and how ineffective intervention often is in doing so."[20] Some neoliberal assumptions also appear to be founded on normative beliefs rather than hard evidence. Keohane acknowledges a normative assumption in modern liberal theory, stating that "the strength of liberalism as a moral theory lies in its attention to how governmental arrangements will operate in practice, and in particular, how institutions can protect human rights against the malign inclinations of power holders."[21] The ability of an institution to promote such outcomes might thus be higher when institutions reflect what Katja Weber calls a heterogeneity of states based on countries' religious, linguistic, cultural, and political backgrounds.[22] From this basis, formal institutions can act as "community representatives" and as "managers of enforcement" of international principles and norms.[23]

Neoliberal institutional theory proposes that, as states seek to coordinate policy, institutions will lower the transaction costs of cooperation in ways that would not be possible were no institution available. This conclusion about transaction costs draws from the assumption that states will assess the costs of bargaining relative to the costs of alternative policy choices. Information sharing is seen as helping states overcome various obstacles to cooperation, while the rules and procedures of international institutions produce efficiency gains in security cooperation.[24] As Keohane demonstrates, international institutions and their functions are best understood as "information-providing and transaction-cost-reducing entities."[25] Celeste Wallander maintains that international institutions can facilitate security cooperation by reducing transaction costs and making it possible for states to cooperate. To Wallander, rules and procedures are "institutional assets" that "enable states to cooperate by providing resources, such as information on intentions or compliance; by establishing rules for negotiations, decision-making, and implementation; and by creating incentives to conform to international standards necessary for multilateral action."[26] Such transaction-cost models assume that states will seek and maintain institutions to increase the efficiency of providing for a common good.

Cooperative Security

As an effort to build inclusive mechanisms for security management without rigid hierarchical architectures, cooperative security views the organized use of military power on behalf of the international community as necessary and acceptable, while at the same time looking favorably on the role of international institutions to coordinate such efforts. The idea became popular in the 1990s as a way to emphasize the ideals that drive multinational security cooperation but without the historical weaknesses of collective security. Cooperative security accepts the basic premise that global security conditions require a complex approach that places a high demand on the management of risk. Underlying cooperative security is a principle of "cooperative engagement," which is a "strategic principle that seeks to accomplish its purposes through institutionalized consent rather than through threats of material or physical coercion. It presupposes fundamentally compatible security objectives and promotes collaborative rather than confrontational relationships among national military establishments."[27] Such an approach emphasizes reassurance over traditional deterrence and containment. The end goal is not a normative world order but rather a division of labor designed to enforce agreed-upon means of preventing war and managing crises.

The concept of cooperative security emerged from a Brookings Institution study in the mid-1990s that stressed five major elements: (1) the establishment of strict controls and security measures for nuclear forces; (2) a regime for the conversion of defense industries whose excess capacity could lead to unwarranted global weapons proliferation and thus exacerbate international instability; (3) cooperative arrangements regulating the size and composition of forces to emphasize defensive configurations and also to restrict the flow of dangerous technologies; (4) the articulation of an internationally supported concept of effective and legitimate intervention, in which the use of force is always multilateral and elected only as a last resort; and (5) the promotion of transparency and mutual interest as the basis for monitoring agreed-upon constraints, including those on the diffusion of advanced technologies.[28] Antonia Handler Chayes and Abram Chayes build on the role of reassurance to show how an ideal type of cooperative security architecture would function. First, they maintain that a strong normative base is necessary for those who participate so that they can have an expectation of fairness and equally applicable procedures. The second core element is a combination of inclusiveness and nondiscrimination. Transparency, the critical third ingredient, entails the availability and accessibility of information about the security arrangement itself and the activities of those working within it. Regime management, the fourth component, requires the collection and analysis of information, review assessment and response to information, capacity building based on known security requirements, interpretation of agreements and settlement-of-dispute capacity, and the ability to maintain adaptability and flexibility to changed security requirements. Finally, a cooperative security order requires the capacity of its members to engage, when necessary, in effective sanction of those who violate agreed-upon norms.[29]

Allen Sens explains cooperative security as a conceptual bridge between the realist and neoliberal frameworks. Based on reassurance and engagement rather than deterrence and containment, cooperative security organizations are inclusive rather than exclusive in nature and aim to engage members and nonmembers as well as like-minded and non-like-minded actors in a larger framework. The primary activities of cooperative security organizations are not directed against a specific external threat but exist for the achievement of shared security objectives. Cooperative security is built on a broadened conception of security in order to promote military and nonmilitary security objectives. Cooperative security also aims to transform and/or adapt existing security institutions. It envisions a cautious, gradual approach to institutionalization, preferring to establish the conditions under which improvised, informal, and flexible patterns of cooperation that are consistent with existing modalities and sensibilities can develop. Finally, cooperative security recognizes the value of other bilateral or multilateral security arrangements in the maintenance of regional security.[30] Sens notes that there are significant challenges to this model—for example, the temptation to free ride. Smaller states may provide suboptimal investments in shared security management, leading to a divergence in capabilities and a willingness to take security risks. In this sense, it may prove difficult to sustain cooperative security architectures in the absence of high agreement on the nature of the challenges being faced.

The divergence of opinion in the international community during the 2002–2003 crisis regarding Iraq's alleged weapons of mass destruction programs illustrates some of the dilemmas inherent in cooperative security. At one level, cooperative security was challenged between 1998 and 2002 because UN weapons inspectors had been kicked out of Iraq, and there had been no penalty for this action. From this perspective, cooperative security was shown to be ineffective as Iraq had violated the norms of the cooperative system on weapons of mass destruction with no serious consequence. The power dynamics of cooperative security did appear to work through early 2003 when the United Nations was able to return weapons inspectors to Iraq aided by the threat of American military intervention. By March 2003, the UN weapons inspectors were close to being able to declare Iraq in compliance with UN resolutions. However, rather than wait for additional information from the United Nations, the United States opted for preemptive war, throwing the existing foundations of cooperative security into disarray. In the eyes of some critics, including some of America's closest allies, by resorting to unilateral actions, the United States violated the principles of reassurance and restraint. Yet, a core premise of the approach was proven as well in that, absent international legitimacy and burden sharing, the United States suffered higher operational, financial, and human costs to its soldiers than it otherwise might have.

Peace through Commerce

Commercial liberalism is based on the perceived benefits of the liberal free market trading system, regional economic integration, efforts to promote economic development in poorer areas of the world, and a presumed positive impact of multinational corporations. Overall, there is a belief that the "spirit of commerce" can promote harmonious international relations through mutual economic gains. This approach differs from neoliberalism in that the truest form of commercial liberalism would seek to limit state involvement in the international economic system. However, commercial liberalism is also pragmatic about the role of nation-states as actors working within the international economic system to manage inefficiencies that might lead to economic instability.

A core objective of commercial liberalism is to promote the maximum amount of economic development for as many people as possible. The more people have access to markets and the more competition is fostered, the more innovation can lead to increased employment and economic development. In addition to fostering international cooperation, liberal approaches to economic development see the expansion of incomes and wealth as a strong deterrent to nationalism and other sources of national, regional, or even global instability. Economic development for a country or people consists of capital accumulation, rising per capita income (with a corresponding falling birthrate), an increasingly skilled workforce, the adoption of new technical styles, and other related socioeconomic changes.[31] The key measure of economic development is the accumulation over time of capital and growth in both gross domestic product (GDP) and gross national product (GNP). Commercial liberals see general gains being made by the expansion of trade, which helps underdeveloped countries grow their economies and integrate into the international trading system. Where necessary, developed states should thus help the less developed grow their economic capacities. Since World War II, this approach has been manifested in terms of foreign economic assistance— significantly, the developmental assistance granted to Western Europe via the Marshall Plan in the late 1940s. Commercial liberalism sees strong prospects for international economic organizations to help states organize themselves for conducting effective trading, managing trade conflicts, and helping to make up for inefficiencies. Some organizations like the European Union have become models for deeply embedded trade, political, and security cooperation at the regional level.

Commercial liberalism posits that corporations that transcend borders— multinational corporations (MNCs)—help to break down the barrier of the nation-state and bring societies closer via economic globalization. MNCs are enterprises that control and manage production establishments located in at least two countries.[32] This relationship reflects more than trading and in fact includes direct ownership of manufacturing plants or resource-extraction and processing operations in a variety of countries. MNCs transcend sovereignty; thus, while commercial liberals see them as beneficial, many others see them as a threat or as a function of one large state's exploitative economic hegemony. Some MNCs are massive and maintain spheres of economic influence that historically were the domain of states. Two thousand of the largest MNCs are based in six of the wealthiest countries in the world, and by the turn of the twenty-first century, the top five hundred MNCs had combined assets of about $32 trillion.[33] By 2010, the largest in the world was Walmart. The fourth, British Petroleum, seemed, to many Americans in 2010, to have more authority over how to manage its massive Gulf of Mexico oil spill than did the United States.

Commercial liberals nevertheless assert that there is an inherent idealism in the expansion of foreign direct investment by MNCs. Such advocates argue that the benefits are split between MNCs and the countries that host them. MNCs often build roads, schools, and other infrastructure that might help a country increase its productivity and thus further meet the needs of its people. Some commercial liberals see MNCs as the principal agents for the exchange of ideas and technology across borders that will lead to a more united world order.[34] MNCs, however, have not always been benign actors, and some states have undermined the sovereignty of others to protect their own home-based MNCs. In Guatemala in 1954 and in Chile in 1972, the United States supported covert action to destabilize governments hostile to American business interests in those countries. Many on the receiving end of their activity see MNCs as harbingers of neocolonialism. Moreover, underdeveloped countries whose people are educated and employed by MNCs risk losing their best and brightest to better economic opportunities outside their homelands. Nonetheless, there is clearly a trend in globalization toward commercial liberalism. Even the most underdeveloped of countries testify that they most want not handouts but rather fair access to compete in developed economies and an opportunity to join the processes of economic globalization.

Democratic Peace and Security Communities

At the core of liberalism lies a normative assumption that republican democracies are inherently peaceful. Immanuel Kant promulgated the notion that democratic government is an important condition for peace. He reasoned that "if the consent of the citizens is required in order to decide that war should be declared . . . nothing is more natural than that they would be very cautious in commencing such a poor game, decreeing for themselves all the calamities of war."[35] Such calamities include paying the costs of conflict out of both society's and their own resources, repairing the painful devastation it leaves behind, and incurring national debt. In modern liberal theory, the "democratic peace" assumes that there is a civilizing function in democracies—where conflicts are dealt with peacefully, using the rule of law rather than brute force. Democracies are transparent: political, economic, and military activity is conducted with a degree of openness and accountability within the political system. This transparency can alleviate relative-gains concerns among democracies and worries about offensive military capacity as other states can take advantage of it to increase their own levels of reassurance. Nevertheless, some analytical confusion emerges over the question of what defines a democracy within democratic peace theory. After all, Adolf Hitler rose to power in the midst of a young German democracy. Although postrevolutionary Iran has incorporated elements of democracy, many adversaries still see it as a threat. The Palestinian Authority holds elections for its leadership, and yet many Israelis still fear the Palestinian political movement. In fact, in 2006, elections in the Palestinian areas resulted in a major defeat for the pro-peace Fatah movement and a major victory for Hamas, which continued to refuse to renounce the use of violence against Israelis. In Turkey, the military intervenes to prevent religious representation in government. Thus, John M. Owen points to the content of democracy and the embedded nature of liberal ideas, not just the institutional mechanisms of democratic processes, as key to democratic peace.[36]

Democratic peace theory generates skepticism because in a number of cases democracies have gone to war with each other. Also, in a number of cases democracies have rushed into or started wars, including the Spanish-American War, the U.S.-Serbia conflict in 1998, the 2003 U.S. invasion of Iraq, Israel's 2006 war in southern Lebanon and its 2008–2009 intervention in Gaza, and the 2008 war between Russia and Georgia (though degrees of democracy in both countries were problematic).[37] Nevertheless, it is true that democracies rarely wage war on each other. Charles Lipson argues that this stems from "contracting advantages" among democratic governments, which allow them to negotiate a separate peace. Lipson demonstrates that "constitutional democracies have a special capacity to make and sustain promises with each other, including those about war and peace."[38] Democratic systems increase the confidence that negotiating partners will uphold promises, as accountability is built into the system. The continuity of governance in democracies promotes stability and predictable behavior. Moreover, high audience costs mean that electorates and legislators will hold leaders accountable if they violate contracts like treaties. Constitutional governance limits the powers of public officials and thus makes it harder for them to move quickly into external conflicts.[39]

Democratic peace theory has an important policy implication. If it is true that there is more peace among democracies, then there should be more democracies. Yet, this assumption creates several dilemmas. First, democracies might opt to overthrow nondemocracies via war in order to spread this strategic logic to other parts of the world—as some who argued for regime change in Iraq before the U.S. invasion advocated. There is, however, no reason to believe that democracy can be imposed—especially via external military force. Second, there is no guarantee that, once begun, the democratization process will breed peace and stability. It can do the opposite if the institutions of democracy and the structural economic and political foundations are not present. Finally, because of their openness, democracies are vulnerable to asymmetric terrorist attacks or insurgencies that could prompt a warlike response and even lead to reduced democracy if the state curtails rights in the name of security. The United States faced a unique dilemma in the Arab revolutions of early 2011 in that popular movements for democratic reform in places like Egypt, Yemen, and Bahrain put America in the position of watching the principles of democracy used to challenge authoritarian governments that it had backed for decades. In March 2011, the United States and its allies went to war to protect civilians in Libya, but many critics asked why it would not do the same in Bahrain and Yemen? Meanwhile, America's most pivotal ally in the region was Saudi Arabia, a despotic monarchy.

A more evolutionary variation on the democratic peace school is the idea of a security community, a concept devised by Karl Deutsch in 1957. Deutsch sought to explain why the prospect for interstate war seemed improbable in certain regions. In countries with high amounts of cross-border communication and similar political identities (such as the United States and Canada or the Scandinavian nations), the prospect for expanding peace based on areas of embedded security communities seemed possible. Deutsch defined a security community as a group of states in a given region with no prospect for war.[40] He focused on "pluralistic security communities" in which states retain their legal independence within a region defined by a group of people who have become integrated. Integration promotes a "sense of community" as well as institutions and practices thought to assure dependable expectations of peaceful change.

Deutsch argued that the North Atlantic Treaty Organization (NATO) might, over time, contribute to the evolution of a transatlantic security community by developing its economic and social potential to become "more than a military alliance."[41] With the end of the Cold War, Stephen Weber asserted that NATO reflected a peculiar mix of alliance and security community. He suggested that a security community can be institutionalized as equivalence is favored over hierarchy, with decisions requiring unanimity and the formal organization existing primarily to enhance transparency and to facilitate the transfer of information among states.[42] The logic of both democratic peace and the security community formed a key argument for advocates of NATO expansion during the 1990s. U.S. Secretary of State Madeleine K. Albright argued in 1997 that "by adding Poland, Hungary, and the Czech Republic to the alliance, we will expand the area within Europe where wars simply do not happen," and "NATO defines a community of interest among the free nations of North America and Europe that both preceded and outlasted the Cold War. America has long stood for the proposition that the Atlantic community should not be artificially divided and that its nations should be free to shape their destiny. We have long argued that the nations of Central and Eastern Europe belong to the same democratic family as our allies in Western Europe."[43]

Yet, as Emanuel Adler has shown, a more likely geographic basis for a well-defined security community is to be found in the European Union rather than NATO.[44] Empirically, while NATO has constrained hostility between Greece and Turkey, so long as the institution includes these two members between which war is a real possibility, it cannot meet the basic criteria for a security community. The agenda of research into the security community concept is highly ambitious, and as yet, it remains more a goal than a guaranteed outcome. As Deutsch put it, "We undertook this inquiry as a contribution to the study of possible ways in which men some day might abolish war."[45]

Emerging Security Paradigms

The study of international security is often divided into the broad paradigms of realism and idealism and variations associated with each. However, both approaches leave unanswered key methodological questions, and each is open to significant challenges by alternative conceptual approaches. As the process of globalization accelerates, new approaches derived from structural power dynamics outside the nation-state and broader utopian concepts have emerged. Some aspects of both realism and, especially, idealism can be found in some of these approaches. However, they are also unique in their characteristics as fundamentally new approaches to understanding international security. Among these new schools are constructivism, transnational civil society, postmodernism, and feminism.

Constructivism

Neither realists nor idealists offer a core explanation of how interests and perceptions of security requirements emerge. Do all states share the same basic needs and concerns? Or are interests relative, shaped by both the domestic and international environments? To what extent does the "identity" of the nation-state shape perceptions of security and insecurity? Sociological approaches to identity formation provide a means to understanding the relationship between the domestic and international sphere of identity and interest formation. As Ronald Jepperson, Alexander Wendt, and Peter Katzenstein note, the international environment in which national security policies are made has at least three layers. First, formal institutions play an important role in reflecting and reinforcing specific norms. A second aspect is the sphere of world politics, which includes basic rules such as sovereignty. Third, international patterns of friendship or enmity also have important functions as the product of social interactions and perceptions. For example, both Canada and Cuba should, by nature of relative power distribution, significantly fear the United States. However, as Jepperson, Wendt, and Katzenstein write, "while one is a threat, the other is an ally, a result, we believe, of ideational factors operating at the international level."[46] Hence the core question in this sociological approach to security: Are the manifold uses and forms of power explained by material factors alone, or are ideational and cultural factors necessary to account for how states decide what is and is not important to their security?[47]

Social theory has been central to the work of Alexander Wendt, who pioneered the school of constructivism. Constructivism addresses the relationship between the international environment and the domestic identity of a nation-state. Constructivists accept the idea of anarchy in the international system but assert that states' own internal identities will affect how they react to it. Constructivists see international politics as a dynamic process in which states simultaneously shape, and are shaped by, the international environment. Anarchy, or at least the degree to which states see anarchy as threatening or benign, is a socially constructed phenomenon. Wendt notes that "people act toward objects, including other actors, on the basis of the meanings that the objects have for them. . . . States act differently toward enemies than they do toward friends because enemies are threatening and friends are not." Moreover, to Wendt, it is "collective meanings that constitute the structures which organize our actions."[48]

In constructivist theory, concepts such as self-help, formal institutions like international organizations and regimes, order, and power exist to the degree that they are consciously chosen to serve the interests of states. Consequently, the international order is simultaneously constructed by and constitutive of state action. However, the content of that order depends on the nature of the actors interacting and shaping the international system. To understand whether anarchy is a threat to security, one has to understand the nature of the actors as defined by their identities and the ideas they hold important. Each actor's identity is defined by the social interaction of the domestic actors within society. What makes this dynamic especially unique is that, while ideas are cultivated within a state and then expressed within the international system, the nature of the international system simultaneously feeds into the domestic sphere of the state.

The role of the nation-state as a protective barrier against international anarchy and as a unitary actor advancing self-interest is thus challenged by ongoing social interactions that transcend the domestic and international sphere of international security. In this constructivist perspective, states exist as a consequence of both their relationship to the structure of the international system and their individual characteristics. The configuration of international structures serves to define what is possible among the existing agents that interact with each other. To Wendt, the international system represents a hierarchy of activity in which the existence of some actors makes possible the existence of others. Wendt provides a framework for understanding the conceptual application of personality to states. States are seen as representing the collective sum of the interactions of society within them—which helps to explain why certain states take on the attributes of "people" as such.[49] This approach makes a major contribution toward explaining why certain kinds of outcomes occur in international security relationships. For example, as Wendt observes, the United States would not be overly concerned with Britain or Israel having nuclear weapons. However, it would perceive the Soviet Union or Iran as a threat. In this sense, the security dilemma is relative and, therefore, a constructed phenomenon. In 2008, Alexander Wendt and Raymond Duvall added to this conceptual framework the "UFO" puzzle, arguing that governments refuse to investigate seriously the scientific evidence for unidentified flying objects in part because the state needs to control the impression that there are things beyond its control.[50]

While constructivism is more theoretical than policy oriented, the approach does have significant practical implications. For example, it allows for the possibility that states can change over time. In this sense, evolving ideas become important shapers of what defines and gives value to power. Consequently, the international system can be an agent of transformation as ideas transcend borders and shape change within a state. If that is the case, then constructivism can explain why the Cold War ended without war—because the ideas of human rights and freedom were ultimately more powerful than tyranny and military force. If enough states were exposed to and inculcated with particular ideas, such as in democratic peace, then powerful dynamics of change could become deeply embedded in the international system. Such embedded norms can expand and transform nation-states. Just over a half a century ago, Japan and Germany were expansionistic, chauvinistic, and war prone. Now, neither state chooses war as a preferred policy. In a constructivist world, states have the capacity to change how they perceive and pursue their interests, and that change can stem from either external or internal forces.

Transnational Civil Society

The idea of an international society is not new. Hedley Bull, for example, examined the social dynamics of anarchy and society to challenge the notion that the two are incompatible. Bull noted that the lack of a universal government or the dominance of the nation-state in providing for security has not limited nation-states' willingness to participate in economic interdependence. Also, war is seen not as an essential part of anarchy but rather as a mechanism of international society for settling political disputes or enforcing commonly agreed-upon international principles and norms. Bull saw international society and anarchy as not essentially in conflict. Balance-of-power systems and other forms of regulative behavior make some degree of regulation in the international system a natural occurrence.[51] Bull focused, however, on the role of the nation-state. New approaches to international society address the role of the state and transnational phenomena.

Contemporary approaches to international society look to the networks of globalization as the basis for the expansion of domestic civil society into the international sphere. The expansion of a transnational civil society implies that rules helping to provide for a peaceful and legitimate maintenance of order (usually associated with a combination of sovereignty and democracy) at the domestic level of politics can be extended internationally. As Jessica Tuchman Mathews writes, in the new security environment, "national governments are not simply losing autonomy in a globalizing economy. . . . They are sharing powers—including political, social, and security roles at the core of sovereignty—with businesses, with international organizations, and with a multitude of citizens groups, known as nongovernmental organizations (NGOs)."[52] At the core of this concept, she argues, is the notion that an individual's security can no longer be reliably guaranteed by the nation's security. Rather, the emerging dynamic of "human security" is competing with national security as a dominant concept that has more to do with the conditions of daily life than the traditional conflicts between states.

The idea of a transnational civil society looks to globalization as facilitating a world shaped by norms that transcend the role of the state as delivering primary goods for individuals. Mathews looks at the rising role of transnational interest groups lobbying on behalf of particular causes as shaping the new civil society. An estimated thirty-five thousand NGOs were operating in developing countries by the mid-1990s; that number had increased to approximately forty thousand by 2010. By the turn of the century, NGOs were delivering more official development assistance than the United Nations.[53] Related to the rise of NGOs is the expansion of their ability to breed new ideas; advocate, protest, and mobilize public support; perform legal, scientific, technical, and policy analysis; provide services; shape, implement, monitor, and enforce national and international commitments; and change institutions and norms.[54] To this extent, knowledge, science, and associated truths become tools to power and influence via global transmission.[55] As Peter Haas shows, a new basis for global change develops with the emergence of transnational networks comprising private experts with scientific or other factual consensual knowledge. This knowledge can then be transferred to bureaucracies within international organizations and then shared with counterparts inside national governments. Such a basis for information exchange can lead to outcomes that otherwise would not have been possible—such as advancing common interests in international environmental protection.[56]

The growth of transnational civil society creates new demands for international law. The codification of principles and norms—for example, the global rejection of genocide—can reflect the emergence of transnational civil society.[57] One key element of civil society is consent to a particular form of legitimacy in governance. The desire among international actors to facilitate cooperation and punish violators of rules is considerably higher in the era of accelerating interdependence. Rather than seeking hard-and-fast traditional international law, states are increasingly open to a new legal principle, "soft law," in addressing new security concerns. Soft laws are, according to Steven Ratner, "precepts emanating from international bodies that conform in some sense to expectations of required behavior but that are not binding on states."[58] The effectiveness of soft law lies in states' ability to conform gradually to emerging international norms and rules in ways that evolve more quickly than traditional legal codification processes but do not carry the immediate threat of punishment.

Hard international law is still practiced, and transnational enforcement procedures are expanding. For example, domestic courts are increasingly utilized for transnational trials. Some governments have granted their domestic courts the power of "universal jurisdiction," which allows for criminal indictment of citizens from other countries. Ratner notes that new sources of international law include private lawmakers, private codes, private rights holders, and private armies. The expansion of transnational civil society also reflects the complexity of new issues requiring regulatory rules, such as trade policy, business, the environment, and human rights.[59] The legal process of building norms can be as important as the development of treaty-based law. "Legalization" is the overall process of establishing binding obligations, precision as to rules, and delegation to third parties for interpretation, enforcement, or the creation of new rules as necessary.[60] Such activity helps to form the basis for the effective role of soft law. Ultimately, soft law provides more flexibility in dealing with the uncertainty of the global security environment. Such outcomes might move states toward compromises necessary for consolidating an effective transnational civil society.[61]

Pacifism and Peace Movements

Many individuals and scholars, as well as some policymakers, deem waging war an immoral and unethical act. Therefore, they prioritize peace above all else. As John Dewey declared, "The only way to abolish war [is] to make peace heroic." Pacifism is the rejection of violence as a means of conflict resolution; it stresses belief in the power of nonviolence. From this perspective, moral authority derives from the promotion of a peaceful world order. St. Augustine writes, "The purpose of all war is ultimately peace." Differentiating pacifism from other approaches to peace is the means through which peace is to be achieved—via a steadfast commitment to the principle of nonviolence. As Martin Luther King Jr. stated, "Peace is not merely a distant goal that we seek, but a means by which we arrive at that goal."

The idea of pacifism begins with the notion that if one individual acts with the moral courage to reject violence, this practice will thrive and spread. In the words of Thomas Merton, "If you yourself are at peace, then there is at least some peace in the world." If the idea of peace grows from one to many, it might also grow at the international level. President Franklin D. Roosevelt, though not a pacifist, enshrined this idea in the statement "Peace, like charity, begins at home." Those who have best understood the ravages of war have often set the template for the goal of peace. Roosevelt's contemporary Winston Churchill declared, "If the human race wishes to have a prolonged and indefinite period of material prosperity, they have only got to behave in a peaceful and helpful way toward one another."

The major religions of the world have, at their core, the ideal of everlasting peace—be it with a deity or among humankind. Many religions emphasize salvation through peace. As the Bible teaches, "Blessed are the peacemakers: for they shall be called the children of God" (Matthew 5:9). In personifying wisdom, the Bible states, "Her ways are ways of pleasantness, and all her paths are peace" (Proverbs 3:17). Isaiah 2:4 declares, "They shall beat their swords into plowshares, and their spears into pruning hooks; nation shall not lift up sword against nation, neither shall they learn war any more." The Catholic Mass contains the greeting among parishioners "Peace be with you," which comes from Genesis 43:23. Such views transcend religious doctrine; a Chinese proverb declares, "When my heart is at peace, the world is at peace." Buddha said, "Better than a thousand hollow words is one word that brings peace." The Dalai Lama states, "I believe all suffering is caused by ignorance. People inflict pain on others in the selfish pursuit of their happiness or satisfaction. Yet true happiness comes from a sense of peace and contentment which in turn must be achieved through the cultivation of altruism, of love and compassion and elimination of ignorance, selfishness, and greed." The Muslim faith aspires to achieve peace as, according to the Quran, "the believers are but a single Brotherhood: So make peace and reconciliation and be careful of (your duty to) Allah that mercy may be had on you." An American Indian

(Shenandoah) proverb states, "It is no longer good enough to cry peace, we must act peace, live peace, and live in peace."

Artists and musicians have also long advanced the cause of peace. Pablo Picasso used his painting *Guernica* to describe graphically the horrors of battle. Filmmakers also have used their medium to illustrate some of the horrors and ironies of warfare. As the Cold War arms race grew during the 1960s, Stanley Kubrick produced *Dr. Strangelove or: How I Learned to Stop Worrying and Love the Bomb*; in one famous scene, the U.S. president interrupts fisticuffs between an American general and a Russian diplomat and, noting their location, declares, "Gentlemen! You can't fight in here! This is the war room!" Francis Ford Coppola's *Apocalypse Now* shows the deep psychological toll the Vietnam War took on its participants. Films from the 1980s such as *The Day After* illustrate the devastating impact that any nuclear exchange between the superpowers would have. During the 1960s and 1970s, musicians like Peter, Paul, and Mary and Bob Dylan sang in protest of war. The Beatles declared, "All you need is love," and Jimi Hendrix asserted in his lyrics, "When the power of love overcomes the love of power, the world will know peace." John Lennon sounded a call to the masses to "give peace a chance," noted that "war is over, if you want it," and appealed, "Imagine all the people living life in peace. You may say I'm a dreamer, but I'm not the only one. I hope someday you'll join us, and the world will live as one." In 2005, the band System of a Down asked in the song "B.Y.O.B.," "Why don't presidents fight the war? Why do they always send the poor?" Michael Franti sang, in 2006, in the song "Time to Go Home," "Those who start wars, never fight them . . . and those who fight wars, they never like them." Country music joined in as Kenny Rogers sang in 2006, "Oh, the last ten years, it's been quite a trip. Over thirty-six-hundred spins around without a cosmic slip. But within the realm of our atmosphere we're 'bout as out of whack as we've ever been in a million years."

Grassroots pacifist movements are not a new phenomenon in international security. As Ben Lowe has shown, a nascent and evolving interest in both the justification for war and the way war should be fought dates back at least to 1340 in medieval England.[62] Some religious movements such as the Christian Quakers and Mennonites hold peace and nonviolence as core elements of their faiths; many practitioners have claimed "conscientious objector" status, and some have avoided military service during a draft. Modern peace movements can be dated to 1815 with the New York and Massachusetts Peace Societies and to the 1816 founding of the Society for the Promotion of Permanent and Universal Peace. Also in the 1800s, Henry David Thoreau proclaimed the necessity of civil disobedience when civil society forces one to doing something immoral or unjust. Thoreau refused to pay a tax that he thought contributed to the funding of the Mexican-American War, which he considered inequitable. Throughout the 1800s, peace activists sponsored a number of private conferences. Prior to the world wars, protests were relatively limited—and some might actually have contributed to war. Many advocates who opposed war—especially in the United States—did so based on isolationist traditions favoring disengagement from global affairs.

Critics have charged well-intentioned movements to avoid war with actually contributing to the outbreak of conflict. Many British students who took the Oxford Peace Union Pledge during the 1930s declared that they would not fight in a war. Critics of that movement accused them of emboldening Hitler by conveying the impression that his aggressive designs would not be resisted.[63] Pacifism thus confronts a dilemma. Would, for example, an absolutist doctrine of nonviolence have defeated Hitler? In the twenty-first century, could pacifism stop suicide terrorism? Alternatively, what if a military intervention undertaken for humanitarian reasons could save hundreds of thousands of lives? Would a pacifist then oppose military force? Ironically, many American and European peace activists who opposed the role of the military during the Cold War became strong supporters of humanitarian military intervention in Bosnia and Kosovo in the 1990s. Yet, many individuals from this same movement also opposed the invasion of Iraq in 2003.

Mohandas K. Gandhi demonstrated the power of nonviolence. Over several decades, he developed a philosophy of nonviolent struggle against tyranny and power that became known as the *satyagraha* movement. In her study of Gandhi's philosophy of conflict, Joan V. Bondurant summarizes the core elements of *satyagraha*. First, truth is essential, and seeking truth is fundamental to understanding one's limitations as well as to exposing violations of honesty and integrity. Second, nonviolence underpins the legitimacy behind the quest for truth and the risk that truth might be relative. By committing to the philosophy of nonviolence, one becomes willing to take the ultimate risk on behalf of "truth" and thus is forced to identify one's own limitations first and foremost. This approach thus forces one into a fuller awareness of one's own honesty and integrity. Closely related to the faith in nonviolence is the commitment to love even people who abuse one—at least to the point where one refuses to harm them in spite of their evil actions. Third, self-suffering in public and private actions is seen as a test of one's commitment to love and truth. Gandhi undertook long, painstaking marches and endured extended and personally devastating fasts to expose truth by way of his own suffering. Finally, *satyagraha* places considerable emphasis on the role of the individual in integrating the first three approaches in a quest for inner truth, self-awareness, love, and peace.[64]

Gandhi's pacifism was guided by a path to peace that began with the individual and sought to expand a general consciousness of truth. Gandhi was also very publicity conscious, however, in his application of nonviolent tactics to remove the British Empire from India. He organized large protests, distributed pamphlets, and used fasts and other forms of peaceful action to expose the truths of brutal colonial rule. "Nonviolence cannot be preached. It has to be practiced," Gandhi concluded.[65] It also included certain imperatives based on a "common honesty" among those who practiced it: they must "render heart discipline to their commander; there should be no mental reservation; they must be prepared to lose all, not merely their personal liberty, not merely their possessions, land, cash, etc., but also the liberty and possessions of their families, and they must be ready cheerfully to face bullets, bayonets, or even slow death by torture; they must not be violent in thought, word or deed toward the 'enemy' or among themselves."[66] In the face of massive nonviolent resistance, many of Britain's actions undermined its colonial legitimacy in the eyes of the world. For example, in 1919 British troops fired into a crowd of unarmed and peacefully assembled Indians (including women and children) protesting in Amritsar, killing some four hundred people.

Other movements have aimed even more specifically to stop armed conflict through public protest and civil disobedience. In the 1960s and 1970s, large segments of the American public protested the Vietnam War. While many protesters were convinced that their actions helped to end the war, critics argued that they had prolonged it by emboldening the enemy to fight on for a better settlement. During the 1980s, large antinuclear movements in Britain and Germany brought to public attention the dangers of nuclear weapons deployments in Europe. However, these movements had also been infiltrated by Soviet intelligence agents seeking to use public opinion to thwart Western governments' Cold War nuclear strategies.

The end of the Cold War marks one of history's most important moments of nonviolent change. One major explanation for its end holds that over many decades, the peoples of Eastern Europe and the Soviet Union were exposed to the Western notions of liberty, human rights, and free markets, as well as to Western goods and cultural products, such as clothing and music. Over time, Western ideas permeated the artificial barrier of the Iron Curtain and became ingrained in the beliefs of political dissidents. By the time Mikhail Gorbachev had consolidated power after 1986, the Soviet leadership had adopted at least some of these Western political, economic, and cultural concepts. Throughout the Soviet Union and Eastern Europe, many dissidents had peacefully resisted oppressive governments and challenged the brutality of Soviet-style dictatorship. Early efforts to quell these pressures for internal change in the Soviet Bloc were met with violence—as in the 1968 Soviet invasion of Czechoslovakia that

ended the "Prague Spring" of democratic reform. However, the ideals of freedom and democracy could not be destroyed. Either imprisoned or in internal
exile, individuals like Lech Wałęsa and Václav Havel maintained their efforts
to bring about a peaceful change within the Soviet system. The importance of
such individuals was made especially evident by Gorbachev, who, as the last
Soviet leader, sought to modernize and reform the system. Whereas Joseph
Stalin had accelerated Soviet economic growth with terror and mass murder,
Gorbachev tried to reform and improve the USSR's political and economic
situation by expanding freedoms and developing a more peaceful international
security policy. Inadvertently, Gorbachev released forces, particularly nationalism, that the Soviet leadership could not control. While considerable nationalist and ethnic violence did occur in the former Soviet space, the overall exit of
the Soviet Union from the Cold War military stalemate was peaceful.

Another major internal transformation that led to a more peaceful international environment was the fall of apartheid in South Africa. Once the
white minority government collapsed, the new leadership there abandoned
its nuclear ambitions. The limits of using popular pressure to change state
behavior were made evident, however, in China's Tiananmen Square in 1989.
Students protesting peacefully for basic liberties were violently dispersed by
the Chinese military, and many were killed or imprisoned. Such was also the
case with massive Iranian street protests in summer 2009 following questionable elections in that country. Meanwhile, the transition of rule away from
Hosni Mubarak in Egypt in 2011 raised concern in Israel about the future
of the peace treaty between the two countries—the foundational pillar of
regional peace.

An important variation on pacifism is found among those who have actually participated in war. While some pacifists are quick to accuse the military
of warmongering, the opposite is more often the case. Military personnel and
veterans who have seen combat are often reluctant to wage war as a result of
their experiences. As a rule, they generally insist that military force be used
solely as a last resort. The armed forces are often the most reluctant to go to
war because their members have to kill, or be killed, in battle. Those who have
to plan and implement wartime decisions are shaped by their experiences.
Retired U.S. general Lee Butler, who commanded the American strategic air
command during the Cold War, called in 1996 for the United States to "make
unequivocal its commitment to the elimination of nuclear arsenals, and take
the lead in setting an agenda for moving forthrightly toward that objective."[67]

Butler's call for nuclear disarmament coincided with a letter signed in late
1996 by nearly sixty retired admirals and generals from the United States and
the former Soviet Union calling for a cutback in existing nuclear stockpiles,
a gradual removal of remaining nuclear weapons from alert status, and a

"continuous, complete and irrevocable elimination" of nuclear weapons. In 2008, a U.S. movement with the goal of achieving "global zero"—zero nuclear weapons—gained strong support across the political spectrum. As Henry Kissinger, George Shultz, Sam Nunn, and William Perry note, "In some respects, the goal of a world free of nuclear weapons is like the top of a very tall mountain. From the vantage point of our troubled world today, we can't even see the top of the mountain, and it is tempting and easy to say we can't get there from here. But the risks from continuing to go down the mountain or standing pat are too real to ignore. We must chart a course to higher ground, where the mountaintop becomes more visible."[68] In 2009, U.S. President Barack Obama stated that movement in the direction of global nuclear disarmament was official American policy—a major reason he was awarded the Nobel Peace Prize in 2009.

Postmodernism

Postmodernism seeks to expose the core meaning of various texts and discourses. A postmodern approach to realism would assert that there exists no single, objective reality but rather a wide range of experiences and perspectives. Humans are thus conditioned to understand the meaning of the content of objects or interests based on their interactions.[69] The postmodernist views the state as a construct of human interaction that only exists so long as it is given meaning by dominant actors and is reinforced through social interactions over time. If, for example, a man walks across the border between two countries and there is no man-made signpost, how will he know he is in another state? A dollar bill only has value because humans assign it one. In reality, it is a piece of paper marked with green ink. Because humans give the dollar bill value, it has power.[70]

Postmodernism seeks to "deconstruct" the nature of objects and interactions by exposing hidden meanings, or subtexts. For example, anarchy is explained not by objective factors but by difference. Individuals define themselves by what they are not, thereby creating a sense of the "outside" or the "other" so that they can learn more about what they are. Such "outside" forces or groups can be seen as threatening to one's own group or identity; thus, anarchy can come to appear threatening because its nature poses challenges to one's sense of self. Postmodernists look at international security relationships and often see a reinforcing hierarchy of power. As governments retain the power of action and diplomacy, and as scholars teach the dominance of realism, neoliberalism, and other state-centric models, they pass on a structure that reinforces preexisting paradigms. By telling students that realism is the dominant approach to security studies, a professor creates a cognitive predisposition toward the state and the content or meaning of anarchy. As Richard K. Ashley writes, "The state as actor assumption is a metaphysical commitment prior to science and exempted from scientific criticism. . . . Despite neorealism's much ballyhooed emphasis on the role of hard falsifying tests as the measure of theoretical progress, neorealism immunizes its statist commitments from any form of falsification."[71]

Referencing the "discovery" of America by Christopher Columbus in 1492, William E. Connolly provides an example of the effort to expose the hierarchy of power embedded within language. The word "discover" was important because Columbus did not invent the new world; he came upon it. But did he actually discover it? And what exactly had Columbus discovered? The land was certainly there before and was, in fact, inhabited by natives who considered it their home. By pure definition, America had already been discovered by its existing inhabitants. Connolly notes that Columbus actually discovered a sense of newness and otherness—something entirely different from the European experience. The "discovery" that mattered was actually the beginning of a new text with new contextual meaning. The explorers who came upon America had to adjust their own assessments and predispositions to a new way of life. Thus, the "New World" had been discovered because the Europeans had discovered a new sense of otherness to which they had to adapt. This adaptation would have lasting impact on the rhetoric and study of international relations as studied in Western traditions.[72]

Or consider the act of placing a topic within the context of "security" and "war." As Ole Waever has shown, the process of "securitization" elevates a certain concept into the realm of security or war as a rhetorical device to raise the level of an issue's importance.[73] This act can increase a domestic actor's power by implying a threat that citizens need protection from. With the end of the Cold War, the "text" of security expanded into a variety of new areas as war rhetoric was advanced to include a "war on drugs" and a "war on terrorism." Whether or not using the word "war," implying a military response and social mobilization, was the best way to manage these problems was highly debatable. Labeling them as war issues would ultimately make it easier for one side in that debate to dominate by calling opponents "weak."

Postmodern theory provides an important tool for understanding a global security order and its implications for the dominance of the nation-state. First, as David Campbell has shown, the concept of contingency implies that varying perspectives embodied in international anarchy are now permeating the traditional boundary of the state. He writes,

> Danger, in short, is no longer capable of just being written as "out there." Security is not to be found "within." This is more than just a result of inter-

dependence, the proliferation of threats, or the overflowing of domestic issues onto the world stage (the conventional response). This is an irruption of contingencies which renders all established containers problematic. It makes little sense to speak of politics occurring in terms of a distinct "inside" or "outside" (such as a "Third World" which is spatially beyond our borders and temporally backward) when, for example, US economic policies encourage "Third World export processing zones" in Los Angeles where manufacturers stamp their auto parts "made in Brazil" and the clothing goods "made in Taiwan" to attract lower tariffs; when the demographic changes that have made non-white children majorities in the California and New York school systems, and will make whites a minority in the United States by the year 2056; and when the poverty and poor health care in Harlem makes the area a "zone of excess mortality" with a death rate for black males higher than their counterparts in Bangladesh.[74]

Second, postmodernism provides important insights into the foundational nature of a technologically conditioned global security network. If the modern era was shaped by large industry and massive armies, the postmodern era is defined largely by the new networks of power—particularly regarding the role of information technology and the power of ideas. By exposing the meaning of power and its origins, postmodernists hope to expose a more basic structure of reality embedded within the way the question of the meaning of security is both asked and answered.

Feminism and Gender

Feminist scholarship—or, more broadly, gender studies—also provides unique perspectives on international security. Feminist approaches note the traditionally male composition of the major actors in international security. The basic assumption behind this approach is that gender matters in understanding international security. The task of understanding the dynamics of international security must also expose overt or hidden assumptions about gender. As a policy issue, gender studies looks at some of the unique challenges that women face in terms of the new security environment. Feminist scholarship challenges premises of "universal assumptions" in major approaches to international security such as realism. A critical approach would note that the realist focus on power and interest derives from the fact that nearly all major realist scholars are men. Gender-based approaches to international security challenge scholars and students to determine how their gender affects their analyses and how this perspective is passed on to others. Feminist scholars seek to break down the political barrier between the "public sphere" of politics and the "domestic or private sphere" symbolic of the home, where traditional women's roles predominate.[75]

J. Ann Tickner shows that realists in particular have tended to view power as domination. Feminist scholars, however, view it as a relationship of mutual enabling requiring a reconceptualization of power to include realist notions and a more multidimensional approach that sees power in cooperative terms. Tickner notes, unlike realist claims, that most of the world's population views security in terms of the need to satisfy basic human needs rather than, or in addition to, protection in traditional military terms. Tickner sees economic development and basic human-needs satisfaction, as well as environmental concerns, as security dynamics consistent with feminist approaches to security. By reassessing security along such lines, a more comprehensive means of alleviating the security dilemma might be accomplished. As Tickner writes, "Thinking about military, economic and environmental security in interdependent terms suggests the need for new methods of conflict resolution that seek to achieve mutually beneficial, rather than zero sum, outcomes."[76]

Tickner offers six elements of a feminist approach to international security. First, a feminist perspective believes that objectivity, as it is culturally defined, is associated with masculinity; thus, "objective" assumptions claimed by realism only represent a partial, masculine view of human nature. Second, the national interest is multidimensional and contextually contingent. Third, power cannot be infused with meaning that is universally valid and thus must consider the possibility of collective empowerment. Fourth, it is impossible to separate moral issues from political action. Fifth, a feminist perspective hopes to find common moral elements in the aspirations of humanity. Sixth, a feminist perspective denies the autonomy of politics from the international sphere; thus, any effort to build a worldview that does not rest on a pluralistic conception of human nature is both incomplete and masculine.[77]

Feminist approaches to security issues are not monolithic; in fact, various schools of thought all derive from basic approaches that emphasize the gender dynamics of security. Essentialist feminism focuses primarily on the values that women bring to international security dynamics and stresses the unique contributions of women as women. A normative content to this school asserts that women are, by nature, more effective in conflict-resolution and group decision-making dynamics. Essentialist feminists see real and positive differences between the potential contributions of women and the male-dominated world of international security. Liberal feminism sees gender differences as marginally important but instead stresses the political agenda of equality in politics. This school especially deplores the traditional exclusion of women as actors in international security. However, this approach has no fundamentally normative element as liberal feminists do not necessarily believe that the inclusion of women in international security will change basic outcomes.

Nevertheless, the lack of full representation of women in the security realm is seen as a basic inequity given that women make up more than one-half of the world's population. A third school, postmodern feminism, looks at the structure of power and the social activity that reinforces it. Postmodern feminists see the language of security discourse as reinforcing a hierarchy of power reflective of the persistent dominance of masculinity in international society.[78] Postmodern analysis explains why some of the most war-prone leaders in world politics have been women, including Margaret Thatcher, Indira Gandhi, Golda Meir, and Benazir Bhutto. The United States' first female secretary of state, Madeleine K. Albright, was an advocate of war in President Bill Clinton's administration and led the charge for U.S. war against Serbia in 1999. At one point during her tenure as U.S. ambassador to the United Nations, Albright challenged the masculinity of Cubans who shot down a civilian airplane, arguing that they had no "cojones." While running for president in 2008, Senator Hillary Clinton denied regretting her 2002 vote to authorize war in Iraq and said she would be prepared to "obliterate" Iran if necessary. Meanwhile, candidate Obama was characterized as "weak" for preferring diplomacy. Postmodernist feminists would assert that, even if women hold positions of authority, the dominant structure of world politics reflects the text and discourse of a power hierarchy that reinforces the power position of men. Though joking, American political consultant James Carville summarized this view well in November 2010 when he said, "If Hillary [Clinton] gave up one of her balls and gave it to Obama, he'd have two." Much media debate after the United States launched air strikes against Libyan forces in March 2011 focused attention on the fact that the strongest advocates for military force were women around President Obama—Hillary Clinton, Susan Rice, and Samantha Power—while most of the men involved in national security decision making had opposed it or expressed reservations. Some analysts also noted that the women's support had nothing to do with gender but rather reflected their common experiences and lessons from the 1990s Rwandan genocide and the nature of their respective jobs as secretary of state, UN ambassador, and assistant to the president for multilateral affairs.

Revolutionary Approaches

If one follows the logic of postmodern assumptions about power to its conclusion, the only prospect for change toward a more peaceful order is through a radical and fundamental reconceptualization of the distribution of power toward a new paradigm of human existence. Global security dynamics have produced a reservoir of popular discontent, provoking radical movements that include anarchists and terrorists as well as faithful and idealistic pacifists. Some schools draw on Marxism, advocating the radical redistribution of wealth as the best means of ending economic disparity and conflict. Thomas Homer-Dixon illustrates an important reality about what people like Karl Marx spoke of as imbalances of economic power. Homer-Dixon points out that in 2006, there were "793 billionaires with a combined wealth of $2.6 trillion—equivalent to 20 percent of the United States' annual gross domestic product (GDP). Between 2003 and 2006, the number of billionaires increased 66 percent, and their total net worth rose 86 percent. If they'd liquidated this wealth in 2006, they could have hired the poorest half of the world's workers—the 1.4 billion workers who earn a few dollars a day—for almost two years."[79] Interestingly, in 2008 and 2009, the United States went through a massive income distribution—from its taxpayers to large corporate banks that had been fundamentally broken by unregulated capitalist excess. Other schools advance the idea of world government and the abolition of the state. The idea of revolutionary Marxism has receded with the end of the Cold War, though its proponents see merit in Marxist explanations for economic and social injustice.

Summary

Liberalism offers a range of concepts and policy frameworks while recognizing areas where realism still has an important role to play. Other approaches seek less direct policy applications and instead try to expose the essential foundations of particular international security trends. While often maligned, the broader idealist search for peace is a constant in international security. Even those leaders who have often engaged in the assertion of military power have also spoken on behalf of the ideal of peace. As American president and war hero Dwight D. Eisenhower stated in 1953, "Every gun that is made, every warship launched, every rocket fired signifies, in the final sense, a theft from those who hunger and are not fed, those who are cold and are not clothed. . . . This is not a way of life at all, in any true sense. Under the cloud of threatening war, it is humanity hanging from a cross of iron."[80] Idealists are often criticized for naïvely and dangerously prioritizing peace over the capabilities and strategies necessary for true security. History is riddled with failed efforts to build a peace that reflects the goals and principles of idealism. Nevertheless, humankind continues to aspire to the aims articulated by idealists. The most intense analytical disputes entail how exactly to achieve more peaceful and just international relations, not whether peace should be the end goal.

Suggested Reading

Baldwin, David, ed. *Neorealism and Neoliberalism: The Contemporary Debate.* New York: Columbia University Press, 1993.

Der Derian, James, and Michael J. Shapiro. *International/Intertextual Relations: Postmodern Readings of World Politics.* Lanham, MD: Lexington Books, 1989.

Doyle Michael, and G. John Ikenberry, eds. *New Thinking in International Relations Theory.* Boulder, CO: Westview Press, 1997.

Fukuyama, Francis. *The End of History and the Last Man.* New York: Free Press, 1992.

Keohane, Robert O. *Power and Governance in a Partially Globalized World.* New York: Routledge, 2002.

King, Mary. *Mahatma Gandhi, and Martin Luther King Jr.: The Power of Nonviolent Action.* United Nations: UNESCO, 1999.

Lipson, Charles. *Reliable Partners: How Democracies Have Made a Separate Peace.* Princeton, NJ: Princeton University Press, 2003.

Slaughter, Anne-Marie. *A New World Order.* Princeton, NJ: Princeton University Press, 2004.

Tickner, J. Ann. *Gendering World Politics.* New York: Columbia University Press, 2001.

Wendt, Alexander. *Social Theory of International Politics.* Cambridge: Cambridge University Press, 1999.

U.S. Secretary of Defense Robert M. Gates reviews the People's Liberation Army Honor Guard as part of an arrival ceremony honoring his visit to Beijing, January 10, 2011. Source: Department of Defense photo by U.S. Air Force MSG Jerry Morrison.

4

Great Powers and Grand Strategy

THE DISTRIBUTION OF POWER AMONG THE MAJOR STATES in the modern international system reflects general stability and peaceful relations a decade into the new millennium. Only the United States has the capacity to project military power on a global basis. Nevertheless, Russia, China, and the European Union all have relative power capabilities that make them major actors in shaping the global security environment. Despite occasional resentment of the reach of American power around the world, there has been little evidence that other powers are willing to counterbalance it overtly. There are, however, limits on the reach of U.S. power. The possession of nuclear weapons, in particular, by the other major powers still makes direct great power war a losing proposition. Nor is the United States' financial capacity for international intervention limitless; debt and a rise in isolationist sentiments are placing increased constraints on American power. By 2010 it was increasingly apparent that the United States was no longer in a financial position to maintain all of its continued expensive overseas military operations. There is thus no guarantee that the current international system will remain stable should the United States enter a major period of retrenchment. American power could recede, and new powers could emerge. Although the threat of great power conflict seems low, a number of regional conflicts could draw great powers into conflict. This chapter surveys the strategic trends and military capabilities of the major powers—the United States, Russia, China, and the European Union—in the early twenty-first century.

The United States

The United States alone has the military, political, and economic capacity to influence events on a truly global basis. Though isolation from world events characterized its previous history, since World War II the United States has grown into a position of global primacy. American power serves as a measure of both the country's capabilities and, historically, the attractiveness of its political system and strategic restraint. During the Cold War, the United States cultivated an extensive network of regional alliances and created institutional mechanisms to involve allies in decision making. Much of the legitimacy of American power in the world stemmed from the U.S. commitment to a defensive doctrine. After the Cold War, the United States found itself facing few external and internal constraints on its ability to shape the international environment, should it choose to exercise its power. Much of the question for the United States revolved around not whether but rather how to exercise that power. This changed radically, however, after the cost of the wars in Iraq and Afghanistan, combined with the deep financial crisis that began in 2008, opened a new debate in the United States over whether it was time to retrench.

During the 1990s, the United States pursued a grand strategy of "enlargement and engagement" under President Bill Clinton. The idea was to consolidate global alliances, enlarge the zone of countries with policies favorable to U.S. interests, engage states that could challenge the United States, and deter states that lay outside the norms of the international system. Where possible, the United States also engaged in peacekeeping and humanitarian operations. The country found itself in an awkward position as it sought to promote a normative agenda of democratic values and free markets. However, its interests also compelled it to stay out of major humanitarian crises. The challenge was to foster positive relationships with potential adversaries such as Russia and China. On the other hand, the United States also wanted to ensure that no other state could become strong enough to challenge American primacy. Meanwhile, the United States found itself confronting the dangers of nuclear weapons proliferation among possibly threatening states such as Iraq, Iran, and North Korea. The United States did eventually deploy significant military forces in dangerous humanitarian conflicts in Somalia, Haiti, Bosnia-Herzegovina, and Kosovo in the 1990s. By 2003, the United States was occupying Iraq in the largest nation-building project since World War II.

The United States is well equipped to address conventional challenges posed by any peer competitor or regional challenger. In fact, the United States faces no major conventional military threats to its territory. The September 11, 2001, terrorist attacks on New York and Washington, DC, however, showed the United States was ill prepared to meet a new dimension of security challenges. Suddenly, the United States faced a new enemy in al Qaeda, one that American power was not aligned to manage. Rather than retreat into a new isolationism as the terrorists appear to have hoped, the United States initially invaded Afghanistan and then Iraq to overthrow unfriendly governments. Under President George W. Bush, the United States adopted a new doctrine that any state harboring international terrorists would be considered to be supporting them. "Either you are with us, or you are against us" was the rallying cry to the world. This perspective would expand to incorporate an offensive doctrine of preemptive war. The United States had committed to eliminating possible threats before they emerge. By 2010, however, the United States remained entrenched in a war in Afghanistan that had lasted longer than the conflict in Vietnam. In 2011, Washington launched a new military campaign in Libya—with the stated intention of playing the "lead role" for "days, not weeks" and then turning responsibility over to its European allies. Since the transition was to the American-dominated NATO, many critics wondered why the operation was not a European-only one from the outset.

The American offensive doctrine rejected deterrence and constituted a major departure from the traditional defensive American posture. In the case of Iraq, the United States went to war over the strong opposition of much of the world, including its closest European allies. American credibility was undermined when much of the intelligence evidence it presented to justify the 2003 invasion proved to be wrong. The military mission of toppling the government of Saddam Hussein was easier than many observers expected. However, the limits and costs of this new strategic action became clear as 90 percent of postwar rebuilding efforts would be carried out by American troops, and the United States would pay 90 percent of the costs. Speculation about other rationales for the war remained rife, with motivations ranging from a desire to control oil flows to attempts to spread democracy in the Middle East through a grand political-sociological experiment. A surge of American forces and a new counterinsurgency approach helped to achieve stability in Iraq in 2006. In 2010 the United States formally ended combat operations. However, it still had to maintain tens of thousands of soldiers, and, realistically, Iraq remained a nation in turmoil and with an uncertain future.

The international campaign against terrorists also prompted the United States to review international defense relationships. Cold War alliances like the North Atlantic Treaty Organization (NATO), while still of political value, were not initially engaged in the American-led coalition military operations in Afghanistan and Iraq. In August 2004, the United States announced that it would begin a phased reduction of about seventy thousand troops that had been permanently based in Europe and Asia. Meanwhile, new priorities emerged as the United States engaged new (but often unreliable) allies, such as Pakistan, in its efforts to destroy international terrorist networks. By 2004, however, America's ability to wage war against terrorists with primarily military power had reached its limits. A leaked memo from U.S. Secretary of Defense Donald Rumsfeld suggested that the United States could not kill terrorists as quickly as they were being created; nor was it clear that the Department of Defense was the agency best suited for the lead role in the campaign against terrorism. Nevertheless, America's defense budget had reached $708 billion per year by 2010. Overall, the United States accounted for about 48 percent of global defense spending, yet it killed Osama bin Laden in 2011 with over two dozen Navy Seals.

During the 1990s, U.S. military doctrine was based on fighting and winning two major regional conflicts at the same time. The United States would maintain forward-deployed equipment and force-projection capabilities to fight major wars simultaneously in the Persian Gulf and on the Korean Peninsula. As forces would be deployed in substantial numbers for other conflicts, such as in the Balkans, this policy took on the posture of a win-hold strategy, whereby a war in one region could be fought and won, while a crisis in another region was contained. This approach was put in place during the 2003 Iraq War when the United States deployed an array of troops and equipment to the Persian Gulf by taking assets from other key parts of the world. However, in a public show of deterrence, the United States also sent long-range bombers with nuclear capability to Guam as a signal to North Korea that it should not take advantage of the war in the Middle East. The degree to which forces were stretched thin had actually become clear during the 1999 war in Kosovo when the U.S. European command had difficulty reallocating resources from other theaters of operation. When an aircraft carrier was moved from the Pacific Fleet, the Pacific Ocean was left unguarded by an American aircraft carrier for the first time since World War II. This commitment to a relatively rigid two-war doctrine thus required a significant realignment of strategy and resource commitments even before the war against terrorism commenced.

By 2010, the United States continued to maintain unchallenged military capability in relation to these global presence objectives but had also added to them the mission of combating international terrorism and the occupation of Iraq and Afghanistan. Active-duty U.S. forces totaled just over 1.58 million with 864,547 reserves. The American strategic command included 336 submarine-launched ballistic missiles in 14 submarines, 500 intercontinental ballistic missiles, 71 B-52 Stratofortress bombers, and 19 B-2A Spirit long-range bombers. Active-duty army forces included 553,044 troops, 329,390 naval forces, 204,261 marines, 334,342 air force personnel, and 46,119 special forces. The United States was also able to exert a regular global presence with substantial airlift capability for troops, including 1,376 planes in the civil reserve air fleet, 11 aircraft carrier battle groups, long-range ballistic and tactical submarines, and 2,708 combat-capable aircraft, including 154 with long-range strike capability.[1] The U.S. Navy had proposed increasing the size of its total fleet to 313 ships by 2020, with a total expenditure of $13 billion per year. The focus on naval expansion would be targeted toward rapid deployment on a global basis, including deployment of fifty-five small combat vessels operating in shallow coastal areas and an additional thirty-one amphibious assault ships, while maintaining eleven aircraft carriers.[2] By 2011, American defense officials began talking increasingly of the greater utility of air and naval power. In a speech at the U.S. Military Academy at West Point, Secretary of Defense Robert Gates said that anyone thinking of launching a ground war in Asia or the Middle East should "have his head examined."

Despite the economic crisis and a growing disconnect between the utility of military power and international influence, the United States continued to increase defense spending under President Barack Obama. The 2010 U.S. budget included a 3.4 percent increase in regular defense spending plus an increase in funding for operations in Iraq and Afghanistan. The total 2010–2011 defense budget was $708 billion, including an additional $159 billion for "overseas contingency operations." President Obama also asked Congress for a supplemental increase of $33 billion to pay for the thirty thousand troops he opted to send to Afghanistan in late 2009.[3] The regular defense budget and new allocations for Iraq and Afghanistan would come on top of the other costs of the Iraq War—including over four thousand American soldiers killed and more than thirty thousand wounded. The Iraq War alone had cost $700 billion by 2010, and one credible study showed that it would eventually cost the U.S. economy $3 trillion as a "conservative" estimate.[4] The most serious threats to American national security over the long-term were global economic trends and particularly the country's $14 trillion debt. Yet, Washington trended toward increased international commitments and more defense spending. As one estimate by Kori Schake suggests, the annual defense budget could be cut by $35.4 billion without sacrificing global technological and conventional supremacy. Democrats, however, fearful of being labeled soft on security, seemed unwilling to cut defense budgets. Thus, Schake (a principal foreign policy adviser to John McCain's presidential campaign in 2008) argued that "conservatives need to hearken back to our Eisenhower heritage, and develop a defense leadership that understands military power is fundamentally premised on the solvency of the American government and the vibrancy of the U.S. economy."[5] Secretary of Defense Gates announced a five-year plan for reductions in the growth of defense spending in early 2011, but this was not a real cut in actual spending but rather an estimation of future savings.

While American military commitments were growing exponentially, the American willingness to sustain them was in decline. According to a Pew Research public opinion poll released in December 2009, the U.S. public had moved sharply toward isolationism.[6] According to the survey, 41 percent of Americans believed the United States played a less important role in world affairs than it had ten years previously. This was the highest number ever recorded by a Pew Research survey in answer to this question. Some 44 percent of the American public incorrectly viewed China as the world's leading economic power, while only 27 percent correctly saw the United States as such. Just one year previously, 41 percent had placed the United States, and only 30 percent had placed China, in that role. A majority of Americans (57 percent) believed the United States should sustain its position as the world's sole military superpower; yet, the number who said that the United States should "mind its own business internationally and let other countries get along the best they can on their own"—a measure of isolationist sentiment—reached an all-time high of 49 percent. In December 2002, only 30 percent of Americans agreed with this perspective. There was also a significant disconnect between the views of the elite and the general public as 69 percent of members of the Council on Foreign Relations strongly supported an assertive U.S. role in global affairs.

In February 2010, the U.S. Department of Defense released the *Quadrennial Defense Review* (*QDR*), which emphasized partnerships in overseas military operations. It was, however, unclear if these were intended as a strategy for continuing expansive American primacy, developing burden-sharing responsibility, or creating a means of transitioning security management to allies and partners.[7] The December 2009 draft of the *QDR* stated, "The rise of China, the world's most populous country, and India, the world's largest democracy, will continue to shape an international system that is no longer easily defined—one in which the United States will remain the most powerful actor but must *increasingly rely on key allies and partners if it is to sustain stability and peace*" (emphasis added—in the final published version, the phrase "rely on" was dropped and replaced by "cooperate with"). Partnership had continued value in that it could enhance burden sharing and make more efficient military-to-military relations as the global security environment shifted. Meanwhile, partnership allowed for continued *realpolitik* with transitioning countries, such as China and Pakistan. Significantly, partnership would also be important in places like Pakistan and Yemen, where the United States had national security interests in combating terrorism but where a visible American presence would fuel local resentments. The *QDR* also stated, "The ability of the United States to build the security and governance capacity of key partners and allies will be central to meeting 21st century challenges. . . .

Building the capacity of allies and partners, together with efforts to prevent and deter conflict from beginning or escalating, can help reduce the need for large and enduring deployments of U.S. forces in conflict zones." In this sense, the ongoing wars in Iraq and Afghanistan and the heavy force presence that each continued to require by 2011 indicated that capacity building among partners could also be very expensive and long lasting with a heavy overseas military footprint.

Senior Pentagon officials, including the chairman of the Joint Chiefs of Staff, said publicly that the national debt was a major vulnerability for American security. However, the *QDR* appeared to have been drafted in a vacuum that took little account of America's relative decline in the global economy. For example, in its core mission, the Defense Department "extend[ed] a global defense posture comprised of forward-stationed and rotationally deployed U.S. forces, prepositioned equipment and overseas facilities, and international agreements." This activity is generally achieved via foreign military sales and financing, officer-exchange programs, and educational opportunities at the lower end. Security-force-assistance missions provide "hands-on" efforts "conducted primarily in host countries to train, equip, advise, and assist those countries' forces in becoming more proficient at providing security to their populations."

Models of this kind of partnership outreach include U.S. forces working in Iraq, Afghanistan, the Philippines, Africa, Colombia, and Pakistan under the rubric of counterinsurgency (COIN) operations. Traditionally, the *QDR* notes, such missions have involved special operations forces. However, this goal is largely mission dependent—as the decision to increase the U.S. force commitment in Afghanistan in fall 2009 demonstrates. In the *QDR*, COIN lies at the heart of an expanded American global military engagement. Major mission initiatives to support building partner capacity for COIN include (1) institutionalizing general-purpose force capabilities for security force assistance; (2) enhancing language, regional, and cultural ability; (3) strengthening and expanding capabilities for training partner aviation forces; (4) strengthening capacities for ministerial-level training; and (5) creating mechanisms to facilitate quicker transfer of crucial material. Missing from this assessment is the common refrain about wars like Afghanistan: these conflicts will not be resolved militarily but rather through diplomacy, economic progress, and especially civilian capacity.

Beyond operations in Afghanistan and Iraq, in 2010 U.S. peacetime forces included approximately four hundred thousand military personnel who were either forward stationed or rotationally deployed to "help sustain U.S. capacity for global reach and power projection." At the same time, the *QDR* indicated that the United States must be prepared to respond to changes in the international security environment and could not accomplish its goals alone, given the diffusion of power in the world. Thus, the Defense Department would "seek a new architecture of cooperation, one that generate[d] opportunities for the United States to work together with allies and partners on shared regional and global security opportunities and challenges." In particular, the United States would "continue to develop its defense posture to enhance other states' abilities to solve global security problems." The assumption was that the U.S. military presence overseas provided a "powerful catalytic effect in promoting multilateral security cooperation and regional security architectures that serve[d] both the U.S. and partner states' interests." This assumption did not test the proposition that this presence simultaneously promoted security dependence and substantial costs for the United States, depleted its resources in strategic reserve, and did long-term damage to its economic security. As U.S. Ambassador to Afghanistan Karl Eikenberry (a retired army general and NATO commander) argued in the fall of 2009, U.S. troop increases would bring "vastly increased costs and an indefinite, large-scale, U.S. military role in Afghanistan." Ambassador Eikenberry concluded that the expanded U.S. role would "increase Afghan dependency, at least in the near term, and it [would] deepen the military involvement in a mission that most agree[d] [could not] be won solely by military means."[8] Ambassador Eikenberry found it most disconcerting that a core prerequisite for COIN operations in Afghanistan—the presence of a reliable "partner" in the Afghan government—did not exist at the time (and does not as of this writing).

In terms of nuclear weapons, as of 2011, the United States had dramatically reduced its nuclear arsenal over the twenty years since 1991. Through the 1990s it kept nuclear capabilities as a reserve component of military doctrine based on continued application of deterrence and mutual assured destruction—though at much lower levels. In 1991 the United States took its strategic bombers off alert (during the Cold War it had kept 30 percent on strip alert ready to fly). During the 1990s, the United States also removed nuclear weapons from its ground forces. Overall, the United States reduced its nuclear weapons by 90 percent from Cold War deployment levels while also negotiating with Russia and China to discontinue targeting nuclear missiles at each other. The United States also announced that it would no longer be developing or testing nuclear weapons. The United States signed, but did not ratify, an international treaty that would have banned nuclear weapons testing. However, it has abided by the spirit of the goal of restraint by not testing nuclear weapons since the early 1990s.

In 2002, the United States and Russia negotiated deep cuts in their total nuclear weapons counts and agreed to achieve by December 2012 an aggregate number of nuclear weapons not to exceed 1,550 warheads for either party.[9]

This was an easy treaty for both sides to negotiate as the Russians wanted deep cuts to save money and the United States was already moving toward unilateral cuts. For Washington, this treaty also served to soften Russian opposition to U.S. plans to build a national missile defense. The United States had, in 2002, completed a review of its nuclear posture, recognizing that the Russian nuclear arsenal was no longer a major threat. Thus, the United States could afford to cut its arsenal significantly without making itself vulnerable. This force included fourteen Trident ballistic missile submarines, five hundred Minuteman III intercontinental ballistic missiles, seventy-six B-F2H bombers armed with cruise missiles and gravity bombs, and twenty-one B-2s armed with gravity bombs. While cutting programs, the United States had also started enhancing nuclear-test readiness, revived nuclear warhead advanced concepts efforts at the national laboratories, and accelerated planning and design for a modern weapons-grade-plutonium production facility.[10]

Critics noted that the basics of the United States' nuclear posture had not changed and merely continued at lower, but still very dangerous, levels. Also, tactical nuclear warheads were not part of any treaty structure. Alternatively, some critics asserted that American strategic thinking had not done enough to support new uses of nuclear capabilities. According to a study and recommendations from the Pentagon's Defense Science Board during the Bush administration, plans for nuclear weapons use did not sufficiently consider greater precision, reduced radioactivity, or the ability to dig deep into the ground to get at hard targets (a capacity not currently feasible technologically). This study recommended developing special-purpose nonnuclear weapons: long-range heavy conventional bombs for hitting precise targets within minutes, submarine-launched nonnuclear missiles, and a new sensor system for finding small, moving, and hidden targets.[11] This approach could, however, have drawbacks as other countries, Russia and China in particular, might not be able to recognize the difference between a conventional and a nuclear intercontinental ballistic missile. Thus, they could mistake a conventional attack, even on another country, as a nuclear attack, which would risk an accidental nuclear war.[12] Also, in September 2005, press reports indicated that the U.S. Defense Department was expanding its guidance for the use of nuclear weapons in combat to include preemptive strikes against terrorist organizations or nations in the planning stages of using unconventional weapons against the United States.[13] By 2010, President Barack Obama was establishing a new set of priorities around nuclear weapons in American national security. However, he too was looking at substantial funding for modernization of the force, especially under pressure from Republican senators, whose support he needed for ratification of further U.S.-Russian arms reductions. Nuclear policy has become a partisan issue in American politics;

thus, it was increasingly difficult for other countries to predict what plans the United States would develop over the long term. Also, in 2010, the Obama administration announced a new element of the American nuclear policy: the United States would only consider use of nuclear weapons against other states that had nuclear weapons, states not in compliance with the Nuclear Non-Proliferation Treaty, or states that were not members of that treaty. While deterrence remains important, the primary threats are seen as potential nuclear terrorism and the proliferation of nuclear materials.

Russia

Russia no longer sits at the top of many assessments of international security trends because it no longer carries the political, economic, or conventional military capacity to exert power within the international system as it did during the Cold War. There have been growing indicators that Russia is modernizing parts of its military, especially its nuclear arsenal. Moreover, while its conventional power is limited, Russia was able to conduct a sophisticated, integrated military operation against its neighbor Georgia in summer 2008. Russia has also increased cybercapabilities and demonstrated willingness to intervene in the domestic politics of neighboring states from the former Soviet Union. Russia has gained new regional influence via its flows of energy—on which its immediate neighbors as well as major parts of Europe are highly dependent. Meanwhile, the West has struggled with determining how far to push for human rights and democracy in Russia versus maintaining the nearer-term benefits of predictability and stability under the combined leadership of President Dmitry Medvedev and Prime Minister Vladimir Putin.

The primary, albeit least usable, capability placing Russia among the top major powers in the world is its nuclear arsenal. As its conventional capabilities have declined, Russia has increasingly relied on its nuclear weapons for deterrence. By 2008, Russia commenced production of new intercontinental ballistic missiles (ICBM) that Moscow says could change speed in flight as a means of avoiding missile-defense systems. This missile would carry as many as ten warheads with a range of five thousand miles. Russia also threatened in November 2008 to deploy Iskander missile brigades in Kaliningrad as a response to (since rescinded) American plans to put ballistic missile–defense systems in Poland and the Czech Republic. Russia also threatened to withdraw from the 1987 Intermediate-Range Nuclear Forces Treaty over this issue. This reliance on nuclear weapons to apply diplomatic pressure is potentially destabilizing as Russia's nuclear arsenal has ongoing maintenance and security problems combined with a deteriorating early-warning system. Command-and-control issues have also raised concerns about accidental launch or a possible nexus between nuclear smuggling, organized crime, and international terrorism.

Although the country continues to play a significant role in international security affairs, Russia has suffered from a general tension over its geopolitical position. Russia is caught between West and East while seeking to leverage influence within its area of influence in the former Soviet Union. Generally, when forced to choose, Russia has aligned with the West and sought good relations with Europe. It has often turned a weak power position into a successful negotiating tool by staking out hard-line opposition to some international policies and seeking payoffs for accommodation. For example, Russia strongly opposed NATO's enlargement during the 1990s but could do nothing functional to halt it. However, by assuming a strong diplomatic posture, Russia managed to negotiate favors in exchange for its cooperation. Moscow also made gains as the West turned a blind eye toward the redeployment of Russian conventional forces in the Caucasus region. Russia also received renewed promises from NATO not to station troops or to build nuclear weapons infrastructure or deploy nuclear weapons in new NATO members' territories and to create a NATO-Russia council that would give Russia limited say in NATO activities. Despite its not being formally related to NATO's enlargement, the Group of Seven (G7), the forum comprising the seven leading global economic powers, expanded to include Russia, becoming the G8, though Moscow's participation was limited to political discussions.

Much of Russia's diplomatic posture in the 1990s was, however, generated by lost prestige and shaped by domestic politics. Russia's leaders initially had to tread carefully in order to keep the military reasonably satisfied and out of politics—in other words, to avoid coups. In 1993, Russian tanks intervened domestically and opened fire on the Soviet-era parliament, which was challenging elected president Boris Yeltsin for power. More broadly, the deep decline in military prestige from the days of Soviet world power was a significant aspect of political frustration that nationalist and former communist leaders could manipulate. In Russia's first parliamentary election following its independence, in 1993, the public voted in favor of a majority-party government led by a nationalist-fascist, Vladimir Zhirinovsky. Yeltsin stood down on New Year's in 2000, handing power to his chosen successor, Vladimir Putin. Putin, a former KGB agent, promised stability while centralizing power over Russia's regions and asserting heavy influence over the Russian media and business leaders. While communism was dead, the tradition of a strong central government persisted under Putin, raising concerns in the West of a drift toward authoritarianism in Russia.

Russia sees its general strategic interests as building a multipolar world order and working against the idea of one country having sole primacy in international affairs. Russia also asserts regional freedom of movement in neighboring states to include a right of preemptive intervention without UN approval. The military was also given, in 2003, a role within the borders of Russia to protect the territorial integrity of the country from breakaway areas such as Chechnya. A sustained war against the independent-minded Chechen Republic preoccupied the Russian army in the 1990s. While the rest of the world looked the other way, the Russian army leveled major Chechen cities such as Grozny. Russian official doctrine defines major threats as including territorial claims by other post-Soviet states to lands held by the Russian Federation; local wars and armed conflicts near Russia's borders; the proliferation of weapons of mass destruction and their means of delivery; infringements on the rights of minority Russians living in other former Soviet republics; and the enlargement of external military blocks such as NATO.[14] To the Russians, these matters came to a head with the summer 2008 invasion of Georgia, designed both to protect Russian-friendly minorities in South Ossetia and to send a broader message to other former Soviet republics like Ukraine. A clear signal also went out to NATO that Russia was in fact quite serious about additional red lines regarding NATO enlargement. Meanwhile, at the broader level, Russia maintained its long-term intelligence apparatus, as evidenced by the breakup of a major Russian sleeper cell inside the United States in 2010.

Overall, Russia seeks a stable global situation so that it can focus on rebuilding and modernizing its economy while gaining international support and investment for that goal. Russia's security policy has thus focused primarily on developing stable relationships with the other major powers while at the same time exerting influence within its periphery—or the so-called near-abroad area of former Soviet republics. After the Soviet collapse, Russia initially made substantial overtures to the West under Foreign Minister Andrei Kosyrev in the early 1990s. However, as domestic political and economic crises led to a more nationalist perspective at home, these pressures placed constraints on Moscow's relationship with the West. Moscow and the West do have a common threat assessment in transnational terrorism. Moscow also requires investment from the West to grow its economy while seeking entry into international economic institutions. Meanwhile, the West requires Russia's assistance in controlling nuclear proliferation and managing the rise of China's power. Russia's assistance to and partnership with the United States in the international war on terrorism has enhanced Moscow's bargaining power. At a crucial moment in fall 2001, Moscow acceded to American overflight of Russian territory and did not raise strong objections to the basing of U.S. military personnel in several former Soviet republics. By

2010, Russia was making clear it would assist further in facilitating logistical access to Afghanistan for American and allied forces. At the same time, Russia was signaling that it could turn off that cooperation at will. In the long term, Russia's massive untapped oil and natural gas reserves could make it a major supplier of energy in the twenty-first century, significantly growing its relative power capabilities.

Russia is an ethnically and religiously diverse country covering a massive geopolitical space with varying levels of economic development. Suspicion of the outside and fear of external encirclement have historically influenced Russian national security policy. Most of Russia never underwent the periods of enlightenment and modernization that Western Europe experienced centuries ago. The serfs were only freed in 1867, electricity only came to Russia after the Bolshevik Revolution in 1917, and the subsequent large urbanization and industrial growth occurred under the totalitarian rule of Joseph Stalin. Russia and the larger Soviet Union were attacked twice during the twentieth century by Germany—which took the fight right to the borders of Moscow during World War II. A long-standing tension has also existed on Russia's border with China. From a security perspective, Russians believe their country lost the Cold War and their military returned home with very little to show for its efforts. Then, little of the promised Western assistance in economic reform and democratization materialized. The United States led the expansion of NATO right to Russia's borders in 2003, when the organization took in the former Soviet republics of Lithuania, Latvia, and Estonia. Meanwhile, American forces remain in Japan and South Korea, while China is rising to Russia's south.

The Russian military was largely left to decay for lack of funding during the 1990s. The accidental sinking of a Russian nuclear submarine in the North Atlantic in 2000 and the death of its 118 crewmen highlighted the severity of the problem. In August 2005, a Russian submarine became entangled in fishing nets near Japan, and rescue only became possible when American and British equipment and experts arrived at the scene. In 2004, 25 percent of all deaths within the ranks of the Russian army resulted from suicide.[15] During the 1990s army officers and their families returning from Eastern Europe (and then the former Soviet republics) were cramped into barracks, and Russian conscription yielded a high rate of no-shows. Further reflecting the dramatic decline in Russian military capabilities in the decade following the end of the Cold War, Russian air force pilots trained on average for 30 to 50 hours per year as compared to the NATO standard of between 180 and 260 hours. In 1994, the air force received only fifty new aircraft, and in 1995 it got less than twenty-five.[16] Russia also began selling off equipment, becoming a major weapons exporter. The country has gone for considerable periods with no satellite coverage to provide early warning of an incoming nuclear attack, and during the Year 2000 computer date turnover, Russia sent military personnel to the North American Air Defense Command to better monitor its own air space. It often seemed that due to its weak economy, Moscow could not see far past the sale of its equipment. For example, Russia sold technology to Iran that could be used to build nuclear weapons that could ultimately be targeted back at Russia. Indeed, in December 2005 Russia was reportedly preparing to deliver over $1 billion in tactical surface-to-air missiles and additional military equipment to Iran.[17] Iran has also sought to acquire Russian nuclear-capable, intermediate-range, strategic air-launched cruise missiles.

The Russian economy has improved, driven upward by high oil prices. Russia's gross domestic product (GDP) grew by 7.2 percent in 2003, its budget surplus grew by over $30 billion in the same year, and its trade surplus increased by 32 percent between 2003 and 2004.[18] While much of the world was in deep economic decline in 2010, Russian GDP was expected to continue to grow as energy prices rose.[19] The Russian defense budget has also increased—from about $22 billion to $42.5 billion in 2010. Nonetheless as a percentage of gross national product (GNP), Russian defense spending was still low at 2.4 percent. Without a major—and politically and economically painful—reform of its armed forces, Russia's ability to act as a significant military power remains limited to its internal security operations, some engagement in nearby countries, and its nuclear deterrent.

Russia has accelerated the training of its soldiers with ground forces tactical training time at the company level increased by 50 percent, air force flying time increased by 11 percent, and naval sea training increased by 25 percent. In 2010, Russia had total active armed forces numbering 1.027 million based on a conscription service of twelve months. Total reserves, with an obligation to age fifty, comprised about 20 million people, 2 million of whom had served within the previous five years. Russia's strategic deterrent troops included 80,000 troops servicing 224 missiles in 14 nuclear submarines and 30,000 strategic missile force troops servicing 385 ICBMs. The Russian army had 395,000 troops, including 190,000 conscripts. The navy had 142,000 in service; the air force, 160,000. Russia also had about 449,000 active-duty paramilitary forces, including the border guard service numbering 160,000.[20] In early 2011, Russia announced plans for a $650 billion increase in defense spending over the coming decade. This increase would include six hundred new fighter planes, one thousand helicopters, and additional force modernization and streamlining of personnel.

Russia's international deployments dropped dramatically from the hundreds of thousands stationed outside the USSR during the Cold War to include, by 2010, some 3,214 troops in Armenia, 3,400 troops in Georgia, 500 troops in Kyrgyzstan, 13,000 troops in Ukraine, and 1,500 troops in Moldova. Russia also sent token troops to UN operations in Sudan, Liberia, Democratic Republic of the Congo, Serbia, Liberia, Central African Republic, and Côte d'Ivoire.[21] Russia's incapacity to project power significantly reduces its ability to commit troops far from home territory. For example, in 1999 about two hundred Russian soldiers moved from Bosnia to Kosovo to establish an area of control near the Pristina airport—apparently to give Russia some leverage in further negotiations during a postwar phase in Kosovo. However, once the troops arrived, no reinforcements were available. Any efforts to reinforce from Russia would have entailed violating NATO member Hungary's airspace.

As of 2011, the Russian armed forces maintained a heavy land component with large numbers of tanks, including about twenty-three thousand main battle tanks that had not been updated significantly since the early 1990s. Russia had stockpiles of artillery pieces numbering 26,121, but much was in storage and useful mostly in outdated Cold War scenarios. Russia had fourteen strategic and fifty-two tactical submarines, as well as fifty-seven surface-combat naval vessels, including one aircraft carrier and fourteen destroyers. Russia maintained significant long-range and tactical aviation but with minimal new equipment and very little training time for pilots (about eighty to one hundred hours for long-range and twenty-five to forty hours for tactical training). Transport air command included 293 planes with additional planes available from the civilian fleet.[22] Overall, however, airlift capabilities were severely limited, and remaining Russian airpower largely consisted of medium-range bombers and operational-tactical missiles.[23] If Russia found it necessary to deter attacks on forward-deployed forces, it might have little choice but to resort to the use of tactical nuclear weapons. Indeed, Russia had reversed its prior political commitment to not being the first to introduce nuclear weapons in conflict. By 2010, Russia was maintaining its previous commitments regarding nuclear weapons, but language in its military planning signaled a lower emphasis on the conditions in which nuclear weapons might be used.

The rise of organized crime in Russia has combined with the decline of the role of the military to create a significant black market for illegal arms trafficking. By one account, some twenty-seven thousand firearms have been stolen from military units in Russia, which had recorded 53,900 crimes involving illegal weapons trading by 2001.[24] Some two hundred of the largest criminal gangs in Russia are global networks. These groups are pervasive in the economy and influence politics heavily, contributing to a significant international investment chill. There is a risk that such groups might engage in the trafficking of nuclear materials by exploiting corruption and often subhuman living conditions in the Russian military and at its nuclear facilities. Less likely, but possible, is the theft of an actual nuclear weapon or components via military transport vehicles that are not searched. Some short- and medium-range conventional missiles have been smuggled out of Russia successfully.[25] While it was not confirmed, a former Russian general claimed in 1996 that about one hundred so-called suitcase tactical nuclear weapons were missing from the Russian arsenal. These small nuclear devices had apparently been intended for paramilitary activity behind enemy lines during the Cold War.

During the 1990s, on multiple occasions petty criminals smuggled below-weapons-grade nuclear material out of Russia. A case containing 5.6 kilograms of Russian-produced plutonium 239 (enriched to 99.75 percent purity) was discovered unprotected in a garage in Tengen, Germany, and a large quantity of beryllium was found in a vault in a bank in Vilnius, Lithuania.[26] Between 1993 and 2002, the International Atomic Energy Agency confirmed eighteen instances of seizure of small quantities of weapons-grade nuclear material.[27] Ironically, in the nuclear decommissioning that accompanied the end of the Cold War, many of the warheads dismantled from missiles are still awaiting destruction and are both risky and expensive to store. The United Nations estimates that "dangerous" levels for making a fissionable nuclear device are 17.6 pounds of plutonium or 55 pounds of uranium—though 2.2 pounds of uranium would probably be enough to cause severe blast damage. The U.S. Department of Energy estimates that there are about six hundred tons of weapons-grade separated plutonium and highly enriched uranium outside of nuclear weapons in Russia. This material is located at fifty-three locations across eleven time zones.[28] This weapons-grade material can be reprocessed or locked away, but it cannot be destroyed. The combined land- and sea-launched nuclear capacity in Russia has an explosive power 120,000 times that of the bomb dropped on Hiroshima in World War II.[29]

Russian nuclear workers have, at times, earned as little as $100 per month, and military and nuclear personnel have on occasion gone months with no pay. Pride and patriotism keep the vast majority of Russian military and scientific experts working to keep nuclear material safe and secure.[30] According to the Nuclear Threat Reduction Initiative, six key problems nevertheless exist with management of nuclear weapons and material in the former Soviet Union: (1) the stockpiles are not all secure, and many are poorly accounted for; (2) inadequate measures are in place to find and recover stolen nuclear materials or to prevent their being smuggled across borders; (3) stockpile custodians receive low pay, face the prospect of mass layoffs, and work in an underfunded and oversized nuclear complex; (4) management of stockpiles remains shrouded in secrecy, making clear understanding of the problems and effective implementation of solutions far more difficult; (5) more weapons-usable material continues to be produced; and (6) the stockpiles of nuclear weapons and materials now in existence are far larger than needed, while only slow progress is being made toward reducing them.[31] In 2001 and 2002, two nuclear-warhead storage sites and two transport trains were found to have been under surveillance by terrorist groups, and one group made plans (not carried out) to seize a reactor at the Kurchatov Institute in Moscow.[32] On a more positive note, in 2010, Russia announced it had closed its last operating weapons-grade-plutonium manufacturing plant—located about twenty-five hundred miles to the east of Moscow—at a cost of about $2.5 billion.

Russia also faces serious challenges with the deteriorating command-and-control and early-warning infrastructure of its strategic nuclear arsenal. Although the risk is low, Russia could still launch an accidental or unauthorized nuclear attack on the United States. While both countries (and China) agreed to detarget their nuclear missiles during the 1990s, they could be retargeted in a matter of minutes. Moreover, it is not 100 percent safe to assume that all nuclear weapons are always in completely competent hands. Even in the United States, some four thousand military personnel were removed from nuclear weapons responsibility between 1975 and 1990 for drug, alcohol, or psychological problems. In both 1979 and 1989, a computer malfunction in American missile-alert systems led to false indications that massive Soviet nuclear attacks were inbound toward the United States.[33] If these situations have occurred in the United States, one can reasonably assume that similar problems exist in the far weaker Russian system. In January 1995, Norway launched a satellite into space that Russian early-warning systems falsely identified as an inbound nuclear attack from NATO. Russia's top political leadership had eight minutes to determine whether this was a preemptive NATO attack—then four minutes to decide whether to launch a retaliatory attack. Despite lower numbers of nuclear weapons, the United States and Russia continue to maintain the basics of the mutual-assured-destruction and launch-on-warning nuclear-response strategies. Poor early-warning systems make this an especially dangerous condition.

Russia maintains Delta IV ballistic missile submarines as the major component of its submarine fleet—each with sixteen multiple independent reentry vehicle (MIRV) missiles on board. An isolated launch of weapons—due either to a breakdown in communication or the rogue actions of a ship—is a slim possibility. Even one such incident would be devastating. According to one study, if four missiles failed for technical reasons but twelve (with a total of forty-eight warheads) were launched, they would reach their primary targets: American cities. The immediate blast would kill everyone in a three-mile radius and create—within hours, depending on wind direction—a forty-by-three-mile area laced with lethal radiation. If such an event occurred in New York City, an estimated 3 million would be killed; in San Francisco, 739,000;

in Washington, DC, 728,000. The study concluded that if missiles hit all of these cities, in a conservative estimate, 6.838 million Americans would be dead within hours, followed by a national breakdown of delivery systems for food, water, electricity, and medicine, leading to millions more deaths in the aftermath.[34]

Russia has yet to affirm its own place in the general scheme of major power relations. When pushed, Moscow has aligned with the West, though it has used the possible withdrawal of that cooperation as a leveraging tool to achieve diplomatic gains. Russia and the West share common threats from terrorism as well as a strong interest in nuclear safety and preventing proliferation. Yet, Russia itself is one of the likeliest sources of an eventual proliferation of nuclear weapons material. The greatest danger Russia poses to the world entails not its marching columns of soldiers and tanks in Red Square. Rather, the most significant threat from Russia continues to stem from its relative weakness at home and abroad. Nonetheless, Russia is massive, has resources, and is in a position to exert its influence in ways that it could not for the first twenty years after the Cold War. Russia plays a significant role because, while it cannot dominate global security outcomes, it can shift alliances between the United States and China or between Europe and the United States. It can threaten an alliance with China to extract gains from the United States or align itself with the United States if its fear of China becomes too great. Alternatively, Russia can work more closely with Europe than it does with the United States, furthering the vision of a world in which no one power dominates.

China

The People's Republic of China is the one country that, by the mid-twenty-first century or sooner, could emerge as a significant geopolitical challenger to the United States. By 2010, it had already moved past Germany and Japan as the second-largest economy in the world, after the United States. A population of over 1.2 billion people, coupled with rapid economic development, has made China a significant emerging power. At the same time, it has historically been an inward-looking, predominantly peasant-agrarian society lacking in economic modernization. As it enters the globalized international economy, China confronts a period of generational change that puts pressure on the government to reform and to respect human rights. Nevertheless, the Communist Party continues to govern the country, holding onto power with the support of the military and appealing increasingly to nationalism for popular support. While the rise of China appears likely, the kind of China that will emerge remains open. For example, might population pressures push China toward aggression as a tool for gaining access to vital resources? Or might China's entry into the global economic system facilitate economic growth and foster internal change toward democracy and a peaceful security policy? Furthermore, in countries like the United States, domestic politics have generated an increasingly anti-China mood as politicians have sought scapegoats for the outsourcing of jobs and American economic weakness. At the same time, however, though the United States bemoans Chinese influence in terms of financing its debt, the same United States put its bonds up for sale in the first place. In reality, by 2011 a strong codependence between the United States and China was emerging, and one global security scenario sees the two countries combining their efforts at the top of the international system for the foreseeable future, with mutual economic interests being the critical link.

At the core of Chinese tradition lies a desire to ensure national unity, stability, and sovereignty. Consequently, China has traditionally focused on defensive measures to prevent invasion and secure its periphery. China's recent historical memories include invasion by Japan in World War II. China did venture into a variety of Cold War engagements, supporting some like-minded communist countries in the underdeveloped world; however, China and the Soviet Union competed over leadership of the communist world and engaged in territorial disputes regarding their common border. The United States successfully exploited these differences during the 1970s as U.S.-Chinese relations were normalized following overtures to China by President Richard Nixon. During the 1980s and 1990s, China gradually sought to engage the international community, though it faced serious external criticism for its internal disregard for human rights.

While much of the analytical focus on China's rise to power stresses its role as a potential challenger to the United States, the major countries most immediately affected by China's growth are Russia, Japan, and India. Russia and China share a four-thousand-mile border. In 1969, competing territorial claims provoked a small shooting conflict at that border. After the Cold War ended, Chinese officials looked at Russia's initial democratic reforms as a model to avoid when implementing internal political and economic change. China rejected Moscow's model of combining market and political reform in the 1980s, preferring gradual market liberalization, carefully managed by the Communist Party. Russia has become an important supplier of arms, for example, selling China fighter planes and associated equipment. China has, in turn, modernized this older Russian equipment for its own use and for further export. The Russia-China relationship is complicated in that while Moscow would like to advance a multipolar world order, an unchecked rise in Chinese power could be as threatening to Russia as to anyone. In the post–Cold War era, Russia has leveraged its relationship with China as a hedge against American power. At the same time, Russia is vulnerable to movements of Chinese populations into eastern Siberia and a growing Chinese interest in diverting Caspian Sea energy supplies toward China. In 2004, some Chinese officials publicly considered purchasing Russia's largest oil company, Yukos, as it appeared Russia might favor a deal with Japan to construct a pipeline to fuel East Asian energy needs.[35]

So long as the United States has maintained a troop presence in Japan (by 2011 the number stood at about thirty-six thousand), Tokyo has relied on its alliance with the United States for protection—which includes sharing the benefits of America's shield of nuclear deterrence. During the 1990s, however, the United States began developing a "strategic partnership" with China that raised concern in Japan about American priorities in Asia. When President Bill Clinton traveled to China in the late 1990s, he did not stop first in Japan to consult with what had been one of America's closest allies. While China's economy had been growing, in large part as a major exporter to the United States, the Japanese economy was in deep decline for most of the 1990s. Although Japan has remained committed to its alliance with the United States, the relative rise in China's power, combined with questions about the American security guarantee, could eventually lead Japan to rebuild its military capability and, in theory, even pursue its own nuclear deterrent. This outcome would increase Chinese national security concerns considerably. At the same time, in late 2010, Japan finalized a new defense strategy that reflected its own worries about the growing power of China. Japan now increasingly emphasized China as a primary concern in terms of defense planning.

Geography has historically kept India and China from conflict, and each has had other strategic priorities. As the two countries are separated by the Himalayas, direct conventional conflict between them has been a difficult proposition. Nevertheless, India has developed nuclear weapons with ranges that can hit targets in China. India has been concerned about China's support for Pakistan and alleged role in facilitating the development of that state's nuclear weapons. China and India also share a border near the areas of key dispute between India and Pakistan. Meanwhile, the origins of freshwater supplies in the Himalayas are a potential source of conflict in the area. Should China ever overtly side with Pakistan, security concerns in India would be significantly elevated. Conversely, China has to pay careful attention to India's expanding naval power and missile and space technologies. India's economy has considerable potential for development, its population now rivals China in size, and its ties to the United States have grown considerably. The manner in which China and India define their relationships in the early decades of the twenty-first century will thus form a key element in the overall dynamics of regional security in South Asia.

China's rise in power is generally associated with the potential to translate economic power into military capabilities. Between 1980 and 2000, China's economy grew by a factor of five annually, average incomes quadrupled, and 270 million people emerged from absolute poverty. China's growth rate in 2009 was 9.1 percent, at a time when much of the rest of the world was in deep recession. Nevertheless, China still remains a predominantly agrarian society, and annual incomes averaged around $6,600 in 2010. Of particular interest to China observers is that, by 2010, China had already passed a range of economic markers that it was generally not expected to reach until about 2020.[36] Meanwhile, China has reformed its economy to facilitate future growth by opening large sectors to external competition and by lowering trade barriers as it established strong trade relationships with Australia, South Korea, and Japan—traditionally the United States' strongest allies in the Asia-Pacific region.[37] In 2004, Chinese prime minister Wen Jiabao predicted that China's trade with Southeast Asia would reach $100 billion by 2005—approaching the $120 billion that the United States does each year in the region.[38]

The potential for China to translate economic gains into military power is generated by its size, location, and population, which could prompt Beijing to adopt a more outward-looking national security policy. Already China has implemented significant increases in defense spending, with annual growth of about 17.5 percent in both 2001 and 2002 and 11 percent in 2003. In 2004, China announced an additional 11.6 percent increase in defense spending. By 2010, China spent about 4.3 percent of GNP on defense, although the relative rate of growth in defense budgets began to decline in that year. Overall, China's defense spending—at between $100 and $150 billion a year—equaled about one-sixth to one-seventh that of the United States. In terms of contemporary capabilities, China has not developed a large capacity to project power beyond a regional basis. However, China does have the capacity to shape events in the South China Sea, in South and Southeast Asia, and on the Korean Peninsula. China has decommissioned or moved large-scale deployments of troops away from the border with what was the Soviet Union. Redeployments or new capabilities have mainly focused on enhancing China's military means of influencing events in Taiwan, over which China claims territorial sovereignty.

China's perceived interests vis-à-vis its relationship with the United States will be key to the future development of Chinese military potential. Momentary tensions often disrupt U.S.-China relations; however, both states share an interest in a healthy economic relationship. China has been concerned about America's building a national missile defense and about American support for Taiwan. At the same time, China appears to prefer the stabilizing role that the United States has played in South Korea and especially Japan. Some analysts in the Chinese military tend to view the United States as the principal obstacle to a rise in Chinese power and as a potential threat to China's regional interests. China views American intervention in other countries—for instance, during the Kosovo and Iraq wars—with concern that new precedents regarding sovereignty are being set that have possible implications for Taiwan, Tibet, and Xinjiang Province. The 1999 Kosovo War unleashed significant, albeit momentary, expressions of Chinese nationalism manifested in popular protests, the burning of a U.S. consulate in Chengdu, the defacing of British and American embassies in Beijing, and informal boycotts of Kentucky Fried Chicken and other American fast-food outlets.[39] Within ten years, Chinese protesters had gone from emulating the American Statue of Liberty in Tiananmen Square to expressing large-scale public anger at the United States.[40] Meanwhile, popular sentiment toward China has hardened in the United States due to concerns about outsourcing and perceptions regarding unfair trade arrangements.

A lack of transparency in defense planning makes obtaining precise measures of Chinese military power difficult; thus, assessing whether China is a partner, competitor, or future threat to other states is hard to gauge. When China releases defense budget information, the detail does not include the amounts spent on weapons purchases, research, and a variety of additional costs.[41] China emphasizes four areas for military reform to make its armed forces more professional and efficient, including a ban on army engagement in private business activities, the introduction of regular auditing and accounting procedures, market-based procurement bidding, and zero-based budgeting. Salaries for officers and regular soldiers have been increased by 84 and 92 percent, respectively. Spending has been increased both on social benefits for servicemen and on training and equipment enhancements.[42] Equipment purchases have focused on adding fighter aircraft via Russian purchases, but China is also moving to produce its own aircraft and naval destroyers.

By 2010, China indicated that it sought a more ambitious role for its naval forces as a means of showing a greater global strategic presence. Called "far sea defense," this evolving concept involves building long-range capabilities to show Chinese presence in major shipping lanes and other key locations around the world. The core of this policy entails developing an extended naval capacity to protect Chinese commercial interests. Early indicators of this approach included the establishing of ports of calls by Chinese naval vessels in Myanmar and Abu Dhabi. During the Libyan crisis of early 2011, China sent a naval vessel to patrol waters off the Libyan coast; this missile frigate was there to facilitate the departure of Chinese citizens but also sent a strong message about new Chinese naval-power-projection capacity. Since 2008, China has maintained three naval vessels in the Gulf of Aden. In addition to a longer-range surface fleet, the Chinese are developing a submarine capacity with longer reach. As of 2011, China was not yet in a position even to begin to challenge American naval primacy in the Pacific region, but it was increasing its ability to frustrate it. Furthermore, Chinese advances in this area had moved, by 2011, considerably faster than expert analysis had previously anticipated. The result was increased concern both in the United States and in Japan, which had observed Chinese vessels passing very close to its territory in 2010.

By 2010, China had 2.285 million active-duty armed forces and about 510,000 reservists, making it the world's largest army. China had about one hundred thousand personnel working on strategic missiles located at twenty-seven interballistic missile sites. China also had about thirty-five intermediate-range missile launch sites and one submarine-based nuclear missile system. The army numbered about 1.6 million troops, although it is reducing the number of conscripts (about 800,000 in 2010). China's navy had about 255,000 personnel, in addition to sixty-five submarines and eighty principal surface combatant ships, including twenty-eight destroyers and fifty-two frigates. By 2011, China likely had 260 ships in total. An important element of Chinese military engagement involving Taiwan would be amphibious landing forces, though China only had eighty-three amphibious vehicles. The Chinese air force included 300,000 to 330,000 troops, though the ability to project power via air was limited as training ranged from 100 to 150 hours. China also had 660,000 active-duty paramilitary forces, most of them devoted to internal security functions. China maintained a limited number of overseas deployments in Côte d'Ivoire, Democratic Republic of the Congo, Lebanon, Sudan, Timor-Leste, and the Western Sahara. However, in terms of defense ties or defense-industry relations, China had by 2011 developed military relations with over 140 countries.[43]

China has also embarked on the modernization and expansion of its nuclear deterrent. China's intercontinental nuclear deterrence has historically been based on a limited deployment—historically about twenty-four hardened-silo nuclear missiles. However, to overcome American missile-defense systems, China is apparently expanding its nuclear arsenal and making it mobile with MIRV systems. A priority for Chinese espionage in the United States has been the successful theft or purchase of advanced nuclear missile and warhead technology. In 2004, China also launched its first new class of submarine, "Type 094," designed to fire an ICBM and likely outfitted with a new missile known as the JL-2 with a range of over forty-six hundred miles. This would mark a significant upgrade from China's existing submarine capability, which had comprised one submarine carrying missiles with a six-hundred-mile range.[44]

China's nuclear strategy has traditionally focused on maintaining a minimal deterrent capability via a limited array of missiles that could strike territory anywhere within the United States. China has kept its missile numbers low but has also been willing to use its nuclear capabilities for political ends. In 1996, senior Chinese military officials interviewed in American newspapers asked rhetorically which major cities the American public was prepared to lose to defend Taiwan. The traditional core of China's nuclear forces comprised two dozen aging Dong Feng 5/5A ICBMs, which are liquid-fueled, silo-based, single-warhead systems.[45] China also likely had by 2010 as many as fifteen hundred short-range ballistic missiles in range of Taiwan and could deploy land-attack cruise missiles targeted at the island nation.[46] Hardened-silo nuclear positions would make missiles vulnerable to a preemptive attack by the United States, and an American missile-defense shield could neutralize China's nuclear deterrent posture. China has developed the capacity to build a larger force, has attained MIRV technology, and, according to one American government study, could deploy "upwards of 1,000 thermonuclear warheads on ICBMs by 2015."[47]

Chinese military planners became acutely focused on the challenges of modern warfare and the need for military modernization following the American-led NATO war in Kosovo in 1999. They noted NATO's application of laser-guided precision munitions employing active homing and direction-finding devices as well as satellite-guided bombs that could deliver one-thousand- to twenty-five-hundred-pound warheads with accuracy within a few meters. Chinese analysts also took note of microwave bombs that could sabotage electronic equipment, missile target seekers, computer networks, and data transmission lines.[48] While the 2003 U.S. invasion of Iraq confirmed Chinese suspicions about precision weapons and airpower, they also observed the new rapid-movement role of ground forces accompanying the invasion as well as the integration of psychological operations with air and rapid ground operations.

Of unique concern to Chinese defense planners was the reality that the United States could now wage wars from significant distances with great precision. The Chinese military had focused mostly on planning for large land battles on its soil or in a nearby territory. China's naval reach, extending only about two hundred nautical miles offshore, could only disrupt, not defeat, an American presence.[49] China might have purchased some weapons, such as surface destroyers with long-range antiship missiles, for the purpose of preventing U.S. aircraft carrier battle groups from intervening in any conflict between mainland China and Taiwan. China also appeared to be enhancing its missile capacity to include ranges encompassing American bases in Japan, likely with the goal of making it more difficult for Japan to support American military activity in the region.[50] As of 2011, the Chinese were studying a range of new capabilities and doctrines, including mobile systems, solid-fuel propellants, advanced guidance systems, warhead miniaturization, space-based capabilities, enhanced radiation and directed energy weapons, antisatellite munitions (leading to the shoot-down of one of China's own satellites in January 2007), and ballistic missile-defense countermeasures.[51] Such programs appear to fall under the rubric of what China calls an "assassin's mace," which it would apply to any conflict involving Taiwan in particular.

China gained from cooperation with the United States in the global campaign against international terrorism.[52] Also, while China had reservations about America's 2003 invasion of Iraq, it did not campaign actively against it. China also benefits heavily from America's role in Afghanistan, which promotes stability in an area where China would otherwise likely have to pay high costs to engage. Chinese strategic doctrine tends to draw on a cultural-historical experience that emphasizes patience and thinking in terms of decades, not months or years. If the United States had initially succeeded in Iraq, it would owe China a debt for not actively opposing the invasion; conversely, if America became bogged down in Iraq—as it did—and had to devote large elements of its active military to the Middle East, this could erode America's general military and economic power and create a long-term relative gain for China. And if the United States had to finance its wars—as it did—by borrowing from China, this too would increase China's power substantially. Secretary of State Hillary Clinton stated the reality of the U.S. situation clearly when she indicated, on her first official visit to China in 2009, that none of the two countries' differences (i.e., over human rights) could surpass their shared economic interests.

Even if China's rise to power does not eventually create new military threats, its consumption of energy could prove just as destabilizing. As recently as the early 1990s, China was a net oil exporter. By 2009, it was the second-largest net importer after the United States. China will likely need to import up to 600 million tons of oil per year by 2020, which is three times its expected domestic productive capacity.[53] The use of energy and the resulting impact on international prices, as well as the environmental consequences, could have rippling effects on the global economy. Alternatively, China's abuse of its own environment could have as negative an impact on its growth trends as anything else. If China's economic potential goes unfulfilled or many citizens are left behind, nationalism could impact China's strategic thinking. Indeed, China's growth is not a win for all Chinese. As China adjusted its economy to join the World Trade Organization, it expected to lose some 10 million farming jobs and 1 million jobs in the automobile and machine manufacturing sectors.[54] In effect, there is no certainty that China will emerge as the global challenger many people anticipate as internal crisis could keep it very inwardly focused for decades to come. China's patience and long view of economic development and international objectives might be its greatest asset, drawing on the advice of Deng Xiaoping, who laid out general principles of Chinese strategy: "Keep cool-headed to observe, be composed to make reactions, stand firmly, hide our capabilities and bide our time, never try to take the lead, and be able to accomplish something."[55]

The European Union

The major European states—Britain, Germany, and France—are individually no longer the world powers they once were. Also, within Europe, traditional security dilemmas have largely been resolved. Some areas of the region have experienced significant destabilizing events, such as the Balkan wars, economic crisis, and major al Qaeda terrorist attacks in Madrid and London. Overall, however, the European continent knows a degree of peace unlike any it has experienced in history. At the core of the general peace in Europe has been Franco-German reconciliation, deeply embedded within international institutions including NATO and the European Union. Nevertheless, Europe does face critical strategic and operational questions about its future security. The central issue is whether the European Union will have enough integrative pull to establish Europe as a collective economic and military power. This question is made all the more crucial by accelerating U.S. military disengagement from European security. Further complicating these dynamics is a general public perception that Europe need not invest overly in military capabilities and might be best served by staying out of military engagements promulgated by the United States. While Europe could rise to become a significant global actor, it equally could remain unable to coalesce and develop common strategies to advance the shared interests of EU members. The danger in this scenario is that, at the very moment when America is disengaging from Europe, no strong institutional mechanism exists to fill that void. This leaves Europe confronting significant external challenges with no effective means of organizing to meet them. The situation became even more pronounced in 2010 when Europe faced serious budget and banking crises in Greece, Ireland, Portugal, and Spain. Budget problems would force a new government in Britain to make major cuts in defense spending in 2010.

Individually, Europe's countries are not significant military actors. Only Britain and France have high-end military capabilities that allow them to project significant power at far ranges. Most European armies are large conscript forces, which were well suited for the Cold War but lack the professionalism, efficiency, and deployment capabilities necessary for modern combat operations. Collectively, Europe spends about two-thirds the amount the United States does on defense but only has one-third of America's capacity. Since the 1950s, European powers have expanded the foundations of economic integration into a European defense capability. However, such efforts were often stymied by a lack of cohesion among the Europeans or by opposition from the United States. Contemporary trends show, however, that the United States is reorienting its forces away from Europe and no longer sees European security as a primary concern. The transatlantic relationship remains vital to both Europe and the United States, and the political and economic ties between the two are strong. Nevertheless, public opinion across Europe opposed America's 2003 invasion of Iraq. Europeans tend to prioritize diplomacy over the use of force in international affairs and view threats such as international terrorism as best solved via intelligence and policing rather than military power. Europe is also undergoing significant demographic changes, with large immigration influxes from North Africa and the Middle East.

Since 1992, EU members have committed to achieve a Common Foreign and Security Policy and to build an independent military capability. The European Union began by appointing a senior official to manage foreign affairs, the first being former NATO secretary general Dr. Javier Solana. However, EU members quickly saw that diverging national security priorities would make it difficult to achieve common foreign and defense policies. France, for example, declared its intent to lead the European Union in opposition to the 2003 U.S. invasion of Iraq only to find that many EU countries refused to follow its lead. The United Kingdom, Italy, and Spain, as well as most countries about to join the European Union from Central and Eastern Europe, initially supported the United States. Germany, however, had already embarked on an unprecedented unilateral opposition to the American policy.

The economic incentives to pool military resources among the EU countries are strong. In 2010, Britain and France announced plans for a pooling of major defense assets, and the two were key lead allies in the March 2011 air assault on Libya. A larger, common EU defense capability can provide these states with a measure of influence in global security that, alone, none would have. The European Union includes twenty-seven countries that, combined, spend over $150 billion per year on defense. EU membership includes two nuclear powers and over 2 million troops from among the member states. In December 1999, the European Union agreed on an ambitious plan to create a rapid-deployment force of fifty to sixty thousand troops for use in humanitarian and rescue tasks, peacekeeping, and crisis management. The EU has set up small battle groups of integrated forces for crisis deployment as a way of building toward this goal.

Politically, the European Union faces decision-making problems. Arriving at collective decisions among twenty-five members is problematic in the best of times, let alone when confronting a military crisis. Additionally, increasing European defense capabilities will require substantial investment of resources and money. Establishing a workable industrial base for European defense is a significant challenge as nations tend to want to protect their own defense industries. One of the European Union's signature projects, the Eurofighter Jet, was only procured in 2003, ten years after it was first scheduled for completion. The European Union has only several long-range transport planes, while the United States has several hundred. Consequently, Europe finds itself tempted to free ride on American power capabilities while simultaneously wishing for more autonomy.

European defense investment, when compared with that of the United States, is clearly weak. Assessing, in 2006, just the United Kingdom, France, Germany, Italy, and Spain (which accounted for 80 percent of all defense spending in Europe), U.S. naval tonnage was three times greater than that of these five EU members for nuclear-fueled ballistic missile–bearing submarines and surface combatants and four times greater for operational transport and support ships. The United States had sixty-six nuclear-fueled submarines; these five EU countries had eighteen. The U.S. navy had twelve catapult-launch aircraft carriers and twenty-nine cruisers; the EU leading five collectively had one of each. America has four hundred frigates; the main five EU members have about one hundred. American ships are produced as one single type and displace twenty-eight hundred tons; the European frigates are of various makes, and a third of them displace only thirteen hundred tons or less. In terms of modern aircraft, the U.S. advantage over the main five EU members was 3.5 to 1 in numbers, and two-thirds of the EU member planes are C-160 Transalls (a third smaller than the C-130, the smallest U.S. transport aircraft). The ratio for tanker aircraft was around thirty to one. The United States had seventy-six hundred main battle tanks, all variants of the MA Abrams; the five main EU members had forty-eight hundred main battle tanks comprising six highly different brands. The U.S. Air Force has 366 A-10 ground-attack aircraft, for which the Europeans had no equivalent at all. Similar disparities existed in command-and-control and intelligence capabilities.[56]

The European Union established a modest military-planning center to coordinate national contributions to a future European military force. The objective was to harmonize national contributions to be coordinated by the EU high representative for foreign and security policy. The European Union had a political and security committee as well as a military committee with military staff. While formally intended as a complement, not a competitor, to NATO, it nevertheless could plan for and control military operations not involving that body.[57] Since fall 2003, the European Union had moved forward with three principal activities: (1) it had deployed a small group of operational planners to NATO headquarters in Mons, Belgium; (2) those states most ambitious about European defense cooperation had worked to accelerate cooperation on military capabilities; and (3) the European Union had agreed to a renewed collective defense commitment while reaffirming that NATO was the primary tool for collective defense in Europe.[58] The EU members agreed to a "headline goal" of capability commitments that governments aimed to achieve by 2010.[59] The planned projected force contributions to the Helsinki force goals included the following: Germany, 13,500; the United Kingdom, 12,500; France, 12,000; Italy and Spain, 6,000 each; the Netherlands, 5,000; Greece, 3,500; Austria and Finland, 2,000 each; Sweden, 1,500; Belgium, Ireland, and Portugal, 1,000 each; and Luxembourg, 100.[60] Subsequently, the European Union undertook small but important missions in Macedonia. The deployment there included 320 troops and eighty civilians. In fall 2004, the European Union took over command responsibility for all forces in Bosnia-Herzegovina.

The European Union has developed strategic partnerships with Russia and opened a working relationship with China. Missions to the Middle East, Iran, and North Korea have also enhanced the diplomatic profile of the European Union. Meanwhile, Europe is also developing a niche capability in postconflict civilian police missions. In 1997, the European Union took responsibility for organizing a multinational police-training mission in Albania and in 2003 organized the European Union Police Mission in Bosnia-Herzegovina (which included nine hundred personnel with five hundred active police officers). The European Union also undertook Operation Artemis in eastern Congo, with control over eighteen hundred (mostly French) forces deployed to Bunia, and played the lead role in antipiracy operations off the coast of Somalia in 2010. Overall, the European Union has coordinated sustained deployment of fifty to sixty thousand troops in and around the European areas, including more than twenty countries in Southeastern Europe, Afghanistan, Central Asia, Iraq and the Persian Gulf, and Africa. The total numbers deployed just in 2003 and 2004 averaged around seventy thousand, and if British deployments in the Iraq War are counted, the number rises to ninety thousand. An additional ten thousand troops from ten countries joining the European Union in 2004 also contributed to these missions. These deployments were not without significant risk. By January 2004, European countries had sustained ninety fatalities in postconflict Iraq. Germany had lost fourteen soldiers and Denmark had lost three in Afghanistan by the end of 2003. Germany's first combat fatality from hostile fire since World War II occurred in Georgia in 2001.[61] Still, difficulties in coordination remained and became clear very early in the Libyan air campaign in March 2011. Britain and France were at the front of the air assault, but it could only be sustained with major American support. While the United States sought to turn over command in a matter of "days" of the bombing's commencement, quick disagreements emerged. France said the mission should not be conducted by NATO, Italy said it had to be, and Turkey raised concerns about the entire operation. Germany abstained from supporting the attacks at the United Nations and pulled its naval patrols from NATO's Mediterranean command once the war began.

The major European powers have significant variations in military capability, though all share declining defense investment. By 2010, France had 352,771 forces and 70,300 reserves. It devoted four thousand personnel to its strategic nuclear forces, which maintained forty-eight submarine-launched ballistic missiles on three submarines, twenty-four nuclear-capable naval aircraft, and three air force squadrons with sixty Mirage 2000 planes with nuclear capacity. France's nuclear force is minimal and designed largely to establish French independence and pride of place among the larger nations of the world. In 2010, France had about 134,000 army personnel, including 7,700 in its foreign legion and about 2,300 special operations forces, 193,376 paramilitary troops, 2,500 marines, 46,195 serving in the French navy, and 57,600 in the French air force. France's primary means of power projection included its nuclear submarines and an aircraft carrier battle group. France had forces abroad, including 2,800 in Germany, 775 in Gabon, 1,000 in the Indian Ocean, 575 in Senegal, and 1,435 in French Guiana. France also had UN and other peacekeeping forces deployed (at levels ranging from just several to several thousand observers) in Afghanistan, the Persian Gulf, Bosnia-Herzegovina, Central African Republic, Democratic Republic of the Congo, Haiti, Kyrgyzstan, Lebanon, Liberia, and Serbia.[62]

As of 2010, Germany maintained an active force of 250,613 with 163,962 conscripts and an additional 161,812 reserves. Its army had 163,962, its navy had 24,407, and its air force had 62,244. After Germany rearmed in the early 1950s, its military's primary function was to deter aggression against the inter-German border by the Soviet Union. The unification of Germany and the end of the Cold War rendered this mission obsolete. As of 2011, Germany maintains a very large land army but also has self-imposed constraints on the external use of force, reflected by both training and equipment. Meanwhile, the conscription component of the German military has historically been seen as an important function for civil society, national service, and the maintenance of civilian-controlled armed forces. Germany's history of aggression and the legacy of the Holocaust have shaped this strategic culture to the extent that the German public remains wary of external force projection. Germany had engaged in lower-end military deployments by 2010, including minor deployments to Poland.[63] Germans have been increasingly engaged in non-combat peacekeeping operations, which have included assuming command responsibility of NATO forces in Afghanistan for a period. By 2010, Germany had deployed 4,365 troops in Afghanistan, 129 in Bosnia-Herzegovina, 459 in Lebanon, 2,486 in Serbia, and 104 in Uzbekistan. Germany continues to host international forces in its territory from Canada, France, the Netherlands, the United Kingdom, and the United States.[64]

As of 2010, of the European countries, the United Kingdom had the most modern and capable forces, though these too were cut dramatically during that year. British active-duty armed forces totaled 175,690 with 199,280 reserves. One thousand troops were assigned to strategic forces that included forty-eight nuclear missiles in four submarines, though with less than 160 operationally available warheads. The British army included 100,290, the navy 34,650, and the air force 39,890 personnel. As an example of British fighting capabilities, a British pilot received anywhere from 210 to 290 flight-training hours per year compared with 150 for Germany. Equipped to project power on a limited global basis, Britain is the primary European country able to accompany the United States in its global military actions. Britain can project power through its nuclear force's four submarines and eight additional conventional submarines, two aircraft carrier battle groups, six surface destroyers, and three hundred combat tactical aircraft. Britain maintains ongoing overseas deployments in Afghanistan, Cyprus, Canada, and Germany. By 2010, Britain also had troops deployed in varying numbers in Kuwait, Gibraltar, Nepal, and the Netherlands, as well as conducting peacekeeping operations in Bosnia-Herzegovina, Democratic Republic of the Congo, Moldova, Serbia, and Sierra Leone. Britain also deployed 458 military advisers to twenty-six countries.[65] Though Britain was at the forefront of the allied campaign against Libya in early 2011, the vast majority of cruise missile and air strikes were launched by the United States in the early days of the operation.

In summer 2004, Britain announced that it would be cutting twenty thousand military (and civilian defense) personnel by eliminating four infantry battalions, three Royal Air Force squadrons, and twelve surface warships. Some key additions, however, would eventually include deployment of two new aircraft carriers (though in 2010, this funding was in question). With these initial cuts, Britain could still extend its reach, but for far shorter periods and with far less impact. While Britain would be able to apply modern, highly sophisticated technology, it would not be able to provide the same high-level ground-troop deployments that had made its role in places like postinvasion Iraq a crucial element of peace-support operations, giving Britain some influence over American tactics, if not strategic choices. Britain's doctrine was to plan for three concurrent military operations—one being an ongoing peace-support operation in addition to large-scale operations alongside the United States and other allies. Realistically, the Iraq operations had already made such a multitask commitment unlikely by 2006, and any additional pressures on the British military would likely place major strains on the army. This concern became increasingly important in 2010, when Britain announced an additional round of defense cuts totaling an 8 percent reduction in spending and a decrease of at least seven thousand soldiers and additional equipment purchases. These reductions were actually much smaller than many observers had anticipated, as earlier in the year the British press reported that defense spending cuts as high as 20 percent were being contemplated.

Summary

While the risk of great power conflict leading to war seems very low, it is not nil. The major powers still maintain significant military capabilities, which serve as a deterrent but also make hypothetical confrontation scenarios appear very dangerous. The world still exists in a condition in which two major nuclear powers, the United States and Russia, base their structural security relationship on the concept of mutual assured destruction. While this architecture has worked historically, the declining state of Russia's military, particularly its nuclear arsenal and early-warning systems, provides reason for concern about the stability of mutual assured destruction. Meanwhile, the United States is shifting policy away from classic deterrence to incorporate a doctrine of preemptive war. China's power is growing and has already altered the general balance of power in Asia. Nonetheless, whether economic attractiveness or military threat will define China's power remains to be seen. Europe is poised to emerge as an important actor in global security, though it faces military deficiencies that could make translating its political and economic power into diplomatic leverage increasingly difficult. Many common global security challenges unite the interests of all the major powers and can thus play a role in easing tensions over issues that would otherwise divide them in a traditional world of great power competition. At the same time, the reality of significant regional hot spots means that these major powers could find themselves in wars they would rather avoid.

Suggested Reading

Brown, Michael, Owen R. Cote Jr., Sean Lynn-Jones, and Steven E. Miller, eds. *America's Strategic Choices.* Cambridge, MA: MIT Press, 2000.

Fisher, Richard. *China's Military Modernization: Building for Regional and Global Reach.* Stanford, CA: Stanford Security Studies, 2010.

Goldgeier, James M., and Michael McFaul. *Power and Purpose: U.S. Policy toward Russia after the Cold War.* Washington, DC: Brookings Institution Press, 2003.

Herspring, Dale R., and Stephen K. Wegren. *After Putin's Russia: Past Imperfect, Future Uncertain.* 4th ed. Lanham, MD: Rowman & Littlefield, 2009.

Mandelbaum, Michael. *The Frugal Superpower: America's Global Leadership in a Cash-Strapped Era.* New York: Public Affairs, 2010.

Priest, Dana. *The Mission: Waging War and Keeping Peace with America's Military.* New York: W. W. Norton, 2004.

Reid, T. R. *The United States of Europe: The New Superpower and the End of American Supremacy.* New York: Penguin Press, 2004.

Shambaugh, David. *Modernizing China's Military: Progress, Problems, and Prospects.* Berkeley: University of California Press, 2004.

Swaine, Michael D., and Ashley J. Tellis. *Interpreting China's Grand Strategy: Past, Present, and Future.* Santa Monica, CA: RAND Corporation, 2000.

Szayna, Thomas, Daniel L. Byman, Steven C. Bankes, Derek Eaton, Seth G. Jones, Robert E. Mullins, Ian O. Lesser, and William Rosenau. *The Emergence of Peer Competitors: A Framework for Analysis.* Santa Monica, CA: RAND Corporation, 2001.

The guided-missile destroyer USS Chung-Hoon (DDG 93), Singapore frigate RSS Stead-fast (FFG 70), high-endurance cutter USCGC Mellon (WHEC 717), and Singapore corvette RSS Vigilance (90) line up during a surface gunnery exercise in the South China Sea on July 12, 2010. Source: Department of Defense photo by PO1 Kim McLendon, U.S. Navy (Released).

5

Regional Flash Points

VARIOUS GLOBAL FLASH POINTS present complex challenges for the quest for power and the search for peace in the twenty-first century. These primary areas include India and Pakistan, the Korean Peninsula, Taiwan, the Middle East, and Eurasia. Potential regional conflicts in these areas have the capacity to impact the interests of the great powers directly. War in these cases is not inevitable. Indeed, some destabilizing events, such as the attainment of nuclear weapons by India and Pakistan, could also deter conflict in a crisis and provide the basis for negotiation. This chapter therefore aims not to predict whether these specific conflicts are likely to occur. Rather, it illustrates why these areas had become the world's key flash points for potential major conflict by 2011 and to show how serious the consequences would be.

India and Pakistan

India and Pakistan represent the most dangerous potential for interstate war at the beginning of the twenty-first century. These two countries are the most likely to use nuclear weapons in anger, and they face a growing combined threat from terrorists seeking to destabilize their relationship. These two regional powers have demonstrated a willingness to fight, primarily over the disputed territory of Kashmir, an Indian-controlled region on the countries' shared border to which Pakistan also stakes a territorial claim. As India threw off the yoke of British colonial rule in 1947, a major portion of the Muslim population left Hindu-dominated India for what became the new state of Pakistan. Some

12 million refugees fled their homes; eventually 1 million were killed in related hostilities. The differences that developed between these two neighbors with common histories but religious and cultural differences grew over time. The two went to war in 1947, 1965, and 1971 and came very close to war in 1987 and 1990. History shapes the environment in which they assess their security needs, and while both sides have a deep interest in peace, both prepare for armed conflict. The American decision to increase its role in Afghanistan in 2009 was in large part designed to provide an anchor of stability and ensure that a broader regional conflict did not erupt, drawing in India and Pakistan.

The global security environment has also shaped perceptions of security requirements for India and Pakistan. India positioned itself outside the Cold War distribution of power and sought to lead the "neutral and nonaligned" countries of the world, though it looked toward the Soviet Union for military and economic assistance. By the 1980s, India had shifted its strategic focus toward the West. However, India found itself largely ignored as the United States and Europe looked to China for economic engagement. Pakistan has pursued less ambitious goals, driven mainly by fear of its large Indian neighbor. During the 1980s, Pakistan sought ties both to the United States and to China for military and economic support. Pakistan became an important country for the United States, which needed assistance in containing Soviet aggression in Afghanistan. The United States provided economic and military assistance to Pakistan on the condition that it would verify its status as a nonnuclear country.

India and Pakistan have been engaged in a classic security dilemma that neither can afford. Both countries face high poverty rates and severe challenges to economic development. By the time both countries became declared nuclear powers in 1998, each was devoting a high percentage of its economy to military spending. India spent about 17 percent and Pakistan about 33 percent of its overall budget on defense. While India has civilian control over the military, Pakistan has shifted to and from military governments that have occasionally seized power in extra-constitutional coups. Illustrating the depth of internal threats in Pakistan, the popular leader Benazir Bhutto was assassinated in 2007 while campaigning for national election. In November 2008, radical Islamist terrorists based in Pakistan attacked the popular Taj Hotel and other sites in Mumbai, India, killing 175 people. In both countries, the political leadership has used the appeal of nationalism to generate popular support for government, and both have been willing to exacerbate tensions over Kashmir to suit near-term political calculations. Conversely, by 2006, both India and Pakistan were also engaged in high-level and grassroots diplomatic efforts to lessen the risk of war, and every time the two parties were pushed close to conflict, calmer heads prevailed.

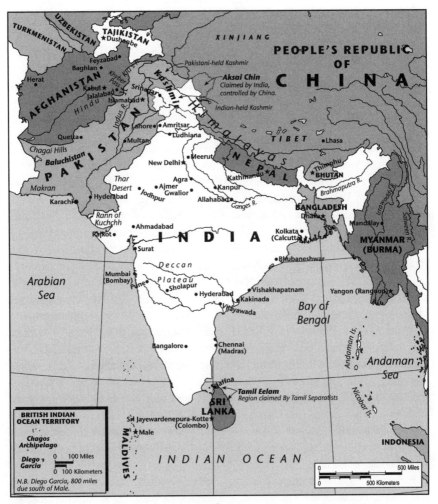

South Asia

The Balance of Power and Nuclear Weapons

India has significant military advantages over Pakistan, with active-duty armed forces numbering 1.325 million and 1.555 million reserves by 2011. Largest among the services is the Indian army, which numbers nearly 1.123 million. The Indian navy has 58,350 personnel and includes sixteen submarines, one aircraft carrier, eight destroyers, and twelve frigates. The Indian air force numbers 127,200 and includes 632 combat aircraft. The Indian air force is well trained, averaging about 180 flying hours per year. India also maintains just over 1.3 million active-duty paramilitary forces, including 208,422 border security forces.[1] Pakistan has a smaller armed forces structure, including 617,000 active-duty servicemen. The army has 550,000 troops. The navy has twenty-two thousand and includes eight submarines and seven frigates as its main surface fleet. The Pakistani air force numbers forty-five thousand with 383 combat aircraft. The Pakistani air force is also highly trained with about 210 annual flying hours per pilot. Pakistan has large numbers of paramilitary forces, ranging up to 304,000 on active duty with a national guard of 185,000.[2]

The balance of power significantly favors India, which has four times the territory and seven times the population of Pakistan, in addition to greater political and economic stability.[3] However, as India does not position all of its forces toward Pakistan alone, there has been a roughly equal balance of power near the India-Pakistan border. Since the 1960s, both sides have sought to gain advantage over the other via nuclear weapons development. For several decades, both India and Pakistan existed as de facto nuclear powers—each knew the other had the capacity to produce nuclear weapons, but none were tested or deployed. Lack of materials and financial obstacles had constrained both sides in their nuclear efforts. However, both sides also made their position clear by not signing the Nuclear Non-Proliferation Treaty and later refusing to sign the Comprehensive Test-Ban Treaty. India began to develop its nuclear weapons program in 1964 and by the 1970s was able to yield domestically produced plutonium. In 1974, India conducted what it called a "peaceful" nuclear test that, while not formally a weapons test, illustrated the technological advances the country had made. India also developed a variety of missile systems with the delivery capacity to target either Pakistan or China. The Indian air force is an available tool of weapons delivery, and India has developed a space program that, if pushed forward, could lead to intercontinental ballistic missile (ICBM) capability.

Pakistan began its nuclear program in 1971 and accelerated it after India's 1974 tests. Pakistan does not have a domestic plutonium-production capacity; instead, it embarked on a clandestine effort to procure uranium and then became self-sufficient in its ability to upgrade it. Pakistan likely received assistance from China in the 1980s; however, the extent of China's involvement in the Pakistani nuclear program is not publicly known. Pakistan's primary means of delivering weapons has been short-range missiles and aircraft purchased from China, the United States, and France. Both India and Pakistan developed fission-based nuclear weapons similar to those deployed by the United States against Japan at the end of World War II. Explosive yields are likely five to twenty-five kilotons.

In spring 1998, tension between these two countries reached a peak as each tested nuclear weapons. The result was the most serious nuclear standoff since the 1962 Cuban Missile Crisis between the United States and the Soviet Union. India was the first to test its nuclear weapons. While these nuclear tests caught the international community by surprise, they should not have. India's newly elected political party, the Bharatiya Janata Party, or BJP, ascended to power on a nationalist agenda, and one of its primary campaign promises was to test nuclear weapons. However, India had kept the tests hidden from outside surveillance, and when it conducted a series of underground nuclear test preparations, the world was caught off guard. Pakistan, in turn, faced extraordinary domestic pressure to respond to India's tests. While a parade of Western officials offered Pakistan economic and political incentives not to test weapons, nationalist passions and a desire to rebalance the strategic equation pushed Pakistan into its own nuclear tests.

Limited Deterrence

The Cold War notion of nuclear deterrence rested on pillars largely missing from the India-Pakistan equation. Neither India nor Pakistan has substantial second-strike capability, and the relative numbers of weapons for each is low (between seventy and ninety for Pakistan and around eighty or one hundred for India), though Pakistan has developed its arsenal at a faster rate. In this situation, either side would have a strong incentive to strike first and hope to eliminate the other's nuclear retaliatory capability. The low numbers of nuclear weapons remove the possibility of mutual assured destruction and thus make the use of nuclear weapons an option in battle. The proximity of India and Pakistan to each other—they share a fifteen-hundred-kilometer border—means that any small crisis could escalate with very little warning. Both countries' capital cities are within four hundred kilometers of the other's territory. Lahore, Pakistan, is only thirty kilometers from the Indian border.[4] This circumstance differs greatly from the U.S.-Soviet nuclear stalemate, where two large oceans separated the two states. Also, neither India nor Pakistan has developed sufficient early-warning capabilities or civil-response plans to help provide warning and preparation for an incoming attack. Moreover, both sides have strong strategic rationales for using nuclear weapons first. If India massed troops near the Pakistan border, perhaps to isolate Kashmir, Pakistan would have a strong incentive to use nuclear weapons on those forces. India would in turn have a strong incentive to attack first to eliminate Pakistan's nuclear weapons.

The U.S. government has conducted simulations of potential conflict between India and Pakistan. These war games consistently predict eventual escalation into a nuclear war once conventional conflict breaks out. Most scenarios begin with a conflict involving Kashmir. If concerned that Pakistan might move forces and equipment to the east of Lahore to isolate Kashmir, India might launch preemptive attacks to secure its access to the region. To do so, it would have to push deep into Pakistani territory, prompting Pakistan to use nuclear weapons against advancing Indian troops to make up for disparities in conventional forces. Pakistan could even wait and drop nuclear weapons on Indian troops concentrated inside Pakistan's territory following an Indian invasion. Pakistan might then claim the moral high ground politically, having only attacked invading troops on its own territory. Variations on that scenario have India launching preemptive attacks on areas where it believes Pakistan's nuclear weapons are located. While it might not be successful, India might be convinced that this strategy would prevent nuclear escalation. However, fear of such attacks could as easily prompt Pakistan to launch its weapons first in a "use-it-or-lose-it" scenario.

In one simulation, the United States would intervene to prevent a conflict by deploying a peacekeeping force between India and Pakistan. This scenario (initially simulated to be set in 2010) would see the United States bring a temporary peace to Kashmir, which Pakistan interprets as reinforcing the existing status quo favoring India. Pakistan could move to isolate U.S. peacekeepers, putting long-range artillery pieces parallel to the Indian corridor to Kashmir, thus cutting off that access. Then, according to the scenario, Pakistan would place guerrilla fighters with Stinger antiaircraft missiles near Kashmiri airports. In the simulation, a U.S. cargo jet is shot down by Pakistani guerrillas operating in the area. War begins when an Indian force chases the guerrillas and engages with the Pakistani military. Indian and Pakistani air strikes on each other's troops and facilities would follow, leading to an Indian attack against Lahore and then a Pakistani decision to launch its nuclear weapons. Eventually, perceiving that the United States is aligning with India, Pakistan asks Iran to come to its aid; Iran responds by crossing Pakistan and attacking Indian troops in the Thar Desert to block their advance. Follow-on forces, including American troops landing on the western Pakistani shore, would seek to cut off the Iranian force's supplies, leading Iran to attack that force and escalating the conflict dramatically.[5]

On several occasions since they tested nuclear weapons, India and Pakistan have come to the brink of war. India has complained about what it sees as Pakistan's support for cross-border terrorism into Kashmir, and even into India proper, targeting Indian troops and citizens. India moved large numbers of troops toward Pakistan's borders in early 2002, with the two sides deploying a combined 1 million armed personnel to the India-Pakistan border. This crisis was de-escalated, though each took different lessons from it. Pakistan appeared to conclude that its credible threat of nuclear deterrence—manifested by missile tests and public statements—had convinced India that it could not risk an escalation. India, meanwhile, appeared to conclude that the overwhelming nuclear and conventional balance of forces favoring it had compelled Pakistan to settle the crisis in accordance with India's demands.[6] India played a high-stakes game by elevating the crisis into a "global drama," which appeared to pay off with Pakistan promising to end support of groups using violence in Kashmir.[7]

Both India and Pakistan appear to recognize the dangers of war, giving some credence to the role of deterrence. By 2004, India and Pakistan had restored diplomatic relations and instituted a number of confidence-building measures. Nevertheless, while neither side wanted a war, they remained perilously close to conflict. For Pakistan, there appeared to be four major "thresholds" beyond which it would introduce nuclear weapons: (1) conquest of large parts of its territory, (2) destruction of a large portion of its land or air forces, (3) economic strangulation, and (4) domestic political destabilization or large-scale internal subversion. India maintains a formal "no-first-use" policy; however, it also leaves open the option to use nuclear weapons in retaliation for attacks on Indian troops "anywhere." India appears to rely on its ability to contain any escalation, a numerical advantage in nuclear and conventional weapons, and its geographic size as decisive advantages in any possible conflict with Pakistan. Meanwhile, both sides continue to develop a range of nuclear-capable ballistic missiles, with India testing 150- to 250-kilometer-range missiles and longer-range multistage rockets that can range between 700 and 3,000 kilometers. In summer 2004, India tested a new missile system able to carry a one-ton warhead with guided capability. Pakistan has tested a 2,000-kilometer-range, solid-fueled, two-stage, nuclear-capable ballistic missile as well as shorter-range missiles reaching 180, 300, and 700 kilometers. In August 2005, Pakistan tested its first cruise missile, and in 2006 it tested shorter-range missiles capable of carrying nuclear warheads. In 2008, Pakistan tested air-launched cruise missiles with nuclear capability and short-range ballistic missiles with ranges of about three hundred kilometers. Eventually, Pakistan has hinted, it will begin development of intercontinental ballistic missiles. India has more advanced missile capabilities (some developed with Russian assistance), including an ability to target most of China and the theoretical ability to build ICBMs. At longer ranges, however, India has experienced problems at the testing stage, with one test missile failing on the launch pad in September 2010.

India and Pakistan remain in a missile-delivery arms race, though both are also constrained by how much they can spend.[8] India has also increased its influence in Afghanistan, seeking to keep Pakistan facing north, while Pakistan has maintained informal intelligence ties to the Taliban as the two countries seem to fight a proxy conflict there. To many American supporters of a continued U.S. presence in Afghanistan, the risk of a regional conflict between India and Pakistan has provided the primary justification. Meanwhile, although Pakistan has benefited greatly from American financial and military assistance, many in the United States do not see it as a reliable ally against global terrorists. To Pakistan, U.S. commitments to help India develop peaceful nuclear energy raise significant concerns about American intentions in the region. The US-Pakistan relationship was to be seriously tested when Osama bin Laden was found to be living comfortably inside Pakistan in May 2011.

Nuclear Dangers

Any exchange of nuclear weapons between India and Pakistan would have devastating repercussions. A Natural Resources Defense Council assessment of a possible nuclear exchange reviewed two scenarios—one with ten Hiroshima-sized explosions with no fallout and another with twenty-four nuclear explosions with significant radioactive fallout (findings are derived using comparative population data based on the Hiroshima weapon's impact in Japan). In the first scenario, a minimal nuclear exchange, ten bombs exploded over ten cities in India and Pakistan, assuming five in each country, would produce the outcomes shown in table 5.1. In this scenario, the nuclear weapons would be exploded above ground, destroying much of the radioactive fallout.

Twenty-four nuclear bombs exploded on the ground would result in greater explosions and more fallout. In this scenario, radioactive fallout would be dispersed into the air. Depending on the amount of radioactivity and the prevailing winds, this scenario estimates that 22.1 million people in India and Pakistan would be exposed to lethal radiation doses of six hundred rems or more in the first two days after the nuclear exchange. Another 8 million would receive additional doses between one and six hundred rems, causing severe radiation sickness and possibly death. A total of 30 million people would be at risk for exposure to radioactive fallout.[9] Most likely, such an exchange would lead to substantial declines in global agricultural productivity and could also accelerate global warming trends as fallout entered the atmosphere and got caught up in trade winds across the Pacific.

Pakistan's acquisition of nuclear weapons raises concerns over command and control of its nuclear arsenal and related materials. While Pakistan's army insists its nuclear weapons are secure, security is heavily dependent on armed guards and gates rather than high-technology capabilities. Three specific scenarios might threaten the Pakistani nuclear arsenal and would have major international repercussions. First, there exist insider threats in Pakistan: those working with the weapons could transfer, or assist the transfer, of weapons or nuclear materials to militant Islamists or terrorists who oppose the government. Second, an outside group, like al Qaeda, could attempt to steal nuclear

Table 5.1.   Scenario Involving Nuclear Weapons Exchange between India and Pakistan: Ten Bombs over Ten Cities

	Dead	Severely Injured	Slightly Injured
India			
Bangalore	314,978	175,136	411,336
Bombay	477,713	228,648	476,633
Calcutta	357,202	198,218	466,336
Madras	364,291	196,226	448,948
New Delhi	176,518	94,231	217,853
Subtotals	1,690,702	892,459	2,021,106
Pakistan			
Faisalabad	336,239	174,351	373,967
Islamabad	154,067	66,744	129,935
Karachi	239,643	126,810	283,290
Lahore	258,139	149,649	354,095
Rawalpindi	183,791	96,846	220,585
Subtotals	1,171,879	614,400	1,361,872
Totals	**2,862,581**	**1,506,859**	**3,382,978**

Source: Natural Resources Defense Council.

weapons or material. Third, the secular government could fall and be replaced by an Islamic regime, which would then be in control of Pakistan's nuclear weapons, materials, and expertise, all of which could then be purposefully proliferated or used.[10] In such an event, other countries, including India as well as the United States, might launch preemptive attacks against Pakistan's nuclear weapons facilities. Pakistan could even interpret an accident at one of its nuclear facilities as a preemptive attack by India, prompting Pakistan to launch an erroneous retaliatory response.

The Korean Peninsula

The Korean Peninsula includes two hostile and very well-armed countries that face each other across a common border. The situation also involves vital U.S. interests, as well as the regional influence of China, Japan, and, to a lesser degree, Russia. By 2011, North Korea had one of the few remaining totalitarian governments in the world, headed by a deeply isolated regime with little experience in the nuances of world politics and international diplomacy. Its leadership was also increasingly unclear, as Kim Jong Il, apparently in declining health, appeared to appoint his inexperienced twenty-seven-year-old son as his successor. During the early 1950s, as communists consolidated power in North Korea, the country divided into northern and southern portions. The United States and its allies intervened on behalf of the South Koreans. After several years of war, the North Koreans were driven to the 38th parallel, which eventually became the legal dividing line between the two Koreas. The two countries never signed a peace treaty and remained in a legal state of war. South Korea has been a strong ally of the United States, which stationed troops in the demilitarized zone between the two states to deter a North Korean invasion. These forces stand opposite North Korean forces that are poised to attack and are within close range of the South Korean capital, Seoul. North Korea elevated this already dangerous situation to a new level by striving to become a nuclear power with long-range missile capability. The reality of ongoing war became clear in March 2010 when North Korean forces fired a torpedo that sank a South Korean ship and killed forty-six sailors. Then, in November 2010, North Korea fired artillery shells at a South Korean island, killing four people, including two civilians. South Korea responded in December 2010 with live-fire military exercises, and the United States sent additional military forces to the region. Once again, this highly combustible situation had the potential to explode.

The North Korean Threat

North Korea entered the second decade of the twenty-first century as an economic disaster, largely due to mismanagement of resources by the government, which had a general disregard for the welfare of its 22.7 million people. As many as 2 million people died as a result of food shortages in the 1990s. Human rights abuses, torture, public executions, slave labor, and forced abortions and infanticides in prison camps were regularly reported. There may be as many as two hundred thousand political prisoners in North Korea.[11] Meanwhile, North Korea spends at least one-third of its gross domestic product on the military, though accurate assessments are difficult to assertain.[12] The North Korean leadership depends heavily on support from the military, which thus receives significant rewards. The military serves as the largest employer, purchaser, and consumer in the country.[13] The heavy investment in the military has seriously weakened North Korea's civilian infrastructure, leading to major energy and food shortages. Declining human and economic conditions could lead to large-scale social unrest, prompting massive internal disruption or even civil war. Alternatively, this could provoke North Korea into a desperate invasion of the South to achieve the forceful reunification of the Korean Peninsula.

Over several decades, North Korea amassed military capabilities to achieve strategic and operational surprise in wartime to sustain breakthrough operations in the South. North Korea appeared to see massive firepower with artillery barrages, multiple rocket launchers, and surface-to-surface missiles as central to this strategy. In war, North Korea apparently would seek to isolate Seoul and capture all air and naval facilities supporting lines of reinforcement into South Korea. North Korea would also likely seek to neutralize enemy airpower. Finally, North Korea would attempt to instill confusion, panic, and fear as a means of imposing reunification of the peninsula on its terms.[14] By 2011, North Korea had the world's fourth-largest military. Its active-duty troops totaled 1.106 million forces and about 4.7 million reserves. The army has about 3,500 main battle tanks, 2,500 armored personnel carriers, and a total of 17,900 artillery pieces. Naval and air forces are much smaller, with 63 submarines, 3 frigates, and 329 coastal combatants and an air force of 110,000 troops. The air force has limited equipment and between ten and twenty hours average for annual training. There is a 189,000-strong active-duty paramilitary force as well as a 3.5 million worker and peasant guard.[15]

South Korea, with a population of 48.5 million, had in 2011 some 687,000 active-duty forces, with 560,000 conscripts, and 4.5 million reserves. The army numbered 420,000 troops and included 2,750 main battle tanks, 2,780 armored personnel carriers, and 3,500 towed artillery pieces. The South Korean navy numbered 68,000 personnel, including 25,000 marines, 13 submarines, and 47 surface combatants. The air force had 64,000 personnel and 490 combat aircraft. South Korea also had 4,500 active-duty paramilitary forces and a civilian defense force of 3.5 million, including qualified men up to age fifty. The United States had 25,374 troops based in South Korea, including 17,130 army, 254 navy, 7,857 air force, and 133 marine personel.[16] Working together with the South Korean forces, both in command structures and regular training exercises, the U.S. forces provided important capabilities in the areas of airlift and sealift; prepositioning of heavy equipment and supplies; battlefield command, control, and communications; advanced munitions; aerial refueling; intelligence, surveillance, and reconnaissance; and counterfire against artillery attacks. Joint U.S.–South Korean military cooperation included major live-fire exercises, combined defense planning, intelligence integration and sharing, logistical interfacing, educational exchanges, and defense-industry cooperation.[17]

North Korea has maintained an offensive troop posture, designed to act with surprise to quickly seize large parts of South Korean territory. The objective would appear to be to make an American reinforcement of South Korea's forward-deployed troops impossible. The general parameters of a major conflict would commence according to several realistic scenarios. North Korea could use a peace initiative or other diplomatic overture as a ruse to launch a surprise attack.[18] In another scenario, the United States would launch a preemptive attack on North Korean nuclear facilities. In response, North Korea might attack into South Korea. Perhaps the most likely scenario would entail a major miscalculation by North Korea (i.e., the use of small military attacks to prompt diplomatic attention), which in the end would lead to an inadvertent escalation. In either scenario, the U.S. and South Korean forces would seek to slow a North Korean invasion and protect Seoul. This goal could be hampered by a lack of early warning, the narrowness of the Korean Peninsula, mountain terrain well-known to the North Korean forces, and the North's launching a two-front invasion into the South. North Korea could seek to terrorize South Korea by using mass artillery fire against Seoul, incorporating chemical, biological, and nuclear weapons. If enough ground could be seized, the North Korean military would likely hand a victory to its political leaders in the North, who could then negotiate a settlement favorable to them.[19]

If the U.S. and South Korean forces could frustrate the North Koreans for long enough, they would eventually be reinforced by American troops based in Japan and the United States. However, by 2011, the U.S. military was also deeply engaged in Afghanistan and recovering from its war in Iraq, fighting in Libya, and providing relief to earthquake-stricken Japan raising questions about its capacity to deploy large conventional forces in a timely manner. Medium- and long-range airpower would thus also be employed against North Korean artillery and troop concentrations. Then, the United States would likely counterattack by seizing key territory. In a final phase, a major counteroffensive would be engaged to destroy the North Korean military. In most estimates, U.S. forces would eventually reverse a North Korean invasion of South Korea. However, the costs of combat would be extraordinary. U.S. forces pushing into North Korean territory would find the countryside a virtual fortress with hardened bunkers and massive tunnel complexes. Meanwhile, North Korean forces would have quickly dispersed into South Korean territory, perhaps mixing in with the civilian population. As much as 65 percent of North Korea's troops and 80 percent of its military firepower are deployed within one hundred kilometers of the border with South Korea, so North Korea would be able to concentrate forces quickly and make its supply lines less vulnerable to air attack. Several thousand artillery pieces and three hundred missiles are within target range (about fifty miles) of Seoul from North Korea and would be employed, likely with chemical and biological weapons. North Korea is believed to have stockpiled about five thousand metric tons of nerve gas, as well as choking, blister, and blood agents. North

Korea likely has the capacity to weaponize some biological threats, including anthrax and the bacteria that cause plague and cholera.[20]

Without any movement of its artillery, North Korea could likely sustain fire of up to five hundred thousand rounds an hour against South Korean and American defense forces over a period of several hours.[21] As many as 1 million people could be killed in the early stages of a surprise attack against Seoul.[22] In 1993, the United States made tentative military plans for a possible attack on North Korean nuclear facilities. The U.S. Department of Defense estimated that victory would require four months of high-intensity combat using over six hundred thousand South Korean troops and five hundred thousand American reinforcements. Within the first ninety days of combat, predicted U.S. casualties ran as high as fifty-two thousand. In addition to massive casualties, the economic and war-related costs were projected to range into the trillions of dollars.[23] By 2011, there was no reason to think that this basic scenario had changed, except for the worse, with the greater likelihood of nuclear weapons use by North Korea. Unforeseen events, like the tremendous national crisis caused by the March 2011 earthquake and nuclear crisis in Japan, could also impact the strategic environment as the leadership in Pyongyang calculated its security situation and assessed the allies' ability to react to North Korea.

In another scenario, North Korea might take advantage of American deployments during a conflict elsewhere. In such a circumstance, America's ability to send massive numbers of reinforcement troops to South Korea would be even more limited. The United States has introduced plans to redeploy large numbers of forces away from forward areas and rely instead on prepositioned equipment and rapid-deployment capacity. The United States can project power from the U.S. mainland to Korea, combined with bases in Guam and Japan. If, however, the United States were deeply engaged in another major troop deployment, its military options against North Korean artillery might be limited. The United States might then have to introduce nuclear weapons as the only available means of stopping North Korean advances or artillery bombardment. The United States has run simulated bombing missions for precisely this scenario using a squadron of F-15E fighter jets conducting mock bombing runs between North Carolina and Florida with simulated B61 nuclear bombs.[24]

The Nuclear Environment

In late 2002, North Korea indicated that it was processing materials that could be used to make nuclear weapons. This announcement ended North Korea's 1993 promise to stop processing nuclear fuel if the United States provided it with economic assistance and light-water nuclear reactors for energy.

At that time, the International Atomic Energy Agency (IAEA) monitored North Korea's adherence to the Nuclear Non-Proliferation Treaty. However, North Korea eventually indicated that it would no longer respect its commitments under this treaty, and nuclear inspectors departed. North Korea seemed to elevate regime survival over unification and argued that it sought nuclear weapons for the defensive purpose of preventing a preemptive American attack. North Korea did offer to give up its nuclear arsenal, or large parts of it, if the United States would commit to a nonaggression treaty with North Korea. Nuclear weapons have also helped North Korea drive a wedge between South Korea and the United States. In the late 1990s, South Korean leaders embarked on an overture toward the North known as the "sunshine" policy. A new generation of South Koreans wanted to end tensions, and if North Korea could make its nuclear issue a bilateral question between it and the United States, then Washington might be blamed by the South Korean population for a failure of diplomacy. Nuclear weapons could also be useful to North Korea as a tool for blackmail—perhaps via an offer to relinquish only some of them in exchange for economic aid. Or, in a dangerous circumstance, North Korea could purposefully proliferate nuclear weapons for profit; there was some evidence that it had developed initial contacts with Myanmar for this purpose by early 2010. Finally, such weapons might be considered a tool of warfare against transportation locations in South Korea, transit points and American troop deployments in Japan, and even the U.S. homeland.

By 2006, North Korea had likely developed at least several nuclear weapons and had a rudimentary capacity to hit targets near or in American territory. During April to June 2003, North Korea announced it had begun reprocessing nuclear fuel rods containing enough plutonium for two to five nuclear weapons, though it did not then claim that it had actually created a nuclear weapon. In October 2006, North Korea declared it had conducted its first successful nuclear weapons test. In May 2009, it carried out a second successful underground nuclear test. By 2011, North Korea had likely produced enough weapons-grade nuclear material to build twelve nuclear bombs and could probably produce enough material to build five to thirteen weapons per year, depending on conditions within its production facilities. In 2010, an American scientist from Stanford University disclosed that while he was on a visit to the country, North Korean officials had shown him a new, large, and secret uranium-production facility. Meanwhile, North Korea also deployed about 120 short-range Scud B/C missiles, which can reach most of South Korea, and forty medium-range No Dong missiles, which can hit targets in Japan. North Korea's missile inventory totaled around three hundred missiles in 2005. North Korea also developed the Taepodong-1 rocket, which has three stages. This missile was tested successfully for flight but not for deployment of payload or accuracy at long ranges. However, if it proceeds to develop a second generation of this missile, North Korea will eventually be able to deliver nuclear weapons to American cities.[25] On July 4, 2006, North Korea conducted a number of missiles tests, including a failed Taepodong-2 missile test that, had it been successful, would have shown a range that could hit U.S. targets in Alaska.

The North Korean acquisition of nuclear weapons significantly alters the security framework in Northeast Asia. Washington has preferred not to engage in direct negotiations with the North Korean government and thus encouraged a multilateral diplomatic framework (including South Korea, China, Japan, Russia, North Korea, and the United States). As of 2011, this approach appeared to force North Korea to constrain some of its more virulent rhetoric so long as it hoped to enhance its relations with China and South Korea. However, it also frustrated North Korea's efforts to isolate the United States and to extract a nonaggression promise. The United States has a military option and could eliminate, or at least dramatically set back, the North Korean program with precision air strikes. Another alternative, explored by Pentagon planners, would be to conduct preconflict maneuvers that would strain the North Korean military with the hope of prompting a coup. For example, one U.S. plan (OPLAN 5030) would be to fly RC-135 surveillance aircraft very close to North Korean airspace. This action might force North Korea to deploy interceptor aircraft and thus use up their jet fuel, prompting North Korean forces to disperse from their bunkers and deploy troops, exposing positions and depleting supplies. Other elements of this alternative would include disrupting the North Korean financial system and engaging in disinformation actions to play on paranoia among North Korean leaders.[26] The danger of such a program is that it could also give North Korea the false belief that it was actually under attack, prompting it to launch its own.

In 2011 there were, therefore, really no good military options for addressing this explosive region. Diplomacy and deterrence, combined with incentives for cooperation, thus comprised the preferred path. By 2010, it appeared that outlines for a diplomatic agreement to end North Korea's nuclear production would have to include the following: (1) North Korea gives up its nuclear program and opens itself again to international inspections; (2) the United States provides a written security guarantee that it will not launch preemptive attacks against North Korea or attempt regime change; and (3) the international community, including the United States, gives financial assistance to aid the emergency economic situation in North Korea and gradually engages North Korea in international transactions that will hopefully reduce its sense of insecurity.[27] In reality, however, only China had the economic capacity to exert leverage on North Korea, and even Beijing argued that its ability to

East Asia

influence the North Koreans was limited. The United States and North Korea were engaged in a high-stakes relationship complicated by a lack of effective communication and understanding. Nuances such as language translations led to confusion over what North Korea revealed about its nuclear weapons programs. Ideological blinders in the North assuming a hostile international environment were enhanced during the administration of President George W. Bush by American rhetoric labeling North Korea as an "evil" state governed by a madman. Washington also appeared to assume the North Korean leaders were crazy, whereas much of their desire for nuclear weapons might be explained by basic deterrence theory—a paranoid but almost purely driven survival instinct. In that sense, American beliefs that North Korea is using its nuclear weapons merely as a bargaining chip might be misguided; the North Koreans may well see them either as a useful deterrent or as actual weapons of war.[28]

Averting Conflict—or a Nuclear Chain Reaction?

Several longer-range questions could also impact the potential for conflict on the Korean Peninsula. A new generation of South Koreans, for example, does not have the same fear of North Korea as its forefathers. This generation is increasingly more likely to challenge South Korea's historical alliance with the United States—and some view the United States as the source of the country's security problems. Alternatively, if South Korea finds that the American commitment to its security becomes ambivalent or hollow, South Korea might develop its own nuclear deterrent. In summer 2004, the South Korean government disclosed that some of its scientists had experimented with enrichment capacity for nuclear fuel, which could be made into weapons-grade material. South Korea had explored a nuclear option in the 1970s but dropped those efforts and instead joined the Nuclear Non-Proliferation Treaty. However, the South Korean message implies that the capacity exists to obtain a nuclear deterrent. Another consequence of a declining American commitment to Northeast Asia could be a decision by Japan to nationalize its military and develop its own nuclear deterrent. Any decision by Japan to go nuclear could raise significant security concerns in China, setting off either a regional arms race, a new balance of power, or, in a worst case scenario, a nuclear chain reaction. Meanwhile, a wild card scenario for which no one seemed prepared in 2011 was a North Korean collapse and the resulting chaos. In that scenario, South Korea might move north quickly and itself become a nuclear power, raising alarm in both China and Japan. Or worry about chaos and instability could prompt China to move into North Korea with land forces that might eventually confront South Korean and American troops moving north. In many respects, the tension between the need for a new regime to see things differently in North Korea conflicted with the near-term preference in the region for stability and predictability.

Taiwan

Tensions between mainland China and the island of Taiwan date to the communist revolution when the pro-American and British leader Chiang Kai-shek was defeated by communist rebels led by Mao Tse-tung. In 1949, Chiang and his political allies fled to Taiwan and claimed to be the true representatives of China. The government of mainland China treats Taiwan as part of its territory. Taiwan's status is contested as many of its citizens and international backers see it as potentially a sovereign state, though it has not claimed to be. Taiwan has some attributes of independence, including its own constitution, representative government, and military. Taiwan has not declared formal independence for two reasons. First, mainland China sees maintaining its sovereignty over Taiwan as justification for using military force against the island. Second, the United States supports Taiwan's autonomy and has made a defensive commitment to it—but only in the event that it does not provoke China by declaring independence.

One China or Two?

The United States, like most of the international community, has an official "one China" policy. However, Washington is pressured by a strong pro-Taiwan domestic lobby and wants to expand arms sales and other exports to the island. This relationship makes it more difficult for the United States to balance its position on Taiwan with its significant economic interest in a good relationship with China. Meanwhile, Taiwan has transitioned from an authoritarian government to a representative democracy, and some political leaders have advanced a more independence-minded agenda. A failure by the United States to defend Taiwan would risk ceding America's position in Asia, perhaps causing Japan to doubt its alliance with the United States. If mainland China had full access to Taiwan, Beijing would have an anchor from which to project power throughout East Asia. China could expand its maritime position via an extended defense perimeter that would run from North to South Asia. China would also gain major influence over the South China Sea, through which about 50 percent of the world's shipping passes.[29]

Taiwan has a population of 22.9 million and total armed forces of 290,000 active-duty personnel and 1.657 million reserves. Its main forces are assigned to the army, with 200,000 troops in defensive positions utilizing 926 main battle tanks, 950 armored personnel carriers, and 1,815 artillery pieces—to name only some of its major capabilities. Taiwan's navy numbers 45,000 and includes 4 submarines, 4 destroyers, and 22 frigates. The navy also includes 61 missile craft for patrol and coastal defense and 12 mine-laying vehicles, as well as 290 amphibious landing craft. The air force numbers 55,000 and includes 32 combat aircraft with 180 annual flying hours for pilot training. Taiwan also has 17,000 paramilitary forces.[30] The quality of Taiwan's equipment is mixed: some of it is very good, and some is second or third generation. American-built F-16 fighters and French-made Mirage jets are very capable, and their Taiwanese pilots well trained. However, Taiwan's submarines are aging, and its coastal defense radar and interceptor forces are vulnerable. Budgetary pressures have also led to cuts in the Taiwanese navy and air force. In January 2010, the United States announced that it would be selling a new package of weapons systems to Taiwan worth a total of $6.4 billion, including communications systems, antimissile systems, minesweeping vessels, and sixty Blackhawk helicopters. China reacted negatively to these sales—with some officials threatening to dump U.S. treasury bonds as punishment. China suspended military cooperation with the United States and said it would place economic sanctions on U.S. companies doing business in China.

The military balance across the Taiwan Strait increasingly favors China. Though China's military capabilities for external power projection are limited, it has focused most of its military planning, modernization, and exercising on scenarios involving fighting a war with Taiwan. China has shown a willingness to use military threats to affect public opinion and electoral outcomes in Taiwan and has made clear it will use military force against Taiwan if it declares independence. Taiwan has become a focus of nationalism and pride in China. China's leaders also worry about the cohesion of all China as Tibet and Xinjiang Province also have separatist movements. If China failed to respond to assertions of independence by Taiwan, its leaders might lose the confidence of the military and risk internal strife. Thus, mainland China and Taiwan have serious domestic pressures that could prompt a war both would likely prefer to avoid.

As China has reduced army deployments at its border with the former Soviet Union, many of its capabilities have been reoriented toward Taiwan. China's armed forces of 2.25 million significantly outnumber Taiwan's. China's jet fighters outpace Taiwan's by ten to one (though it had, by 2010, begun eliminating older aircraft and emphasizing fewer, but more modern and capable, jets), and China has seventy submarines compared to Taiwan's four. Taiwan has three times fewer fourth-generation jet fighters than China—though Taiwan's pilots are far better trained. Despite improvements, by 2010, China still lacked significant sustained naval power and, in particular, adequate amphibious landing capacity that would allow it to launch a major invasion across the Taiwan Strait. As China reorients its military capacity for force projection, it has focused on a near-term effort to enhance missile technology to inflict immediate and painful damage in a conflict. China had, by 2010, deployed over twelve hundred short-range ballistic missiles in range of Taiwan and was already capable of deploying an additional seventy-five per year.[31] China could institute a naval blockade of Taiwan via submarines and fighter aircraft. China also has made significant advances in information warfare, electronic warfare, and special operations.[32]

China has important reasons to avoid military action against Taiwan. China places a high priority on economic growth, and thus engagement in the global economy might be viewed as more important than Taiwan. China might thus be more likely to use diplomatic isolation, increasing Taiwan's economic dependence on mainland China, and seek to affect domestic public opinion in Taiwan.[33] Meanwhile, China's major military weaknesses are in naval power and amphibious craft, which are both necessary for an invasion of Taiwan. China also lacks sufficient air cover to protect landing craft. China also does not have experience with joint operations coordinated among various services. Chinese logistics would, for example, be vulnerable to confusion and counterattack. Moreover, despite its large army, only about 50,000 troops would be available for any land operations in Taiwan (going up to 250,000 if China reallocated forces and drew on reserves). The United States does assume that China could win an engagement in Taiwan. However, doing so would require China to commit massive capabilities over an extended period, to bank on no third-party intervention, and to be prepared to accept significant damage to its economy and global diplomatic standing.[34] Finally, China also had, by 2010, engaged in a number of territorial sea disagreements with Japan, requiring that Tokyo not deplete its attention overly from areas in the North Pacific.

Unconventional War and Strategic Consequences

China may be developing strategies and capabilities consistent with other options besides a conventional invasion. In this scenario, China could rely on strategic surprise designed to cut off the leadership of Taiwan with a direct assault on the capital city of Taipei. Such a decapitation strategy would combine precision attacks by prepositioned special operations forces and airborne troops, as well as a barrage of missiles and fast achievement of air superiority—perhaps in as little as forty-five minutes. By attacking leadership and command-and-control capacities in Taiwan, as well as targeting selected civilian infrastructure, China would hope to cause massive confusion. By the time Taiwan's regular army troops could coordinate and respond, it might be too late. China could simultaneously create panic and chaos in the general population by launching missile attacks across the Taiwan Strait—possibly employing selective use of weapons of mass destruction. Using conventional missiles, including some carrying chemical and biological agents, would exacerbate the psychological impact and could also temporarily shut down airfields, preventing elements of the Taiwanese air force from launching. China might engage in small amphibious attacks as a ruse to distract the Taiwanese army from the real action, which would remain focused on leadership and command-and-control facilities.[35] Meanwhile, some form of pro-Beijing uprising could be cultivated as a political showing of public support for China's actions. An early objective would be to capture a major landing strip to deploy Chinese rapid-reaction troops, who would then conduct operations with air support launched from mainland China.[36] From there, China would appeal to a pro-Beijing leader, who would then shift policy away from independence and perhaps toward unification on China's terms.

In order to actually invade and occupy Taiwan, China would have to combine an effective capacity to land ground troops and use airpower to subjugate Taiwanese defenses before reinforcements could be organized. China's existing capability makes this a very difficult proposition. For example, its ballistic missiles are highly inaccurate. To attack Taiwan's runways and prevent its mustering an air defense would require a sizeable deployment of China's missiles. China's air force would not be able to fly during the night, and any massing of Chinese airpower would be noticed by American and Taiwanese intelligence, eliminating the element of surprise. Once an attack began, Taiwan would likely use nightfall to make short-term repairs to damaged airfields. China's planes lack precision and would have to fly at low altitude, making them vulnerable to antiaircraft fire. Attrition rates as high as 10 percent would not destroy China's ability to attack, but combined with servicing, refueling, and the limited duration of missions, they would constrain its airpower. Most likely, at least half of Taiwan's aircraft would survive even the best of surprise attacks, allowing the Taiwanese to hinder Chinese efforts to achieve air dominance. China's small amphibious fleet would only be able to move about ten thousand to fifteen thousand troops plus their equipment. China might be able to airlift more troops into Taiwan but not large pieces of equipment in a rapid manner. If Taiwan had warning time and could coordinate its active-duty ground forces, it would have a significant advantage over Chinese forces with about one hundred thousand troops facing some twenty thousand within the first forty-eight hours. This imbalance would likely be even greater, however, as China could lose as much as 20 percent of its forces just in approaching Taiwan and fighting its way onto land.[37]

Rather than invading, China could combine economic and military pressure to force a change in Taiwan's political leadership. A blockade or punishment with missile attacks could be used to coerce Taiwan into a pro-Beijing position. Each approach has drawbacks, as it is not clear that China could enforce a blockade, and missile attacks risk escalation and international isolation. If, however, China did launch a surprise invasion, there might be little that the United States could do. Washington could scramble airplanes from within the region and move its aircraft carrier battle group in the Pacific toward Taiwan. The United States could launch air attacks on China's mainland to damage logistical support for ongoing operations. Also, marines based in Japan and on amphibious assault ships in the Pacific might be able to conduct operations inside Taiwan relatively quickly. The problem for the United States is that, by the time it was able to influence events, the facts on the ground might have already been set. The United States would also have to ask whether it wanted to risk an escalation with China.

Taiwan has run computer war game simulations showing that, in a surprise-attack scenario, China might actually defeat Taiwan in as little as six days. This scenario alarmed Taiwanese officials because it was based on an amphibious landing invasion, which Taiwan has anticipated for some time. The drill showed that, in a surprise attack, Taiwan's troops would be able neither to stop a Chinese amphibious landing nor to halt Chinese troops from advancing inland. After one day of simulated Chinese attacks, Taiwan's airport bunkers, harbors, and key government buildings were destroyed by extensive bombings, including the launch of some hundreds of missiles from China.[38] Taiwan could hope to preserve the fighting capabilities of the air force and navy and about 80 percent of the army—allowing it to hold on for two weeks while reinforcements were organized.[39] Military success for Taiwan would require the United States to uphold its promise to defend the island by organizing a response within that two weeks. More likely, the United States would need about one month to organize enough forces to mount a serious counterattack in Taiwan. If, at that same moment, North Korea chose to attack South Korea, then the strategic calculation would be dramatically altered. The United States began to train for this scenario in summer 2004, conducting a major military exercise, "Summer Pulse 2004," which involved 7 aircraft carrier strike groups, 50 warships, 600 aircraft, and 150,000 troops surging simultaneously around the world.[40] This scenario, however, did not account for the sizeable deployments of American forces still committed to Iraq and Afghanistan.

Taiwan's Security Dilemma

Taiwan's dilemmas are complicated by a need to transform its military capabilities. Taiwan's military is organized heavily around its army, which is not integrated into a joint command structure, is not well trained, and is highly politicized. Budget constraints have made major modernization a difficult proposition. Even if missile defenses were put in place, Taiwanese personnel would be insufficiently trained to operate them for some time. Taiwan has a cumbersome national security and planning system, which makes it hard to coordinate flexible and efficient military planning. Initiative and low-level adaptive strategy are not significantly developed in army training.[41] American officials have suggested improvements, including better interservice coordination, a joint perspective on military operations, the capability to deter modern air and naval forces, development of missile-defense and modern antisubmarine-warfare capabilities, modernization of command-and-control systems, appointment or election of effective military and civilian leaders with vision, an effective national security structure, better military responsiveness to civilian control, and a rational procurement system.[42] Improvements that move too quickly might, however, actually accelerate an attack on Taiwan should China fear it stood to lose initiative. China might, alternatively, pursue a strategy of purposeful deception regarding its own strengths in order to lull Taiwan into a sense of security and thereby forestall any serious Taiwanese buildup in defense capability.[43]

Taiwan could also opt for unconventional military action. Taiwanese military experts refer to a "scorpion strategy" against China. If, for example, Taiwan received warning of a Chinese attack, it could launch preemptive strikes against some of China's missile-launch capability. China would have to defend its flank, allowing time for the Taiwanese army and American reinforcements to engage. Taiwan could also choose not to engage China's troops at all but to attack high-value targets deep inside China. In the face of a credible threat to the Chinese mainland, including its civilian population or major infrastructure, such as Shanghai's Pudong Tower or the Three Gorges Dam project, China might think twice about the relative benefits of conquest. China is not likely to take seriously Taiwan's existing capacity to project power at this level. For example, the Three Gorges Dam is fifteen hundred kilometers from Taiwan, while its aircraft have a combat range of only up to about twelve hundred kilometers, and its aging fleet has limited operational capacity. Such an attack—for instance, if carried out by higher-capability F-16 fighters, which Taiwan has sought, unsuccessfully, from the United States— would also likely be labeled by China as a terrorist attack and used to justify an overwhelming military response against Taiwan.[44]

If its vulnerabilities became untenable, Taiwan could develop nuclear weapons. This action would certainly provoke a hostile response from China and do serious damage to Taiwan's relationship with the United States. Some analysts and press in Taiwan nevertheless argue that developing a Taiwanese nuclear arsenal is the only way to ensure China knows it would suffer great damage from an attack.[45] Taiwan engaged in a nuclear weapons research program in the 1970s but abandoned it under strong American and international pressure. Taiwan does periodically make statements to the effect that it has the capacity to produce nuclear weapons quickly if need be. Taiwan could probably build nuclear weapons, but how fast is uncertain. Taiwan would likely need to import separated plutonium or highly enriched uranium.[46] Taiwan is also not likely to develop sufficient numbers of missiles or long-range aircraft that would allow it to truly inflict pain on China.[47]

Interdependence and the Case against War

An important trend between China and Taiwan could dampen the risks of war. Taiwan has increasingly engaged in economic investment in China. Increasing economic interdependence could eventually make war too costly for both. Despite occasionally intense rhetorical hostility, neither side appears willing to risk war. Nevertheless, the threat of war between the two is real. For Taiwan, the issue is a matter of identity and independence. For China, it is a matter of strategic interest and pride. Most Taiwanese recognize the danger of their situation, and public opinion surveys show that nearly 50 percent of Taiwanese oppose fighting to defend the island if a vote favoring independence were to trigger a conflict with China.[48] Even Taiwan's official position on military power is vague, as a Taiwanese white paper on defense demonstrated in 2002: "Menaces to our national security include domestic, destabilizing factors. . . . Some of our people, for example, are confusing foes with friends, or are divided on the issue of national identity, undermining the unity of the people against external threats."[49] Still, in 2008, Taiwan elected a new leadership that campaigned on a nationalist agenda but argued that it could achieve more gains through economic cooperation with China than with confrontation.

The Persian Gulf and the Middle East

Much of the world's economy depends on the steady flow of Persian Gulf oil, which makes the Middle East an area of vital strategic importance. Tensions in the Middle East have led to serious international crises, particularly over

Israel, which found itself in major regional conflicts in 1948, 1956, 1967, and 1973 and engaging in multiple interventions in Lebanon. The right of Israel to exist as a state has been widely recognized in the region, though its occupation of territory seized in war and the broader plight of the Palestinian peoples, combined with major terrorist attacks against Israel, remain an open wound throughout the Middle East. No single state within the region has the capacity to gain regional dominance—although the United States exercises a heavy external influence. The United States maintains close relationships with a range of countries, including Saudi Arabia and the other Persian Gulf kingdoms, as well as the nearby countries of Egypt, Israel, Jordan, and Turkey. Meanwhile, the United States has organized international coalitions to isolate Iran for its efforts to establish nuclear weapons capacity. Most dramatically, the U.S. invasion and occupation of Iraq in 2003 signaled a dramatic new level of engagement in the region.

American Primacy and the Iraq Conundrum

The United States is promoting democracy in the Middle East. However, the combination of America's support for Israel, its strong backing of some authoritarian political leaders—for instance, over decades in Saudi Arabia, Bahrain, Yemen, and Egypt—and its 2003 invasion of Iraq stirred anti-Americanism. The United States promotes democracy and economic progress in the region, but often with little effect. The United States staked its credibility on the building of democracy in Iraq—with the hope that this effort would prompt further reform in the Middle East. Iraq has made halting steps toward democracy, but whether stability will result we will not really know for decades. In 2011, grassroots revolutionary movements spread like wildfire through the region, creating a major new opportunity for a massive transformation. In many respects, the failure of governments to meet the basic needs of their people combined with growing youth bulges and new communications to topple regimes like that in Egypt. Yet, the United States was caught between its historical allies, stability, and the realities of democratic forces transitioning in the region. There is no fundamental reason why the Arab and Muslim countries of the Middle East should not emerge as democracies that dramatically improve the quality of life of the people across the region. However, whether democracy will produce either stability or outcomes commensurate with U.S. and Western interests remains uncertain. Indeed, elections in the Palestinian areas resulted in the anti-Israeli group Hamas's victory in 2006. Ironically, the very notion of democracy as an import from the West may actually undermine its potential in the Middle East.[50] In 2009, the United States began a new effort of outreach, with a major address to the

Muslim world by President Barack Obama in Cairo, Egypt, seeking a "new beginning," which set the tone for many of the movements to come in 2011. President Obama acknowledged where the United States had made mistakes, but he also challenged those in the region to note when America did positive things to help people, including Muslims. Still, the region remains highly in flux and highly dependent on the presence of American power for stability, as the 2011 intervention in Libya showed. Still, for the first time in recent history, the potential to shape the destiny of the region was increasingly in the hands of its people, not outsiders.

The United States is the dominant military power in the Persian Gulf and the broader Middle East. The U.S. Fifth Fleet is headquartered in Bahrain (which, while supported by Washington, led a brutal crackdown on democracy protestors and was then shored up by the Saudi army in early 2011), with forces stationed in the Indian Ocean, Persian Gulf, and Red Sea. This grouping includes an aircraft carrier battle group with six surface combatants, three amphibious assault ships, and mine-countermine vessels. The U.S. Sixth Fleet in the Mediterranean Sea complements those forces deployed closer to the Persian Gulf. The Sixth Fleet includes one aircraft carrier battle group, two nuclear-fueled submarines, two landing aircraft, and a variety of support and transport craft. Also nearby, the United States keeps long-range bombers at Diego Garcia in the Indian Ocean. In Bahrain, the United States maintains 1,447 combined navy, marine, and army forces. Some two hundred army troops are deployed in Djibouti, and the United States maintains command and logistics headquarters which are staffed along with prepositioned equipment in Kuwait. The United States deploys 432 troops in Qatar and eighty-four air force personnel in the United Arab Emirates. Meanwhile, the United States also has long-range force-projection capacities deployed in Europe and the continental United States devoted to contingencies that include Middle East operations—such as the March 2011 Libya intervention.[51]

One major source of tension in the Persian Gulf during the 1990s was the deployment in Saudi Arabia of American troops based there to contain Iraq. This was a source of frustration for Islamic radicals, who saw the holiest areas of Islam being protected by non-Muslims. Removal of the regime of Saddam Hussein in Iraq eliminated the need to base American troops long term in Saudi Arabia. The American presence there was thus reduced significantly from twenty thousand troops and equipment prepositioned during the 1990s to only three hundred by 2006. However, this shift did not resolve the question of America's regional presence, given the subsequent occupation of Iraq, which fed into a larger narrative about American intentions promulgated by Islamic nationalists. By 2005, ongoing U.S. deployment in Iraq included 146,000 troops, and seemingly no end to the war was in sight

The Middle East

as it had evolved into a full-blown insurgency, with al Qaeda attacks coupled with a nascent civil war and increasing Iranian influence in the south.[52] In late 2006, the United States developed a new approach to Iraq that focused on counterinsurgency, and negotiations with local tribal leaders offered financial incentives to turn against al Qaeda. U.S. troops focused on protecting the civilian population. The idea was that once stability was attained, developments like oil sharing, financial reform, power sharing, elections, and regional diplomacy would lead to long-term improvements. Asserting that the stability portion of that concept had been achieved in August 2010, President Obama announced that all combat forces had left Iraq—though nearly fifty thousand troops would remain for training and counterterrorism operations. The goal was to work toward a full withdrawal of U.S. troops in Iraq by summer 2011. The central question nearly ten years after the U.S. invasion was still whether Iraq could maintain stability on its own.

Once the United States was in Iraq, a premature disengagement of U.S. troops might have been the most destabilizing threat to the Persian Gulf. Without the presence of American forces, Iraq could have erupted into civil war, perhaps leading to intervention by neighboring countries. Conversely, the American presence in Iraq energized Islamic radicals in and outside the country, who came to see defeat of America in Iraq as a major ideological imperative. Prior to the American invasion, Iraq had about 389,000 active-duty forces and 650,000 reserves. While much of the military's leadership had patronage ties to the Hussein regime, most of the regular forces were either conscripts or professional soldiers. Nevertheless, the U.S. occupation authority disbanded the Iraqi military in summer 2003, leaving several hundred thousand well-armed people unemployed—many of whom would join a counter-U.S. insurgency. Added to the unemployed military were some fifty thousand members of Saddam Hussein's Baath Party fired from their civil service, education, public health, and media jobs. An estimated 90 percent of these people had joined the Baath Party purely for fear of the consequences of not supporting Saddam Hussein. However, they were rendered unemployed when they could have helped in rebuilding Iraq.[53] Meanwhile, by fall 2004, only $1 billion of $13.6 billion in promised international aid had reached Iraq, and only $1.2 billion of $18.4 billion authorized by the U.S. Congress for reconstruction in 2004 had been spent.[54]

The internal situation in Iraq is complicated by the demographic makeup of the country, which includes a majority (about 60 percent) Shiite Muslim population in the south. Sunni Muslims (about 20 percent) dominate Baghdad and surrounding areas in central Iraq. In the northern part of the country, the Kurdish population (the remaining 20 percent) has long sought independence. In this mix, the United States promised to build a functional representative democracy, though it would be hard for any true democratic process to produce anything other than a Shiite majority. Shiite Muslim influence is ascending in Lebanon, Pakistan, and Saudi Arabia. Indeed, the Saudi government tended to see the elected Iraqi Shiites mainly as agents for Iran, which was already dominated by radical Shiite Muslim clerics.[55] The Sunnis, which dominated the Saddam Hussein government, could be left politically isolated, and the Kurds, unsatisfied with their role in a new Iraqi government, might still press for independence. Kurdish independence was especially problematic because the Kurds also have large separatist-oriented populations in southeastern Turkey. Kurds in Turkey might thus be prompted to unite with Kurds in Iraq. Such moves could prompt Turkey to intervene in northern Iraq to prevent the Kurds from gaining independence.[56] By late 2010, the United States had lost nearly 4,450 personnel killed and nearly 32,000 seriously wounded since the invasion.[57] Over $800 billion had been spent, with final costs estimated to go as high as $3 trillion. Meanwhile, between 2003 and 2010, a range of estimates showed that around 100,000 Iraqis had been killed, and between 2006 and 2010, 1.5 million Iraqis were internally displaced from their homes.

Iran, Israel, and the Geopolitical Balance

The country with the greatest potential to alter the strategic environment around the Persian Gulf is Iran. In 1979, the U.S.-backed government of the shah of Iran was overthrown in favor of a radical Shiite Muslim political movement. Both the United States and many of its allies in the Middle East saw this kind of radical internal change as the biggest threat to regional security. In the 1980s, the United States thus aligned with the secular government of Saddam Hussein in Iraq, which fought against Iran and its brand of Islamic fundamentalism. Iran is a significant regional power with 523,000 active-duty troops and 350,000 reserves. Its army numbers 350,000 (including 1,613 main battle tanks); its navy, 18,000; its air force, 30,000 (though with only about 312 operational aircraft of second and third generation); it has 40,000 to 60,000 paramilitary forces. These assets include 3 Russian Kilo Class submarines; 146 patrol and coastal boats, many with antiship cruise missiles; about 3,000 shore-based antiship missiles with ranges of twenty thousand meters; 14 surface-to-air missile sites; and 35 ballistic missile sites with over 400 Scud B/C and SS-8 missiles.[58] Iran's military is mainly defensive—but if it chooses, the country is in a position to disrupt shipping lanes in the Persian Gulf at the Strait of Hormuz as well as around the Gulf islands of Abu Musa and the Tunbs. By early 2011, the country of Bahrain in the Gulf increasingly appeared to be a staging ground for a proxy power competition between Saudi Arabia's Sunni-backed monarchy and Iran's agitating Shiite population.

Iran has experienced over thirty years of autonomous rule by conservative Muslim clerics, with very little to show for it but international isolation for a well-educated population that would contribute much to the global economy if it could. During the 1980s and 1990s, Iran's support for anti-Israeli terrorists alienated it from the international community. During the 1990s, Iran also saw declining oil revenues combined with growing population demands on the state to deliver basic services.[59] Inflation ran at around 15 percent, and unemployment reached as high as 25 percent. Gradually, Iran began conditioning its support for international terrorists and condemned the

2001 attacks by al Qaeda on the United States. It was also a quiet facilitator of initial U.S. engagement in Afghanistan in 2001. Meanwhile, a new generation of younger people exerted pressure for a less restrictive government and more engagement with international society—as evidenced by massive pro-democracy demonstrations in summer 2009. According to public opinion surveys, some 70 percent of Iranians view opening normal relations with the West favorably. The Iranian newspaper *Yas-e Now* asked in June 2003, "What are the actual demands of the Iranian people?" To that, 13 percent chose the answer "continuation of the present political policy"; 16 percent chose "political reforms and increases in the powers of the reformists"; 26 percent chose "fundamental changes in management and in the performance of the system for an efficient growth"; and 45 percent chose "change in the political system, even with foreign intervention."[60] Unlike the majority of the Arab states in the Middle East, Iran has a legislative democracy, though it is constrained by the heavy influence of religious leaders in the judicial branch of government, whose actions against pro-democracy activists and protestors in 2009 raised serious doubts about the regime's legitimacy.[61]

Iran's role in the geopolitical framework of the Middle East has also been shaped by what appeared, by 2004, to be a sustained effort to build nuclear weapons, or at least to ensure its capacity to do so. Iran has a number of incentives for attaining nuclear weapons. First, as Iranian conventional military capabilities are generally weak and outdated, Iran might seek nuclear weapons as a deterrent against an American preemptive war. Second, Iran's other major enemy in the region is Israel, which is estimated to have about two hundred nuclear weapons. Iran might want nuclear weapons to deter possible Israeli military action and achieve strategic parity with Israel. Third, Iran has nuclear Russia to the north, as well as nuclear Pakistan and India to the east, and China is not far away. Should there be a conflict over access to oil flows from the Persian Gulf or Caspian Sea regions, nuclear weapons would be an important asset significantly elevating Iran's role. Fourth, Iran might want to develop nuclear capabilities to further proliferate the assets for money or to hand weapons over to terrorists. Iran's nuclear program could also be linked to a general quest for prestige in the international community. Some analysts believe that Iran seeks nuclear weapons for the existential goal of pursuing a religiously driven destruction of Israel.

Ambiguity about Iran's nuclear program serves as a force multiplier, given uncertainty about what Iran might, or might not, possess in terms of conventional and unconventional war-fighting capability.[62] Iran's main missile-delivery capacity focuses on earlier-generation Soviet-era Scud missiles. Iran has, however, also been seeking to acquire Russian nuclear-capable, intermediate-range, strategic air-launched cruise missiles (Kh-55 Granat).[63] Iran has not hidden its effort to mine uranium deposits in Saghand and has been constructing a uranium-enrichment facility at Natanz. By 2003, it had as many as ten centrifuge machines assembled, parts for another one thousand, and plans for up to five thousand. Iran still remained substantially removed from having a weaponized nuclear program combined with an effective ballistic missile–delivery system. In Arak, Iran was constructing a heavy water plant that could make up for the lack of this capacity at other facilities (especially in Bushehr).[64] The IAEA indicated that Iran was not fully cooperative or transparent in its weapons programs. In 2008, the United States declared that, in national intelligence estimates, Iran had suspended its nuclear program designs in 2003—though perhaps with the intent of moving to a new stage focused on developing fissile material. In April 2009, Iranian president Mahmood Ahmadinejad announced that Iran had completed the capacity to run its own nuclear fuel cycle and tested advanced centrifuge mechanisms—while still asserting this was all for civilian and peaceful purposes. In March 2009 alone, Iran appeared to have increased its centrifuge capacity by 25 percent to 7,231 centrifuge machines. Still, the IAEA also said in September 2009 that Iran was not near having nuclear weapons capacity and that concern over its development was exaggerated. Yet, in February 2010, the IAEA changed its assessment, asserting that Iran's nuclear efforts could be geared toward weapons programs.

Of particular concern to the broader international community are Iranian efforts to upgrade and expand missile capacity. Iran has an earlier generation of ballistic missile technology purchased largely from North Korea during the 1980s. This program includes components from North Korea's No Dong program, which could provide the foundations for an eventual ICBM system. Iran has also developed an internal ballistic missile program that includes the Shahab-3 missile, which it claims has a range of up to thirteen hundred kilometers. Unconfirmed reports imply that Iran is also researching a Shahab-5 with a twenty-five-hundred-kilometer range.[65] Iran has also launched suborbital rockets, suggesting it has a nascent ICBM capacity though its attempts at space launches have been technically problematic. Iran could by 2011 employ missile systems, but mainly for deterrence, not long-range offensive capability. However, given the radical nature of its regime and historical links to international terrorist movements, it could transfer missile technology and weapons for asymmetric use against adversaries in the Middle East or even Europe. Iran could also pursue more assertive conventional power in the Persian Gulf region with less fear of retaliation. Meanwhile, an Iranian nuclear missile program could prompt Israel to preemptively attack Iran—or set off a chain reaction of nuclear weapons programs spreading to Egypt, Saudi Arabia, Syria, and Turkey.

Iranian acquisition of nuclear weapons would raise particular concern in Israel. In 1981, when Israel learned about Iraq's nuclear program, it launched a preemptive military attack against the Osirak Nuclear Facility in Iraq. Israel similarly could be tempted to eliminate or slow Iran's nuclear advances. Israel does have the capacity to carry out such an action. Israel's total armed forces number 176,500 active-duty troops and 565,000 reserves. Israel's army has 133,000 personnel, and its relatively small navy numbers 9,500, with three submarines and three hundred naval commandos. It has a likely nuclear capability of two hundred warheads deliverable on Jericho 1 and 2 missiles, which can range between five hundred and two thousand kilometers. The Israeli air force is one of the best equipped and trained in the world. It includes thirty-four thousand troops, and its pilots have an average of 180 training flying hours per year. Israel's air force has 461 combat aircraft and eighty-one armed helicopters.[66] Israel is capable of long-range bombing runs if planes are refueled either in the air or on friendly territory. Israel's planes have high accuracy and thus could likely strike deep inside Iran with confidence of success. Overall, however, given the collapse of the Saddam Hussein regime, Israel also faces a lower conventional military threat in the region given a benign Iraq.[67] Israel has thus focused more immediately on the potential for Iranian proxy wars by engaging against Hezbollah in Lebanon in summer 2006 and Hamas in Gaza in the 2008–2009 winter.

If the United States grew concerned that Israel might act unilaterally against Iran, Washington might step in—perhaps preferring to act rather than face the dangerous consequences of an Israeli war with its neighbors. While a U.S.-led coalition assault or UN-mandated attack on Iran might be somewhat less destabilizing than an Israeli one, the risks involved remain extremely large. Iran would likely generate a robust defense of its territory and airspace and possibly counterattack in locations where attacks were launched against it. Depending on the scale of the attack, Iran would likely place its forces on alert, disperse high-value assets, and implement internal security plans to prevent an internal uprising. It might also retaliate by shutting down the Strait of Hormuz. Iran might seek support from other states in the region to attack U.S. assets and threaten oil shipments in the Persian Gulf or impose a general oil embargo against the United States. Iran would likely use the release of any radioactivity into civilian areas due to attacks on nuclear facilities to appeal further to world opinion. In the medium term, Iran would likely pursue a diplomatic strategy identifying itself as the victim of external aggression, courting sympathetic world opinion. Pakistan's leadership in particular would likely face significant internal pressure, given its border with Iran and its own nuclear programs. Tehran might also engage in a campaign of asymmetric warfare on high-value Israeli or American targets, for instance, by working to promote the destabilization of Iraq and Afghanistan. Large-scale domestic unrest might pressure those states in the region that aligned with the United States to distance themselves, perhaps leading to an unraveling of the Arab-Israeli peace process and even the collapse of U.S.-friendly governments in the region.[68] Consequently, while allies in the region, including Saudi Arabia, have urged the United States to consider preemptive attacks on Iran, in reality, a military solution did not, by 2011, meet basic cost-benefit analysis—especially given that success could not be assured.

The best option for attacking Iranian facilities would be covert action carried out by Iranians, perhaps with support from American special operations forces predeployed inside the country—although some Western governments have viewed using a computer virus to set the nuclear program back as an attractive option. Both options require highly precise intelligence, which is not available. A direct attack might succeed but might have to be dramatic in scale and include a significant air campaign to suppress Iranian air defenses; provide combat search-and-rescue services; eliminate Iran's ability to retaliate immediately with air, missile, or naval units; and include follow-on strikes to ensure targets were destroyed.[69] Such an attack could prompt an uprising to overturn the Iranian government, in which case several hundred thousand external troops might be necessary to halt internal fighting and provide long-term stability. The most problematic outcome of a military option is that the opportunity for a peaceful transition away from nuclear weapons in Iran might be lost. Many Iranian reformers have worked for integration into the world community. Yet, Islamic clerics who currently dominate Iran often use the threat of outside attack as a justification for holding back reform movements and suppressing dissent. Domestic changes in the country could be the best means for prompting an internal rethinking of nuclear efforts in the broader context of a new foreign policy that prioritizes integration with the world economy.[70] In this regard, the United States and its allies faced a serious dilemma in summer 2009, given the pro-democratic uprisings, as the best possibility for a deal on nuclear weapons would mean sustained negotiations with the existing government. Overt support for the democracy movements would likely have pressed the government into a more dangerous nationalistic posture and emboldened its pursuit of the nuclear program. Yet, the most favorable long-term outcome would likely be an internally driven democratic change of government, followed by voluntary abandonment of the nuclear program as the nation reintegrated peacefully into the community of nations.

The Saudi Question

The future of Saudi Arabia raises significant questions about the overall stability of the Persian Gulf and has regional and global implications. With 25 percent of the world's oil reserves, Saudi Arabia plays a key role in setting global energy prices. It is also home to the holiest of Islamic sites. Due to challenges posed by instability to the north in Iraq, growing Iranian influence, and internal threats to the dynasty of the royal Saud family, the future of Saudi Arabia is a significant global concern.[71] The more the Saudi royal family perceives external threats, the more its members find themselves reliant on the United States for defensive needs—including a plan announced by the United States in 2010 to sell their government $60 billion worth of weapons systems. However, the more the Saudis align with the United States, the more internal threats to the regime arise in the form of radical Islam. Ironically, the greatest threat to the current Saudi government might actually be a successful transition toward a secular democracy in Iraq and popular democracy movements in Iran and Egypt. If an Arab country eventually emerges as a model for stable representative government, internal pressure for democratic reform could destabilize Saudi Arabia—with a very uncertain outcome. Also, if Iraqi or Iranian oil were to reemerge in global markets and drive down international prices, then Saudi Arabia's primacy in international oil would be challenged. If Iraq or Iran were to fail as a state, Saudi Arabia could be drawn into conflict. Given its size and open desert geography, Saudi Arabia might also find that the fastest and cheapest form of deterrent would be to obtain nuclear weapons.

One of the greatest risks to stability in the Middle East would be a gradual failure of Saudi Arabia as a state. Internal strife or a coup by radical Islamists could produce a dramatic shift in Saudi Arabia's strategic priorities and significantly alter the regional, and even global, balance of power. The most dramatic, though least probable, scenario would involve an abrupt revolution. Despite of the death of Saudi leader King Fahd in July 2005, there remains a strong status quo preference among the embedded leadership and ruling elites and strong international support for internal stability in the country.[72] In order to pacify its population, the Saudi government handed out $30 billion to its people in early 2011. Still, there were some protests, and generational shifts could present near- and long-term questions about the legitimacy of the Saudi monarchy in governing the country. Furthermore, a lack of transparency concerning the remaining reserves of oil could raise doubts about the country's reliability. Saudi Arabian stability could atrophy in the event of an extended and uncertain leadership transition as the older generation of the Saud family passes on, accompanied by internal and external crises—which was demonstrated when Saudi troops entered Bahrain in March 2011 to shore up its allied government there.[73]

An Uncertain Future

When the United States invaded Iraq in 2003, it took a dramatic and costly gamble that it would be able to transform the region. It hoped to eliminate a threat in Saddam Hussein, but American goals almost certainly entailed more than this. Washington hoped to ensure that oil flows would remain open at stable prices. However, oil alone could not explain the policy—especially as Washington could have cut a deal with Saddam Hussein and ultimately lifted sanctions. Perhaps if a major threat were removed to its east, Israel might feel more comfortable in negotiating with Palestinians for a lasting peace. Until this crucial issue is resolved, with the creation of a Palestinian state, it will be hard to erase many of the tensions that affect the broader region. Nonetheless, by 2011, this goal remained elusive as Israel continued to pursue settlements in Gaza and to enforce an embargo that denied provision of supplies to meet basic human needs as well as humanitarian assistance in the area. Washington also apparently hoped to see democracy spread through the region so as to produce governments more responsive to their peoples and, hopefully, amenable to American interests. Only with the passage of time—likely measured in decades—will we know if this transformation has succeeded or not, though it is fair to say that it is one happening before the eyes of the world on a par with the fall of the Berlin wall and that it will have enormous ramifications.

Eurasia

The geographical term *Eurasia* describes the region that reaches from Turkey into western China. Its geopolitics reflect a nascent and shifting alliance patterns among states that have competing interests but tend to reinforce a fragile status quo.[74] This region also contains the second-largest energy reserves in the world and could become a new arena of strategic competition among the great powers. Central Asia is rife with instability driven by weaknesses in state capacity to meet domestic challenges, including transnational terrorism, ethnic strife, environmental degradation, and organized crime. The region remains heavily swayed by residual Russian influence left over from the Soviet system that dominated much of the area during the twentieth century. However, smaller former Soviet republics are exerting their independence through efforts to coordinate policy that would hedge against or balance Russian influence. Meanwhile, expanding American influence has prompted nascent great power coordination between Russia and China. All the major countries engaged in the region perceive a shared threat from radical political Islam and international terrorism, which facilitates a shared interest in stability. Thus, while the potential for great power competition exists, it is not assured.[75] Nascent structural alignments that have emerged in early twenty-first-century Central Asia—regional hegemony and balancing and great power maneuvering—illustrate the dominance of existing geopolitical trends.

Russian Hegemony and Balancing

Russia has, since the collapse of the Soviet Union, sought to build a regional mechanism for exerting its influence via the Commonwealth of Independent States (CIS), a residual structural legacy of the Soviet Union. Established through the 1991 Minsk Treaty, the CIS emerged as a loose confederation of twelve countries seeking to harmonize various economic and security policies. In 1993, Russia completed a military doctrine according to which the frontiers of the former Soviet Union defined the boundaries of Russian influence. In 1995, a presidential statement identified Moscow's goals in the CIS as making the region an exclusive area of Russian influence, minimizing the expansion of external presence and influence on CIS territory, facilitating regional crisis management, and protecting Russians living outside Russia within the CIS.[76] For non-Russian members, support for the CIS has varied from Belarus's enthusiastic embrace to the reluctant compliance of Ukraine— where Russia has been overt and covert in exerting its influence in elections. In the absence of significant Western assistance, weak states like Ukraine have often been left with little choice but to maintain their deep economic dependence on Russia, which Moscow has used to leverage power within the CIS. In 2010, Ukraine abandoned its bid to join the North Atlantic Treaty Organization (NATO), preferring to pursue neutrality instead.

Russia's exercise of power in the region is primarily economic and accomplished through the residual personnel and economic networks of the Soviet era. Power is often exerted through policy regarding fuel and energy, which Moscow can turn on and shut off, depending on how cooperative CIS members are. To pressure Georgia into allowing a continued Russian presence in military bases on its territory, Moscow periodically shut off the flow of natural gas. When Georgia refused to allow Russia to enter the Pankisi Gorge area on the border with Russia's breakaway republic of Chechnya, Moscow retaliated by introducing visa restrictions on Georgian citizens in Russia and halting gas

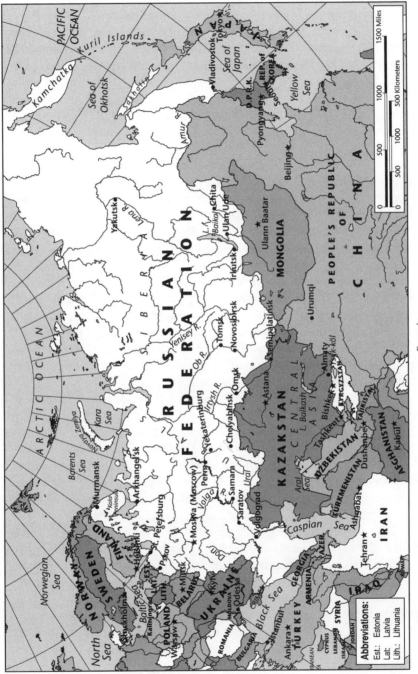

Eurasia

flows until past debts were repaid. In 2008, Russia opted for full-on military operations in South Ossetia inside Georgia. Russia has also used the flow of energy supplies as a means of pressuring Ukraine and Moldova to make payments on debts to Moscow and used threats of gas-supply disruption to the Czech Republic to influence public attitudes there toward American plans for missile-defense systems.[77]

Russia has sought to develop within the CIS a customs union, economic integration, converging standards of international economic legislation, a payments union, integration of production in science and technology (and the defense industry), common legal conditions, and a common capital market.[78] Russia has sought to destabilize uncooperative CIS states via a range of intelligence activities, blackmail, coercion, subversion of problematic political leadership, and support for violent groups amenable to Russian influence.[79] Russia's overall military power in the region is, however, in significant decline. By 2011, Russia maintained 5,500 troops in Tajikistan, 3,214 in Armenia, 3,400 in Georgia, 1,500 in Moldova, and 13,000 in Ukraine.[80] However, Russia has declining capacity to project military power within the CIS. Russia hopes to develop a fifty-thousand-member rapid-deployment corps at the Russia-Kazakhstan border, but whether it can fund and sustain readiness is doubtful. Airlift capabilities are severely limited, and what remains of Russia's air capacity consists mostly of medium-range bombers and operational-tactical missiles.[81] In a worst case, Russia might, given its conventional military weakness, have to rely on tactical nuclear weapons to deter attacks on forward-deployed troops, though this scenario is highly unlikely.

While Russia's overall military influence in Eurasia is declining, most states in the region continue to lean toward Russia to meet their security concerns. The trade-off for Russian influence is the provision of general stability. This is especially the case for countries like Kazakhstan and Tajikistan, whose postcommunist leaders draw from their Soviet backgrounds to gain economic benefits they can then distribute within their own political patronage systems. Even non-CIS states have moved closer to Russia to enhance their own relative interests. For example, in June 2001, Turkey began construction of the Blue Stream Natural Gas Pipeline with Russia. This pipeline would increase its dependence on Russian natural gas from 66 to 80 percent (Turkey imports 98 percent of its energy needs). By late 2010, total flows exceeded 51 billion cubic meters of gas. This deal was completed over strong objections from Turkey's main ally, the United States.[82] EU countries like Germany and Poland are also dependent on Russian energy flows and have generally preferred a positive relationship with Moscow, regardless of Russia's actions in its own neighborhood, like the 2008 invasion of Georgia and political and economic pressure on Ukraine.

To improve reception of Russia's presence within the CIS, Moscow presents its efforts as a cooperative approach to regional security. In 1992, Russia negotiated the Collective Security Treaty with most CIS members. While little substantive follow-on effort emerged, in 1999 the CIS developed the Joint Air Defense System based in Moscow and headed by the Russian Air Defense Forces Command. This move largely institutionalized what already existed in the previous Soviet air defense system that covered Russia, Belarus, Azerbaijan, Armenia, Kazakhstan, Kyrgyzstan, Tajikistan, and Uzbekistan. CIS security functions received additional bolstering when an agreement was reached to create a joint rapid-reaction force consisting of troops from Russia, Kazakhstan, Kyrgyzstan, and Tajikistan to respond to regional crises and to fortify porous border areas against terrorist incursions. Russia has pushed for the CIS to expand its military role, to facilitate rapid military deployments in crises, as well as the transfer of military equipment and technology, and to limit the influence of alternative arms marketers, particularly the United States. For Russia, the CIS has also served as a means of signaling its security interests to the United States and its worries about expanded U.S. influence in Eastern Europe and areas of the former Soviet Union.[83] Ultimately, the CIS has allowed Moscow to extend a defense perimeter away from its borders via air defense, border guards, and the development of small-scale rapid-deployment forces.

The most significant attempt at regional balancing was the grouping of Georgia, Ukraine, Uzbekistan (which suspended its membership in 2002), Azerbaijan, and Moldova (GUUAM); however, this never amounted to more than a political declaration of common goals. The GUUAM members described their alignment as a "strategic alliance designed to strengthen the independence and sovereignty of these former Soviet republics."[84] GUUAM was significant as the only regional security cooperation in the former Soviet space that did not include Russia. Western officials generally viewed GUUAM as an anti-Russia alliance. Moscow shared this perspective as it watched cooperation in GUUAM accelerate during the 1999 NATO war in Kosovo in side meetings held at NATO's fiftieth-anniversary summit in Washington, DC. The GUUAM alliance began informal consultations and produced joint declarations beginning at the Conventional Armed Forces in Europe Review Conference held in 1996. GUUAM's status as a cooperative structure was formalized at the 1997 Council of Europe summit meeting in Strasbourg.[85] The central organizing elements of GUUAM included promotion of political interaction, the avoidance of separatism, peaceful resolution of conflicts, peacekeeping activities, and the development of a Eurasian-Transcaucasian transport corridor. Strategically, GUUAM members signaled their intent to hedge against Russian power through their integration into Euro-Atlantic and European structures of security and cooperation, including "the development of a special relationship and dialogue with NATO."[86] The fluctuating level of member interest in GUUAM, however, prevented it from becoming much more than a loose affiliation of states. Both Moldova and Uzbekistan engaged inconsistently, with Uzbekistan suspending its membership in 2002. Conversely, Georgia pushed its ambitions so far as to provoke the Russian invasion of its territory and a shooting war in summer 2008, while in 2010 Ukraine declared neutrality and abandoned its quest to join NATO.

Great Power Alignments

In June 2001, the leaders of China, Russia, Kazakhstan, Kyrgyzstan, and Tajikistan transformed an informal grouping established in 1996 and known as the "Shanghai Five" into a formal international institution, the Shanghai Cooperation Organization (SCO), which was expanded to include Uzbekistan. Its official objectives are to promote trust, stability, and mutual understanding between members, including confidence building in the military sphere and mutual reductions of armed forces in border areas.[87] The SCO is a potential balancing mechanism that China and Russia could use to frustrate America's role in Eurasia and to coordinate common interests in grand strategy. The founding document promotes multipolarity as a core objective. Both China and Russia use the advancement of multipolar international relations to constrain American power. This objective is reinforced by the specific requirement that each state accept the primacy of the United Nations, with respect for sovereignty and noninterference in the domestic affairs of states. While specifying that it is not directed against any other states, the SCO embodies important elements of geopolitical alignment. For example, to bolster Russian and Chinese efforts to frustrate U.S. plans for national missile defense, SCO members agreed to preserve the global strategic balance and stated that they all saw the 1972 Anti-Ballistic Missile Treaty as crucial to that objective.[88] The orientation of the SCO toward this global balancing goal, even with a combined Russian-Chinese position, had little impact as the United States began deployment of a missile shield in 2004. The SCO's balancing potential can thus be overstated.

Russia's interest in the group may also be guided as much by a desire to constrain the growth of China's influence in the region as to hedge against American power. Russian-Chinese accommodation should be viewed in light of the two countries' history of deep tensions and rivalry for influence in Northeast Asia. Also complicating the SCO's balancing functions is members' shared interest with the United States in combating the spread of radical political Islam and international terrorism. The SCO agreed to create an antiterrorist center in Bishkek, Kyrgyzstan, and to organize a two-thousand-soldier unit of Russian, Kazakh, Kyrgyz, and Tajik troops. Thus, the SCO is as likely to move closer to common American interests as it is to balance American power. This trend line is true for Russia, which has suffered a steady campaign of separatist-oriented terrorism, and China, which has a significant ethnic separatist movement in its northwestern Xinjiang Province. China asserts that the al Qaeda terrorist organization supplied Islamic groups in Xinjiang with money, arms, and leadership and that as many as one thousand Chinese Muslims may have trained in terrorist camps in Afghanistan.[89] Uzbekistan has also had to manage an al Qaeda–affiliated terrorist threat in the Islamic Movement of Uzbekistan. Given the proximity of the SCO states to Afghanistan and other terrorist bases, the SCO could even complement American interests as the organization pursues its own campaign against terrorism. Conversely, Russia and China could use the SCO to ensure that the United States does not gain a permanent foothold in Eurasia justified by its counterterrorism efforts. Russia agreed in 2010 to facilitate transit routes for American equipment into Afghanistan, which, at the same time, implicated that it could as easily frustrate this flow of American military power. The SCO members have also created mechanisms to accept additional members, and Iran has shown interest.

Beyond the Status Quo?

Generally, Central Asia favors stability over major confrontation. Even the dramatic Russian invasion of Georgia in 2008 indicated the limits of Western power more than anything else, given that the United States and its NATO allies could or would do very little to assist beyond providing humanitarian aid and political and economic support. And while Russia showed it could organize and conduct major joint military operations in its immediate vicinity, its capacity was still limited. Thus, no single power has the capacity to dominate the region. Current alignments work in concert to hedge against any one country's dramatically overturning the status quo. While American interests have expanded in Afghanistan, the United States has also indicated that it will begin to draw down its presence in 2011 and end combat operations by 2014. Shared interests in constraining radical political Islam and combating international terrorism might favor cooperation rather than competition among the great powers, especially as the United States disengages. Major shifts in energy demand or the stoppage of oil flows from the Persian Gulf, however, could create incentives for states to assert their interests in natural resources around the Caspian Sea. A dramatic heightening of American power in the region could strengthen Russian and Chinese cooperation. Alternatively, a dramatic increase in China's power could move Russia closer to the United States. And, importantly, its ability to pivot between the United States and China also gives Russia important leverage with which to gradually build its own gains over time.

Summary

A close look at these major regional flash points illustrates the role that power plays in both conflict and peace. These early-twenty-first-century flash points are complex regional affairs. Moreover, each could have dramatic global consequences. A major dilemma emerging from these potential crises involves the United States' key role in all of these areas. Yet, the United States cannot be everywhere at once. Thus, a central question is whether it can sustain this level of global engagement. And if the United States had to choose regional priorities, what would they be? To be certain, eruption of these flash point crises is not inevitable, and in some cases, it might even be improbable. They are less likely to become true catastrophes if the risks involved are well understood and creative solutions are generated. A crucial question is, Can America afford to play a stabilizing role in key areas like Asia and the Middle East? If not, then who will lead and with what consequences?

Suggested Reading

Kang, David. *China Rising: Peace, Power and Order in East Asia.* New York: Columbia University Press, 2009.

O'Hanlon, Michael, and Mike M. Mochizuki. *Crisis on the Korean Peninsula: How to Deal with a Nuclear North Korea.* New York: McGraw-Hill, 2003.

Pollack, Kenneth. *The Persian Puzzle: The Conflict between Iran and America.* New York: Random House, 2004.

Ricks, Tom. *The Gamble: General David Petraeus and the American Military Adventure in Iraq, 2006–2008.* New York: Penguin, 2009.

Roy, Olivier. *The New Central Asia: Geopolitics and the Birth of Nations.* New York: New York University Press, 2007.

Schofield, Victoria. *Kashmir in Conflict: India, Pakistan, and the Unending War.* London: I. B. Taurus, 2010.

Shlapak, David, David T. Orletsky, and Barry A. Wilson. *Dire Strait?: Military Aspects of the China-Taiwan Confrontation and Options for U.S. Policy.* Santa Monica, CA: RAND Corporation, 2000.

Sperling, James, Sean Kay, and S. Victor Papacosma, eds. *Limiting Institutions?: The Challenge of Eurasian Security Governance.* Manchester, UK: Manchester University Press, 2003.

Suh, J. J., Peter J. Katzenstein, and Allen Carlson, eds. *Rethinking Security in East Asia: Identity, Power and Efficiency.* Stanford, CA: Stanford University Press, 2004.

Tucker, Nancy Bernkoph. *Dangerous Strait: The U.S.-Taiwan-China Crisis.* New York: Columbia University Press, 2008.

Astronaut Dale A. Gardner, on an extravehicular mission, holds up a "For Sale" sign refer-
ring to the two satellites Palapa B-2 and Westar 6, which they retrieved from orbit after
their Payload Assist Modules failed to fire. Source: NASA.

6

Technology and the Business of Security

IN WORLD WAR II, IT TOOK THE UNITED STATES nine thousand bombs, weighing two thousand pounds each, dropped by fifteen hundred B-17 aircraft to destroy a five-hundred- to one-thousand-foot target. By 1970, it took 176 bombs to do this, flown by eighty-eight F-4 aircraft. In the 1991 Persian Gulf War, the same outcome could be achieved with one or two laser-guided bombs launched by just one F-117 aircraft.[1] The networks of globalization allow for the proliferation and application of entirely new concepts of technology, which can radically reshape global security. These networks have, in effect, become part of the modern battlefield—or, more appropriately, battle space. This chapter examines the relationship between technology, trade, and modern security challenges by surveying the revolution in military affairs, the relationship between information and security, and the military use of space. It then examines how the business of technology and trade relationships affect the supply and demand of weapons proliferation, the role of transnational networks in organized crime and proliferation, the privatization of security, and the security impact of international economic sanctions.

Revolution in Military Affairs

A revolution in military affairs, or RMA, occurs when the combination of technological advances with economic transformation brings about dramatic innovative changes in weapons, tactics, and strategies.[2] There have been more than a dozen revolutionary innovations in military capability, including the chariot, Iron Age infantry, Macedonian Age, stirrup, artillery/gunpowder, Napoleonic Age, railroad, rifle, telegraph, dreadnought and submarine, air superiority and armored warfare, naval airpower, and nuclear weapons.[3] The twentieth century witnessed especially dramatic changes in the role of military technology. By the end of World War I, for example, the tank had emerged as a new means of combat that was applied heavily in World War II. Yet, the tank was of little use to American fighters in the jungles of Vietnam. The nuclear revolution illustrates the enormous implications some technologies can have. The contemporary evolution of technology focuses primarily on the combination of existing tactics integrated into multiple systems utilizing advanced capabilities and integrated platforms to guide precision weapons and engage in new dimensions of warfare. Information warfare, cyberwarfare, advanced psychological operations, electronic warfare, biometrics, robotics, pilotless aircraft, integrated intelligence systems, and space assets reflect a few of the emerging tools of modern warfare. In some areas, the impact of these changes could be so dramatic as to fundamentally alter core concepts of fighting. Meanwhile, the control of information can be a liability—as the United States learned in 2010 when Wikileaks began publishing damaging diplomatic cables, a move U.S. Secretary of State Hillary Clinton called an "attack" on the world.

The Limits of Technology in War

The modern revolution in military affairs creates several new dynamics in war fighting for those states that possess the capacity—and there is no guarantee that technology is always a net asset in conflict. By integrating information with weaponry, a state with advanced technology can attain dominant situational awareness on the battlefield. Possessing advanced technology, however, does not guarantee success unless it is coupled with advances in military doctrine. In the 1973 Yom Kippur War, Israel emerged victorious—but not because of its significant technological superiority. Israel's surveillance technology showed that Egypt was mobilizing artillery, tanks, and bridging equipment, but the Israeli military rejected this information, refusing to believe that Egypt would attack. Even when Israel intercepted Egyptian commanders' discussion of invasion plans on open communication channels, it ignored the intelligence. Israel had modernized its technological capacity but not its doctrine or assumptions about the nature of threats. It won the war, eventually, based on the quality of Israel's military leadership, troops, and national spirit—not because of its technology.[4] Faulty information in 1993 led the United States to bomb, with great precision, a meeting of Somali warlords believed to be plotting attacks on UN peacekeepers in Mogadishu.

Actually, it was a gathering of moderate local political leaders planning possible negotiating strategies. This attack turned much of the local population against the United States. In the 1999 Kosovo War, bad information led to the inadvertent targeting of the Chinese embassy in Belgrade by the United States, resulting in the deaths of a number of Chinese and severely damaging the embassy building.

In 2003, the United States and Britain went to war against Iraq based on intelligence that showed Iraq to be developing weapons of mass destruction. The U.S. National Security Agency intercepted e-mails, telephone calls, and military communications and presented them as proof of the existence of illegal weapons. However, they could not actually tell who was talking to whom or what about. Unconfirmed information was included in a formal presentation by U.S. Secretary of State Colin Powell at the United Nations. Satellite imagery of trucks presented by the U.S. intelligence community as "signature" evidence of nearby chemical weapons use turned out to show water tankers or fire trucks.[5] After the Iraq War, an inquiry into Britain's use of intelligence showed that (among other problems) (1) there was significant doubt about a "high proportion" of human intelligence sources and the information they gave, which was passed on to decision makers; (2) sources were not adequately double-checked; (3) third-hand information regarding chemical and biological weapons programs was relied on; and (4) information from another country's intelligence agency on Iraqi biological and chemical agents was "seriously flawed." A claim by the British government that Iraq could deploy weapons of mass destruction within forty-five minutes had been based on dubious intelligence.[6]

Still, uncertainty about Iraq and its capabilities and intent was a problem for American decision makers. The United States had discovered just after the 1991 Gulf War that Iraq had been much closer to attaining nuclear capability at the time than had been understood. This previous finding created high uncertainty about what might not be known at the time in 2003, given past experience. When pressed in early 2003 by President George W. Bush about the quality of intelligence on Iraq, the director of the Central Intelligence Agency, George Tenet, stated emphatically that it was a "slam dunk" case. Senior officials, including Vice President Richard Cheney, made declarative statements of fact that Iraq had weapons of mass destruction. Secretary of Defense Donald Rumsfeld said with confidence that the weapons' location was well known. In reality, Iraq was mostly in compliance and had disarmed.

Despite enormous technological advances, the United States did not have accurate situational awareness before the Iraq invasion in 2003. Abundant public information actually countered U.S. and British claims regarding Iraq. UN weapons inspectors and public media reporting had largely revealed the information needed to determine that Iraq had no weapons of mass destruction.[7] During the war, poor human intelligence illustrated the limits of technological advantage. The United States launched about fifty air strikes against high-value Iraqi leaders with precision-guided munitions. None of these attacks hit their intended targets, despite what was thought at the time to be solid intelligence. Information provided by satellite telephone from an Iraqi source reported that Saddam Hussein was hiding in a bunker at a compound south of Baghdad. This report prompted an acceleration of the fighting in the hope that the leadership could be "decapitated," leading to quick victory. After the war, it was discovered that no such bunker existed.[8] Throughout the war, frontline American troops lacked access to surveillance and intelligence data due to computer failures. In one case, a lieutenant colonel was told to expect one Iraqi brigade advancing south from Baghdad but instead encountered three separate brigades advancing from three different directions. This was the most significant Iraqi counterattack during the war. While the United States won the battle, it did so because of greater firepower, not advanced technology. U.S. troops often suffered from a "digital divide": technology gave division commanders a good sense of the battlefield but left frontline commanders blind. Common problems included lengthy download times, software failures, and a lack of access to high-bandwidth communications. In several circumstances, Iraqis attacked American troops that had stopped moving to download computer data on enemy locations.[9]

Despite such limitations, advances in information technology are also a significant strategic asset. The contemporary information revolution creates conditions in which the modern military can achieve close to total battlefield situational awareness. The integration of satellite technology with soldiers on the ground can provide information in almost real time to command-and-control centers. This capacity can help with targeting as well as with postbattle damage assessment. Technologically advanced militaries can achieve an integrated analysis of air, land, subterranean, and above- and underwater areas. Thermal imaging and pinpoint satellite technology as well as audio sensors can gain a full spectrum of information about an enemy. Advanced radar imaging and night-vision capability allow an advanced military to do most of its fighting at night. A political decision to employ technology is also often necessary. During the 1994 Rwandan genocide, the United States considered electronic jamming of radio programming that was promoting the mass murder of civilian populations. Washington decided not to take this action, which would have violated international radio broadcasting agreements. On the other hand, senior officials in the Bill Clinton administration argued that they did not act early to stop the genocide because they did not have full information about its scope—despite detailed memos from the United Nations and daily front-page reporting in the *New York Times*.

Battlefield awareness can give an attacker significant advantages. For example, the ability to deploy a tactical Internet system—an integrated system of computers, radios, satellite terminals, switches, and software that constantly passes information both horizontally and vertically, automatically and on demand, throughout a military force—can give a force real-time communications interlinked with command-and-control authorities.[10] In the U.S. military, this force integration can clarify for units exactly where their friendly allies are in the battlefield while identifying enemy locations through unmanned aerial vehicles and integrated surveillance. These integrated systems can provide precise, accurate, and evolving battlefield updates.[11] The American Land Warrior system makes a single troop part of an integrated digital battlefield via a helmet eyepiece that folds down and presents a computer screen with display or sighting from a camera on the soldier's rifle. The Land Warrior then wears a personal computer and two radio systems with a ballistic protection vest equipped with a folding handgrip that serves as a computer mouse.[12] Technological development for war fighting is both accelerating and radical in its implications. On the other hand, these enhancements are primarily limited in that, while one can kill a terrorist leader with a pilotless drone aircraft with a five-hundred-pound bomb attached, that leader will most likely be replaced. And, dropping bombs inside sovereign countries—like Pakistan or Yemen—risks alienating populations essential to winning hearts and minds, especially when civilians are inadvertently killed. The danger is that technology can be seen as a quick fix when in reality it is just one item in the box of policy tools.

From Science Fiction to Modern War

Scientific and technological advances in fields usually not associated with warfare, such as biology and genomics, increasingly have applications for modern conflict. Medical advances mean that far more soldiers can survive injuries that would once have been fatal; on the other hand, this increases substantially the number of traumatic injuries (i.e., to the brain). Biological entities are being found to have military applications as scientists have researched the use of insects, shellfish, bacteria, and weeds to act as "biosentinels" to warn of biological or chemical attacks; for instance there are heat-sensing beetles and bees that can smell explosives like TNT and Semtex.[13] In the Persian Gulf, the United States deployed a team called Mark 6 comprising a group of dolphins used to detect, locate, and mark threats such as underwater mines. Protein-based bacteriorhodopsin is a biological material that changes shape when exposed to light; each change has unique spectral properties that might be used in an electronic device. Protein-based electronics could produce three-dimensional memory devices. With this technology, every soldier in a unit could be provided with a wearable computer system that would store seven to ten gigabytes of digital data in a $1 \times 1 \times 3$ centimeter polymer vial and withstand virtually any environmental conditions. A protein-based photovoltaic converter could coat a soldier's helmet and generate energy to run a laptop computer in the field. Other bioengineering applications currently envisioned by American military planners include engineered bone and accelerated wound healing. Integrating the biological basis of organisms such as abalone could conceivably lead to impact-resistant materials for armor. Some bird feathers and fruits have foundations that could be integrated into military clothing and enhance concealment. Biosensors, perhaps embedded in a wristwatch, might help identify when a soldier has been exposed to a biological or chemical agent, as well as provide information about how well he or she can withstand a particular climate or environmental setting, such as high-altitude mountain terrain.[14]

Technology can also mimic or extend beyond biology via the emerging science of nanotechnology. Minute airborne platforms could, for example, simulate the swarming behavior of insects, dramatically impacting an enemy troop concentration or civilian population that lacked countermeasures. Nanotechnology would, if functional, combine individual atoms and molecules into electrical and biological machines smaller than can be seen through a microscope, or about fifty billionths of a meter in size. Advanced states are investing heavily in nanotechnology research, with investments estimated to exceed $1 trillion per year by 2015.[15] Envisioned nanotechnology applications include molecular-sized robots that could repair individual human cells.

Already, in late 2004, Japanese scientists had successfully conducted a surgical operation on a single living cell using a "nanoneedle" two to three hundred nanometers in diameter. This procedure included successful insertion of the needle into the cell's nucleus.[16] Supercomputers could be made too small to see even with a powerful microscope. Nanodetectors could be used to identify airborne biological phenomena such as viruses or noxious chemicals. In theory, billions of nanotechnology-based sensors could be deployed to revolutionize the notion of intelligence. Multidimensional information dominance would be radically enhanced. Via nanotechnology, virtual reality systems might revolutionize training simulations. Weapons proliferation might be better monitored by nanotechnology sensor nets, which might also function in missile-defense systems.[17] In 2004, Dust Networks Inc. concluded a contract with Science Applications International Corporation to deliver "smart-dust sensors" for perimeter security systems using tiny battery-powered, wireless sensors. These sensors can integrate information to track surrounding conditions and transmit them to a device, which then assembles important data via the Internet. Such sensors can take pictures, serve as a thermometer, detect whether an individual is carrying a gun, or ascertain whether a tank is nearby.[18]

Automation and advanced robotics are already widely available—for example, for diffusing bombs, clearing minefields, or flying unmanned airplanes—allowing for combat or dangerous activity without harm to troops. In Iraq, the United States introduced a robotic airplane called the ScanEagle, which carried out more than one thousand hours of intelligence and reconnaissance work for the U.S. Marine Corps in 2003 and 2004. The plane is four feet long with a ten-foot wingspan and flies for up to fifteen hours on just two gallons of fuel. Its surveillance capacity allows it to send to U.S. troops real-time video images detailed enough to show the facial expressions of enemy soldiers.[19] Further advances in these areas, combined with nanotechnology, will have a dramatic effect on the battlefield. By 2010, the U.S. Army was envisioning robots serving as antisniper warriors and sentry guards, interestingly raising the specter of the Terminator as the future of modern warfare. With pilotless robotic aircraft, the war fighter becomes a military or intelligence officer living a normal suburban life in the United States, in effect pushing a button to kill a target thousands of miles away in real time. Microrobots, as small as toy cars, can be used for complex battlefield imaging or to get into small spaces for tactical surveillance. By 2010, over fifty countries around the world were developing robotic-warrior technology. Meanwhile, enemies also employ a much simpler variation—for example, insurgents in Iraq used mobile telephones or garage door openers to trigger deadly improvised explosive devices.

A range of military research focuses on the development of nonlethal weapons. Research into the bioeffects of beamed energy and sonic wavelengths, which might be able to affect human behavior without killing people, has advanced considerably. Lasers to blind enemy soldiers and sonic weapons to stun or nauseate people or to create severe gastrointestinal crises have been successfully developed.[20] In 2004, the U.S. government warned airline pilots that terrorists might seek to crash airplanes by shining lasers (common in a variety of industries, including outdoor light shows) into cockpits, blinding pilots during landing or takeoff.[21] Lower-tech concepts include delivering electric shocks from a distance, spreading slippery material on roads to make them impassible, or dispersing foam to limit access to or disable machinery. Tactics used by domestic police also can have military applications. Such tools include tear gas and pepper spay; rubber bullets, propelled balls, and beanbag rounds; flash grenades, which create a bright light and loud bang but do no damage; Tasers; and weapons that use light, sound, heat, or smell for diversion.[22] These applications would be especially useful in hostage situations, when combatants hide among civilian populations, and when crowd control is needed.

Other nonlethal weapons include audio devices that can disable an enemy. The United States has developed a megaphone that can operate at 145 decibels and project an ear-splitting tone from three hundred yards. This technology could rid a cave or building of terrorists or insurgents concealed inside. While the wider civilian impacts have not been fully vetted, the United States first deployed this capability in Iraq in 2004.[23] A simpler version of screeching noise was used to the same effect in 1989 when invading U.S. forces cornered Gen. Manuel Noriega in the Vatican embassy in Panama City. U.S. troops set up large speakers in a nearby street and blasted the embassy with heavy metal rock that the beleaguered general was known to detest. Noriega soon surrendered. In Iraq, American trucks with massive audio equipment blasted AC/DC songs to drown out the mosques calling fighters to jihad against American troops during the battle of Fallujah in fall 2004. Chemical weapons that can be used to put a building's occupants to sleep have been used by Russia and are under further development in the United States. The United States is researching a microwave weapon whereby a millimeter-wave beam mounted on a military vehicle would penetrate skin to a depth of about one-sixty-fourth of an inch, heating water molecules and producing intolerable pain.[24]

The Dilemma of Advanced Technology

Only a few states possess the spectrum of advanced capabilities or research-and-development methods to deploy advanced military technology. Globalization does, however, allow for the proliferation of technology so that a state might skip entire generations of conventional military evolution and focus on high-tech capabilities. Many of the innovative technologies used to enhance modern military operations have dual-use civilian functions and can be purchased on international markets. Militaries must also struggle to employ technological experts who can make more money in the private sector. Traditional measures of military power might not be adequate to define the relative power or capability that a particular state possesses. A related problem arises in coalition fighting. If one state makes technological advances, it can become less capable of entering combat interoperably with other nations' military equipment. During the 1999 Kosovo War, the United States found that its pilots' communication systems were incompatible with older systems used by its NATO allies. The United States could not always utilize its technological advantages in that war, a cost deemed worth paying to gain the benefit of a larger political coalition. Another operational dilemma posed by advanced technology is the high degree of expertise required to operate modern military systems. A more advanced education might be at least as important for military recruitment as combat skills. Finally, for all the precision technology, large bombs and conventional ground forces still matter. In 2004, the United States asked defense contractors to develop a precision-guided thirty-thousand-pound bomb to be called the Massive Ordnance Penetrator—informally known as Big Blue.[25]

As technology makes combat more precise, war itself might come to seem like a painless exercise, perhaps making it more likely as a policy option. Because technology enables the projection of military power from far-off platforms and the appearance of minimal casualties is established in the public mind, war might be more probable. A premature resort to war on such assumptions could lead to quick military solutions to otherwise intractable problems—or just as easily result in an unwinnable quagmire. The latter in particular will become a problem if overreliance on technology diverts planning and investment away from important military tools, such as land armies. If, due to an impression that war can be fought and won via airpower alone, ground options are not available, military commanders could be denied a critical tool for achieving victory. Winning a war with airpower is possible, but securing a long-term peace on the ground will likely require ground troops. If these are not there to secure a peace, the war might not have been worth fighting in the first place. Even then, technology has its limits, as Israel discovered in its 2006 war in southern Lebanon, where Hezbollah forces used minimal firepower to wreak major damage on Israeli armored vehicles while intercepting Israeli communications. Rather than fighting like guerrillas, the Hezbollah fighters challenged the Israelis using more conventional warfare combining low- and high-end technology and tactics.

Underdeveloped or collapsing states and rough terrain can reduce target opportunities and make it harder to deploy advanced technology. In the initial 2001 war in Afghanistan, the United States could attack a very limited number of targets with precision weapons. Fighting in a desert or mountain environment could make it very difficult, for example, to deploy a tactical Internet system when high mobility raises problems establishing a network and rugged terrain is not amenable to effective computer use. The war in Afghanistan did produce new high-technology innovations, such as the arming of unmanned aerial vehicles (previously used only for high-resolution surveillance) with bombs for pinpoint attacks with conventional munitions; by 2009 these were being deployed across the border into Pakistan as well. Also, American intelligence agents were able to use satellite communications to guide precision air strikes to create fear among local Afghan warlords who required persuasion to cooperate more fully with the United States.[26] Combatants, however, might simply choose not to fight against the high-tech aspects of their more powerful adversaries, instead drawing them into urban areas or jungles where the technology will be less effective. Fighting at night in close quarters, insurgents in Iraq used bright red and blue flares to blind Americans wearing night-vision equipment. Technology can also be constrained or degraded by atmospheric conditions, including weather, dust, and smoke.[27]

Advances in communication and surveillance could jeopardize privacy among average citizens. The United States had, by 2002, begun using its military surveillance capability for a variety of domestic activities, ranging from observing individuals and groups of people at large, symbolic events to mapping important cities for emergency preparedness. The U.S. National Geospatial-Intelligence Agency has assembled visual information on more than 130 urban areas.[28] Human knowledge and freedom can grow as technology facilitates interconnections and communications across borders; however, knowledge and freedom can also be eroded as states seek modern technological means of gaining military advantage. To modernize both its economy and its military, China is seeking advanced technology; yet, this technology is also proliferating within Chinese society, allowing citizens to gain access to the outside world. This trend makes it harder for the state to control the flow of information. An example from the Tiananmen Square crisis, where Chinese troops cracked down on public demonstrations calling for liberty in June 1989, illustrates this challenge. A man named Wang Nan left his home on the morning of June 3 with a camera in hand, innocently thinking he could take some photographs of a historic moment in Chinese history as students and others gathered to protest Communist Party rule. Wang Nan witnessed the military opening fire on civilian protesters and took out his camera. The soldiers firing on the people saw him with the camera and shot him, killing him with a bullet to the head.[29] The Chinese government continued to see new threats in the flow of information, requiring Google to censor its search engine in China. Google initially complied but changed course in early 2010, when it announced that it had sustained a major cyberattack emanating from China. Meanwhile, in early 2011, multiple press reports indicated that a highly effective computer virus had been used to set back major aspects of the Iranian nuclear program, though the details on that were not fully made public.

New surveillance technology known as radio frequency identification (RFID) can allow for instant tracking of goods and people on a global basis in near real time. For example, law-enforcement officers have used RFIDs on Texas schoolchildren to monitor their movements. Just as it can enhance children's safety, this technology could also be used to invade individuals' privacy and perhaps violate civil liberties, such as the freedom of movement.[30] By 2014, 1 trillion objects could be linked electronically, and remote sensors and microscopic radio transponders could be placed virtually anywhere, including inside people's bodies. The degree to which states will use technology to enhance control—or lose control because of technology—remains to be seen. Also uncertain are the health and environmental implications of technological advances—such as the effect of residual waste from discarded cell phones.

Information and Security

Modern developed societies have so dramatically expanded the role of information systems that a definition of power must incorporate knowledge and communication as key elements. At the turn of the twenty-first century, in 2002, 2.8 billion cellular phone and 1.2 billion fixed-line subscribers worldwide made about 180 billion minutes of international telephone calls via several hundred satellites orbiting Earth.[31] In 2009, the total number of international phone minutes used had ballooned to 406 billion. It took radio broadcasting thirty-eight years to reach 50 million people and thirteen years for television to reach the same number. It took the Internet four years to reach 50 million users. By March 2000, 300 million people worldwide were using it.[32] In 2010, this number had grown to about 1.9 billion. In 2002, an estimated 31 billion e-mails were sent worldwide every day.[33] In 2006, daily e-mail volume exceeded 60 billion. The number of e-mail accounts was estimated to have grown to 1.2 billion by 2006.[34] The advent of videoconferencing and Skype for personal calls further enhances these communication flows, accounting for about 12 percent of all international telephony. The information revolution increases demand to integrate the military and civilian life beyond weaponry. This military-civilian interface includes advanced telecommunications systems and computerized databases. Networks where the storage, transmission, manipulation, and dissemination of electronic digital information, including satellite communications systems of microprocessor production and software development, transcend this nexus between the civilian and military worlds.[35] From these trends, the dynamics of information power have come to assume a major strategic importance.

Information Power

As information has become a tool of power, it has increasingly been applied to modern warfare. Information warfare has five basic elements: intelligence-based warfare designed to subvert or confuse an adversary's knowledge gathering; electronic warfare using technology to degrade an adversary's information infrastructure; hacker warfare, which includes attacks on an enemy's computer system either to spy on the enemy or to turn his own systems against him using disinformation; command-and-control warfare using targeted violence to destroy command centers and their links to the battlefield; and psychological operations, which use information to demoralize enemy forces or to affect an enemy population.[36] While these operational concepts are appealing strategic tools, they are also complicated and have limitations. For example, ascertaining how an enemy uses information and interlinks information can be difficult. State and private-sector activity can be protected by encoding and creating systems redundancy. It is also difficult to know when an information-warfare strike will have the maximum impact and to assess success or failure. Finally, one has to be cautious about crippling an enemy's ability to communicate. For example, destroying an enemy's command-and-control system might make it difficult for him to command troops to lay down their weapons. Destroying an enemy's telephone and television capacity can make it more difficult to get information out to the public to gain its compliance with peace-support operations or occupation.[37] Meanwhile, Web-based "reporting" on sites like Wikileaks can expose national security secrets in ways that states have not had to grapple with before. Reportedly one potential source of the leaks about Afghanistan in 2010 on Wikileaks simply downloaded the secret documents onto a CD marked "Lady Gaga" with no questions asked.

In addition to the United States, there are four emerging centers of global communications power: India, China, the EU, and Russia. Indonesia, Brazil, Kenya, and Romania are also engaged in communications infrastructure. Power within this system can shift and indicate relative gains for one state or region. For example, in 2002, American companies owned 85 percent of the undersea communications infrastructure; by 2004, China had bought control of major assets including Level 3 Communications, PSINet, Asia Global Crossing, and Global Crossing.[38] In December 2004, China's Lenovo Group announced that it was purchasing the personal computer business of IBM Corporation, making it the third-largest seller of personal computers in the world. The shifting geopolitics of the information revolution creates new opportunities for states like India and China to accelerate their economic and political power in the twenty-first century. Meanwhile, this creates vulnerabilities for the United States, which has seen information- and technology-driven jobs migrate to these countries, which can provide similar services with lower-wage workers. Some regions have been left substantially behind, for example, in the area of broadband development. However, this began to change in Africa as SEACOM began laying infrastructure lines for broadband in East Africa in 2009.

Increasing global reliance on a new generation of solid-state electronics, as well as rapid information processing and transmission, creates a heavily integrated network of targets for those who might seek to attack an enemy. Banking, stock markets, telephone switching networks, electric power grids, and air-traffic control systems can combine so that information becomes both a strength and vulnerability in a modern society.[39] Critical security questions arise including, What constitutes an information attack? When is an information attack an act of war? How is an information attack verified? How is the attacker identified and verified?[40] A state or nonstate actor can attack information systems from within the territory of a third state or cross several states in the process of attacking from various directions. For example, in 2007, Estonia came under a massive disruption-of-service cyberattack on a scale that many assumed could only have been mounted by Russia, though that country's involvement was not fully proved. Over thirty thousand personal computers are involuntarily recruited each day into secret networks that spread spam and viruses. Viruses such as Mydoom and Bagle conduct an online battle for control of information via malicious viruses that can capture and control an individual computer. These particular attacks originated from private sources in Latvia, Macao, and Israel.[41] The American Department of Defense estimates that, in 2001 alone, it faced about forty thousand Internet attacks. While most cyberattacks on the U.S. military fail, in 2000, 715 achieved some degree of access to Department of Defense systems.[42] During the 2008 presidential election in the United States, the campaigns of both Barack Obama and John McCain were hacked into—with evidence that the source came from inside China.

The heavy investment in civilian and military systems makes the modern state vulnerable to novel uses for traditional weapons. For example, exploding a nuclear device at a high altitude (between forty and four hundred kilometers above Earth's surface) would do little damage in terms of blast and radioactivity. But the objective could be to generate an electromagnetic pulse (EMP) from the interaction of the nuclear explosion with Earth's atmosphere, ionosphere, and magnetic field, resulting in a general shock within the atmosphere and on Earth that would disable electronics and destroy or damage the systems they drive. The impact would be particularly devastating to the electrical power and information systems on which modern society depends. The infrastructural effects would include a shutdown of a nation's financial system and delivery systems for food, water, and medical care. The trade and production of goods and services would also be severely affected.[43]

Even natural phenomena like solar flares from the sun could cause massive, perhaps wholesale, disruption to electricity supplies around the world.

In a country like the United States, whose electric power grid is interconnected in several regional clusters, an EMP event over the Midwest could disrupt about 70 percent of the country's power supply. An EMP attack would also significantly damage or disrupt civilian telecommunications systems in areas exposed to the effect. Surviving networks would be stressed beyond their capacity to function properly. Interbank fund transfers, securities transfers, and payment services would be dramatically affected, as would automated banking operators. Even a shutdown lasting for a few minutes to a day would have a potentially catastrophic impact on the American financial system. Severe effects would also ripple through the transportation sector, including massive traffic light malfunctions in major cities, confusion in railway traffic, a breakdown in loading and unloading and security measures at seaports, and a failure in air-traffic control systems, leading to a national backup in air travel. The region affected by an EMP event would likely encounter food-distribution problems over a period of weeks or even months, creating potential for large-scale public unrest and disorder to emerge as a major public-security crisis.[44] In cities where freshwater is generated by electricity, drinking water would be in short supply.

Knowledge and Power

The spread of instant communications is exposing regions of the world to a variety of new ideas and information. For example, the Middle East is open to information with the potential to engage publics in ways previously unknown in the region's politics. In 1979, Iranian revolutionaries spread their messages via small cassettes—advanced technology at the time. By 2010, the Internet, including Facebook and Twitter messaging, had combined with new uses of older technologies, such as satellite television, to transfer ideas and images across borders where the state traditionally controlled access to information. Newspapers are no longer able to serve as government mouthpieces as they are challenged by independent voices. Some newspapers published outside the Middle East, such as *Asharq Alawsat* and *al-Hayat*, link Arab communities to a global discussion that bridges ideas from within and outside the Arab world. Television has also been altered by the Al Jazeera network, which uses satellite technology for independent broadcasting. This change was key for the revolution in Egypt in February 2011, for, while state television broadcast propaganda, Al Jazeera provided independent news about the role and scope of protest movements. On the other hand, many terrorist groups like al Qaeda slip under the radar by relying on close-knit courier groups among their followers. Although the Internet is available to varying degrees in every country in the Middle East, television remains the primary source of information in the region.[45] This has changed for younger generations, which also used Facebook as a major initial rallying tool in the case of Egypt in 2011. However, clandestine networks, including terrorist organizations, use Internet access and television imagery to get their messages out, and some have used online chat rooms to build contacts and recruit people to their causes. Conversely, these cybertools also give power to the expansion of ideas, innovation, and commercial and economic development—especially among new, Internet-savvy generations.

The purposeful use of disinformation can help states or other international actors advance particular strategic objectives in shaping public attitudes. For example, in October 2004, the U.S. military in Iraq let CNN know that it planned to begin military operations in the insurgent stronghold city of Fallujah. That particular report was in fact false (though the United States would eventually engage insurgents in a major battle at Fallujah). This was an intentional use of the media to deceive the enemy into thinking an attack was imminent and to trick him into exposing defensive tactics. Such tactics can raise concerns about the credibility of military reporting and its use as a source of propaganda during a state at war. However, as a U.S. official told the *Los Angeles Times*, "information is part of the battlefield in a way that it's never been before.... We'd be foolish not to try to use it to our advantage."[46] In 2001, the U.S. Department of Defense abandoned a plan to create an Office of Strategic Influence tasked with planting pro-American—and possibly even false—news stories in foreign media outlets, including those of allies. Nonetheless, the use of psychological operations utilizing new media sources persisted in planning mechanisms. Such activities included planting news stories in the foreign press and creating false documents and websites in Arabic to discredit mosques and religious groups that promulgated anti-Americanism.[47]

The Military Use of Space

Space harbors great unknowns, though exploration continues to expand knowledge of the final frontier. The unknown can breed optimism and fear at the same time—but the urge to develop and expand technology to explore space continues to grow. The exploration of Mars and Earth's moon raises new possibilities for human life. Mars, it appears, might have once held water, the essence of life. The moon could be a major source for energy production through mining of the helium-3 isotope, which can be attained there. If accessed, the isotope would have a cash value of as much as $4 billion per ton in terms of its equivalent in oil energy production. There are an estimated 1 million tons of helium-3 on the moon—enough to power Earth for thousands of years.[48] Hollywood films like *The Day the Earth Stood Still, War of the Worlds, Independence Day,* and *Mars Attacks* show the future of space as requiring defense from external threats. But other images portray a more peaceful future in which space exploration, as envisioned in *Star Trek,* unites humanity to expand knowledge and embrace diversity. Programs like *Star Trek* have also stimulated thinking about new technologies, from desktop computers to cell phones to laser weapons.[49] The growing use of space—which includes about five hundred operational satellites orbiting Earth—creates the additional challenge of space debris and other hazards. An estimated nine thousand pieces of space debris that pose threats to satellites or spacecraft can be tracked from Earth. There is also considerable "microdebris," perhaps more than one hundred thousand undetectable particles less than ten centimeters in length that can do damage.[50] In the most extreme case, space threats can also include meteorites: the collision with Earth of an asteroid ten kilometers in diameter likely contributed to the extinction of the dinosaurs.

Spacepower

Outer space, the area beyond Earth's atmosphere, is considered the common heritage of humankind and is—both by tradition and treaty—free of military deployment. While space has not been weaponized—no actual weapons are deployed in or from space—it has been militarized for many decades. Indeed, the use of space contributes significantly to increasing security. Satellites provide early warning about nuclear weapons launches, which helps states avoid misinterpretations leading to deadly conflict. The same satellite technology can also be used to monitor the destruction of weapons according to treaty obligations or to study global environmental challenges. International cooperation and the use of communications technology in space facilitate a global perspective on security challenges. Humanity has also been served by the advent of satellites used for enhanced astronomy, atmospheric study, search-and-rescue capacity, space exploration, and weather forecasting.

Many countries benefit militarily from space activity: satellites using the Global Positioning System (GPS) help with mapping; aerial refueling and rendezvous; geodetic surveys; search-and-rescue operations; communications; arms-control verification and monitoring of nonproliferation activity; early warning; intelligence, surveillance, and reconnaissance; and weather prediction. The United States relies heavily on space activity to support its modern military. American military command-and-control capacity is enhanced by the ability to coordinate troop movements and help troops on the ground determine their location, facilitate targeting and weapons guidance, and provide communications for unmanned aerial vehicles. New concepts may include antiballistic missile laser technology, precision-guided bunker-buster bombs, kinetic energy antisatellite weapons, space-based lasers, and a space plane.[51] The future use of space raises questions about how "spacepower" will develop and what new challenges will accompany it. In civilian technology industries, the commercial sector, the defense industries, and intelligence gathering, states are increasingly competing over strategic advances in spacepower—though in every area of space, the United States has nearly complete dominance.[52]

Heavy reliance on space also creates new vulnerabilities. For example, a relatively crude satellite could be launched privately or by a country. Already by 2004 relatively heavy private rockets had been tested, which could eventually be launched into space. A satellite or rocket packed with pebbles or nails could be detonated in proximity to or set to explode on contact with a critical satellite or spacecraft.[53] Such an attack might eliminate an existing space-based advantage or undermine intelligence-gathering capabilities as a precursor to other military actions on the ground. While terrorists could not likely gain access to space capacity, they could use conventional weapons or weapons of mass destruction on Earth against critical links that control satellite-guidance and communication networks. More likely, terrorists would use space-based technology such as GPS to target precision attacks or coordinate cells worldwide. To deal with this concern, the United States has planned for the capacity to disable the entire U.S. network of global positioning satellites during a crisis so as to deny that technology to anyone who might use it to aid terrorist activity.[54] Satellite imagery available for purchase on the Internet, for instance, from Google Earth, can also help in planning attacks on particular targets. Finally, states seeking power in the international system could build advanced space weapons, such as antisatellite or laser technology, as a means of achieving strategic parity or advantage.[55]

Space weapons are military tools based in space or with an essential element based in space. These include directed-energy weapons that can propagate destructive force at very high speeds and mass-to-target weapons that deliver a hard device, such as an explosive, to a target in space or on Earth.[56] Space-applicable weapons can also include metal projectiles called hypervelocity rod bundles for hitting ground targets from space.[57] These bundles were often referred to in debates over space weapons as "rods from God." Missile-defense or antisatellite systems can be based on Earth for use in space. There are three basic kinds of space-applicable weapons. The first includes ground-, sea-, and air-based missile-defense interceptors, which use low-Earth orbital space to destroy ballistic missiles; this kind of system is being simultaneously researched and deployed by the United States. The second type of space-based weapons is under consideration for future development and testing; it includes kinetic kill interceptors designed to destroy missiles by collision and space-based lasers that send high-powered beams at rising missiles to destroy them. The third type includes antisatellite systems, such as missiles launched into space or space-based systems that would enter the same orbit as deployed satellites to launch or explode some form of conventional explosive.[58]

States have sought to avoid developing the capacity to destroy satellites, but it is an increasingly tempting area. Even a small-scale disruption of one satellite can have enormous economic and social impact. For example, in May 1998, a single Galaxy IV satellite failed, causing 80 percent of pagers in the United States to stop working and affecting 27 million users.[59] A worst-case scenario would involve a high-altitude nuclear detonation, which could disable all low-Earth-orbit satellites within line of site of the explosion by burning out their electronics. Eventually, all nonhardened satellites would be exposed to transient-radiation and system-generated electromagnetic pulses as they orbited near the area of the initial explosion.[60] By attacking American satellites, an adversary might be able to gain a degree of parity on the conventional battlefield given the growing U.S. reliance on satellites to coordinate military activity. American reliance on missile-guidance technology has increased significantly. During the 1991 Persian Gulf War, the United States launched 228,000 air-to-ground munitions, only 4 percent of which were laser guided. In the 1999 Kosovo War, some 23,700 air-to-ground missiles were launched, and 30 percent were either laser or GPS guided. In the 2001 Afghan conflict, the United States launched eighteen thousand air-to-ground missiles, of which 56 percent were laser- or GPS-guided munitions.[61] Since the 1990s, the United States has been engaged in the development and deployment of stealth satellite technology that would make it much harder to detect the location and orbital path of satellites.[62]

Space Dominance

The United States is the dominant space power, but there is no internal consensus as to how it should approach the military use of space. "Space doves" oppose all military use of space and seek treaties to forestall future development. "Militarization realists" believe that warfare will eventually entail some form of combat involving space and that it is best to prepare for it. "Inevitable weaponizers" argue that every area of the battle space has previously been developed for weapons use, and there is no inherent reason why the same rule should not apply to space. Thus, states can reasonably be expected to prepare to conduct military operations involving outer space. "Space hawks" are enthusiastic about all development of space weapons and oppose most constraints on research and deployment.[63] One key element of the space debate is the financial power of the space industry. Space-technology industries generated $125 billion in profits in 2000, and total American investment in space technology was about $600 billion per year by 2010.[64]

The United States has embarked on a concerted effort to continue, develop, and expand space dominance as a key objective in the twenty-first century. It controls 95 percent of all global military spending on space and dominates two-thirds of the commercial space industry. The United States maintains twenty-four to thirty-two GPS satellites to coordinate and locate troops and targets. Imagery intelligence is provided by the KH-11, which has a resolution of four to six inches in daylight and several feet at night, and the Onyx system, which provides night and all-weather imaging radar. As many as seven signals-intelligence satellites are also used to intercept radio and television broadcasts, cell phone communications, radar transmissions, and other electronic signals. A satellite network provides real-time communications for the military and includes a nuclear-hardened, antijam communication link between the military, the White House, and the Department of State without ground-based assistance. Nine satellites comprise a tactical mobile communications network for naval communications and other fixed and mobile terminals. Early-warning systems are provided by a constellation of satellites that detect and track missiles throughout all phases of their flight around the world.[65]

The U.S. Space Command concludes that "just as land dominance, sea control, and air superiority have become critical elements of current military strategy, space superiority is emerging as an essential element of battlefield success and future warfare." The vision for 2020 is that the United States should succeed at "dominating the space medium and integrating space power throughout military operations."[66] The U.S. Strategic Command (STRATCOM) identifies space as essential to America's security and well-being and carries the mission of protecting the nation's space capabilities, interests, and investments. STRATCOM oversees a global network of satellite command and control, communications, missile warning, and launch facilities for U.S. space systems. Specific missions are divided into four major categories. Space Force Support includes launching of satellites and high-value payloads into space. Space Force Enhancement provides weather, communications, intelligence, missile warning, and navigation to all aspects of American military service operations worldwide. In the Afghanistan and Iraq wars of 2001 and 2003, virtually every military platform used was linked by satellite through STRATCOM. Space Control involves using technological advantage to ensure unfettered movement in and use of space and denial of use to adversaries. This function includes surveillance of space, protection of space forces from hostile threats and environmental hazards, and prevention of unauthorized exploitation of space capabilities. This function can include negation of space systems hostile to the United States and its allies. How this is to be done remains left unspecified in public literature.

STRATCOM notes that the United States might find it necessary to disrupt, degrade, deny, or destroy enemy space capabilities in future conflicts. The United States does confirm, however, that there is no current means to operate antisatellite weapons. More likely, conventional weapons could be used to strike an adversary's space-launch or ground-relay facilities while antisatellite research is ongoing. In February 2008, the United States used ground-based interceptors to shoot down its own satellite before it could reenter the Earth's atmosphere. While officially done to ensure that potentially hazardous debris did not hit the ground, for all practical purposes this was also an antisatellite operations test. STRATCOM also includes Space Force Application in its planning and operations. It identifies future roles and missions involved in the evolving battlefield, which could encompass combat operations in, through, and from space.[67] Notably, antisatellite weaponry need not necessarily be space based and, as such, would not necessarily violate existing international understandings related to the weaponization of space.[68] Symbolizing, both to supporters and critics, the scope of spacepower, Acting Air Force Secretary Pete Teets said in 2004, "We haven't reached the point of strafing and bombing from space—nonetheless, we are thinking about those possibilities."[69]

In 2005, the United States began considering a new policy that would authorize the air force to implement its research, development, and eventual deployment of space weapons. However, it is also possible that while policy might change, implementation might still be a long way off. The extreme difficulty, even danger, of operating in space is a major obstacle to deployment of systems. Additionally, the costs of deployment are likely to be high, constraining any actual decision to deploy weapons. In fact, there is no guarantee that the United States will prioritize space as a major investment area beyond its existing dominance. Domestic or other global security priorities on Earth could prompt a redirection of resources away from space programs. Conversely, there is also some evidence that space might not actually be the center of gravity of future military operations that its proponents assert. For example, the American space shuttle fleet has been diminished in value as an expensive safety risk. America's satellite launch capacity is heavily dependent on a declining commercial-sector demand in order to stay economically viable.[70] The United States did announce in 2005 that it intended to return to the moon by 2018—though the estimated price tag of $104 billion proved too high relative to other priorities. In 2010, President Barack Obama cancelled this new moon initiative. Still, American spending on space remained high, at about $18 billion, while the next potential serious competitors—Russia and China—were spending about $2 to $3 billion by 2010, with India spending about $900 million.

The Space Race

Sixty countries in the world have some kind of space program activity—most involving satellites. Only a handful, however, have the assets to deploy men into and work in space. France, Japan, and Israel all have self-contained space-launch capabilities. Australia also has the potential to provide launch facilities for Russia and the United States. France, the United Kingdom, Germany, Italy, Japan, and Israel have their own satellite industries and technologies. Japan has launched a set of four satellites for information gathering over North Korea. These satellites can also monitor any point on Earth twice a day. Japan is also developing a two-layer missile-defense shield.[71] Europe has moved forward with its Galileo project, which provides a global-tracking navigational satellite system that allows users around the world to know their location with precision. The European Space Agency (dominated by France) provides Europe with access to launch facilities as well as a variety of remote-sensing satellites.[72]

A second tier of space-capable countries includes India, which has its own access to space; Pakistan, which has developed missile technology and deployed a communications satellite (with plans to deploy an observation satellite); and Brazil, which has its own indigenous space launch programs. Among these states, however, only India has a comprehensive space program.[73] India was the first developing nation to achieve space-deployment capabilities. The degree of India's military use of space is unclear beyond the development of surveillance capacity. In October 2003, the chief of the Indian air force said that India had begun development of a command station for an eventual space platform for nuclear weapons. He later retracted the statement under pressure from his civilian leadership.[74] Brazil maintains a nascent space program and has significant military involvement in a rocket-development program. Brazil has also worked with China to develop and launch two remote-sensing satellites for real-time, civilian, environmental monitoring.[75] In 2009, Iran tested rocket capacity that would allow it to deploy satellites and was moving forward in developing additional elements of a nascent, home-grown space program. Even smaller countries like Algeria have begun to enter into the commercial satellite arena. For these countries, as well as many first-tier countries, a major driver of the investment in space technology might also be the ability to sell access or equipment for profit.

The United States' main potential competitors for space dominance are Russia and China. Russia maintains significant Soviet-era space capabilities. About two-thirds of Russia's spacecraft in orbit are used for military purposes. Russia has announced plans to modernize its communications, navigation, and reconnaissance satellites. However, Russia has also cut its overall space investment by two-thirds since the end of the Cold War, and about 80 percent of its satellites should have expired by 2010. Russia has five types of imagery reconnaissance satellites—none of which were in orbit by 2004—though a new reconnaissance satellite system began launching in 2006. Russia also has a series of electronic intelligence satellites, but they have short life spans and have also begun to expire. In 2009, an American satellite collided with a nonfunctioning Russian military satellite—the first ever such collision—and created a debris cloud that posed a threat to other satellites passing nearby. Russia does maintain active orbits for its military communications satellites, though not all of those available are operational. Only about 50 percent of Russia's navigation satellite capabilities were running in 2004—though the country has indicated a commitment to revitalize its overall satellite capacity. Russia's ballistic missile early-warning and space-monitoring systems have been in significant decline since the collapse of the Soviet Union. Much of the infrastructure for Russia's early-warning satellite network was spread around the former Soviet Union, and not all former Soviet republics have cooperated in upgrading radar systems. Only in 2003 was Russia able to activate the Volga radar station, based in Belarus. Previously, the entire northwestern sector of missile surveillance had been exposed due to the shutdown of a radar station in Latvia in the mid-1990s.[76]

In 2003, China joined Russia and the United States as having placed a human into orbit around Earth. Chinese leaders say they envision a moon landing by about 2017 and the eventual deployment of a project to measure the capacity for accessing helium-3 on the moon. China also foresees deploying a moon-based telescope and robotic space explorers.[77] China has communications, navigation, and imaging satellites. A number of its communications satellites are integrated into military command, control, communications, computer, and intelligence systems. China has one imaging reconnaissance satellite, one meteorological satellite, and one remote-sensing microsatellite, all of which can be used for civilian or military purposes. China has also established an engineering and research center that would allow it to implement large-scale production of small satellites. China plans to produce six to eight small satellites per year and to launch over one hundred by 2020 to provide complete surveillance of the country. According to the Xinhua news agency, the purpose would be to have a "large surveying network" to monitor water reserves, forests, farmland, city construction, and "various activities of society."[78] In January 2007, China used ground-based interceptors to shoot down a failing satellite about five hundred miles into space—effectively a demonstration of antisatellite capacity.

Strategic Dilemmas in Space: Missile Defense and Antisatellite Weapons

Two technological advancements under development in the early twenty-first century cross the divide between the militarization and weaponization of space: missile defense and antisatellite warfare. Missile defenses, the ability to destroy incoming missiles, were banned during the Cold War by the 1972 Anti-Ballistic Missile Treaty between the United States and Soviet Union, the logic being that missile-defense systems could make a nuclear war more possible if one side felt it could strike first and survive a retaliation. In the 1980s, the United States revisited the idea under President Ronald Reagan, who called for the Strategic Defense Initiative, or SDI, known to detractors as "Star Wars." The United States conducted research but agreed not to deploy such systems through the 1990s. George W. Bush ended America's commitment to the treaty and commenced plans to deploy interceptor systems in California and Alaska (with support elements in Greenland and the United Kingdom) and pressed Europe to accept a system deployed in Poland and the Czech Republic. President Barack Obama continued to accept the premise of ballistic missile defense but preferred to begin with local and regional capabilities. Thus, in summer 2009, he announced plans to scrap the systems planned for Eastern Europe and emphasized a regional deterrent emphasizing medium-range capabilities that Iran might deploy. In November 2009, America's NATO allies agreed to this concept, and Russia indicated it would participate in its development.

Ballistic missile-defense systems would have serious technological limitations. If accomplished using ground-to-space interceptors, ballistic missile defense effectively entails hitting a bullet with a bullet. Space-based options are equally problematic, relying on the creation of lasers to destroy missiles from above. Rather than building space-based assets, using the Aegis ship-based system would enable knocking a missile out in its boost phase—just as it is launched and before it entered space and accelerated. At launch, rockets are close and slow, making them easier to hit. This tactic, however, would require almost instantaneous knowledge of a launch and a missile-defense platform within range; thus, it would have to integrate satellite surveillance accurately. There is also research into an airborne laser program that would place lasers on a Boeing 747–400. However, this system's capacity would be limited by range, beam power, the type of ICBM rocket used, and countermeasures.[79]

U.S. deployments in North America and Washington's initial plans for deployments in Europe have proceeded on an acquisition model of "spiral development," which includes deployment of existing capabilities before their effectiveness is proven. This plan assumes that an initial threshold capacity will gradually be improved over time. As a result, systems are being deployed without a clear end cost or proven capacity for success and with major questions about how American allies might be engaged. As testing has progressed, limited-theater missile-defense capacity has improved. Ballistic missile–defense testing has also yielded technological advances, including against incoming missiles with decoys attached. Between 2001 and mid-2008, the Missile Defense Agency asserts it conducted successful tests with thirty-four out of forty-two attempted intercepts. Six of nine tests successfully eliminated long-range targets. Of those six, four used warhead decoys as countermeasures.[80] However, there has also been a reduction in the complexity of tests involving decoys. Furthermore, the actual number of intercepts is more realistically eight of fourteen because the Missile Defense Agency does not include tests in which interceptors did not launch.[81] In fall 2008, for example, an intercept successfully occurred. However, the decoys on the inbound missile failed to deploy. Thus, the definition of a "successful" test is open to interpretation. In any event, the system is not battle tested for serious war-fighting conditions.

The proliferation of weapons of mass destruction and missile-delivery systems is no doubt a serious international security threat in the early twenty-first century. Of particular concern is the acquisition of these systems by states that have not abided by expected norms of behavior within the international system. By 2007, there were over 120 ballistic missile launches worldwide— though mostly by American and European allies.[82] Iran, however, has a long record of hostility toward the interests of NATO member states and has the largest force of ballistic missiles in the Middle East and the second-largest in the underdeveloped world after North Korea.[83] About thirty countries worldwide have missiles with ranges of up to one thousand kilometers, and eleven have ballistic missiles with longer ranges.[84] There are also roughly seventy-five thousand cruise missiles around the world for which ballistic missile–defense systems have no relevance. Despite this proliferation threat, disagreement exists over whether missile defenses are the best policy response—particularly given technological limitations. As Philip Coyle and Victoria Samson note, "Shooting down an enemy missile is like trying to hit a hole-in-one in golf when the hole is moving at 17,000 mph. . . . And if an enemy uses decoys and countermeasures, missile defense is like trying to hit a hole-in-one when the hole is moving at 17,000 mph and the green is covered with black circles the same size as the hole."[85] Some states worry that rather than providing purely defensive postures, missile defenses would make offensive military action more likely by states possessing them as such states would not be concerned about retaliation. Even limited systems could cause states to perceive this threat and thus build more offensive missiles to overcome these defenses. This could lead to costly arms races that might eventually include deployment of weapons in space and other expensive technologies. Finally, even if ballistic missile defenses were effectively deployed, these systems would not stop cruise missiles, which fly low and fast and can carry a nuclear payload, or terrorists with a weapon parked on a boat in a harbor.[86] A state might also detonate a nuclear weapon just above Earth's atmosphere. If North Korea were to detonate a fifty-kiloton nuclear warhead 120 kilometers over its own territory, within fifty days the number of commercial satellites surviving in low-Earth orbit would decline from about 450 to zero.[87] Consequently, some space security experts have advocated a middle position: the development of purely defensive capabilities for space deployments, perhaps guaranteed by an international treaty limiting space weapons deployments.

A missile-defense capability has a secondary application if these systems are also used to attack satellites orbiting Earth. Attacking satellites, which travel in well-known orbits that can be tracked from ground positions, would be considerably easier than intercepting incoming missiles. If, for example, a ground-based missile-defense interceptor were launched straight up, it could lift to an elevation of about six thousand kilometers and hit satellites in low-Earth orbit with little difficulty.[88] The nondevelopment of antisatellite weapons has been respected as an international norm since the Soviet Union abandoned work on their production in the 1980s. The Soviet systems, the plans and designs for which remain in Russian hands, involved launching a missile armed with conventional explosives into an orbit close to a target. When the warhead exploded, the debris would destroy any nearby satellite. The United States developed some nascent antisatellite programs in the 1980s and 1990s but has not deployed such capability. These included the Air-Launched Miniature Vehicle, ground-based kinetic energy, and Mid-Infrared Advanced Chemical Laser programs.[89] In February 2004, the U.S. Air Force released its Transformation Flight Plan, which identified antisatellite weapons and weapons that could strike Earth from space as areas for research and eventual deployment after 2015. In reality, as the Chinese and Americans have both shown in shooting down their own orbital satellites, the capacity already exists for this kind of space war. Other specific weapons systems under consideration by the air force are air-launched antisatellite missiles, ground-based laser, the Orbital Transfer Vehicle, space-based high-energy radio-frequency weapons, the Space Maneuver Vehicle, the Space Operations Vehicle, and hypervelocity rod bundles.[90] Once developed, antisatellite weaponry could potentially open a new arms-race era in space. It is hard to imagine some countries standing idly by while others advance the capacity to destroy their satellites and other space assets.

The Business of Security

Global military spending by 2010 totaled $1.5 trillion per year—an increase over the previous decade of 50 percent but actually a decline of 8 percent from the previous year. The United States accounted for the vast majority of global military spending and weapons sales. The United States outspends the next nineteen nations combined—almost all of them are allies—on military capabilities, accounting for 43 percent of all global defense spending. The total value of the global arms trade for 2009 was $57.5 billion. Developing nations accounted for $45.1 billion of all international arms deliveries. Russia was second in worldwide arms sales, with $10.4 billion, and France is third with $7.4 billion.[91] Such expenditures can be opportunity costs that weaken a society in other vital areas such as education, domestic infrastructure, or debt payment—thus undermining the economic foundations of security.

Supply, Demand, and the Networks of Trade

During the latter half of the twentieth century, there were some 160 wars globally in which 24.5 million people were killed—primarily through the use of conventional weapons.[92] The dangers posed by conventional weapons proliferation were illustrated for the United States in postinvasion Iraq. Though the United States invaded Iraq to rid it of weapons of mass destruction, the major threat to American forces came from conventional weapons. Most of the nearly forty-five hundred American troops killed by late 2010 had been killed by revolvers, rifles, pistols, rocket-propelled grenades, and improvised roadside bombs. By one estimate, Iraq had 3 million tons of bombs and bullets; millions of AK-47s, other rifles, rocket launchers, and mortar tubes; and thousands of more sophisticated arms, including ground-to-air missiles. As many as 8 million small arms might have fallen into citizens' hands, then either used by or sold to insurgents.[93]

Another danger of small arms proliferation includes man-portable air-defense systems (MANPADS), which pose a threat to military and civilian aircraft. These light, portable systems are hard to counter and can fire infrared-guided missiles that target a heat source, such as an airplane engine. There are estimated to be five hundred thousand shoulder-fired surface-to-air missiles of about thirty different types worldwide. An estimated six thousand are considered to be outside governmental control, including some four thousand that were unaccounted for following the U.S. invasion of Iraq in 2003. In illegal weapons markets, MANPADS have been known to sell for between $1,000 and $100,000 a piece.[94] By one estimate, MANPADS were responsible for four hundred casualties in twenty-seven incidents involving civil aircraft during the 1980s and 1990s. By 2010, MANPADS had been fired at civilian jets in over forty incidents. During the Soviet invasion and occupation of Afghanistan, some 2,698 Soviet aircraft were shot down; MANPADS accounted for 56 percent of these hits and 79 percent of aircraft damage. In November 2002, two rockets were launched at an Israeli passenger plane via MANPADS in Mombasa, Kenya.[95] A related proliferation concern is cruise missile technology. Some seventy-five thousand cruise missiles in arsenals around the world could be launched from private vessels, naval ships, or aircraft.

The supply-and-demand example of conventional weapons trade is but one example of the globalization of international transactions driving the world economy. This system relies heavily on a complex web of transnational networks that constitute the lifeblood of the global trading system. These networks include the flows of goods, services, and people, as well as the transportation nodes at which they all interconnect. Such networks can be identified by their physical characteristics, such as roads, pipelines, shipping lanes, and ports. They can also be thought of as less tangible identities, such as the flow of money, information, and ideas.[96] These networks can become a target for attack in a global security dynamic and are vulnerable to disruption by states or nonstate actors seeking advantage in a conflict. Trading networks can be disrupted through direct attacks on transportation nodes. For example, detonation of a nuclear weapon in the port of Los Angeles would dramatically disrupt America's imports and exports. More than 95 percent of America's non–North American foreign trade arrives by ship. At the turn of the century, some eight thousand ships were making more than fifty-one thousand U.S. port calls annually.[97] Alternatively, destruction of major geographical choke points for shipping—such as the South China Sea, the Panama Canal, or the Strait of Hormuz—could severely damage the flow of international goods and services.

The Internet also provides criminals or terrorists engaging within the networks of global trade new means of stealing, moving, or hiding financial resources. In February 2000, denial-of-service attacks on two major websites illustrated the potential to cripple the Internet industry. By securing access to a number of unprotected computers, hackers instructed them to send a massive number of e-mails to websites, which overloaded capacity and caused collapse. Yahoo! was shut down for five hours, causing a major disruption for its 8.7 million daily users and to its service as a portal to other Web pages and search engines. Buy.com was also attacked the same day and shut down for six hours. The next day, Amazon.com, then visited by 892,000 users per day, was shut down for nearly 4 hours; the CNN website, with 642,000 users daily, was shut down for 3.5 hours; and eBay, with 1.68 million users each day, was shut down for 5 hours. A day later, the E*Trade brokerage site, with 183,000 users each day, was closed for nearly three hours, and ZDNet, with 734,000 daily users, closed for over three hours. The financial costs of these attacks were estimated to run, at minimum, into the hundreds of millions of dollars.[98] In October 2000, a group of twenty people working with an inside contact created a digital clone of a Sicilian bank's online function. The group planned to use it to divert $400 million, then launder it through other financial institutions, including the Vatican Bank and banks in Switzerland and Portugal. This scheme only failed because one of the plotters informed the police.[99]

Transnational Networks and Organized Crime

The use of transnational networks for illicit activity, particularly organized crime, represents a new security challenge fomented by globalization. Such networks comprise communication channels and interconnected nodes, which can be individuals, organizations, firms, and computers connected in significant ways.[100] Networks can range in size from several to hundreds of individuals involved in anything from drug trafficking to money laundering to prostitution to weapons trading. A UN study concluded in 1999 that "from the perspective of organized crime in the 1990s, Al Capone was a small-time hoodlum with restricted horizons, limited ambitions and merely a local fiefdom."[101] The United Nations notes three classifications of transnational organized crime: (1) groups that can be specifically identified, (2) clusters of criminal groups that originate from specific geographic localities, and (3) the markets toward which transnational organized-crime groups gravitate and within which they operate.[102]

Transnational criminal networks can operate clandestinely or hide behind legitimate front groups. They are inherently dispersed and lack an identifiable physical infrastructure. Such groups are able to exploit differences in national laws and regulations and are highly resilient and redundant. If one part of the network is taken down, the remainder will stay in place. Transnational criminal networks tend to have a core, based on some form of kinship or close operational ties among a leadership group. This core is often located in weak states that serve as safe havens. The core group then tends to have peripheral affiliates that range from organizational leaders to couriers and transportation personnel. Such networks organize to gather information as an early warning against infiltration by law enforcement and might engage in collaboration with other networks while also exploiting corrupt officials within governments for operating means and information gathering. These networks can thus become virtual entities including organizers, insulators, communicators, guardians, extenders, monitors, and crossovers who are recruited from legal activity and maintain their official positions.[103]

Transnational organized crime is especially problematic as a conduit for the illegal weapons trade. For example, North Korean officials have openly boasted that they will sell fissile nuclear material and even weapons for the right price. North Korean intelligence agents have already been identified in international illegal drug trafficking and counterfeiting. Some North Korean ambassadors fund their embassies through black-market trading of missile technology and drugs.[104] Russia presents the most serious danger for the convergence of organized crime and proliferation. By the turn of the century, there were an estimated eight thousand criminal gangs in the former Soviet Union, two hundred of which had global ties.[105] Much of this organized crime emerged with the end of the Cold War, when the Soviet security apparatus, the KGB, was reduced in size. The downsizing of the KGB left a cadre of about one hundred thousand people with expertise in international clandestine activity, such as money laundering, looking for employment. There were at least eighteen known attempts of nuclear weapons trafficking from Russia in the decade following the Soviet collapse. Military trucks have been used by narcotics and weapons smugglers, including to transport short- and medium-ranged missiles, as they are not typically searched by Russian internal security forces.

Nuclear weapons technology presents a particular challenge created by the nexus of supply, demand, and transnational networks. There are some 22,400 strategic and tactical nuclear weapons in the world. By the turn of the century, stockpiles of separated plutonium were estimated to contain 470 tons of the material—enough for roughly one hundred thousand bombs. Stockpiles containing nearly sixteen hundred tons of highly enriched uranium could produce over 130,000 additional bombs. Aside from the nuclear states or suspected nuclear states, enough plutonium was available for civilian use to create more weapons in Belgium, Germany, Japan, and Switzerland; there were also about twenty tons of civilian highly enriched uranium at over 130 operational, and an unknown number of closed, civilian research facilities in more than thirty countries.[106] Russia alone had an estimated six hundred tons of weapons-grade separated plutonium and highly enriched uranium located in 252 buildings at fifty-three sites spread across eleven time zones.[107]

Most attempts at smuggling nuclear material from Russia have been relatively small-scale criminal efforts. The network of organized criminal activity has, however, moved closer to nuclear facilities. For example, at Russia's main storage facility for plutonium and highly enriched uranium, counterintelligence officers closed down an organized-crime ring supplying illegal drugs to security forces there. Russia and its surrounding former Soviet republics all have significant weaknesses in their customs and border patrols. Few border crossings have nuclear weapons detection equipment and even fewer have the personnel trained to use it.[108] The biggest problem from Russia has nevertheless been the illegal transfer of conventional weapons and equipment. By 2004, an estimated twenty-seven thousand firearms had been stolen from military units in Russia, and 53,900 crimes involving illegal trading in weapons were reported in 2001 alone.[109] According to the U.S. General Accounting Office, fifteen hundred Russian customs officers were fired in 1998 for corruption, and at one border crossing, personnel agreed to turn off radiation-detection equipment in exchange for alcohol.[110]

The A. Q. Khan Nuclear Shopping Center

Transnational networks facilitate the growing danger of a black market in nuclear weapons technology. In 2004, this risk was exposed in the form of the nuclear trading network of Pakistani scientist A. Q. Khan, the scientific pioneer of the Pakistani nuclear weapons program. Khan, who the Pakistani government says worked without its approval, developed, over several decades, a covert transnational network to profit from the sale of nuclear weapons technology and designs. The market focused on obtaining non-weapons-grade uranium, which can be purchased legally, and illicitly traded centrifuges. These centrifuges can process uranium into weapons-grade material by spinning away impurities and retaining U-235, which can then be used to create atomic reactions to detonate nuclear warheads. Uranium is widely available around the world, and efforts to keep it under control have not been successful. For example, the mining operation in Democratic Republic of the Congo that provided uranium for the atomic bombs dropped on Japan in 1945 has been closed. Yet, thousands of diggers continue every day to hack at open earth, filling thousands of burlap sacks with soil rich in cobalt, copper, and radioactive uranium. This activity provided $1 billion in business in 2002 for poverty-stricken Congo. Near the mine, businessmen from Africa, India, and China have set up smelting mills that then ship their products to Zambia and later overseas.[111]

A. Q. Khan's role illustrates the danger that, once attained, scientific knowledge of how to build nuclear weapons can be hard to contain. Khan gained expertise in nuclear design technology in the 1970s when he worked on centrifuge designs in the Netherlands. He returned to Pakistan, where it is believed he soon applied his knowledge, via stolen designs, to the Pakistani nuclear program. Khan became well known in Pakistan as a strong supporter of the global Islamic movement and a critic of the restrictive positions of the existing nuclear powers. Khan widely published information in scholarly papers about how to make centrifuges effective. In the 1990s, he began to advertise the sale of used equipment from his laboratory in Pakistan. Contacts between Pakistani nuclear experts and potential recipients began as early as 1987, when Pakistan transferred centrifuge design information to Iran, North Korea, and Libya. Khan apparently made at least thirteen personal trips to North Korea, which offered to send its missile technology to Pakistan in exchange for centrifuge designs and equipment.[112]

The Khan network was small and efficient and profited enormously from the transfer of nuclear weapons technology. It began to unravel when, in April 2003, a ship with a cargo of superstrong aluminum tubing was stopped in the Suez Canal by German authorities that had determined it was headed toward North Korea. The tubes were consistent with Khan's centrifuge designs. In October 2003, a German-registered ship bound for Libya was stopped by the United States, which discovered thousands of parts for uranium centrifuges linked to businesses in Turkey and Malaysia. This exposure, combined with diplomatic pressure on Libya, led the country soon thereafter to announce it was abandoning its nuclear weapons program. The International Atomic Energy Agency (IAEA) was granted access to Libya's programs and was thus able to explore how this nuclear weapons proliferation network operated.

The shipment to Libya had come from Dubai via a middleman working for Khan. This same agent had previously offered Iraq assistance on its nuclear program in 1990.[113] He offered to provide Iraq with nuclear bomb designs and uranium-enrichment equipment in exchange for $5 million. Iraq rejected the offer, believing it likely to be a scam.[114] The Khan network, working out of about a dozen different locations, was organized to trade components for uranium-enriching gas centrifuges. Libya acknowledged that it had purchased parts for at least four thousand advanced centrifuges. This would have allowed it to enrich enough uranium to make several nuclear bombs per year—though only a small portion of the necessary parts actually reached Libya. Libya also lacked rotors, rapidly spinning tubes needed for the core of a centrifuge.[115]

The Khan network consisted mostly of legitimate businesses spread across a variety of countries. Khan largely served as a salesman negotiating the parameters of a nuclear-technology deal and then promising delivery of parts in exchange for money. A variety of middlemen would then find suppliers for the necessary components, and finished parts were shipped to Dubai, where they were assembled. The suppliers included businesses in Malaysia, South Africa, Japan, the United Arab Emirates, and Germany. Components were produced independently and included a range of electronics, vacuum systems, and high-strength metals.[116] In Malaysia, Scomi Precision Engineering (a subsidiary of Scomi Group Berhad, a prominent and publicly traded conglomerate) manufactured components for export to Libya. They produced fourteen semifinished components, shipped in four deliveries to Libya between December 2002 and August 2003, in exchange for $3.4 million.[117] This business produced a total of 330 tons of quality aluminum purchased from a German firm in Singapore legally.[118]

Chartered flights were used to deliver the cargo organized by a network of middlemen that included three German businessmen and a Sri Lankan. The Sri Lankan associate, Buhary Syed Abu Tahir, told Malaysian police that Khan had asked him to send two shipping containers of used centrifuges to Iran from Dubai aboard a merchant vessel owned by an Iranian company. The Iranian individual receiving the shipment provided two briefcases with $3 million in cash, which was then stashed at a residence owned by Khan in Dubai. A British national living in France also helped obtain material for Libya via Spain and Italy. Tahir described the Khan organization as a "loose network without a rigid hierarchy or a head and a deputy head," with some Khan associates dating to the early 1970s.[119]

Khan, who pled guilty and was pardoned by Pakistan's former president Pervez Musharraf, insists that only old, second-rate technology of little actual use was transferred. In the case of Libya, however, nuclear weapon blueprints were included—for $50 million. This information would have allowed Libya to bypass a considerable number of steps in developing a self-run uranium-reprocessing program and given it explicit detail about how to assemble an implosion-type nuclear bomb to place atop a large ballistic missile. The blueprints were detailed down to the level of what torque to use on the bolts and what glue to use on the parts.[120] Some of these blueprints were well-engineered, but second-generation, documents originating from China.[121] Through the transfers, Khan earned millions of dollars and lived a lavish lifestyle beyond the means of a Pakistani government scientist.[122] Hundreds of millions of dollars were exchanged in this nuclear-technology network over a period of about fifteen years.[123]

The dangers of the network were illustrated by the high degree of legal activity integrated into an illicit trade. As a Malaysian police report on the network's activity concluded, "To untrained eyes, such components would not raise any concern as the components are similar to components that could be used by the 'petro-chemical industry' and 'water treatment' and various other industries."[124] When the IAEA received documents pertaining to its investigations in Libya, they were handed over in two white plastic shopping bags from a Pakistani clothing shop called Good Looks Tailor.[125]

Countries like Russia or networks like the Khan smuggling ring are not the only challenge regarding the proliferation of nuclear weapons technology. In 2004, government auditors in the United States disclosed that the United States had made insufficient effort to recover large quantities of weapons-grade uranium—in total enough to make about one thousand nuclear bombs. This material had been distributed to forty-three countries—including Iran and Pakistan—over several decades. This uranium was loaned, leased, or sold to countries beginning in the 1950s to help promote the peaceful use of nuclear energy. The intention was to recover the materials, but the effort to do so was lax. The audit estimated that the government had recovered only about 2,600 of 17,500 dispersed kilograms, leaving about 15,000 remaining overseas. The material is currently under the control of governments, universities, and private companies in twelve countries not expected to participate in programs to facilitate the material's return, including Iran, Pakistan, Israel, Mexico, Jamaica, and South Africa.[126]

Security Privatization

The expansion of transnational networks in security reflects an increasing trend toward the privatization of security. This particular trend poses significant challenges to the ability of nation-states to control the security agenda. Private companies have taken on the role historically played by mercenaries. Some states are ceding direct control over important security operations to the private sector.[127] These private contractors have played an especially important, and sometimes illegitimate, role in recent wars in Afghanistan and Iraq. Finally, private interest groups have also shaped agenda setting by focusing international attention on particular security problems that states might otherwise have ignored.

Private Security Companies

Private security firms are increasingly present in international conflict situations where states find it easier to outsource some security operations. Hiring private security companies can be less costly than training large numbers of troops. Moreover, as contractors exist outside the control of nation-states, they lack the accountability that military or intelligence personnel might have. Private contractors might thus do things that states could not get away with. Private contractors can, alternatively, venture into war zones where states might not be willing to go, providing security protection for humanitarian aid groups and political leaders seeking to consolidate peace but who are at risk.[128]

Contracting to private logistics firms might also save governments money or allow them to assign more pressing tasks to formal soldiers.[129]

American companies have taken the lead in assuming private military functions. Military Professional Resources Inc. employed seventeen retired U.S. generals and sent 182 former Special Forces personnel to train and equip Bosnian military forces in the 1990s. This operation was supplied with $100 million worth of surplus American military equipment. The Vinnell Corporation, a subsidiary of the large military manufacturer Northrop Grumman, has trained the Saudi National Guard and received a $48 million contract to train the Iraqi military. Executive Outcomes, which eventually went out of business, sent six hundred soldiers to Angola and three hundred to Sierra Leone to combat insurgency movements that local governments were unable to manage. Executive Outcomes included its own air force with Mi-8, Mi-17, and Mi-24 helicopters and MiG-23 fighters. This group was central to outcomes in a number of African conflicts during the 1990s. Comprising primarily former South African military officials, Executive Outcomes had a permanent staff of only thirty people but could deploy a fully supported battalion of 650 fighters within fifteen days. Between 1993 and 1998, the number of private security companies operating in Angola alone grew from six to eighty.[130]

By 2008, the United States had spent about $100 billion on private contractors to complement and support military operations in Iraq and employing about 180,000 people. Though increased considerably under President George W. Bush, reliance on such contractors was also sustained by the Obama administration, especially in Afghanistan. The best known of such contractors, Halliburton, provides a range of logistical support for military operations, including security operations for the oil industry; it had $5 billion in contracts in Iraq by 2004 and employed forty thousand people there by 2008. The Halliburton subsidiary Kellogg, Brown & Root was a major logistics component in U.S. operations in Somalia in the early 1990s. This company became the number one employer in Somalia by 1993 with twenty-five hundred locals on its payroll. By September 2003, Kellogg, Brown & Root had billed, over two years, about $950 million for work done under contracts in Iraq, which are capped at $8.2 billion. Kellogg, Brown & Root was also set to earn additional income from contracts to maintain U.S. bases ranging from the Balkans to the Horn of Africa and stretching east to Afghanistan and Kyrgyzstan. It also built the U.S. detention facility for captured terrorists in Guantánamo, Cuba. A number of specific operating systems are heavily dependent on contracting for their operations, including the American F-117 stealth fighter, M1A1 tank, Patriot missile, and Global Hawk unmanned drone aircraft.[131]

Other companies in Iraq included DynCorp, which was given a $50 million contract for law-enforcement support, police training, and prison-guard duty. DynCorp also won a lucrative contract to provide security for the leading government figures in Afghanistan. Custer Battles (which by 2010 had gone out of business) received a $16 million contract to provide security at the Baghdad airport, and the British firm Erinys received $39 million to protect Iraqi oil fields.[132] In Colombia, six different companies have received a share of $1.2 billion annually from the United States to fly planes that spray coca fields and monitor smuggling with radar. British firms also account for a large number of private security companies, such as Global Risk International, which provided Nepalese Gurkhas, Fijian paramilitaries, and former British Special Air Service veterans to guard the American headquarters in Iraq.

The increasing role played by private security companies in military operations raises questions about the ability of states to control and protect personnel who act in the states' interest but are not subject to oversight or even direct legal liability. For example, if a soldier wearing a uniform were to commit a crime in a foreign land, he would be the legal responsibility of his command authority—the military under which he served. If, however, a private security employee commits a crime, even while employed by another country, he is subject to the local laws of the state he is in. Because many of the places where such private security forces operate are, in effect, failed states with no local legal apparatus, these individuals often operate outside the rule of law.[133] In one case, a number of American contract employees in Bosnia-Herzegovina were implicated in criminal activity including rape and operating a sex-slave racket involving trade in girls as young as twelve years old. Several of these contractors were fired from their jobs, but none were prosecuted. The only court case involved the whistle-blowers, who were fired for publicizing the illegal activity.[134] Military command-and-control questions arise: Should contractors carry weapons? If they abandon their work, are they deserters? Do they get rights as prisoners of war if they are captured? Do they have to obey the laws of war if they are doing guard duty at a prison?

Outsourcing War

In the postinvasion peace-support operations in Iraq, private security companies were assigned significant roles in the U.S.-led military occupation. Numerically, private contractors were the second-largest coalition member—with about twenty thousand working in Iraq. By spring 2004, assignments for private security companies in Iraq included guarding reconstruction projects, providing security for senior American officials, escorting supply convoys through hostile territory, and defending key locations, including fifteen regional authority headquarters and the primary American base in central Baghdad. These private security companies cost about 25 percent of

$18 billion authorized for reconstruction in Iraq by the U.S. government in 2004—significantly more than an initial estimate that contractors would account for only 10 percent of spending.[135] As much as 30 percent of primary military support services were being supplied by private contractors in the Iraq mission by 2003. Included in this mix were eleven work orders valued at $66.2 million awarded to CACI International Inc., which provided interrogation support and analysis work for the U.S. Army. These contractors were assigned tasks including debriefing of personnel, intelligence report writing, and screening and interrogation of detainees at established holding areas. Interrogators were assigned to coordinate and work in conjunction with military police and military intelligence interrogation units. Due to a lack of trained interrogators, the U.S. Army contracted this task—only to find that few of the CACI personnel had any formal training in military interrogation policies and techniques.[136] CACI had hired some of these contractors after five-minute phone interviews with no resume, fingerprinting, or criminal-background checks.[137]

Using private contractors for intelligence activities carried a high risk as private contractors could be working for other governments. These individuals' loyalty, accountability, and professional training could not be as certain as in the formal military command structure. In a December 2000 internal memo, the U.S. assistant secretary of the army instructed the deputy chief of staff for intelligence that contractors' involvement in intelligence should be restricted. The memo noted that "private contractors may be acquired by foreign interests, acquire and maintain interests in foreign countries, and provide support to foreign customers," and "reliance on private contractors poses risks to maintaining adequate civilian oversight over intelligence operations."[138] Yet, no subsequent formal effort was made to place such restrictions in the U.S. military field manuals governing the activity of private contractors. In fact, the Pentagon hired a private contractor, Military Professional Resources Inc., to write the rules for contractors in the field.

Private contractors in Iraq participated in human rights abuses at the Abu Ghraib prison. In summer 2004, it became known that American personnel had used torture and psychological tactics to humiliate Iraqi prisoners of war. While a number of U.S. military personnel were tried for their involvement in these activities, none of the contractors present had violated the Geneva Conventions regarding prisoners of war. CACI International provided more than half of all the analysts and interrogators at Abu Ghraib, and all the translators there were employees of Titan Corporation. Contractors were actually supervising military officers.[139] The only investigation of abuse by contractors was carried out by CACI itself. Even before that investigation was complete, the U.S. government had extended an additional $23 million contract to

CACI. Another company, Erinys, discovered that four of its guards killed while working in Iraq were former members of governmental security forces of apartheid-era South Africa. One of these employees had admitted to crimes in an amnesty application to the Truth and Reconciliation Commission there.[140] In 2007, contractors from the company Blackwater were found to have killed seventeen civilian Iraqis. However, murder charges were dismissed in an American court. In Afghanistan, three Americans were sentenced to extended prison sentences for running a private prison and torturing Afghan detainees. The leader of the group, Jonathan Idema, a former member of the U.S. Army Special Forces, presented a defense that showed video of him being greeted by high-level Afghan officials and meeting with a U.S. Army officer. Idema asserted that all of their operations had been approved by either corps commanders or regional governors. However, the Afghan court concluded that there had been no authorization for these men's activity.[141] As the United States began its withdrawal of combat forces from Iraq in summer 2010, it ironically became even more reliant on military contractors in the country. Likewise, as it surged concurrently into Afghanistan, so did the contractors. Interestingly, Barack Obama had kept his campaign promise to end combat operations in Iraq and to focus on Afghanistan; at the same time, he had violated his promise to end the heavy emphasis on private contractors in American military operations.

The New Agenda Setters

An additional, expanding private component of twenty-first-century security is the role played by international nongovernmental organizations. Activist movements and independent research institutes generate transparency about the activity of states and their military-security activities. This work complicates the ability of states to act but also provides citizens with information based on which to judge their governments. Issues such as human rights and the environment owe their place on the global security agenda to the efforts of nongovernmental activist movements such as Amnesty International, Human Rights Watch, Freedom House, the Rainforest Action Network, and the Worldwatch Institute. In the early 1990s, a hunger strike by American activist Randall Robinson focused the attention of the U.S. government on Haiti—the kind of place that a great power would have previously ignored. The Nobel Peace Prize was awarded in 1997 to Jody Williams, who worked to coordinate the International Campaign to Ban Landmines. This effort resulted in a global treaty banning the production and use of these weapons, which kill indiscriminately. Meanwhile, websites offer, for private use, satellite imagery and information on a wide array of technologies, tactics, and strategies that once were the classified domain of nation-states. Indeed, there is little information about international security that cannot be found via a good Internet search engine. Efforts by governments to maintain secrecy are thus also fundamentally challenged by the growing pressure for transparency.

Sanctioning Security

The use of sanctions to enforce international standards or to project state power heightens the relationship between security and trade. International economic sanctions entail the stoppage of any trade or financial relationship between two or more international actors, typically with one state or international organization targeted by another state or group of states. Sanctions are a popular tool for exercising power because they help to send a serious political message without resort to force. International sanctions have been seen as a legitimate tool of modern diplomacy since they were enshrined in the Covenant of the League of Nations and used by the United Nations as instruments of collective action among states. States have applied multinational or bilateral sanctions to promote or compel change in international behavior. With the end of the Cold War, sanctions became a popular tool of the United States, which had imposed over sixty different sanctions on countries by the turn of the century.[142] The United Nations had also imposed economic sanctions on Iraq, Libya, the Balkans, and North Korea, as well as on Iran over its nuclear program on four separate occasions by 2010. Opinions about whether sanctions on Iran would work depended on one's assessment of that country. No doubt these sanctions caused pain there—but this might not matter if the nation was driven solely by Islamic ideology. Sanctions might work in a rational country making policy based on cost-benefit determinations.

The Sanctions Dilemma

Despite the increasing use of sanctions as a policy tool, there is considerable disagreement about their utility. The question as to whether sanctions work depends largely on what states seek to accomplish. Evidence suggests that sanctions have been the least successful at promoting the fall of governments or the overthrow of dictators. There has also been minimal success at getting governments to change policies perceived as fundamental to their interests. However, sanctions might play a more positive role in achieving policy change with regard to positions that states are not fundamentally committed to. Sanctions have been shown to help weaken governments' ability to carry out aggressive plans by denying key resources.[143] They are also thought to have had a number of unintended consequences and thus are increasingly controversial.[144] For example, sanctions are often thought to hurt those people whom they are intended to help—for instance, a dictatorship being denied goods and services is likely to pass on the pain of sanctions to the general population rather than allowing those who hold power to suffer. Sanctions can also hurt the interests of the state imposing them if they are not universal. Those who are most negatively damaged in that circumstance are producers inside the sanctioning country who lose access to markets. By the turn of the century, the United States was estimated to be losing about $20 billion per year in export profits due to sanctions. This, at the time, cost American workers about two hundred thousand well-paying jobs.[145] Sanctions can also deny states the tools of diplomatic engagement and economic leveraging to work with countries to change particular policies.

According to a survey conducted by the Institute for International Economics, international sanctions have been most effective when the goals are relatively modest, the target country is much weaker than those imposing the sanctions, a significant amount of trade is cut off, the sanctions are sustained for a long time, force is used to implement them, and they are multilateral. The institute surveyed 116 cases of international sanctions and found them to be effective about 33 percent of the time.[146] The direct correlation between sanctions and increased security is thus limited. The best-known case is South Africa, on which the United Nations imposed a comprehensive sanctions regime in the 1980s for its official apartheid policy segregating whites and blacks. Sanctions worked, largely because they were universal and those who suffered under them—the black majority in the country—were willing to bear the cost as a path to long-term change.

In numerous cases, well-intended sanctions have led to significant decreases in security. In 1991, the United Nations imposed sanctions on the Balkans via an embargo on the sale of weapons into the region. The problem, however, was that one side in the conflict, the Serbs in Yugoslavia and their brethren in Bosnia-Herzegovina, had inherited weapons and associated equipment after the collapse of the Yugoslav national army. This left the Croatians and Muslims, who had seceded from Yugoslavia in search of independence, largely undefended. By 1993, the United Nations had sent twenty-five thousand peacekeepers, mainly British and French, into the region to uphold cease-fire agreements. Once these troops were on the ground, the countries contributing them became deeply opposed to lifting the arms embargo because they feared that their forces would be caught in a spiraling cross fire of ethnic payback. Once in place, the arms embargo could not be lifted without British and French approval in the UN Security Council. These same countries had also recognized the legal independence of Slovenia,

Croatia, and Bosnia-Herzegovina, which were granted statehood but denied the most important component of legal sovereignty: the right to self-defense. The end result was an ethnic slaughter in which over two hundred thousand were killed or went missing.

The case of Iraq in 1990 illustrates both the potential benefits and the dangers of using trade sanctions as a security tool. The UN Security Council levied severe economic sanctions on Iraq following its invasion of Kuwait. Only food and humanitarian goods were permitted to flow into the country. The sanctions, it was agreed at the United Nations, could not be lifted until the Security Council had determined through intrusive weapons inspections that Iraq had met a number of postwar requirements, including complete elimination of weapons of mass destruction programs. However, the primary victims of these sanctions were the citizens of Iraq, not the leadership. According to UN estimates, while Saddam Hussein lived comfortably in his palaces, the sanctions contributed to the deaths of over 576,000 children, and Iraq's infant-mortality rate doubled during the 1990s.[147] By 1998, it appeared that the sanctions simply were not working. The Iraqi government told UN weapons inspectors it had complied with their mandates and then kicked them out. The period between 1998 and 2003 led to a growing sense of insecurity, particularly in the United States, that Iraq had reconstituted its weapons of mass destruction program. Only after the United States invaded and overthrew Hussein's government did it become clear that, regarding weapons of mass destruction, the sanctions had actually worked—there were no such weapons in Iraq, and the country's conventional military power was dilapidated. As one senior Iraqi scientist put it after the war, the material conditions for developing weapons of mass destruction were considerably worse than when the programs had been in full development in the 1980s. Abdul Noor, a major developer of Iraq's earlier nuclear program, said, "We would have had to start from less than zero. . . . The country was cornered. We were boycotted. We were embargoed. The truth is, we disintegrated."[148]

Are Sanctions Better Than Nothing?

The use of sanctions as a tool to leverage trade for security illustrates a moral dilemma. The United States, for example, imposed harsh sanctions on Myanmar to punish its military for denying basic human rights to its people. Yet, the denial of trade contributed to the loss of employment for some one hundred thousand Burmese people while the military dictators remained in power. This economic dislocation occurred in a country where one child in ten dies before age five, 44 percent of children are malnourished, and 58 percent of pregnant women do not receive adequate medical care. Many of the women rendered jobless as a result of U.S. sanctions had little choice but to earn their living in the sex industry, thereby risking exposure to and proliferation of HIV/AIDS.[149] Yet, even in such a circumstance, alternative policies such as doing nothing or using military power are unpalatable.[150] The case of Iraq also suggests that, while morally abhorrent with regard to their effects on the Iraqi people, the sanctions did accomplish their purpose of forcing the disarmament of Iraq. In the case of India and Pakistan, the world community could not agree on effective sanctions regarding either potential nuclear development or nuclear testing. After India and Pakistan tested nuclear weapons in 1998, the immediate international response was a call to apply sanctions. Yet, this raised a major strategic question: What gain was there in sanctioning India and Pakistan when they already had the weapons? They were not going to roll back their weapons programs. Harsh international sanctions would only serve to make already poor and potentially unstable countries even poorer and more unstable—only they would then be armed with nuclear weapons and isolated from the international community. Indeed, Pakistan emerged as a vital ally in the U.S.-led war on terrorism beginning in 2001 and became a major recipient of foreign economic assistance. Notably, the threat of sanctions did nothing to deter either country from pursuing nuclear weapons technology or to persuade them to give up their weapons.

Summary

This chapter illustrates ongoing transformations in the nature of technology and the business of global security. The intersection between the evolving network of ties between the civilian and security trading worlds is illustrated by the challenges of commerce mixing with transnational organized crime and nuclear proliferation. The particular power dynamics of the supply-and-demand equation are illustrated both by the demands for proliferation and also by the growing privatization of security operations. Finally, the relationship between trade—or the stoppage of trade via sanctions—and security outcomes shows that actions states take to exert their power in this integrated network of transnational information and commerce can have unintended consequences. These examples of new dimensions of security show that an encroaching nexus between the civilian and military worlds blurs the two and creates a host of new targets for anyone engaged in conflict—as well as new opportunities for peace.

Suggested Reading

Allison, Graham. *Nuclear Terrorism: The Ultimate Preventable Catastrophe.* New York: Times Books, 2004.

Arquilla, John, and David F. Ronfeldt, eds. *Networks and Netwars: The Future of Terror, Crime, and Militancy.* Santa Monica, CA: RAND Corporation, 2001.

Gansler, Jacques S., and Hans Binnendijk, eds. *Information Assurance: Trends in Vulnerabilities, Threats, and Technologies.* Washington, DC: National Defense University Press, 2005.

Hitchens, Theresa. *Future Security in Space: Charting a Cooperative Course.* Washington, DC: Center for Defense Information, 2004.

Hufbauer, Gary Clyde. *Economic Sanctions Reconsidered.* Washington, DC: Peterson International Institute for Economics, 2005.

Hundley, Richard O. *Past Revolutions, Future Transformations: What Can the History of Revolutions in Military Affairs Tell Us about Transforming the U.S. Military?* Santa Monica, CA: RAND Corporation, 1999.

Libicki, Martin. *Cyberdeterrence and Cyberwar.* Santa Monica: RAND Corporation, 2009.

Nolan, Janne, Bernard I. Finel, and Brian D. Finlay, eds. *Ultimate Security: Combating Weapons of Mass Destruction.* New York: Century Foundation, 2004.

Singer, P. W. *Corporate Warriors: The Rise of the Privatized Military Industry.* Ithaca, NY: Cornell University Press, 2004.

———. *Wired for War: The Robotics Revolution and Conflict in the 21st Century.* New York: Penguin, 2009.

7

Asymmetric Conflict

THE DIFFUSION OF GLOBAL POWER provides new avenues for states, substate groups, terrorists, and individuals to shape global security. Conventional military conflict may no longer be the most useful way to win wars, and it could even be a liability if not used with precision. This chapter examines the dynamics of asymmetric power as applied in the cases of genocide, ethnic cleansing, terrorism, and insurgency movements. It shows that responding to asymmetric threats creates new security demands involving military intervention and preemptive war, homeland defense, and peacekeeping and peace-support operations. In a world where asymmetries in conflict are increasing, the effort to increase security can paradoxically create more insecurity. When the likelihood of asymmetric threats is high, the quest for power and the search for peace can become increasingly complicated, for as security in one area is accomplished, entirely new threats can emerge.

Strategy and Tactics of Asymmetric Conflict

Asymmetric threats are best understood as stemming from a relationship between strategy and tactics conducted outside accepted international norms, often by nonstate actors. Asymmetric tactics are employed to strengthen a weak actor in its pursuit of broader goals. The refusal to play by the rules is not new and can be an effective means of leveling a major imbalance of power. The story of the Trojan horse shows what can happen when an enemy uses tactics that enhance surprise. American Revolutionary minutemen hid

The Taj Hotel is engulfed in smoke during a gun battle resulting from a major terrorist attack in Mumbai, India, on November 29, 2008. Source: Reuters/Arko Datta.

in forests and attacked in a way that flummoxed the British. Mohandas K. Gandhi fought an asymmetric battle against the British by engaging them not with weapons but with nonviolent action. Some asymmetric acts use barbaric behavior to shock a society—consider the Rwandan genocide or the 2001 al Qaeda attacks on the United States. In 2009, the United States engaged in a major initiative to defeat the Taliban insurgency in southern Afghanistan, which had resurfaced as a substantial threat to regional stability. But whether the United States—or anyone else—had the capacity to "win" against this kind of insurgency was unclear. Asymmetric conflict is a tactic in the exercise of power, and the proliferating networks of globalization make its use both more likely and more dangerous.

Asymmetric warfare involves the application in conflict of tactics that are outside the norms of accepted rules of combat and designed to weaken an enemy's resolve or ability to fight. When asymmetric warfare is implemented, traditional defensive barriers such as military power and deterrence may decline in value. Asymmetric attacks might take advantage of an opponent's unwillingness or inability to adapt to asymmetric challenges due to self-imposed restraint. The use of asymmetric warfare is driven by the perception of relative power available to a combatant as well, possibly, as by expectations about what an attacked country or group of people will tolerate when confronted with the choice to fight or capitulate. An attacking group or country might, for example, employ barbaric tactics that violate the laws of war to achieve a particular objective. Examples of offensive asymmetric tactics include the murder of noncombatants, the use of concentration camps, and purposeful bombing of nonmilitary targets. Defensive strategies can also apply asymmetric tactics, such as guerrilla insurgency, that seek to impose costs on an adversary without marshaling a massive military force. Such offensive or defensive approaches are not designed to bring about an enemy's conventional military defeat but rather to target the hearts and minds of its people and to destroy their will to fight.[1]

Those who use asymmetric warfare are often engaged in what they see as a heroic, life-and-death struggle to defend not only themselves but a larger worldview. Nationalism and religion can, for example, help those who use barbaric tactics convince themselves that their efforts are just. Extreme forms can include terrorism; hostage taking; biological, chemical, and radiological warfare; deliberate large-scale attacks on civilians; indiscriminate targeting; hiding military or paramilitary forces near schools or churches; false representation; cyberwarfare or infrastructure attacks; and deliberate environmental destruction.[2] Every conflict situation has some degree of asymmetry; symmetry in the balance of power is rare and, in fact, more likely to produce stability than conflict due to mutual deterrence. Thus, asymmetric conflict is best understood in both general and operational terms.[3]

Asymmetric tactics are often conducted against states with self-imposed constraints on their own concepts of morality and war fighting. Terrorists or insurgents might have no reservations about killing large numbers of innocent civilians, whereas modern states often operate under legal, public, and ethical constraints that prevent them from responding in kind. Nevertheless, states also can use asymmetric tactics to attain general objectives, such as using technological advantages that an enemy does not possess. Asymmetric tactics can thus be force multipliers in the exercise of state power. The major asymmetric challenges of the twenty-first century often combine military objectives with attacks on civilian society in a combustible and deadly mix of tactics and proliferating targets.[4] There can be direct targets such as attacks on large civilian populations via nonmilitary techniques ranging from ethnic cleansing to the use of rape and torture to psychologically terrorize a population into some form of concession or capitulation. In the extreme, genocide has been used to destroy entire populations. Rather than fighting against large armies, a country or group can draw an enemy into urban conflict where the benefits of heavy armor, artillery, airpower, and technology are substantially reduced. In such settings, those fighting with asymmetric insurgency tactics have an advantage as they know and have mobility within the terrain. Asymmetric tactics also include using the visual consequences of asymmetric attacks to impact a target audience. News media, the Internet, and other forms of mass communication can help movements draw attention to their causes. In this sense, asymmetric attacks might be limited in their physical effects, but various media dramatically multiply the intended political impact of asymmetric attacks—often on a global level.

Understanding the dynamic between strategy and tactics is essential to engaging in asymmetric conflict because wars are not won by overcoming an enemy's tactics. Wars are won with winning strategies. For example, American troops won the 1993 Battle of Mogadishu in Somalia, killing scores of Somali fighters. However, battlefield victory turned into strategic retreat for the United States when scenes of dead American soldiers being dragged through the streets were broadcast on worldwide television. Creating scenes of chaos and fear in the streets for a television audience was the tactic; forcing an American withdrawal was the strategic goal. Destroying the World Trade Center in September 2001 was an asymmetric tactic by al Qaeda to accomplish the likely strategic objective of mobilizing Muslims against the West and prompting internal regime change in Saudi Arabia and Pakistan.[5]

Asymmetric warfare tools might be employed at the periphery of a conflict with the intent of striking at the center of gravity of an enemy's political will.[6] Generally, the goal is to affect an enemy's willingness to fight or to effect some other change in policy or behavior. The will to fight can also have an operational component that drives asymmetric tactics. Those who are desperate or face overwhelming weaknesses might be more willing to accept huge losses in conflict and to pursue dramatic and escalating forms of violence. Certain virtues can enhance asymmetric strategies and tactics. For example, the will to fight on against overwhelming odds can often be stronger than a state's willingness to bear the human and financial costs of certain policies. Patience is a particular advantage—and an area in which religious groups employing asymmetric strategies and tactics have an advantage. If one side in a conflict expects quick and easy outcomes, it might be defeated by an adversary prepared to fight for years, if not decades.[7]

Organizational functions can also provide asymmetric dilemmas. The North Atlantic Treaty Organization (NATO) took over responsibility for operations in Afghanistan in 2005, but as an institution, it had no experience with counterinsurgency and a minimal willingness to engage in combat. Most NATO allies that contributed forces sent too few, and many put major restrictions, or caveats, on what their members could do. Only the United States, Britain, the Netherlands, and Canada supplied combat forces. As a result, by 2009, the situation in Afghanistan had gotten so bad that the United States felt compelled to adopt an entirely new approach and send in an additional thirty thousand troops. While in 2010 NATO set a goal of ending combat operations in Afghanistan by 2014, this was more an expression of hope than real policy as the insurgency there showed little sign of breaking, while NATO remained divided on the war—a fact the enemy was able to exploit. Beyond groups like the Taliban, some states also might support asymmetric tactics to achieve objectives without directly engaging in conflict themselves.[8] Iran and Syria, for example, have each provided third-party support for anti-Israeli terrorist networks. Indeed, one of the major problems in Afghanistan was that the Taliban's main areas of support were inside Pakistan. In March 2011, NATO then assumed command and control for a no-fly zone over Libya, naval action, and protecting civilians as part of a handoff from an initial American-led air campaign to halt a slaughter of rebel forces by the government. Realistically, even in NATO, the asymmetries of power suggested that the operation remained largely underpinned by American, not allied, capabilities, and as the operation ran into serious problems, it was more likely to become an American responsibility.

Combating asymmetric challenges requires using unconventional frameworks for conceptualizing security challenges. Linear thinking can risk perpetuating dangerous outcomes and even exacerbate an asymmetric threat. In particular, overly militarized responses to asymmetric threats can provide short-term tactical gains but cause long-term problems. For example, Russia responded to Chechen demands for independence with a massive and punishing military campaign. However, this did nothing to sway the aspirations of Chechen rebel fighters. In one instance, after Moscow intervened with military force in Chechnya in 1994, a Russian tank became separated from its main unit. When the driver stopped to ask a group of civilians where he might buy some cigarettes, they shot and killed him.[9] Ten years later, some two hundred thousand Chechens were dead, and Russian citizens were dying in a barrage of Chechen-backed terrorist attacks around Russia, including at a school in Beslan, North Ossetia, where 334 hostages, including 186 children, were killed. Heavy reliance on conventional military power in a world of proliferating asymmetric opportunities can be self-defeating. Fighting a war against a tactic, rather than developing a clear plan to defeat a strategy, can play into the hands of the enemy.[10]

Genocide and Ethnic Cleansing

Barbaric actions, such as genocide and ethnic cleansing, exist far outside norms of acceptable international behavior and can have horrifying consequences. Genocide is the purposeful targeting for murder of a particular group of people based on a shared political, ethnic, national, or religious identity. Ethnic cleansing is the purposeful movement, by means of threatened or actual force, of a population from a particular territory. The Holocaust of World War II, in which 6 million Jews as well as gypsies and other minorities were killed in Nazi death camps, led the international community to define such actions as crimes against humanity. Nevertheless, genocide and ethnic cleansing remain major tactics in modern asymmetric warfare. They are asymmetric because they include the purposeful use of military force or other forms of violence mainly against unarmed civilian populations.

Nationalism oriented around ethnic or religious traditions has been a common factor behind genocide or ethnic cleansing. Nationalism sees the most important source of conflict as identification with a particular group—either ethnic or religious or both. Nationalism arises as a historical phenomenon when a group of people acquires a certain territory that has symbolic value as a "homeland" and wants to defend that land against external threats. Religion can play an important, though not always essential, part in heightening a sense of difference between groups desiring to control territory. Over time, a mythology of victimization and superiority can emerge within a group, leading to overt tension or even conflict with outsiders. Modern communication can facilitate and accelerate the expression of such ideas surrounding identity, culture, and religion. Nationalism is not necessarily a negative phenomenon; it can be a crucial means of establishing a cultural identity. The modern international system, indeed, owes much of its existence to the organizing role that nationalism plays in identification with nation-states. Nationalism as a sub-state or transnational phenomenon, however, can erode state authority and even contribute to state collapse. Close proximity among ethnic and religious groups can heighten an emotional sense of threat or victimization, leading in turn to independence movements, transborder disputes, and even dramatic acts of genocide and ethnic cleaning.[11]

The use of either genocide or ethnic cleansing as a tactic in warfare becomes particularly likely in the absence of a clear distinction between offensive or defensive military capabilities among parties to a conflict. When there are multiple identities and weak states, activists or political leaders can use heightened fear of the future to mobilize members of a group to defend against a perceived threat. Such actions can then create similar fears in other groups.[12] One group that feels threatened by another has an incentive to strike first and decisively; therefore, the second group also has an incentive to strike first.[13] A side choosing to use offensive action will have an incentive to use any power advantages—be it via shock tactics leading to capitulation, ethnic or religious relocation, or genocide—to eliminate the threat posed by its opponent. The resulting model of conflict spirals toward use of severe tactics that can be both massive and intractable in their consequences.[14] A weaker side will have equal incentive to inflict pain and psychological trauma on a more powerful enemy to reduce its will to fight. As they engage in barbaric tactics, both sides will likely feel victimized, and their positions can harden into immutable worldviews that only total annihilation of the enemy will satisfy.

The Balkans

A decade of ethnic-nationalist conflict in the Balkans illustrates the severe dangers inherent in some forms of nationalism that apply asymmetric tools to achieve political outcomes. In 1991, Slovenia and Croatia withdrew from the constitutional architecture of Yugoslavia. These former Yugoslav republics used democratic processes to determine their own statehood, though Croatia had a sizeable Serb minority population. Meanwhile, Serb politicians had, since the mid-1980s, increasingly used nationalism as a rationale for their ongoing control of the remaining Yugoslav government. The Serbs responded to these moves toward separatism with a short war in Slovenia and a more extended conflict in Croatia. Croatia reacted by displacing several hundred thousand ethnic Serbs in its territory. Another former Yugoslav republic, Bosnia-Herzegovina, was roughly divided between three major ethnic groups: 43 percent Muslim, 32 percent Serb, and 17 percent Croatian. By summer 1993, Serb forces in Bosnia, aided by Serbs in Yugoslavia, began a major campaign against the largely defenseless Bosnian Muslims. Serb forces ethnically cleansed entire regions of the country, organized death camps, used rape as a tool of warfare, and regularly shelled civilians in major cities. Serb authorities have admitted to committing Europe's worst atrocity since World War II: the killing of seven thousand Muslims in the city of Srebrenica in 1995.

Eventually, a Croat-Muslim alliance beat back Serb forces in Bosnia, which created a new balance of power on the ground and facilitated peace negotiations in 1995. Once the war ended, the depth of the damage in Bosnia became clear. Entire cities had been cleansed of males of fighting age. An estimated 6 million landmines needed to be cleared. The impact on the country's infrastructure was dramatic, with some 80 percent of power generators damaged or out of operation, 40 percent of bridges destroyed, and no national telecommunications system; 30 percent of health-care facilities, 50 percent of schools, and 60 percent of housing had been destroyed or seriously damaged. Average citizens were surviving on a per capita income of $500 per year, and 80 percent of the population was dependent upon external humanitarian assistance. An estimated 2 million people were displaced from their homes within Bosnia-Herzegovina, and another 1 million had fled as refugees. In addition to the over two hundred thousand estimated dead, there were also two hundred thousand wounded, of which 25 percent were children.[15] The entire population—Muslim, Croat, and Serb—suffered severe psychological trauma from the warfare and destruction, which will take generations to heal.

The Balkan story did not end, however, after the negotiated cease-fire in Bosnia. In 1987, Serb nationalist leader Slobodan Milošević had visited a site in the region of Kosovo inside Serbia, a province in what remained of Yugoslavia, with a 90 percent ethnic Albanian population living under Serb rule. Milošević delivered an impassioned speech that stirred the historic memories of Serb nationalism, a tool he exploited to establish his political power in Yugoslavia. During the 1990s, the Kosovo situation simmered as Serb authorities usurped local Albanian rights. In response, a violent Albanian independence movement grew: the Kosovo Liberation Army (KLA). Targeting Serb military and civilians, the KLA hoped to raise the costs of Serb control and provoke international intervention on their behalf. By spring 1998, the KLA had prompted a growing Serb backlash. The Serbs relied primarily on paramilitary forces to frighten Kosovar Albanians into giving up their claims to independence—culminating in a gruesome attack on Albanian civilians in January 1999 in which about two dozen were killed in a grotesque fashion. The Serb forces hoped to deter a NATO intervention to stop human rights abuses by suggesting that, if NATO attacked, Serbs would ethnically cleanse the entire province. When NATO did go to war, the Serbs forcefully expelled some eight hundred thousand Albanians from Kosovo into neighboring Albania and Macedonia. By 2008, Kosovo had declared its independence—which was of course widely celebrated there but generated concerns among states like Russia and China that also had potential breakaway regions.

Rwanda

The Balkan story unfolded somewhat less tragically than it might have because it took place in the backyard of modern Europe. The conflict simply could not escape the attention of the United States and its European allies. This condition stood in contrast to the completely unchecked genocide in Rwanda that occurred at the same time. In this case, the world stood by while an estimated eight hundred thousand people died in barbaric ethnic and tribal warfare. The conflict in Rwanda culminated years of power struggles between the Hutus and the Tutsis—the dominant tribal groups in the country. By 1990, these struggles took the form of a movement by Rwandan Tutsi refugees (who had been trained by and fighting for Uganda) who invaded Rwanda in October 1990. As these rebels were combated, prominent Tutsis were arrested, and the Hutu government looked away while private militias carried out escalating harassment, in some cases massacring Tutsis. A near-term settlement was negotiated by the Rwandan Hutu leaders and Tutsi rebels, and France, Belgium, and Zaire sent peacekeeping forces. By 1993, however, the Tutsi rebels had regrouped, and the Hutu leadership of Juvenal Habyarimana was challenged internally by militant nationalists. In April 1994, his plane was shot down. Hutus blamed Tutsis, though it has not been determined who was responsible; it could have been Hutus looking for a reason to begin an organized campaign of genocide.[16]

Genocide resulted when dominant Hutu forces decided to use paramilitary militias to kill and terrorize Tutsis. These forces were specially trained in such tactics as the burning of houses, tossing of grenades, and hacking up of dummies with machetes.[17] According to a UN informant, whose warnings were passed on to, but ignored by, senior UN officials, military and paramilitary training focused on discipline, weapons, explosives, close combat, and tactics. This training, the informant indicated, was designed to take advantage of the registration of all Tutsis in the Rwandan capital of Kigali—most likely for the purposes of extermination. The informant estimated that the personnel he was working with could kill one thousand Tutsis in twenty minutes.[18] Additional evidence that the actions were premeditated to achieve a total victory against Tutsis included ethnic entries on identity cards; numerical codes painted on homes in the capital city; radio broadcasting of violent, anti-Tutsi messages; a Hutu extremist party operating with presidential backing; civilians being armed through party militias; militia members surveilling Tutsi families; and the preparation of death lists. The Hutu militias were armed and supplied by the Hutu-led Rwandan Ministry of Defense.[19]

Hutu militias promulgated an ideology of "Hutuness" for all of Rwanda. They presented a "final solution" of mass murder—not as a way to create suffering but, they claimed, as a tool for alleviating it.[20] The dramatic intent behind the killing became evident when it was not limited to Tutsis but also targeted moderate Hutus.[21] An American intelligence assessment conducted as the genocide raged concluded that the attacks appeared designed to eliminate all potential opposition, including those who favored negotiation, and to "raise the costs" of any Tutsi takeover of Rwanda.[22] The conditions for genocide were set and quickly spiraled out of control. Hutu propaganda, broadcast over national radio, identified Tutsis repeatedly as "animals," "cockroaches," and "snakes" and asserted that Tutsis were not true Rwandans but invading Ugandans who had a superiority complex. All Tutsis were thus a direct threat to all Hutus and, in this view, had to be killed before they could kill average Hutus.[23] A perspective had grown within both tribal communities that the other was a threat to its survival; thus, the solution for each was to eliminate the other. The balance of forces favored the Hutus, who were on the offensive. The genocide was carried out by about thirty thousand active-duty Rwandan army forces and an additional fifteen to thirty thousand Hutu militiamen organized against about twenty thousand Tutsi rebel forces. The Tutsi force could not do much to counter Hutu movements, however, as the Tutsis were located in one small area of northern Rwanda.[24]

About eight hundred thousand were killed in one hundred days during the Rwandan genocide—an average of 333.3 murders per hour, or 5.5 lives taken each minute. Added to this were uncounted numbers of maimed who lived with their wounds. Many female Tutsi survivors were raped as a tool of systematic terror.[25] The situation had accelerated rapidly because Tutsis initially came together in groups, so that within several days, more than five hundred thousand Tutsis were gathered in large concentrations throughout the country. This gave the Tutsis an advantage in the short-term as the initial Hutu attackers were poorly armed. However, the tactic of gathering together backfired against the Tutsis when Hutus from the regular army, reserves, and Presidential Guard arrived at these Tutsi locations. This heavy congregation tilted the balance of power toward the better armed Hutus and resulted in 250,000 Tutsis killed in just two weeks.

Hutus avoided attacking Tutsis in areas where the world community was likely to witness the events. In areas where Tutsis survived, this most likely stemmed from the presence of international observers. Hutus also cut landline telephone service in the country to prevent outside communication and set up roadblocks to check civilian identification and prevent people from fleeing the country.[26] After the major fighting ended, the United Nations organized an international response to set up refugee camps. However, during this time, thousands of Hutus were killed in Tutsi retaliatory attacks. One account described the pure brutality of the actions taken by each side as including the use of machetes, which "often resulted in a long and painful agony and many people, when they had some money, paid their killers to be finished off quickly with a bullet rather than being slowly hacked to death. . . . Mutilations were common."[27]

As in the Yugoslav case, the Rwandan application of genocide as a tactic failed as strategy. The initial Hutu goal appeared to be the creation of an unstable enough situation that any international presence would withdraw, and Tutsi leaders and Hutu moderates could then be systematically eliminated. In the near term, this approach appeared to succeed. Several weeks into the campaign, with about one hundred thousand dead, the UN Security Council agreed to withdraw 90 percent of its peacekeepers. UN military officials on the ground, however, said the rapid deployment of about five thousand UN troops might have prevented the entire genocide. Absent even a signal of intent to engage from the international community, the violence spiraled out of control, while only 450 poorly trained and lightly equipped UN troops remained in the country. Six weeks after atrocities began, with 328,000 dead, the United Nations authorized deployment of five thousand African peacekeeping forces into Rwanda—though few countries offered troops. This deployment was also delayed, however, as the United States bickered with the United Nations about who would pay for the use of American armored personnel carriers. Eleven weeks into the genocide, the UN Security Council authorized France to create a safe area within Hutu-controlled regions. Eventually, Tutsi rebels had regained the initiative and fought their way to Kigali. The Hutu government eventually fled to Zaire, along with a massive exodus of Hutu refugees. In one hundred days of fighting, the barbaric Hutu tactic of killing innocent civilians was successful. The tactic also worked in that the horrific nature of the activity prevented the international community from reinforcing what minimal presence it had in Rwanda. Indeed, as the crisis escalated, UN forces withdrew. Yet, in the end, the Hutus lost the war and fled.

Never Again?

Genocide and ethnic cleansing are far more common than the world would have expected following the promise never to let it happen again after World War II's Holocaust. Often the meaning of "genocide" is disputed in part to avoid responsibility for stopping it when no high-priority national interests are involved. Nevertheless, the organized mass murder of innocent civilians is reasonably easily identified when it occurs. In Bangladesh, Cambodia, Equatorial Guinea, Ethiopia, the Balkans, and Rwanda, the organized mass killing of innocents has taken place since World War II. Millions of men, women, and children have been killed, abused, or dislocated as a result of genocide or ethnic cleansing. When the international community noted the tenth anniversary of the Rwandan genocide in 2004, strong lessons were debated as to why it happened and how it could have been prevented. Yet, at the very same time, genocide was happening again in Sudan. Meanwhile, advocates of keeping American troops in both Iraq and Afghanistan argue that the instability and civil wars that would likely result from their departure would probably end in genocide.

Terrorism and Insurgency

Terrorism and insurgency are asymmetric tactics applied to achieve broader political or other objectives. Historically, the impacts of terrorism and insurgencies are more confined than those of genocide and ethnic cleaning. However, if combined with the proliferation of weapons of mass destruction, terrorism and insurgencies could create catastrophic consequences. Both are asymmetric tools available to weak actors seeking to level the playing field by causing dramatic and shocking political events. Terrorism targets innocent civilians without discrimination. Clandestine fighters use insurgency to attack military targets during an occupation. Complicating the distinction of terrorism from insurgency is the fact that one person's insurgent, who might have local political sympathy or external support against an occupying power, is often another person's terrorist. Context matters when identifying the role both play as tactics. Nonetheless, as tactics, both are asymmetric, and both can be barbaric in nature, especially when insurgency combines with terrorism and technology.

The Meaning and Use of Terror

Terrorism is designed to achieve a political objective by using violence against civilians to generate fear. Its objectives have evolved over time, as have its methods and targets. However, the dynamics of asymmetric power that drive it—as a struggle along a continuum of central versus local power, big versus small power, modern versus traditional power—have remained constant.[28] The principal purpose of a terrorist attack is to destroy a target, as well as to create fear in an audience by perpetrating dramatic and shocking acts.[29] In that sense, the selection of a target and how and when it is hit are critical components of both tactics and strategy. Such was the case with the use of airplanes as missiles on September 11, 2001, and the choice of the World Trade Center and Pentagon as highly symbolic targets. The medium for generating fear would be the proliferation of imagery of the attacks on worldwide television. Targets are thus generally selected to be consistent with the objective, available resources, and relative potential for success in an attack.[30]

The use of terror has been commonplace as a means of securing power and stability for governments. After the French Revolution, terror was used to restore order following the overthrow of despotism. Modern terrorism, however, specifically uses the murder of private citizens and the destruction of public and private property to achieve a broader political objective. The purpose can range from using violence for nationalist or state ends to advancing specific transnational interests such as drug cartels or other organized crime. In the case of Afghanistan, all of these elements had converged by 2010.[31] Religious zealots, many of whom espouse philosophies ranging from dominance to Armageddon—and take it on themselves to bring these about—add a new dimension to the use of terrorism. While terrorism can be defined differently based on context, it is best understood as an asymmetric tactic designed to advance a strategic goal. It is most often associated with a political objective; uses violence or the threat of violence; is intended to have a psychological repercussion beyond the actual target; is often conducted by organizations with a chain of command, though acting without uniform or insignia; and most often has been perpetrated by a subnational group or nonstate entity that seeks to overcome power disparities in order to shape a public agenda.[32]

Insurgency and guerrilla warfare have also increasingly adopted asymmetric terrorist tactics as tools of attrition. Insurgency and guerrilla movements comprise small armed groups fighting for a particular piece of land or political objective. They are often differentiated from terrorists in that insurgent and guerrilla fighters generally confine their attacks to military targets rather than killing civilians. Nevertheless, civilians have been directly affected by these movements. In its struggle for Algerian independence, the Front de Libération Nationale (FLN) killed about sixteen thousand civilians and kidnapped about fifty thousand. The FLN also killed an estimated twelve thousand of its own members in internal purges. Similar activity took place among the Vietcong during the Vietnam War.[33] The Irish Republican Army (IRA) in Northern Ireland saw itself as a legitimate guerrilla campaign, but many of its targets over several decades were civilians. The IRA bombed bars and timed attacks on civilians to do economic damage to the United Kingdom.

Insurgents and guerrilla fighters have in some circumstances gained legitimacy, depending on the conditions under which they operated. During the
Cold War, the United States and Soviet Union supported insurgent and guerrilla movements in the underdeveloped world to advance their competing
agendas. Nicaraguan insurgents and guerrilla movements fighting a socialist
government in the 1980s were called "freedom fighters" by the United States,
which also backed the right-wing government of El Salvador in its campaign
to suppress insurgents and guerrilla fighters. Yet, the government of El Salvador supported paramilitary groups that used barbaric tactics, including rape,
disappearances, and other forms of violent intimidation.

Insurgent and guerrilla movements can thus take on a variety of rationales.
These movements are, however, increasingly turning to terrorism as a tool for
accomplishing their objectives. While insurgency and guerrilla movements
are not regular armies, they organize, operate, and select targets as if conducting a military campaign. Insurgency often aims to prevent an external power
or local government from exerting effective control over a certain territory or
even a whole country. Thus, a central objective of insurgents is to create confusion, chaos, and fear to show that those in power cannot govern effectively.
Whether such movements are global (e.g., the al Qaeda terrorist movement)
or local (e.g., groups advocating for the Palestinians, the Basques in Spain,
or the Chechens in Russia), all are aided dramatically by the dynamics of
the global security environment. Transportation technology accelerates the
pace and capacity for such movements to organize and act. Communications
technology has played a similar role as a force multiplier for contact among
members of an organization and as a means of publicizing actions and agendas via the media. The deregulation of both the international economy and
the means of exercising global trade helps to weaken the traditional role of
the state and facilitate the flow of money and weapons. Migration also plays
an important role as ex-patriot organizations can provide members of such
movements with support or safe haven. The spread of modern cultures—especially Western versions that dominate contemporary popular television,
movies, art, and food—serves to fuel backlash. This reaction can tip someone
toward insurgency or at least provide a rallying cry for those who claim to
defend local cultures against intrusion from outside forces.[34]

Terrorist tactics applied by insurgent and guerrilla forces are potent when
employed in weak states or states experiencing major internal transitions.
Weak or failing states create fertile ground for armed gangs or militias to
coalesce into organized insurgent or guerrilla movements seeking to consolidate power—by 2010, for example, al Qaeda was mainly present in places like
Pakistan, Somalia, and Yemen. As an asymmetric tool, these tactics can be
crucial means to redress substantial power imbalances. The Liberation Tigers

of Tamil Eelam (LTTE) in Sri Lanka, for example, developed a well-organized campaign that recruited and trained individuals to carry out terrorist attacks, including a 1987 airplane bombing that killed sixteen, a 1997 targeting of a ship, which killed thirty-two, and a 1997 truck bombing that killed eighteen. The Tamil Tigers had, by 2003, conducted over two hundred bombings of places of worship, office buildings, and transportation centers. The Tamil Tigers asserted that these kinds of attacks were the only means available to fight given the military dominance of the Sri Lankan army.[35] In 2009, the Tamil Tigers announced a cease-fire, officially out of concern that continued fighting would cause unnecessary killing of civilians by the government.

States in transition toward democracy are vulnerable to insurgent movements and guerrilla forces that can use terrorist tactics to intimidate civilians and harass or assassinate political opposition. Moreover, targets in transitioning states might also include international aid workers and the staffs of organizations seeking to build civil society, such as UN employees. The objective in this case would be to create the circumstances that would lead outside forces to withdraw, leaving a political and security void for insurgents to fill. This was the case in post-Hussein Iraq, where an insurgency opposed to American occupation emerged in 2003 and grew steadily through 2006. Targets for terrorist bombing attacks included average citizens lining up to join Iraqi police forces, the headquarters for UN operations, and civilian aid workers and contractors. Many of these innocent victims were kidnapped and then beheaded; their murders were sometimes videotaped and sent out for viewing on the Internet. Such attacks are consistent with an asymmetric strategy driven by a combination of will, capability, and goals. In the case of Iraq, the strategic objective appeared to be either to facilitate the conditions under which Iraqis would abandon support for outside intervention or possibly to prompt a civil war from which insurgents might emerge to govern. In late 2006, the United States adopted a specific new doctrine for its military forces built on a theory of how to fight counterinsurgency warfare. At the core of this plan was a surge of thirty thousand troops and a new emphasis on providing stability by emphasizing protection of local populations. The idea was mainly tactical as the larger purpose was to create an environment in which longer-term political reconciliation, oil-revenue sharing, and regional diplomacy could develop, allowing the United States to leave. By 2010, the United States had drawn down to just under fifty thousand troops, and advocates of the counterinsurgency concept claimed success. Critics, however, argued that even before the surge, there had been a new balance of forces on the ground as populations in Iraq had been moved, and local populations had been bribed with American money to turn against insurgents. Politically, the advocates of counterinsurgency won this argument as their doctrine became the policy foundation for another surge of thirty thousand troops into Afghanistan in late 2009. Meanwhile, Iraq remained highly unstable, and Afghanistan showed few sustainable signs of improvement, absent American and allied forces.

The Evolution of Modern Terrorism

Terrorism took its modern form during the post–World War II decolonization movement. During the 1960s, terrorism grew among some sub-state groups as a means of expressing opposition to particular policies or of advancing particular ideologies. While many movements professed their commitment to revolutionary ideas, in no single case did their zeal actually succeed in advancing an ideological doctrine.[36] In the 1970s, a number of organizations emerged and used terrorist methods to bring attention to causes advancing independence for particular territories or to protest the actions and policies of particular governments. Movements such as the IRA, the Palestine Liberation Organization, and Basque ETA in Spain became well known for their use of brutal terrorist methods in sustained campaigns designed to weaken the public resolve to support existing policies. These movements did have some degree of sympathy from within their own communities and saw themselves as advancing a legitimate fight against oppression. Terrorism thus fostered a vicious cycle of attack and retribution. Some elements would become so deeply entrenched in this cycle that they would favor war over peace. When the Israeli leader Yitzak Rabin negotiated a peace settlement with the Palestinians, he was assassinated—by a Jewish zealot.

By the 1980s, these anticolonial trends in terrorism were accompanied by the growth of state sponsorship of some terrorist organizations. Some states, such as Iran and Syria, had direct ties to anti-Israeli groups; however, other states labeled in the international community as sponsoring terrorism had only minor or nonexistent ties to terrorist groups. Some states that did have ties to terrorist groups were often not identified as such because they were allied with great powers—especially the United States. The United States conducts an annual review of which states sponsor international terrorism. If a state appears on this list, it is to be denied trade and international loans, among other penalties. While some have gone on and off, the primary states on this list have been (over time) Cuba, North Korea, Iran, Iraq, Syria, Sudan, and Libya. Among these states, Cuba and North Korea were largely on the list as a consequence of their domestic leaderships (Libya and North Korea were removed for diplomatic reasons). Iraq (before the U.S. invasion) was on the list due to its connection with a 1993 plot to assassinate former U.S. president George H. W. Bush; there was no evidence of direct Iraqi involvement with international terrorist organizations, despite regular, dubious assertions by

American officials implying the existence of a relationship between Saddam Hussein and al Qaeda. Two states that did provide some support for international terrorist groups were not on the list as they were American friends. Saudi Arabia was known to have provided financial resources to anti-Israeli groups while profiting from the sale of oil to American consumers. Prior to September 2001, Pakistan provided recognition and support for the Taliban government in Afghanistan, which harbored al Qaeda. Pakistan had also been accused (mainly by India) of engaging in informal support of cross-border terrorist organizations operating against India in Kashmir. Elements within the Pakistani intelligence services were also well known to have ties to the Taliban in Afghanistan. Indeed, the Taliban had, some American officials argued, become a quiet proxy ally of Pakistan by 2010 and, of course, Osama bin Laden was killed in Pakistan after hiding in plain sight for years.

The threat from terrorism is not only the actual damage it does but the deep fear that it can generate. Of about ten thousand terrorist events catalogued between 1968 and September 2001, only fourteen caused more than one hundred casualties. Until 2001, far fewer Americans were killed by terrorists than by lightning strikes. Until the September 11, 2001, attacks on the United States, all deaths resulting from international terrorism occurred outside the United States. The total number of Americans around the world killed by terrorists is about equivalent to the number who have drowned in bathtubs in the United States.[37] Two key dynamics do nonetheless illustrate a major change in the role of international terrorism in global security. First, some major international terrorist networks have moved beyond limited objectives. These global movements also work closely with local political movements to extend their web of influence. In this sense, globalization provides multiple means through which terrorists can organize and operate. Terrorist groups are increasingly able to move and hide money using the international financial system and to transmit messages via encoded communications over the Internet. Dispersed ethnic groups can provide local cover and recruitment for terrorist operatives. Moreover, the perceived negative effects of globalization have expanded the number of discontents looking for some means, even if symbolic, to defend local cultures and traditions. The rise of global finance, the advent of the 24/7 global economy, the growth of transnational ethnoreligious communities, and the ability to hide financial resources in safe havens, traffic in illicit items, and encode communications with advanced technology are all key manifestations of the global networks in which terrorists can now operate.[38]

Second, the appeal of religious convictions increasingly helps leaders of terrorist networks to motivate people to commit suicide terrorism. Earnest religiosity can quickly spiral into fanaticism when combined with other factors like economic deprivation and a sense of social humiliation and isolation.

Religious terrorists often see violence as a moral act that brings them closer to salvation. Religious terrorists hold absolutist worldviews and thus do not necessarily seek stature beyond the notoriety of their sacrifice.[39] Nevertheless, even those people who are advancing a religion have a strategic goal and have convinced themselves that their actions are rational.

The trend toward more religiously driven terrorism is rising. In 1968, a study by the RAND Corporation identified no religiously motivated international terrorist organizations. By 1994, one-third of forty-nine international terrorist groups were classified as primarily religious.[40] Religion is particularly used by terrorist organizers as a recruitment and motivational tool to enlist operatives or political and financial supporters. While terrorism might appear to reflect acts of desperation, they can be rational acts as understood by those who carry them out. In some cases extended terrorist campaigns have led to some political gains—once the movement chose to abandon violence.[41] IRA sympathizers Gerry Adams and Martin McGuinness became acceptable international actors following the end of their struggle against British occupation in Northern Ireland. Likewise, the leader of the Palestine Liberation Organization, Yasser Arafat, became a widely accepted international figure after his group called a cease-fire, condemned terrorism, recognized Israel's right to exist, and engaged in negotiation.

The main group in the world practicing suicide terrorism is not, however, a religious movement but rather the Sri Lankan Tamil Tigers, motivated mostly by a Marxist-Leninist ideology. Of 186 suicide terrorist attacks worldwide between 1980 and 2001, the LTTE accounted for seventy-five.[42] Nevertheless, the mix of religion and terrorism can be extremely dangerous. Religious terrorists see themselves as locked into a permanent struggle of good versus evil. They use violent behavior to honor a commitment perceived as required by a higher being. Religious terrorists consider themselves unconstrained by secular rules or laws. Generally alienated from the dominant social system, religious terrorists are often dispersed and have dispersed supporters, making them harder to locate or prevent from taking violent action—a situation rendered even more difficult to monitor by the use of global contacts via the Internet for recruitment.[43] This was the case with a Nigerian apparently recruited by Yemeni al Qaeda sympathizers to (unsuccessfully) blow up a plane approaching the Detroit, Michigan, airport on Christmas Day 2009.

In terms of the relationship between religion and terrorism, religious cults play an important and dangerous role. Some cults have charismatic leaders who promulgate the concept of a coming Armageddon and salvation. These leaders demand total faith in them as godlike figures who instill the belief that it is followers' duty to facilitate the end of times. The Aum Shinrikyo movement in Japan held such a commitment to its leadership and Armageddon during the 1990s. This group also had considerable financial resources and scientists seeking to develop weapons of mass destruction. The cult included scientists trained in microbiology, who experimented with anthrax, botulinum toxin, Q fever, and the Ebola virus. In the early 1990s, they sought to disseminate biological weapons by outfitting a car to distribute botulinum toxin via its exhaust pipe. They also tried to spread anthrax via a spray system on a roof in Tokyo. Aum Shinrikyo failed in the use of biological weapons distribution, so they resorted to the use of sarin nerve agent in the Tokyo subway, killing eleven people and wounding hundreds while spreading fear across the entire country. On a smaller scale, in the United States in 1984, the Rajneeshee religious movement sought to affect the outcome of local elections in Wasco County, Oregon, by spraying salmonella on salad bars in restaurants, leading to about 750 cases of digestive poisoning though no deaths. The cult's plan was discovered, and its effort failed.[44]

An individual's transformation into a terrorist can result from a variety of factors. Some terrorists see themselves as legitimate actors advancing political or religious values in a war so important that they cannot afford to differentiate between military and civilian targets. Others justify their actions on the basis of historical actions taken by the enemy. Still others have been alienated from society as a result of some direct experience that has brought them to a belief in the legitimacy of violence against innocents. In many cases, a vicious cycle develops; for example, the modern IRA really took off in terms of recruitment and local support when the British army opened fire and killed thirteen innocent people on Bloody Sunday in Derry in Northern Ireland in 1972. After that, Protestant paramilitary forces became more deeply entrenched, leading to decades of spiraling violence and terror.

Such stories are common in a world in which passion for revenge can overpower willingness to resolve differences peacefully. Timothy McVeigh, for example, was a loner who developed deep resentment of the U.S. government following a stint in the military and a tour of duty in the 1991 Gulf War—where he learned to work with explosives. He was seen as too radical in his worldviews, even for some of America's most virulent antigovernment militia movements, which McVeigh had come to idealize. He and a friend conspired to blow up Oklahoma City's Alfred P. Murrah Federal Building, killing 168 people. The dead included schoolchildren attending class on the second floor. One high-level leader of al Qaeda, Dr. Ayman al-Zawahiri, had in his youth been a political activist in Egypt. He was arrested by the Egyptian government for his activity and reportedly tortured over several years in prison. There, his hatred apparently grew deep enough that he took up arms against the United States, which he saw as backing Egypt.

Some anti-Western and pro-Islamic terrorist movements have developed a broader ideological context that also serves as a significant tool to inspire local radical activists to carry out terrorist attacks. This rise toward an ideologically dispersed international terrorist movement stems from an overarching belief that Muslims should take up arms in a holy war against the Judeo-Christian West, a profound sense of indignation at the deaths and perceived oppression of Muslims in Palestinian areas and elsewhere, and a growing conviction that moderate secular governments should be replaced by Islamic political movements. This trend complicates terrorist coordination and makes attacks more likely to be regionally based, smaller in scale, and aimed at "soft" (i.e., easy to kill) civilian targets. While the threat might be smaller in scale and more diffuse, it is also more difficult to combat.[45] There were, by 2004, more than a dozen, and perhaps as many as forty, regional Islamic groups with growing capabilities and aspirations. These groups had established training camps in Kashmir, the Philippines, and West Africa—and their ambitions were growing beyond the local concerns that initially spawned them.[46] Increasingly, "al Qaeda–inspired" groups started taking the lead in advancing terrorist activity—for example, the group Lashkar-e-Taiba carried out, with only a small group of terrorists, a deadly, paramilitary-style assault on the high-profile Taj Hotel in Mumbai, India, in November 2008, killing 175 people.

Al Qaeda

Despite the relatively low incidence of terrorism, its catastrophic potential has been made clear by al Qaeda, which killed nearly three thousand Americans in September 2001. Before September 11, only a handful of massive-scale terrorist events had involved casualties numbering into the low hundreds: 325 killed in the 1985 crash of an Air India flight; over 300 killed in 1993 by car bombs in India; 270 killed in the 1988 explosion of Pan Am Flight 103; 241 killed in the 1983 truck bombing of an American marine barracks in Lebanon; 171 killed in the crash of a UTA flight in 1989; 168 killed by the Oklahoma City truck bombing in 1995; and 115 killed in the 1987 destruction of a Korean jetliner.[47] Terrorists were nonetheless able to kill nearly three thousand people within several hours on September 11. On that single day, nearly half as many people were killed as had died, among all nationalities, in terrorist attacks around the world during the 1980s and 1990s. During that same two-decade period, 856 Americans had died abroad or at home due to terrorist attacks.[48] Al Qaeda had become a resilient, adaptive, and dangerous global terrorist movement that increasingly served to inspire terrorists as much as directly organize them.

Al Qaeda, which is Arabic for "the base," is a transnational terrorist movement inspired by the late Saudi national Osama bin Laden. Bin Laden brought the organization considerable financial resources and organizational skills that he had developed as an engineer. Well educated and experienced in the ways of the West, bin Laden had been brought up living a wealthy lifestyle in a prominent Saudi family. The al Qaeda organization grew out of the anti-Soviet mujahideen movement in Afghanistan and in the 1990s engaged in a close relationship with the fundamentalist Islamic Taliban movement. By the late 1990s, the Taliban had come to control most of Afghanistan. The al Qaeda network also expanded during this time by forging an alliance with a similar Islamic terrorist movement based in Egypt. Al Qaeda set up bases in Afghanistan, perhaps more than a dozen, where as many as one hundred thousand fighters committed to a holy war underwent training. Not all who attended these camps, however, were committed al Qaeda terrorists, and most went on to fight in the Afghan civil war, not to take up a global crusade. Al Qaeda's core group of followers likely numbered about two thousand at the time of the 2001 attack and had an even smaller leadership structure numbering several hundred.

September 11, 2001, marked the first time many citizens around the world had heard of al Qaeda, but this was not the group's first attack. Al Qaeda members were involved in the first effort to bring down the World Trade Center in 1993. Al Qaeda members were also involved in a failed plot to blow up a number of airliners flying over the Pacific Ocean several years later. In 1998, al Qaeda operatives destroyed American embassies in Kenya and Tanzania, killing hundreds of workers—mostly local Africans. Toward the end of 1999, an al Qaeda member was arrested at the U.S.-Canadian border. He was caught with operational devices and plans to explode a bomb at the Los Angeles airport. Later in 2000, al Qaeda members used a small boat to bring explosives alongside the USS *Cole*, which was at harbor in Yemen, killing over a dozen soldiers and severely disabling the ship. In fact, al Qaeda had formally declared war on the United States in 1996. Yet, aside from the expert community focused on international terrorism, the warnings did not register with a sense of urgency. Even when, in August 2001, President George W. Bush received a classified briefing from the Central Intelligence Agency titled "Al Qaeda Determined to Attack Inside the United States," little was done, and the president continued with his vacation in Texas. The American media focused heavily that summer on the dangers of shark attacks.

Al Qaeda initially took on the form and rhetoric of a military organization. It had a high-level political committee that authorized actions; a military committee that proposed targets, gathered ideas and organized support for operations, and managed training camps; a finance committee that provided budgetary resources for training, housing, living expenses, travel, and the movement of money worldwide; a foreign purchases committee that acquired weapons, explosives, and technical commitment; a security committee that provided physical protection, intelligence collection, and counterintelligence; and a public relations committee that organized propaganda strategies and made public statements for the organization.[49] It did not, however, have a hierarchical chain of command. Rather, it identified operations and assigned responsibility to carefully selected clandestine operatives. Of the September 11 hijackers, bin Laden boasted after the attack that only a handful had actually known they were on a suicide mission. Following the initial collapse of the Taliban in Afghanistan, al Qaeda's known numbers were reduced by an estimated two-thirds killed or captured by American and allied forces. It had also lost its home base of operations in Afghanistan. By 2010, however, it had reestablished a relatively free zone of operations in northwestern Pakistan, where presumably Osama bin Laden was in hiding.

By 2004, al Qaeda was evolving from a tightly controlled tactical operation to a larger anti-Western ideological movement. It relied on an expanding group of regional and local terrorist movements with which it could associate. Rather than making command decisions centrally with his closest associates, bin Laden appears to have inspired a hybrid of smaller, regionally based terrorist operations. By 2005, diverse local al Qaeda leaderships were making command decisions and coordinating their efforts with local radical Islamic movements. Attacks in Morocco and Spain in 2003 and 2004 were carried out not by highly trained terrorists organized by Osama bin Laden but rather by uneducated slum dwellers or small shopkeepers with little previous extremist involvement.[50] In 2009 a small group of Pakistanis plotted to blow up subways in New York City, and a Nigerian hid explosives in his underwear to blow up a plane landing in Detroit. In 2010 a lone Pakistani tried to explode a car bomb in Times Square, people in Yemen tried to blow up airplanes with package bombs, and a Somali American was arrested for plotting to blow up a Christmas tree lighting ceremony in Portland, Oregon. Yet, none of these plots were successful. Still, in terms of incidents involving potential risk to Americans, 2009 and 2010 were the most dangerous years since 2001.

While the majority of major al Qaeda attacks had failed, to the organization, the fact that it remained active was evidence of success at meeting the goal of promulgating fear and asserting relevance. Furthermore, some lower-level attempts did succeed, and all of them used local inspiration and organization to deadly effect. The Morocco attacks included the destruction of a Jewish community center, a Spanish restaurant and social club, a hotel, a Jewish cemetery, and a Jewish-owned Italian restaurant. Forty-five were killed, including twelve of the fourteen terrorist bombers. When suicide bombers hit London in July 2005, killing fifty-two people on the Tube and a bus, the bombers were quickly discovered not to be international terrorists but British citizens inspired by the al Qaeda message with only loose connections to the traditional al Qaeda organization. Though it was not classified as a terrorist attack, an American soldier of Muslim background opened fire at Fort Hood in Texas, killing thirteen soldiers and wounding thirty—in protest of U.S. policy toward Afghanistan. The shooter had been corresponding via e-mail with a radical Islamic cleric in Yemen. The future of al Qaeda will remain in flux with the killing of bin Laden by American troops in May 2011.

The Globalization of Terror

Globalization provides modern terrorist networks new means to finance, conduct, and publicize attacks. Al Qaeda's relatively small inner circle was able to multiply its power by forging alliances with Islamic groups in other countries, including Egypt, Libya, Algeria, Saudi Arabia, Oman, Tunisia, Jordan, Iraq, Lebanon, Morocco, Somalia, and Eritrea.[51] While bin Laden brought financial resources to al Qaeda, the organization generated most of its money via legal global fund-raising networks. Al Qaeda relied on well-placed financial facilitators and the diversion of funds from Islamic charities, including large transfers of money to al Qaeda without the knowledge of those giving it. While no government overtly supported al Qaeda, the organization did benefit from some governments turning a blind eye toward its fund-raising.[52] Al Qaeda's money was moved through what is known as the Hawala architecture, a traditional and informal system of transferring money in the Islamic world. Couriers operating in Pakistan, the United Arab Emirates, and around the Middle East also served as conduits for the transfer of funds. Al Qaeda had an operating budget before 2001 of about $30 million, most of which went to supporting the Taliban in Afghanistan, as specific terrorist operations were relatively inexpensive. The 2001 attack against the United States cost an estimated $500,000. The much smaller-scale, but still very deadly, al Qaeda bombings in Morocco that killed forty-five people in May 2003 only cost about $4,000.

A unique attribute of modern transnational terrorist movements is the growing use of the Internet as a communication and propaganda tool. One observer in Afghanistan during November 2001 said that he watched "every second al Qaeda member carrying a laptop computer along with a Kalashnikov" as operatives dispersed around the globe.[53] In December 2003, al Qaeda supporters published on the Internet a manifesto articulating both the strategy and the timing of what became the attacks on commuter trains in Madrid, Spain, the following March. The Internet posting clearly stated al Qaeda's strategy: "Withdrawal of Spanish or Italian forces would put immense pressure on the British presence in a way that Tony Blair might not be able to bear. . . . In this way the dominoes will begin to fall quickly." The March 2004 attacks killed 191 people; a week later, the pro-American Spanish government was ousted in a popular vote. The Internet has served as a virtual base to unite al Qaeda members using encoded programs to facilitate the exchange of information, discussion of strategy, and dissemination of instructions and training methods for terrorist recruits. Overall, there are an estimated forty-five hundred terrorist-related websites in the world. Not only do such Internet sites facilitate coordination and communication, but they have also become virtual training camps—they even include postings of how to build explosives and carry out attacks. In 2010, an al Qaeda supporter even began publishing an online "magazine" called *Inspire*. The first issue featured articles like "May Our Souls Be Sacrificed for You!" and "Make a Bomb in the Kitchen with Your Mom."

The role of the Internet in al Qaeda's network was detailed in summer 2004, when Pakistan detained Mohammed Naeem Noor Khan, a key computer engineer for the terrorist network. Seizure of his laptop led to the arrest of thirteen terrorist suspects in Britain and exposed electronic links between al Qaeda operatives or sympathizers in Pakistan, Europe, and the United States. His computer files included extensive detail on surveillance and information about preferred targets. The tactics al Qaeda employed in using the Internet were not especially sophisticated. The group avoided detection by not using the same Internet café too often and writing messages first in a word processor, then pasting them into e-mails to reduce Internet connection times.[54] The advantage of the Internet is that it provides no center of gravity to retaliate against; yet, it can unite terrorist operatives from around the world. This interconnectedness gives terrorists global reach in recruitment, communication, and coordination. The Internet can also be a tool for spreading false information that could heighten defenses in a country like the United States, costing it billions of dollars in preparation for an attack that has not actually been planned. Terrorists can thus use the Internet to produce "chatter" that wreaks economic and psychological damage on a target society without firing a shot. Elevating the terrorist warning alert level from yellow to orange (a system now scrapped by the United States) drained an average of $1 billion per week from the American economy. Such provocations can also reveal what kinds of threats a target is preparing to defend and how, and terrorists can use that information for further planning. In 2010, the United States opted to drop this color-coded system, moving toward more localized warnings, should they be necessary.

A particularly gruesome application of the Internet to spread terror is the broadcast of recorded hostage killings. The images of the murder of American journalist Daniel Pearl by al Qaeda members in Pakistan were disseminated globally via the Internet. During the occupation of Iraq, images of Western hostages seized by insurgents were quickly sent out over the Web. Barbaric images of beheadings were used to incite others to support a cause and to create humiliation and a sense of helplessness among target audiences. These images also appear to have been used to deter nongovernmental organizations and international organizations from sending workers into the areas where their assistance was most needed to provide long-term stability. Meanwhile, radical Islamic websites could be further used as propaganda vehicles. For example, photos of American soldiers mistreating Iraqi prisoners were widely distributed on the Internet to advance political arguments that the United States sought to humiliate Muslims. Individuals or activists who support the goals of terrorist movements, but do not want to engage in terrorism directly, have quietly engaged in an "electronic holy war" by distributing anti-Western propaganda.[55] With this in mind, the United States opted not to initially make public photos of the dead bin Laden taken in May 2011.

The virtual battle space of global terrorism has also included the advanced technology of cellular telephones, which create both opportunities and vulnerabilities for terrorist networks. For some time, for example, the United States had intercepted the cellular phone communications of Osama bin Laden. This became known after a press leak from the American intelligence community seeming to brag about intercept capabilities. Subsequently, bin Laden went deep underground and resorted to more basic forms of communication, such as couriers. American intelligence also apparently intercepted communications made by bin Laden during the 2001 war in Afghanistan at the battle of Tora Bora. In April 2002, several al Qaeda operatives used a cell phone call as a means of alerting a senior al Qaeda leader of an attack on a synagogue in Tunisia, which killed twenty-one people, mostly German tourists. The phone call was traced to a particular kind of cellular phone used by the senior al Qaeda operative. German officials were able to trace the origin of the phone conversation to a Polish-born Muslim living in Germany whom officials had been monitoring because of his association with known militants at a local mosque. This intercept revealed a preference among al Qaeda operatives for a particular kind of cell phone that included a Swiss chip, known as a subscriber identity modular card, which al Qaeda apparently thought would keep its conversations untraceable. By narrowing the monitoring of traffic to cell phones in Pakistan, the German officials were able to track the senior al Qaeda figure's general location.[56] Eventually, Khalid Sheikh Mohammed, the operational leader of al Qaeda and the mastermind of the September 11 attacks, was captured.

Mohammed's capture led American intelligence agents to his computers, cell phones, and personal phonebook. From this source, authorities traced up to six thousand phone numbers, which provided a virtual map of al Qaeda's existing international operations.[57] Demonstrating how al Qaeda utilized technology in innovative and dangerous ways for communication, its members used a tiny Swiss communications chip. Al Qaeda members thought this particular chip would hide them, but it actually facilitated the monitoring of Mohammed and a number of his associates. Use of cell phone information also helped Switzerland break up a Yemeni and Somali ring of document forgers engaged in human smuggling with ties to a high-level al Qaeda operative. A cell phone obtained from a bomber involved in an attack in Saudi Arabia in May 2003 helped to break up this ring of terrorists. The network was later revealed to have included contact with operatives in France, Italy, Germany, Great Britain, Belgium, the Netherlands, Turkey, Georgia, Saudi Arabia, Yemen, Bahrain, Qatar, Syria, Iraq, Iran, Malaysia, Ethiopia, Somalia, and the Maldives.[58]

The decline of some states' capacity to meet basic human needs and to enforce the rule of law can generate fertile ground for recruiting or training terrorist sympathizers or operatives. Al Qaeda, having lost Afghanistan, increasingly looked to other failing states as new areas for basing activity. Indeed, while the United States was escalating its engagement in Afghanistan in 2010, its own intelligence estimates showed that there were few, if any, al Qaeda operatives in the country. Advocates of the war argued that it was necessary to stay in Afghanistan to prevent it from becoming a future al Qaeda safe haven. However, al Qaeda already had developed safe havens in Pakistan, Somalia, and Yemen. Historically, the collapse or weakening of states in the underdeveloped world did not merit much attention from great powers. However, the absence of the rule of law in some states can allow terrorist networks freedom to organize, train, and carry out attacks. Somalia, for example, has suffered a prolonged crisis of state capacity, a significant rise in criminality, and large-scale disease and drug problems. The country has large numbers of internally and externally displaced refugees, many of whom have found their way to the United States. Somalia also has a long, unpatrolled coastline with a high incidence of piracy. Added to this mix, Somalia has a growing radical Islamic movement from which have stemmed small but significant terrorist actions, primarily carried out by the Al-Ittihad al-Islami, one of at least seven significant Islamist movements in Mogadishu, which has been identified as having facilitated financial transfers to training camps where al Qaeda members have been based.[59] West Africa has seen considerable movement of financial resources, especially from diamond investments made by al Qaeda. West Africa was a particularly popular location as al Qaeda appeared to conclude that such areas provide opportunities to organize outside the purview of traditional Western intelligence operations.[60]

Terrorism and Weapons of Mass Destruction

The risk posed by terrorists with weapons of mass destruction is far more complicated than Hollywood movies might suggest—but it is a legitimate concern for five primary reasons. First, these weapons are the most dramatic means a movement can use to create a sense of massive or divine retribution. Second, the motivations of some terrorists have changed, with an increased role played by religious groups fanatically committed to the perceived "justice" of their cause. Third, the supply side of weapons persists and manifests serious security problems, particularly in Russia, Pakistan, and North Korea. Fourth, chemical and biological weapons capabilities are proliferating, and terrorists could use many dangerous communicable diseases that grow naturally. Fifth, the technology with which to develop weapons of mass destruction is proliferating through the networks of globalization.[61]

The prospect of a transnational terrorist group developing an outright functional nuclear weapon is low. It is, however, somewhat more possible that such a group could steal or purchase one. More likely, the combination of a variety of components from existing weapons would be of value—if only to build something that looks like a functional weapon to use for blackmail. Built-in safeguards in American and Russian nuclear weapons programs are a significant complication in using a full nuclear weapon if one were stolen. Nevertheless, terrorists could acquire a nuclear weapon or the fissile material to make one in at least two hundred locations worldwide.[62] The effective development, assembly, and delivery of nuclear weapons generally requires the apparatus of a nation-state. A terrorist's standard of success for a nuclear blast, damage, and generation of fear is, however, likely to be much lower than that of a state acting according to traditional military doctrine. Chemical weapons are a battlefield tool that most militaries see as a dangerous hindrance to be avoided if possible. However, a chemical weapon dispersed in a subway would produce dramatic panic and fear—highly consistent with terrorist objectives. The ability to use biological agents for targeted attacks was proved in fall 2001, when five people were killed by anthrax sent through the U.S. mail. While these small-scale attacks created significant fear, the limits of anthrax as a weapon of mass destruction were also highlighted. Large states, including the United States and the Soviet Union, worked to weaponize such biological agents but abandoned this pursuit in the 1970s, largely because of the difficulty of delivering them.

The dangers of biological weapons, if deployed, are nevertheless real and serious. Biological agents such as viruses are especially problematic because many grow in nature and are hard to detect until someone has been infected. Terrorists could spread smallpox and forms of the plague, which are among the most virulent of biological threats. A terrorist group could infect an operative with smallpox who would use the global travel system to infect unknowing victims, who would then contract and spread the disease. Of course, this assumes that people would make direct contact with someone obviously infected with smallpox rather than running away. In addition, smallpox has a vaccine, effective after exposure if administered within several days. If an outbreak were successfully contained, the vaccine might prove more dangerous than the disease itself. In the last American outbreak of smallpox in the United States in the 1940s, more people died from the vaccine than from the infection. While its effects were limited, the 2001 anthrax attacks in the United States still wreaked considerable havoc: parts of the U.S. Congress and Supreme Court were shut down; eighteen people were infected, of whom five died; thirty-three thousand people were required to take preventive antibiotics; and $3 billion in damage was done to the U.S. postal service. While anthrax is extremely dangerous if inhaled, it is also treatable with antibiotics if one knows the symptoms. Anthrax must be finely processed using sophisticated laboratory technology to be effective in its most virulent form. Even then, it is vulnerable to wind currents and low levels of radiation (such as that in sun rays). Another biological agent that terrorist groups have experimented with is ricin, which grows naturally. However, it can only be used in attacks on individuals, not as a weapon of mass destruction. A ricin attack would be horrifying. If inhaled, ricin causes death within forty-eight hours due to respiratory and circulatory failure; if injected, it causes immediate destruction of the muscles and lymph nodes near the injection site, with major organ failure and death quickly following. However, to equal one kilogram of anthrax, one would need four metric tons of ricin.[63] Ricin is relatively simple to weaponize, but anthrax and smallpox are not. Turning such tools into weapons of mass destruction would require the apparatus of a modern state. A longer-term concern is that states or individuals might someday be able to alter the genetic code of such diseases, making them resistant to vaccines or antibiotics.

In a nightmare scenario, a functional nuclear weapon would be smuggled, most likely in a shipping container, into a country and exploded—either in a port or an urban area. Alternatively, components of a nuclear device could be delivered separately and then assembled domestically. The threat is a difficult one for a country like the United States, which deals daily with about 300,000 trucks, 6,500 rail cars, and 140 ships that deliver some fifty thousand containers holding more than five hundred thousand items from around the world.[64] In 2004, ABC News reported that for two consecutive years, its reporters had successfully shipped depleted uranium into the United States. Though harmless, depleted uranium would give off a signature similar to that of enriched uranium used in nuclear bombs. In the second test, the reporters shipped the depleted uranium in a teak trunk from Jakarta, Indonesia. It was then placed in a shipping container bound for the United States. Despite newly placed radiation-detection devices, the uranium went unnoticed during a three-week passage across the Pacific and through the port of Los Angeles.[65] The amount of weapons-grade material in the former Soviet Union, the risk of leakage in Pakistan, and the growth of clandestine markets, combined with vulnerable ports, together constitute a serious global security challenge. Just one nuclear bomb exploded by a terrorist group could do extraordinary physical, economic, and psychological damage.

The difficulties of nuclear bomb building and delivery, however, make alternative forms of radiological terrorism more likely. For example, a terrorist attack on a nuclear power plant, such as the Indian Point Energy Center thirty-five miles north of New York City, could have dramatic consequences. Though nuclear power stations have been hardened against airplane crashes, it is not clear what a sustained air attack combined with explosives would do. Alternatively, large ground-assault teams could, in theory, seize a power station and destroy it from the inside. Any circumstance in which a terrorist group instigated a nuclear meltdown at a power station would have dramatic consequences. A study of the effects of an attack on Indian Point estimates that, depending on weather conditions, a core meltdown and radiological release could result in 44,000 near-term deaths from acute radiation syndrome and 518,000 long-term deaths from cancer for people within fifty miles of the plant. Economic damage within one hundred miles would exceed $1.1 trillion in the worst case.[66] The probability of creating a successful meltdown scenario is low—but there is a variation on the threat. Rather, for example, than crashing into a nuclear reactor, a large jetliner could instead target the building housing the spent fuel rods. These are by-products of the production of nuclear energy and are stored in cooling pools of water not far from reactors. A fire created in such a pool by jet fuel could spread radioactivity into the atmosphere in amounts equal to or beyond that released during the Chernobyl disaster.[67] A successful attack on a nuclear power plant would be very difficult for terrorists to achieve—assuming they wanted to. On September 11, 2001, al Qaeda could have flown into any number of nuclear power stations. The organization instead remained focused on the targets it had selected and the political impact of that selection.

Also more likely than a nuclear explosion would be the release of radioactivity via a conventional explosive device—a so-called dirty bomb. The purpose of a dirty bomb is not to cause actual destruction but rather to generate panic and economic damage. In a simulation of a successful dirty bomb attack on London via an explosion of a handful of cesium chloride wrapped around a ten-pound conventional explosive, the potential effects were shown to be significant. Exploding such a device in Trafalgar Square might immediately kill only about ten people. Heated air from the blast would likely carry millions of minute flakes of cesium chloride into the breeze over London. Depending on the wind direction, this would cover Whitehall's government offices, Charing Cross, and then the city of London. Within a half an hour, radioactive dust would reach about six miles toward London's suburbs. As the air cooled, the invisible radioactive particles would fall on people, parks, gardens, pavement, and cars. People within about three miles of the blast, however, would be exposed to a small risk of cancer—about one in one thousand people would have some increased risk. At the point of the blast, the risk would be about one in fifty. The main damage would be economic as panic set in among millions of people. In fact, some people might die from panic-induced heart attacks or from being trampled if a bomb were exploded in a crowd. The cost of a cleanup operation, however, is unknowable as the radiation would likely linger for up to two hundred years if left undisturbed. It might actually be more effective to demolish entire sections of the city and remove the rubble completely.[68]

Even the dirty-bomb risk has to be put into context. Constructing such a bomb is not easy. Absent conditions only a state can provide, terrorists constructing or transporting such a device would be exposed to radiation. They would likely become sick quickly and die from radiation exposure. Also, in terms of the effects of a dirty bomb's radioactive dispersion, humans live every day with tolerable levels of radiation when simply traveling on jets or walking in the sun. Just four medical CAT scans create an increased cancer risk of 0.004—a greater risk than that posed by the London dirty-bomb scenario. Thus, while a radiological device would be an effective tool of terror, it would not be a weapon of mass destruction.[69] A terrorist would likely do far more human and economic damage by engaging in some sort of air or ground assault on a petrochemical facility or stealing and exploding a truck full of chlorine gas. As an example of the damage a leak, let alone an explosion, can do at a chemical plant, in 1984 a toxic leak at a pesticide factory in Bhopal, India, led to seven thousand immediate deaths, and eventually as many as twenty thousand people died. An additional fifteen thousand people died in Bhopal from related diseases between 1984 and 2004.[70] Furthermore, the decision to detonate a nuclear or radiological device by any terrorist group would entail the severe difficulty of acquiring and delivering it. Having decided to organize and engage in nuclear terrorism, a group would then have to obtain either a weapon or the components necessary to build one, while bypassing the safeguards designed to make doing so highly difficult. A terrorist organization would have to move these materials through a wide array of transportation nodes, evading existing (and improving) detection capabilities. Finally, terrorists would have to detonate the weapon successfully. A disruption during any point of this process would cause the entire project to fall apart, making it a high-risk and high-cost venture.[71]

Consequently, while the risk of terrorists obtaining weapons of mass destruction is not zero, terrorists appear to prefer the easiest and least expensive means, such as car bombs, assassinations, and suicide attacks. The reality of this more mundane risk remains a significant threat to modern states. Indeed, the bombs exploded in London in July 2005 were built from materials that anyone could get at local stores. A country like the United States has 600,000 bridges to protect, 361 ports to police, and 14,000 small airports that terrorists could use. There are 4 million miles of paved roadways and 95,000 miles of coastline, in addition to an open 4,000-mile border with Canada. Some 260,000 natural gas wells and 1.3 million miles of pipeline could be attacked. In terms of transportation, 1.2 billion people ride the subway system in just New York City every year, and more than 77 million people use that city's three airports each year. While the United States has hardened its government and military targets, the private sector remains highly vulnerable to attacks designed to generate fear—movie theaters, shopping malls, hotels, sporting arenas, concerts, and schools are just a few possible venues for generating fear through violent terrorist acts.[72]

Defensive Dilemmas

Asymmetric threats create significant defensive dilemmas. By their very nature, asymmetric challenges are difficult if not impossible to deter. From genocide to terrorism, these strategies and tactics are driven by deep passions that cannot be easily overcome. Deterrence in the classic sense does not work when the attacker is willing, even hoping, to die. In fact, the very strength that many nation-states have in terms of conventional deterrence makes them more likely to be attacked asymmetrically. Any strategy that seeks to stop asymmetric threats is challenged to identify the appropriate center of gravity in order to engage most effectively. A response to terrorism that relies on conventional military power actually risks playing into the hands of terrorists. Yet, doing nothing or capitulating to demands would signal weakness and invite more attacks. Striking a balance between offensive and defensive measures for managing asymmetric challenges is a central dilemma for states in the twenty-first century.

One of the most important lessons of genocide, ethnic cleansing, and the rise of terrorism and insurgency is that early, proactive engagement by the international community can prevent escalation. However, prevention creates a variety of challenges that heighten the dilemma posited by asymmetric threats. For example, the conditions that can lead to genocide and ethnic cleansing might be best managed by preventive diplomacy and, if necessary, the use of force to uphold diplomatic settlements. However, as was the case in Kosovo, many of these crises occur within sovereign states. In this sense, sovereignty becomes a barrier against preventing genocide and ethnic cleansing. Had NATO done in 1992 what it did in 1995 and 1999, tens of thousands of lives might have been saved in the Balkans. Had the United Nations moved forces into Rwanda as the violence was breaking out there, genocide might have been avoided. Early international engagement is essential to prevent local or regional violence from escalating. However, such conflicts often occur in parts of the world where great powers have minimal interests. Additionally, regional organizations and countries often do not have the capacity to handle such crises without the help of larger states. This dilemma is further heightened by the fact that it is in some of these no-man's-lands that terrorist organizations are able to move with impunity. A critical concern about Libya in early 2011 was that a failure by the international community to intervene could lead to a failed state, with al Qaeda operating from there. However, debates over whether to arm rebels fighting to overthrow the government backed with NATO air power initially faltered on concerns that al Qaeda operatives were among the rebels who would be armed.

This intervention dilemma is also true regarding the relationship between terrorism and weapons of mass destruction. In 2003, the United States invaded Iraq based on a new doctrine of preemptive war. This doctrine justified offensive attack against a sovereign country based on possible future threats. While the fear that the United States had of such a linkage between states with weapons of mass destruction and global terrorist networks was understandable, it was unfounded. Due to focus on a symptom of the problem in Iraq, the larger threat was left unattended: the potential proliferation of weapons of mass destruction from Russia and Pakistan. Meanwhile, Iran, which did have direct links to international terrorist organizations, made progress toward a nuclear weapons program. A 2001 study by a bipartisan commission, the Baker-Cutler Report, showed that the problem of weapons security in the former Soviet Union could be managed with a total expenditure of $30 billion spread out over ten years. However, the United States was heading toward $1 trillion spent in Iraq (and Afghanistan) by 2010.

The decision taken in 2009 to surge American troops into Afghanistan as part of a new counterinsurgency plan there illustrated the dilemma of using military power against asymmetric threats. Such a plan might have worked in 2006, when the Taliban was only regrouping, but by 2009 its operating area included most of southern Afghanistan and was spreading further into the country. The concept that President Barack Obama's administration adopted in late summer 2009 was built around the same counterinsurgency concepts applied in Iraq in late 2006. Obama signed off despite an internal dilemma in the policy outcome, which was announced in December 2009. First, successful counterinsurgency depends on protecting a target population in support of a legitimate government. However, that could not be said of the government of Afghanistan, which was rife with corruption and had rigged elections to stay in power. Second, even with thirty thousand more troops, there simply were not enough American and NATO forces to accomplish the mission—even just in southern Afghanistan. Third, the key to victory was in winning the hearts and minds of local populations, but there was little evidence in public opinion surveys that this was happening as most Afghani citizens had lost faith in the very government that America was fighting for. Fourth, the NATO allies were not in the fight—leaving America to do the heavy lifting at a time when its own public was turning against the war. Fifth, counterinsurgency doctrine also required a surge in civilian capacity in Afghanistan, but that capacity really did not exist in any large-scale, meaningful way. Sixth, there was little evidence that the Afghan military or police would be adequately trained in a way that would allow U.S. forces to transfer operations over to local capacities.

President Obama made clear in fall 2009 that he was not signing off on a counterinsurgency plan for all of Afghanistan and that the military planned to begin handing over operations in 2011. Yet, by late 2010, there was little evidence that the plan was working. Even worse, by surging forces into southern Afghanistan, the United States had risked turning a local, territorially driven insurgency into a more global terrorist movement within the Taliban. Moreover, while the Taliban had been forced out of southern Afghanistan, its members were as likely go into Pakistan, risking further destabilization there. On the other hand, had the United States not remained in Afghanistan, the country was at high risk for collapse, exacerbating dangers of instability in next door's nuclear-armed Pakistan and India.[73]

Good intelligence that exposes genocidal intentions, ethnic-cleansing operations, insurgencies, or terrorist plots is essential to identify opportunities for early intervention to preempt attacks. If local communities can be convinced to turn against those who perpetrate barbaric acts of violence, then culprits can be captured or killed. However, such efforts can also backfire. As the insurgency in Iraq grew in late 2003, the United States increased the prisoner population at the Abu Ghraib prison from fifty-eight hundred in September 2003 to eight thousand five months later.[74] By arresting large numbers of Iraqis, then using interrogations combined with humiliation techniques and torture, the United States might have hoped to compel prisoners to give up information. Some prisoners released back into the community might even provide intelligence information if they feared that their treatment in prison would become public in a society that placed such an emphasis on shame, particularly regarding sexual matters. The humiliation tactic was a deep psychological intrusion into basic Iraqi cultural and religious mores. Photos were taken of naked men simulating sex with each other, touching each other, and posing in a variety of compromising sexual positions while being handled on dog leashes by women prison guards.[75] Other elements of interrogation included the use of dogs to terrorize captives, dog collars on inmates, wires and electrodes attached to genitals, and physical abuse. U.S. marines in Iraq used mock executions of juvenile prisoners to frighten other prisoners, burned and tortured detainees with electric shocks, and warned a navy doctor that if he treated the prisoners, he would be killed.[76] If defeating insurgents who use the barbaric tactic of terror entailed winning hearts and minds, the United States had handed itself a major defeat.

Interrogation of prisoners can lead to actionable intelligence that might stop asymmetric attacks. One tactic used by the United States has been to send terrorists to friendly countries whose intelligence agents do not have the same restrictions on the use of violence to gain information as U.S. agents. In another controversial method that stops short of direct physical harm, American agents in Guantánamo Bay, Cuba, have had certain detainees strip to their underwear, sit in a chair while shackled hand and foot to a bolt in the floor, face strobe lights, and listen to loud rock and rap music while the temperature is adjusted to maximum levels—for up to fourteen hours at a time. Other techniques have included allowing a captive to fall into a deep sleep, then moving him to another cell, then waiting for him to fall back into a deep sleep, waking him, and moving him again—up to six times a night.[77] Yet, there is considerable dispute about whether the pressures applied in these cases work to elicit good information. Ultimately, the person being physically or mentally coerced is as likely to say what he or she thinks the captor wants to hear. Or a subject might give up some actionable intelligence combined with information that is terrifying but untrue, further spreading baseless fears.

Defensive postures against asymmetric warfare also create unique dilemmas. Using power to deter suicide terrorists is not possible because they do not fear death. Power in this case is useful only if exercised with the ability to kill suicide terrorists before they reach their targets. It is possible to create layers of perimeter security to dissuade a terrorist organization from wasting scarce resources and recruits. For example, the United States has created an integrated data system for using finger scans and photos to match identities of suspicious visitors who come into the country via airports, seaports, and border crossings. This program was expected to affect about 13 million travelers from twenty-seven countries and to cost $15 billion to implement fully by 2014.[78] At the same time, as states perform traditional national-defense functions, they risk encroaching on citizens' human rights and civil liberties. For example, once the International Civil Aviation Organization implements an international standard for facial recognition on all passports, it will have established a database of information on over 1 billion people.[79] In the United States, hundreds of citizens were detained without reasonable evidence following the September 11, 2001, attacks. In 2004, a federal judge ordered Drake University in Iowa to provide records of students who had attended an antiwar meeting. Reconciling the tension between security and freedom is thus a significant challenge of the twenty-first-century security dynamic. By 2010, Americans were increasingly concerned about full body scans and more intrusive pat-downs at airports. Additionally, the growing volume of private information being kept on citizens, or by other citizens, risked a new level of technological intrusion into liberties that seemed to many citizens almost Orwellian in nature.

Summary

Asymmetric conflict challenges the foundations of traditional approaches to power and peace. Wars between nation-states can be significantly altered by the variety of means that small, less powerful, yet dangerous actors have to set the global security agenda. The dangers posed by new threats can be severe to both nation-states and average citizens. Threats of genocide and ethnic cleansing are containable and, if international society chooses to engage them, preventable. The horrors of genocide and ethnic cleansing are real and continue despite international norms that promise intervention to halt these barbaric acts of brutality against civilian populations. In this sense, the solution lies in the willingness of the international community to act. Terrorism too can be both reduced and defeated—particularly when the nature of threats is well understood and placed in the broader context of global security.

Suggested Reading

Barnett, Roger W. *Asymmetrical Warfare: Today's Challenge to US Military Power.* Washington, DC: Potomac Books, 2003.

Bergen, Peter I. *Holy War Inc.: Inside the Secret World of Osama bin Laden.* New York: Free Press, 2002.

Daalder, Ivo, and Michael O'Hanlon. *Winning Ugly: NATO's War to Save Kosovo.* Washington, DC: Brookings, 2000.

Kaufman, Stuart. *Modern Hatreds: The Symbolic Politics of Ethnic War.* Ithaca, NY: Cornell University Press, 2001.

Kuperman, Alan J. *The Limits of Humanitarian Intervention: Genocide in Rwanda.* Washington, DC: Brookings, 2001.

Mueller, John. *Overblown: How Politicians and the Terrorism Industry Inflate National Security Threats, and Why We Believe Them.* New York: Free Press, 2007.

National Commission on Terrorist Attacks Upon the United States, *The 9/11 Report.* New York: St. Martin's Press, 2004.

Pape, Robert A. *Cutting the Fuse: The Explosion of Global Suicide Terrorism and How to Stop It.* Chicago: University of Chicago Press, 2010.

———. *Dying to Win: The Strategic Logic of Suicide Terrorism.* New York: Random House, 2005.

Power, Samantha. *"A Problem from Hell": America and the Age of Genocide.* New York: Perennial, 2003.

8

Human Security

HUMAN SECURITY FOCUSES ANALYTICAL AND POLICY ATTENTION on the problems that affect the basic safety and well-being of individuals. In this case, the quest for power and the search for peace focuses on the conditions of those people who themselves do not have power or are victims of international conditions outside their control. Approaches to human security stress the protection of human rights and democracy as well as physical challenges such as population size, food availability, disease, and the human costs of war. This approach also, however, has significant global applications. Even people who live comfortably are challenged by pressures from external human insecurity crises, which can spill over into modern and developed societies. Individuals are often threatened in the context of asymmetric attacks on civilian populations—frequently by their own governments. This chapter examines the meaning of human security in the context of human rights and democracy, population and migration, food and health, and the human costs of war.

What Is Human Security?

The question of the security, safety, or rights of the individual is not fundamentally new. The increasing number of challenges to human security, however, is new, as is the increasing number of states and nonstate actors working to put the issue at the top of the international agenda. As Canadian foreign minister Lloyd Axworthy noted, Canada explicitly adopted a foreign policy focused on human security after the Cold War to advance a "new

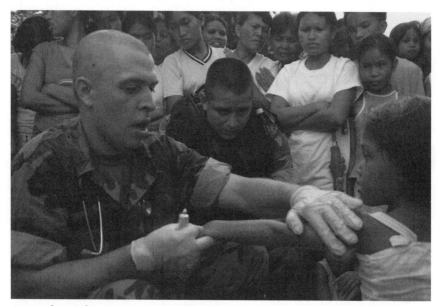

A navy hospital corpsman treats a Filipina girl as a crowd gathers around to watch in the small fishing village of Himbangan, Philippines, on February 2, 2006. Sailors and marines from the amphibious assault ship USS Essex *(LHD 2) and the dock landing ship USS* Harpers Ferry *(LSD 49) were providing humanitarian assistance for the victims of the February 17, 2006, landslide in the village of Guinsaugon on the island of Leyte. Source: Department of Defense photo by PO2 Brian P. Biller, U.S. Navy (Released).*

foreign policy paradigm."[1] As a result, Axworthy said in 2001, "several years ago, few were talking about human security. . . . Today, at every forum I attend or meeting I participate in, states of all station and tradition are using the term, and more important, are accepting the usefulness of the idea."[2] A range of countries, including Canada, Ireland, and the Scandinavian nations, are pursuing a foreign policy that emphasizes human security. International organizations and advocacy groups have also played a major role working outside the traditions of the nation-state system as part of a growing human-security network.

Human-security research seeks to identify conditions under which the actions of states' internal and external policies threaten the safety and security of individuals. The concept can also be applied to nonstate actors and transboundary phenomena that can affect the human condition. Such an approach becomes even more applicable in the era of global security as individual rights often go unprotected in the absence of international guarantees.[3] The human-security concept is also an advocacy agenda—promoting freedom from pervasive threats to people's rights, their safety, and even their lives.[4] Measuring human security, however, is a significant methodological challenge. Generally, human security can be thought to be achieved when and where individuals and communities (1) have the options necessary to end, mitigate, or adapt to threats to their human, environmental, and social rights; (2) have the capacity and freedom to exercise these options; and (3) actively participate in attaining them.[5] The United Nations' Human Development Index focuses on levels of economic development, life expectancy, and level of education as indicators of human insecurity. The application of various data shows that it is possible to achieve relatively significant increases in human security via even small increases in economic development. Taken over twenty years, the 2010 Human Development Index showed that the world had made consistent improvements in human security while at the same time the divide between those who had benefited and those who had not was wider.[6]

Human-security analysis suffers from a divergence among relative expectations of how much security any individual must have in order to be said to have attained a measure of security.[7] A family living in Mozambique or Ethiopia might have significantly different human-security expectations from one living in Egypt or South Africa. Any African citizen might have a completely different set of expectations as regards human security than a citizen from Europe or North America. Within Europe and North America, there are dramatic differences in expectations, for example, between Western and Southeastern Europe and between the United States and Mexico. Citizens in the developed world might worry about a general threat such as terrorism or global climate change. Citizens in the underdeveloped world might worry more about where their next meal will come from.

The UN Development Programme's 1994 report on human development defined a variety of areas of human security that have served as an ongoing foundation for the concept in terms of policy goals. The report identified the core elements of human security as including economic, food, health, environmental, personal, community, and political security.[8] Building on these core aspects of human security, the Commission on Human Security defined human security in 2003 as the "protect[ion of] the vital core of all human lives in ways that enhance human freedoms and human fulfillment."[9] According to Sadako Ogata and Johan Cels, this means "protecting vital freedoms—fundamental to human existence and development. . . . Human security means protecting people from severe and pervasive threats, both natural and societal, and empowering individuals and communities to develop the capabilities for making informed choices and acting on their own behalf."[10] Caroline Thomas notes that human security is about the "achievement of human dignity, which incorporates personal autonomy, control over one's life, and unhindered participation in the life of the community."[11]

Fen Osler Hampson and his colleagues identify three general approaches to human security. The first approach focuses on liberty, human rights, and the rule of law as sources of security. The second stresses achieving mechanisms to provide for the safety of peoples and to create freedom from fear. Such an approach seeks proactive ways to end war and to eliminate the underlying causes of international conflict and violence. The third approach addresses the need for "sustainable human development" by alleviating the economic sources of human insecurity and solving new sources of insecurity, such as HIV/AIDS, drug trafficking, poverty, and environmental problems. The sustainable-human-development approach has three distinct dynamics: (1) the definition extends to a large number of problems not traditionally associated with the concept of security, (2) the new understanding of these threats marginalizes those of an exclusively military nature, and (3) those threats considered to be the most relevant—such as environmental degradation and population growth—are considered to be so relevant within a global context that the national interest itself is a diminishing point of reference.[12]

A catalogue of potential threats to human security could generate an endless list of harmful aspects of the human condition. As Andrew Mack writes, "Conflating a very broad range of disparate harms under the rubric of 'insecurity' is an exercise in re-labeling that serves no apparent analytical purpose. . . . If the term 'insecurity' embraces almost all forms of harm—from affronts to dignity to genocide—its descriptive power is extremely low."[13] In his pioneering work, Mack limits the study of human security to the direct consequences of war and conflict for the human condition. Alternatively, some approaches use a broad definition of the concept that includes the general distribution of power in the structure of the international system. Caroline Thomas, for example, asserts that when power is distributed unevenly, human insecurity results when one person (or group) exercises power in a purposeful manner that harms other people. "Human security," writes Thomas, "is understood not as some inevitable occurrence but as a direct result of existing structures of power that determine who enjoys the entitlement to security and who does not."[14] While a range of specific issue areas can be assessed to measure degrees of human security, dominant issues include human rights and democracy, population and demographic change, food and health, and the human cost of war.

Human Rights and Democracy

Human rights have constituted a major element of the international security agenda since World War II and were enshrined in the establishment of the

United Nations in 1945. There is, however, considerable debate over what human rights are, what degree of rights is sufficient for all people, and the extent to which the exercise of one individual's or group's human rights may impinge on the rights of others. Human rights advocacy also raises general questions about the moral imperative to protect human rights versus the tradition of sovereignty. Moreover, a particularistic concept of human rights—such as the Euro-American concept of individual liberty—might be seen as infringing on the cultural or religious rights of other societies. Economic sanctions or military intervention to stop human rights abuses can also create entirely new sets of humanitarian problems, even when well intended. Closely related to the question of human rights is the degree of political freedoms assured and protected by governments—and as such the degree to which governments are responsive to the needs of their peoples. Thus, the degree of democracy has also become an important measure of human security.

Contemporary Challenges to Human Rights

The global human rights situation improved dramatically with the end of the Cold War. Hundreds of millions of people were liberated from dictatorships in Central and Eastern Europe. The end of direct superpower competition led to a resolution of proxy conflicts—for example, in Latin America—where human rights were persistently violated. The end of the Cold War, however, also resulted in a resurgence of the quest for self-determination in ethnically complex regions. Culture and religion also have emerged as significant human rights questions—particularly in the Islamic world. Is it a human right to exercise religious freedom if that denies individual liberty? Are Islamic women in some societies denied human rights because they often cannot show their faces in public, attain higher education, drive cars, or vote? Or is such a perspective derived from a Western concept of human rights and thus an expression of cultural imperialism and Western domination? Even in the Western world, religious differences highlight a human rights dilemma. In Ireland a woman cannot legally attain information about how to get a safe abortion—a state of affairs consistent with the religious beliefs of Ireland's 90 percent Catholic population but in violation of human rights doctrine as codified by the European Union, which guarantees the freedom to travel. In December 2010, the European Union found that Ireland's restrictive laws did not sufficiently protect the safety of women. Conversely, in China, the government provides strong incentives for women to have only one child—and the result is a high rate of abortions. In this case, China has been criticized for advocating a draconian population-control policy that denies the right to procreate. The United States has also been accused by international human rights groups of violating the rights of immigrants seeking to cross the border from Mexico. Many European states will not extradite criminals to the United States in opposition to the U.S. death penalty, which is seen as cruel and unusual punishment.

Human Rights Watch identifies a range of areas where the United States faces human rights deficiencies, including child welfare, criminal sentencing and drug laws, the death penalty, discrimination against gays and lesbians, immigration and the treatment of noncitizens, labor rights, police brutality, prison conditions, racism and discrimination, and women's rights.[15] At the same time, the United States has served as a beacon of human rights. It has sent its soldiers to die to protect the rights and dignity of other peoples. As a country with interests, however, the United States has had to choose priorities and thus supported authoritarian governments in Pakistan and Saudi Arabia. In 2002, U.S. Secretary of Defense Donald Rumsfeld visited Afghanistan and declared the Herat-based warlord Ismail Khan an "appealing person." Khan had eliminated dissent, controlled the press, and forced women to wear burkas—a custom Washington had claimed would end with the liberation of Afghanistan.[16] Europeans also share this dilemma as they confront a significant increase in European anti-Semitism and anti-immigrant attitudes reflected in increased incidents of violence against North African and Middle Eastern immigrants and gypsies. Whether Muslims should be permitted to wear headdresses has been a consistent source of tension in France and elsewhere in Europe (including in Switzerland, which also sought to ban the building of minarets on mosques). Should their rights as Muslims be respected, or should they be required to assimilate?

The standards for assessing human rights are the guarantees articulated in the Universal Declaration of Human Rights. As Jack Donnelly notes, these rights—such as the values of nondiscrimination and an adequate standard of living for individuals—provide a basis on which to organize action for remedies. The rights (with the exception of the right to self-determination) are specifically rights that are indivisible and not merely a menu from which one can pick and choose. Nevertheless, there is a core tension between such universal rights and the historical right of sovereignty.[17] As Donnelly writes, "Internationally recognized human rights impose obligations on and are exercised against sovereign territorial states. . . . 'Everybody has a right to x' in contemporary international practice means 'Each state has the authority and responsibility to implement and protect the right to x within its territory.'"[18]

The scope of human rights challenges spans all regions of the globe, though some areas are clearly more violation-free than others. Human Rights Watch summarizes regional human rights trends in its annual *World Report*.[19] According to the organization's surveys, Africa faces some of the most severe human rights challenges among the regions of the world. In the new millennium, Africa has hosted 3.3 million refugees; the continent has almost 30 percent of the world's refugee population and about 13.5 million, or more than half, of the world's 25 million internally displaced persons. Africa also was challenged by the relationship between transnational disease (especially HIV/AIDS) and basic human needs (such as access to medical treatment more readily available in the developed world). Between 2000 and 2020, some 25 million Africans were projected to die prematurely. Meanwhile, violent conflict ravaged large areas of Africa. In the Democratic Republic of the Congo, Sierra Leone, and Sudan, warring parties employed gang rape, violent abduction followed by repeated rapes, and amputation of breasts and sexual organs. Africa's efforts to advance a continent-wide human rights agenda were complicated by Libya's role as the region's representative to the UN Commission on Human Rights, which it chaired in 2003. Libya has a long record of detaining government opponents without charge or trial, prohibiting the formation of political parties or independent nongovernmental groups, constraining press freedoms, and torturing political opponents.

Latin America has seen significant improvement in regional human rights trends with the end of the Cold War. Limitations on political dissent remain a particular problem in Cuba and public protests have produced violent government reactions in Venezuela, Paraguay, and Bolivia. Haiti has severe problems resulting from a lack of governance and general instability with competing militias combating each other for power. The situation in Haiti grew catastrophic in 2010 when a massive earthquake hit the country. While the international community rallied to Haiti's aid, the situation was a disaster, including outbreaks of cholera ten months later coupled with political instability. Antigovernment rebels in Colombia (the FARC) have carried out a persistent terrorist campaign that includes targeting of civilians. In one circumstance, these rebels launched a gas cylinder bomb that hit a church in Bojaya where displaced persons were gathered. This attack killed 119 people, including 48 children. Conversely, the government has also used severe tactics against captured rebel members and their sympathizers.

While many states in Asia have moved away from an argument that "Asian values" justify strong state power over restriction of liberties, the global war on terrorism gave many leaders a new rationale to deny individual freedoms. In Afghanistan, for example, the human rights condition improved considerably with the initial ouster of the oppressive Taliban government in 2001. By 2010, however, the overall situation in the country had declined substantially. In Bangladesh and Sri Lanka, massive numbers of displaced persons must worry daily about their personal security—let alone access to education, clean water, and health care. In Malaysia, a political opponent of the prime minister was arrested and given a flawed trial, imprisoned, and subjected to physical mistreatment. In Myanmar, the military government placed long-time dissident Aung San Suu Kyi under house arrest for a total of fifteen years, on and off, beginning in 1989—only restoring her freedom in late 2010. The government in Myanmar also conscripted large numbers of child soldiers and forcibly relocated entire ethnic communities. Hindus in Myanmar have been especially targeted, their homes looted, vandalized, and burned; temples and sacred sites destroyed; and scores of Hindu women and girls gang raped in front of male relatives while the government did little or nothing to investigate or prosecute these crimes. In China, the Communist Party has regularly repressed political and religious freedoms, particularly in Tibet. Meanwhile, North Korea was, in 2011, effectively a massive prison camp under the rule of the world's last remaining totalitarian dictator.

Europe has demonstrated a deep commitment to human rights and a desire to expand them more broadly through Eurasia. When the North Atlantic Treaty Organization and the European Union expanded to include new members from Central and Eastern Europe, these countries had to meet specific criteria for respecting human rights. In a historical reversal, Russian minority populations in former Soviet republics have sought, and received, due regard and protections for their status. Ethnic cleansing in the Balkans has been halted—though the seeds of conflict remain unresolved. Throughout the Caucasus and Central Asia, however, the human rights situation has been grim. A combination of rule by former Soviet crony dictators, competition over oil-driven economic growth in the Caspian Sea region, ethnic conflict and civil war in a number of states, and the general preference for stability over human rights dominates the war on terrorism in this area. Uzbekistan, in particular, was ruled by an authoritarian government that has imprisoned poets and other citizens in a crackdown on political Islam, which has terrorist support in the Islamic Movement of Uzbekistan. Meanwhile, Belarus remains stuck in a Soviet-era relationship with Russia, and Ukraine exists on the margins of instability. In Ukraine and Russia, press freedoms have been severely curtailed. Journalists investigating sensitive governmental activity have been harassed and even murdered. Throughout the European region, there is growing tension regarding the need to protect the rights of immigrants—especially the cultural and religious rights of those coming from North Africa and the Middle East. In October 2010, German chancellor Angela Merkel asserted that her country's effort to build a multicultural society had failed.

The Middle East is one of the world's most problematic areas for human rights. A failure to resolve the long-standing Palestinian question, both in the Palestinian areas and for refugees who fled Israeli occupation, plagues the region. Between 2000 and 2002, some 2,500 Palestinians and over 650 Israelis were killed, and at least 21,000 Palestinians and 2,000 Israelis were injured in ongoing conflict. In the 2006 war in southern Lebanon against Hezbollah, some 1,225 Lebanese and 119 Israeli soldiers were killed. Of these, 510 in Lebanon were civilians, and 40 Israeli civilians were killed. In the 2009–2010 war in Gaza, about 1,400 Palestinians were killed, the vast majority of them civilians, in retaliation for rocket attacks that had killed a relative handful of Israelis and were not coordinated by the Palestinian authority. Some of the most dramatic violations of human rights in the region come from the hands of Arab governments against their own peoples. The lack of legitimately elected and supported governments in Jordan, Morocco, Saudi Arabia, and the smaller Gulf states—combined with the unilateral rule of long-standing political parties in Egypt, Libya, Syria, Tunisia, and Yemen—made progress toward advancing regional human rights difficult, especially when there is a preference for stability. Throughout the region, justice is poorly administered and often takes place outside the rule of law. Peaceful critics of governments have been imprisoned, and press and publishing freedoms severely restricted. These dynamics came to the foreground in early 2011 when popular movements spread from North Africa to Iran, pressing for basic freedoms for people and the fall of authoritarian rule. In the cases of Tunisia and Egypt, that led to an initially smooth transition. However, governments turned military and police force on their own people for sustained periods in Bahrain, Iran, Libya, Syria, and Yemen. During the 1980s and 1990s, secular and Western-leaning Turkey killed twenty-five thousand of its own people in its campaign against Kurdish separatist fighters. Islamists in Turkey wishing to display their faith publicly were barred from public service, and the Turkish military intervened on occasion to oppose the policy of the popularly elected government.

The human rights dimension of human security reflects a mixed record. Improvements might occur in one part of the world, while significant declines occur in others. Much progress depends also on the priority that the world community puts on advancing human rights. When concern about national security is high, then respect for human rights tends to decline. There is a serious dilemma in this approach as near-term support for authoritarian government tends to stir violent opposition in the long-term. In supporting authoritarian governments that help in the campaign against terrorism, the world simultaneously risks the emergence of a new generation of terrorists spawned by the resentment that oppression can breed. Conversely, under what conditions is the international community obliged to intervene in cases of gross violation of human rights inside sovereign countries? While nations acted, for example, to save rebels from brutal military repression in Libya in 2011, they did not do so when the same circumstances occurred in the countries of friendly governments like Bahrain and Yemen.

Degrees of Democracy

Democracy is seen as increasing human security because well-functioning democracies facilitate the peaceful resolution of internal disputes. In democracies, political and military leadership are held accountable for their actions, and it is therefore harder to pursue policies that violate human rights. Democratic institutions alone do not guarantee stability or peace. Indeed, the process of democratization can be highly destabilizing if political, ethnic, or religious groups position themselves—often violently—to attain power. Also, the democratic principle of self-determination can stir separatist movements that often result in violent conflict or civil war. Generally, however, democracies protect basic political freedoms, particularly minority rights, which accord a higher sensitivity to the cause of human security.

Since 1973, Freedom House has conducted annual surveys measuring the level of freedom worldwide, which provides a standard for measuring effective democracy. Freedom House generates rankings of degrees of freedom by evaluating the electoral process, political pluralism and participation, the functioning of government, freedom of expression and belief, associational and organizational rights, the rule of law, and personal autonomy and individual rights. A country with a score of 1 to 2.5 is understood to be "free"; 3 to 5.5, "partly free"; and 5.5 to 7.0, "not free." The areas ranked 6 and 7 have the lowest degree of democratic freedom. A ranking of 6 means that people in a country have severely restricted rights of expression and association, and there are almost always political prisoners and other manifestations of political terror. These countries are characterized by a few partial rights, however, such as some religious and social freedoms and the ability to engage in business activity and to have relatively free private discussions. Countries with a score of 7 allow virtually no freedoms, and there is an overwhelming and justified fear of repression. States ranked in 2010 at the high end of "not free" included Myanmar, Equatorial Guinea, Eritrea, Libya, North Korea, Somalia, Sudan, Turkmenistan, and Uzbekistan.

Over several decades of Freedom House surveys, the Western Hemisphere and Western Europe rank as having the highest degrees of freedom. Worldwide, the number of "free" countries grew from forty-three in 1973 to eighty-nine in 2003 while the number of "not free" states declined from sixty-nine to forty-eight. The area with the highest number of "not free" states is sub-Saharan Africa, though that too has dropped from twenty-eight in 1973 to sixteen in 2003. In non-Muslim countries, the number of "not free" countries has declined from forty-six in 1973 to fourteen in 2003, while the number of "free" countries has risen from forty-one to eighty-seven. Muslim-majority countries have not, however, witnessed considerable change, with twenty-three countries not free in 1973 and twenty-seven not free countries in 2003. In 2003 there were only 9 countries in the Muslim world with electoral democracies, whereas 112 non-Muslim countries have such systems. Thus, the global trend has been toward more democracy—except in the Muslim world. Importantly, Freedom House notes that, as a percentage of the global gross domestic product, "free" countries account for 89 percent, or $26.76 trillion, of annual economic output. Meanwhile, "not free" and "partly free" countries account for a combined 56 percent of the world's population—a decline from 65 percent in 1973.

The relative degree of democracy is an important measure of human security at several levels. First, as a general rule, democracies have been better able to hold governmental authorities accountable for human rights abuses. Second, there is a correlation between lack of democracy and inhibited economic development. Third, in democracies the ability to set the agenda and win arguments via persuasion diffuses power away from central authority and into the hands of citizens who choose to engage in the democratic process. Fourth, there has been negative growth in the degree of freedom and civil liberty in the Muslim world. Often contemporary terrorism is associated with Islamic movements, but it is also the case that many movements evolve out of a sense of oppression by participants' own governments, and religion plays a minimal role.

Reform of authoritarian governments in the Islamic world could provide new outlets for legitimate political expression and become an important means of undermining terrorism. This assumption, though, presents dilemmas because strong governments can be necessary for combating some terrorist groups. At the same time, strong governments that repress citizens' rights can spawn new terrorist movements. Democracies might risk sacrificing some political freedoms in the name of safety due to fear of international terrorism. In that case, while seeking protection from external attacks, governments gain in power at the expense of individual freedoms. This too can spark a backlash and even lead to violence against governments. When he blew up the Alfred P. Murrah Federal Building in Oklahoma City in 1993, Timothy McVeigh was, in his warped view, protesting the encroachment of the federal government on the private lives of citizens. Democracies are uniquely vulnerable to terrorists and other criminals, who can use the freedoms that democratic governments protect in order to move about freely. Reconciling the demand for safety and the maintenance of freedom has become one of the most significant challenges for human security in the twenty-first century.

Population and Demographic Change

The Earth has finite resources and finite space; yet, its population grew exponentially at massive rates during the twentieth century. The world population of 6.8 billion by 2010 was over 3.5 times that at the beginning of the twentieth century. The global population in 2050 will likely be about 9.1 billion. The time required for the global population to grow from 5 to 6 billion—twelve years—was shorter than the interval between any of the previous 1 billion increases. At the turn of the century, the global population was growing at the rate of 371 million—the equivalent of a new Western Europe—per five-year period.[20] India and China both have over 1.2 billion people. China is expected to add over 10 million people per year through 2015.

There are four main approaches to understanding the relationship between population and security. First, states face resource-scarcity problems and might seek to capture new territory to meet their populations' needs. Second, lateral pressure can result when a state extends its interests outside territorial boundaries, leading to a combination of high population growth, high technological capacity, and inadequate resources.[21] Third, military capability is closely related to population in that, for population growth to cause expansionist behavior by a state, some military capacity is necessary. Traditionally, at least in modern, developed states, a sizeable population can be both a source of economic power and an important means of raising large armies. A fourth approach sees positive security consequences resulting from population growth. The growth of population might force innovation and reduce conflict as free trade, technology, and human ingenuity foster cooperation, increased productivity, and efficiency.[22] It is indeed the case that, while there is enormous poverty and deprivation globally, more people in the twenty-first century are living in comfort and relative wealth than at any time in human history.

While population can exacerbate a conflict situation, significant military capabilities may be a necessary ingredient. Thus, population pressure alone may not explain expansionist or aggressive behavior.[23] Also, countries with low technology are more subject to population pressures and resulting conflict than more technologically advanced states. Finally, states do not actually appear to engage in conflict for purposes of acquiring new land for a population. Rather, this is more often an excuse for expansion than an actual cause.[24] Overpopulation is most likely to be a security problem when rapid demographic change within or among populations occurs. Such changes can be indicators of coming violence that might result in international or civil wars. An expanding agrarian population might rise up to protest how land is used by its owners or their treatment of the people living on it. An expanding urban population combined with declining economic growth might turn publics toward protest, crime, and violence. An expanding population of better-educated youths facing limited opportunities can experience internal conflict as its members compete for elite status within society. A large "youth

bulge" in which people aged fifteen to twenty-five come to play a disproportionate role within a population can also lead to large-scale mobility or public
dissatisfaction with the status quo. Migration of a population into an area already settled by another distinct ethnic or political group can breed conflict.[25]
Finally, declining population rates can signal a state's inability to meet basic
human needs.

Population movements can become a security issue for several reasons.
First, international migration is increasing due to a desire either to flee conflict areas or to pursue a better economic future. These movements are aided
by advances in global networks of communication and transportation. Other
factors such as environmental degradation or natural disasters also generate
cross-border or internal movements of people. Second, more people want
to leave their countries than there are countries willing to or capable of accepting them. Third, most of the world's population movement is from one
underdeveloped country to another, and the world's largest refugee flows
have been within Africa, South Asia, Southeast Asia, and the Persian Gulf.[26]
Governments might force emigration as a means of achieving cultural homo-
geneity or asserting the dominance of one ethnic community over another.
Governments have also forced outward migration as a means of dealing with
political dissidents and class enemies. Under Fidel Castro, Cuba managed
some of its internal dissent by opening up prisons and allowing political
opponents to leave the island for the United States. This policy removed a
threat to the Castro government and put significant strain on America's immigration capacity. Ireland has, over time, used outward migration as a way
to manage high unemployment at home. States might also force population
movement as a strategic objective—perhaps to put pressure on a neighboring
state or states. States have also relocated their national populations to secure
territory they have seized. For example, the Soviet Union moved significant
Russian populations into the Baltic states after World War II. By the time of
the Soviet collapse in 1991, 22 million Russians were living in the non-Russian
areas of the former Soviet Union.

Economic migration can also become a security problem if migrant workers' presence fuels nationalist reactions. Legal immigrants have been harassed
and treated violently even in advanced democratic societies such as the
United States and the nations of Western Europe. This condition occurs for
several reasons. When migrants are actively opposed to the regime in their
home country, they can skew political discourse within their country of resi-
dence. Migrants or refugees can also be perceived as political, economic, or
security risks to their host country if they strain state capacity or intend to engage in violence, such as terrorism or other criminal activity. Immigrants can
also be seen as a cultural threat to a host society, exacerbating social, racial,

or religious tensions. A host country might turn on those visiting within it and use them as hostages or human shields to threaten, blackmail, or prevent aggression on the part of their country of origin.[27] The movement of populations across borders also provides new networks of globalization as money flows back and forth between émigrés and their home families. While the vast majority of such financial transfers are legitimate, some have ultimately gone to finance international terrorist movements.

Population Trends and Demographic Developments

Data available from the UN Fund for Population Assistance demonstrates the difficulty of ascertaining and regional disparities in population trends.[28] Sub-Saharan Africa has the most severe population challenges. The region is rife with health problems, human displacements, violent conflicts, and political strife—all compounded by ongoing increases in population. Over the past several decades, sub-Saharan Africa's population grew faster than that of any other region. The population there doubled between 1975 and 2000—rising from 325 to 650 million—and was expected to reach 1.1 billion by 2011 and is expected to double to over 2 billion by 2050. Annual growth rates are 2.2 percent. Nearly half of Africa's population is between the ages of five and twenty-four; thus, future growth in population is likely to remain very high. Only recently has a general acceptance of the need for reproductive-health awareness, family planning, and the use of contraception emerged. The region faces a severe shortage of health professionals, managers, researchers, planners, and technicians to implement population-assistance programs. The absence of significant infrastructure makes it difficult to bring the best means of coping with these challenges into the region—even for the purposes of gaining good data on the nature of the population problem.

The Middle East, which spreads from North Africa to the Persian Gulf, has an overall population of about 300 million, with annual population growth rates of 2.7 percent. The Middle East's population is young, with almost 39 percent below the age of fifteen and 50 percent under twenty-five. The number of women of reproductive age grew from 50 to 69 million during the 1990s. These population trends exacerbate the human-security problem in the Middle East by compounding the challenge of economic underdevelopment. In the Arab world, 62 million people live on under $1 per day, and 145 million live on under $2 per day. There have also been positive demographic trend lines in the Middle East at the dawn of the twenty-first century. The death and infant and child mortality rates have declined in most Arab countries. Fertility rates have also fallen significantly. Nevertheless, poverty has worsened throughout the region with a significant effect on reproductive-health services, education, and employment. Rapid urbanization, changing migration patterns, dwindling financial resources for population programs, and increasing rates of HIV/AIDS infection make the rapid population growth all the more challenging.

Sixty percent of the world's population resides in the Asia-Pacific region, which has also made considerable progress in reducing population growth. The average population growth rate at the turn of the century was 1.3 percent—the lowest in the developing regions of the world. Life expectancy was a relatively high sixty-five years. Nevertheless, five countries in the area were likely to account for nearly 45 percent of the world's population growth between 2002 and 2050: Bangladesh, China, India, Indonesia, and Pakistan. Specific problems include maternal mortality ratios exceeding four per one thousand births and high infant and toddler mortality rates in Afghanistan, Bhutan, Cambodia, India, Laos, Nepal, and Timor-Leste. There are also some 600 million illiterate adults in the region. Rapid urbanization, high levels of water and air pollution, and increases in HIV/AIDS infection are all serious manifestations of population problems in this region. While it had a high number of people under the age of twenty-five, Asia also had the largest percentage of elderly. In Asia, 8.8 percent of the population was over the age of sixty in 2000, a number projected to rise to 14.7 percent by 2025.

Eastern Europe and Central Asia represent a diverse group of countries with many states benefiting from membership in the European Union, while others face declining populations spurred by poor health care and the spread of HIV/AIDS. Countries like Azerbaijan and Kazakhstan are especially challenged by the combination of population and development. There is also a large discrepancy between life expectancy for males and females, as well as declining capacity to care for an aging population. Low-paying jobs and unemployment have also led to a rise in illegal trafficking of women and girls for prostitution. In Russia, average life expectancy for men is in the mid-fifties, and overall population growth was in decline at the turn of the century.

By 2011, Latin America and the Caribbean had a total population of 534 million. The average rate of population growth was 1.46 percent, which was a decline from 1.72 percent during the 1990s. Women's risk of dying during childbirth was high, with a ratio of 1 in 160. Moreover, high risk of HIV/AIDS infection and a high teenage fertility rate (between 2000 and 2005, seventy-one births per one thousand girls aged fifteen to nineteen) adds to a significant pressure on states to do more to meet their populations' basic needs. Latin America is particularly challenged by large population movements toward massive urban centers. Some of these megacities exist on the margins of a complete breakdown in health services and have high incidents of child prostitution and other illegal activity. Trends in Latin America reflect a global increase in urban populations since 1950, when only 750 million (about 29 percent of world population) lived in cities. By 2000, the United Nations projected that the number had quadrupled to about 2.93 billion (48.5 percent of the world's population). Among this new urban citizenry, by 2003, 89 percent lived in underdeveloped countries where the number of urban citizens had multiplied more than six times—to about 40 percent of the world's urban population. The United Nations projects that by 2025 to 2030, people living in underdeveloped countries will account for 98 percent of all new urban dwellers. Over half of Asia's population will be living in urban centers, and another billion people will press the limits of urban population centers over the next twenty years. By 2020, as much as 70 percent of the Chinese population alone will be living in cities. The United Nations estimates that, by 2015, there will be as many as 523 cities, each with 1 million inhabitants, containing 40 percent of the world's population. By 2000, there were fourteen cities with 10 million inhabitants, with a projected twenty-six (twenty-two in underdeveloped countries) by 2015.[29]

Just after the turn of the century, nearly 50 percent of all people in the world were under age twenty-five, and about 20 percent were between ages ten and nineteen.[30] Among adolescents, 87 percent lived in developing countries. Overall, some 238 million children (one in every four) lived in conditions of extreme poverty, while many lived without their parents or had been marginalized by humanitarian disaster, migration, disability, or poor health conditions. About 13 million children under age fifteen had lost one or both parents to HIV/AIDS. Between 100 and 250 million children lived on the streets. One in every 230 people worldwide was a child or adolescent forced from his or her home as a result of war. Meanwhile, 57 million young men and 96 million young women aged fifteen to twenty-four in developing countries could not read or write. Children have also been used widely as soldiers in warfare—particularly in Africa. Women of all ages confront unequal power relations relative to men, and human rights abuses affecting women have proliferated to include forced marriage, child marriage, sexual violence and coercion, sexual trafficking, and female genital mutilation. An estimated 14 million young women between ages fifteen and nineteen give birth each year. For this age group, complications due to pregnancy and childbirth are a leading cause of death—with unsafe abortions being a major risk factor. In countries like Niger and Uganda, the average woman in 2010 was having about seven children in her lifetime—whereas in Japan women had an average of 1.2 children.

Over two people are added to the world's population every second.[31] Relative population growth has, however, actually been declining. The annual average growth rate was approximately 1.2 percent in 2002, a decline from 2.2

percent in 1963 and 1964. This decline is driven mainly by reduced fertility among the world's women, who now give birth to an average 2.6 children over their lifetimes. Still, this number represents about half of a child per woman more than needed to ensure replacement of the population. This level will likely drop below replacement level by 2050 as fertility rates continue to decline. At the same time that fertility is declining, the number of women in their childbearing years is increasing relative to the rest of the world population. These women accounted for three-fourths of the global population growth in 2010. Moreover, age demographics show trends toward growth of younger populations resulting from a relatively high but declining fertility rate combined with a moderate but declining mortality rate. Children (zero to fourteen years of age) represent 29 percent of the world's population; young adults (fifteen to twenty-nine years of age) and women of childbearing age (fifteen to forty-nine years of age) each comprise 26 percent of the world's population.

A critical nexus between demographic challenges and security exists in the Middle East, where young males are becoming dominant among the overall population. The United Nations estimated that, in 2010, in Egypt and Saudi Arabia the proportion of the population aged thirty or younger would approach 60 percent. Young males represent 70 to 90 percent of first-time job seekers and often lack marketable skills. There are twice as many new workers emerging as there are jobs available, which can lead to strong pressures toward economic migration.[32] In already unstable and underdeveloped societies, this leads to economic dislocation, low wages, social free time, anger, and possibly violence. Historically, such demographic pressure troughs have been associated with unrest and violence in Russia (1910s), Japan (1920s), Germany (1930s), and Cambodia (1970s), and similar patterns are repeating in Iran and Saudi Arabia.[33] The population in the Middle East is also aging. Over 20 percent of the population in Egypt and Iran and nearly 15 percent of that in Saudi Arabia is expected to be over age sixty by 2050.[34] Even in modern developed countries, the aging of the current young population will present serious population pressures. For example, an estimated 25 percent of Japan's population will be over age seventy-five by 2050. The pressure to sustain expensive welfare benefits for this aging generation in Europe and Japan will likely strain budgets significantly and could impact long-term economic growth and stability.

Migration and Refugees

As the number of young people expands in places like the Middle East, and as population growth rates decline in Europe and the former Soviet Union, migration pressure will increase significantly in the twenty-first century. Europe will most likely feel the high impact of net migration from North Africa and the Middle East. The result is projected to be the growth of an ethnic socioeconomic underclass in Europe. Instability can thus be imported as immigrants maintain ties to their homelands. They could sustain such links by protecting insurgencies, supporting sides in conflicts in their countries of origin, and solidifying transnational movements.[35] Migration is especially problematic for underdeveloped countries as the pull to leave is highest among the best-trained and most capable people—causing the best and brightest to leave and deterring them from investing their skills in the advancement of their home country's development. According to the Arab Inter-parliamentary Union, some 54 percent of doctors and 26 percent of engineers migrate, and more than 50 percent of Arab and African students who study abroad do not return.[36] Some countries, like South Africa, find themselves deeply strained to meet the needs of their own populations but, at the same time, receive large inflows of economic refugees from places like next-door Mozambique.

The United States is increasingly affected by Latino immigration, which has prompted some controversial analysis and a nativist backlash. This was somewhat ironic, as between 2005 and 2009, net immigration of illegal immigrants into the United States fell by two-thirds. Samuel Huntington argued that "the persistent inflow of Hispanic immigrants threatened to divide the United States into two peoples, two cultures, and two languages."[37] He asserted that the basic values enshrined in American civil culture reflect the white, British, and Protestant traditions of the seventeenth and eighteenth centuries, which give America a clear definition in terms of race, ethnicity, culture, and religion. Huntington saw that tradition being threatened by a new intellectual preference for multiculturalism, combined with the pressures of globalization. He called the end result "the single most immediate and most serious challenge to America's traditional identity" coming from the "immense and continuing immigration from Latin America, especially from Mexico, and the fertility rates of these immigrants compared to black and white American natives." Huntington proposed a scenario of what would happen if Mexican immigration to the United States abruptly stopped. The annual flow of legal immigrants would drop by about 175,000, illegal entries would diminish dramatically, and the wages of low-income U.S. citizens would improve. Those who did immigrate to the United States would come from a much more highly educated stratum of Latin America's population.

Huntington differentiated Hispanic immigration into the United States from the movements of other ethnic groups by focusing on six factors. First, the existence of the shared U.S.-Mexican border makes the issue of immigration an immediate and ongoing problem. Second, the scale of the movement south to north is immense—to the point that Latin Americans have outpaced blacks as the largest ethnic group in the United States. Third, much of the immigration from Latin America is illegal, with estimates of illegal entry by Mexicans into the United States being as high as 350,000 per year during the 1990s. Fourth, Hispanic immigrants have a strong regional concentration in the American Southwest, creating a particularly strong influence on the local economy and politics there. Fifth, the movement of Hispanics northward is persistent. Sixth, Hispanics have a historical claim to the territory in which they are settling—having lost the land initially in the Texas War of Independence and the Mexican-American War. Huntington notes that Latin American immigrants do not assimilate American political traditions and cultural norms but rather persist in maintaining their own. This trend has sparked a growing debate over whether English should be the sole official language or whether Spanish should be adopted as well. According to Huntington, "Continuation of this large immigration (without improved assimilation) could divide the United States into a country of two languages and two cultures," which would "not necessarily be the end of the world; it would, however, be the end of the America we have known for more than three centuries"; further, "Americans should not let that change happen unless they are convinced that this new nation would be a better one."

America was, of course, built by immigrants, including Europeans, Hispanics, and Asians. Raul Yzaguirre, president of the National Council of La Raza, quotes Benjamin Franklin to point to limitations in Huntington's focus. Franklin said, "I have great misgivings about these immigrants because of their clannishness, their little knowledge of English, their press, and the increasing need of interpreters. . . . I suppose in a few years [interpreters] will also be needed in the [Congress] to tell one-half of our legislators what the other half say." Franklin was referring not to the Hispanic immigrants Huntington fears but rather to Germans. Yzaguirre concludes, "Today's immigrants, their children, and grandchildren believe in America. Why can't Samuel Huntington?" However, observers like Fouad Ajami agree with Huntington's analysis. Ajami writes that, when he immigrated to the United States, "the door was open (I walked through it four decades ago), but the assumption was that older loyalties would be set aside. . . . It was, after all, the 'newness' of the New World that had created its magnetic appeal." He adds, "In saying there is no 'Americano dream,' Huntington restates the case for that simpler and older American dream." Another admirer, Patrick Buchanan, writes, "Even as one welcomes the eminent Harvard professor to the oft-derided ranks of those resisting the mass invasion of the United States, let us concede the hour is late. Huntington may have just climbed over an adobe wall only to find himself inside the Alamo."

While socioeconomic pressures drive much of the world's migration, much of it also results from forced population movements due to human action or natural disaster. Refugees are, as defined by the United Nations, "persons who are outside their country and cannot return owing to a well-founded fear of persecution because of their race, religion, nationality, political opinion, or membership of a particular social group."[38] Other "persons of concern" can include asylum seekers, refugees who have returned home but still need help in rebuilding their lives, local civilian communities that are directly affected by the movements of refugees, stateless persons, and growing numbers of internally displaced persons.[39] At the beginning of the twenty-first century, the UN agency responsible for monitoring data and assisting such individuals estimated a worldwide total of just over 17.093 million refugees or otherwise displaced people. Regionally, this includes nearly 6.188 million in Asia, just over 4.285 million in Africa, 4.268 million in Europe, 1.316 million in Latin America and the Caribbean, 962,000 in North America, and 74,100 in Oceania.[40] In 2009, this number had grown to over 42 million, including 26 million internally displaced people.

In its 2003 report "Refugees by Numbers," the UN High Commissioner for Refugees (UNHCR) noted positively that about 3.6 million refugees and other groups assisted by the United Nations had recently returned home. This included nearly 2 million Afghan refugees from Pakistan and Iran, as well as about 750,000 internally displaced people within Afghanistan. Other major homeward population movements occurred in Angola, Sierra Leone, Burundi, Bosnia-Herzegovina, Sri Lanka, and the Russian Federation. The major focus of refugee outflow has been in Africa, with Liberia and Côte d'Ivoire being especially problematic. In Latin America, Colombia has been a source of growing numbers of internally displaced peoples. Meanwhile, nearly half of the total people of concern are in Asia. In 2002, a total of just over 1.014 million people sought protection from another state for fear of persecution at home. The United Kingdom processed 110,700 asylum applications, with main countries of origin being Iraq, Zimbabwe, Afghanistan, Somalia, and China. The United States received 81,100 applications, mainly from China, Mexico, Colombia, Haiti, and India. Meanwhile, a global estimate of 951,000 "stateless" individuals includes permanently displaced war-affected populations or ethnic groups such as the Roma gypsy population in Europe.

Insecurity can result for refugees and displaced peoples at several levels. First, those who have fled their homes often do so as a result of severe violence and are forcibly expelled from long-standing homelands. In 2010, the United Nations reported that the number of forcibly displaced peoples had risen to 43.3 million—the largest number since the mid-1990s. Moreover, the number voluntary returning to their homelands had fallen to the lowest level in two decades. Second, refugee camps have notoriously poor security and overall conditions. Refugees often must flee a situation with only the clothes on their backs and the items in their pockets. Basic human needs must be met upon their arrival—often in dangerous and poorly maintained refugee camps. Third, refugees often find themselves turning to petty crime or getting caught up in organized criminal rackets—with women often falling victim to sexual slavery or resorting to prostitution. Fourth, refugees and asylum seekers often become targets of hatred and persecution based on race or religion in their host countries. Fifth, some international actors might use the threat of violence against refugees as a deterrent or other tool of warfare.[41] Refugees returning to their homes after conflicts end—especially children—can have deep psychological scars. They often need assistance in rebuilding, restarting their lives, and restoring their lost traditions. Even more problematically, refugees returning home can displace those who did the displacing in the first place—potentially sparking new conflict. Military conflict is a primary producer of refugees but other factors can include land reform policy, agricultural development, and natural disasters such as droughts, floods, earthquakes, and large tropical storms. The World Commission on Dams estimates that between 40 and 80 million people have been displaced by dam construction alone.[42] Solving such broader problems is thus also essential to resolving challenges posed by the long-term displacement of peoples.

The problem of internally displaced peoples also poses a major threat to human security both inside states and in areas beyond state borders that experience spillover effects. The United Nations estimates that, by 2003, approximately 25 million people had been forcibly displaced within fifty countries.[43] A comment from a displaced person inside Turkey provides an illustration of internal displacement:

> Soldiers came to our village, they started [with] the village guards. Then the [guerrillas] attacked and killed three village guards. After that, those who had joined the village guards decided that they did not want to be village guards. They wanted to turn their guns back to the army. At that point, the soldiers came and burned the village. . . . There was no possibility to resist. They didn't allow us to take our things. We couldn't gather our animals. They forced us all out. . . . After a few days no one was left. We left everything in our house. It was completely destroyed. They burned everything, the school, the mosque. They burned our fields, our grapes. . . . No one is living in that area now. It is completely empty. . . . We don't have permission to go back.[44]

Internally displaced people are the legal responsibility of their government. But often the problem is caused by the government or by individuals it supports. Internally displaced peoples often suffer some of the bleakest manifestations of the human condition. As the United Nations reports, internally displaced peoples are "to be found in urban slums, squatter settlements, camps for the internally displaced, host families, railroad boxcars, converted public buildings—and a majority of internally displaced are women and children, ethnic or religious minorities, indigenous people and the rural poor."[45]

Responsibility for managing the plight of displaced peoples lies with governments and the United Nations. However, state sovereignty limits what the United Nations can do beyond facilitating relief. Even in cases in which international relief is permitted, aid workers are often attacked by combatants or taken hostage and find it very difficult to operate due to difficult terrain or a lack of infrastructure. Between January 1992 and March 2001, 1,998 UN civilian staff members—including from the United Nations Children's Fund (UNICEF), World Food Program, and UNHCR—were killed, and 240 were kidnapped or taken hostage. The International Committee of the Red Cross has also been attacked, with six medical staff killed in Chechnya in 1997, four killed in Burundi in 1997, and six delegates killed in 2001 while delivering supplies in the Democratic Republic of the Congo.[46] A symbolically tragic and personal loss for such aid workers came in the murder of Silvio de Mello and many of his staff in a terrorist attack carried out by insurgents in Iraq. De Mello, the former UN director for humanitarian issues, had deferred his appointment to head the UNHCR in order to develop humanitarian-assistance programs in postinvasion Iraq in 2003. In October 2009, a terrorist bomb targeted UN officials in Pakistan, killing three aid workers there. Even when humanitarian relief can be established, there remains great danger, for example, in camps set up for internally displaced people. Insurgents or government forces often attack refugee camps in search of their enemies. Alternatively, some governmental or nonstate groups raid displaced persons camps to steal relief supplies.[47]

Food and Health

Food security is affected by the relationship between food supply and the rising demands of the planet's growing population. Some regions of the world face immediate and severe food shortages. In Africa, over thirty countries are experiencing significant food-security problems. Worldwide, in 2010, over 925 million people were undernourished, including 146 million children. Each year, 15 million people die around the world from malnutrition. On average, a child dies of hunger somewhere in the world every five seconds. By 2008, on average, twenty-five thousand people died every day around the world due to lack of food. Malnutrition makes societies vulnerable to the effects of famine and disease as people's immune systems become weakened by poor nutrition. In the underdeveloped world, the lack of adequate medical services exacerbates this problem. Even for those who are well fed and have excellent medical care, transnational disease has become a significant human-security challenge as the networks of globalization accelerate the spread of deadly diseases like HIV/AIDS and SARS. In 2009, the world was gripped by fear over the rapid spread of the H1N1 virus. Transnational disease can contribute to declining state capacity to meet basic human needs, possibly leading to large-scale instability in a country or region.

Food supplies have, overall, become more plentiful globally due to technological advances in production. By 2011, however, some basic food products, like wheat, had also become increasingly expensive—and the cost of wheat was even a factor in prompting the street protests in Egypt in early 2011. However, major disparities exist around the world. For example, in 2004 the average person in developed countries consumed 10 percent more calories daily (2,947) than the average person in the developing world (2,675). As a relative comparison, in Tanzania, per capita household expenses were $375 in 1998, of which 67 percent went to food. In Japan, per capita household expenditures were $13,568 in 1998, but only 12 percent went to food. This disparity in income and food spending between the developed and underdeveloped worlds is illustrated by the $17 billion spent in the United States and Europe each year on pet food versus the $19 billion needed in annual investment to reach UN development goals for the elimination of hunger and malnutrition.[48] Given annual costs of about $30 billion for treating medical ailments associated with malnutrition, the United Nations estimates that an annual funding increase of $24 billion in international support for food programs would result in a fivefold increase in global productivity and income.[49]

As per capita incomes increase worldwide, households are purchasing more meat and animal products, the consumption of which doubled in the developing world between 1995 and 2000. As incomes grow and basic food consumption improves, other demands will increase—for example, grain production will need to increase 50 percent by 2050 to keep pace with population growth. By 2010, major changes in local climates had affected grain production in Russia, and worldwide the cost of grain had increased substantially. Even if food production and trade evolve progressively with growing demand, an estimated 135 million children under the age of five are likely to remain hungry in 2020, with Africa and South Asia being hit especially hard.[50] According to the World Bank, these areas will likely require as much as $100 billion per year through 2050 to adjust for lost agricultural capacity due to climate change. Food security also has immediate relevance to the quality of food consumed. A variety of diseases affecting farm animals can have an impact on humans. Even the fear of such diseases can have dramatic consequences for food availability: when the H1N1 virus was found to be associated with human contact with animals at pig farms, Egypt killed its entire pig population—unnecessarily. New food technologies, particularly the creation of genetically engineered food products, raise questions regarding food quality. While some states explore new means of designing foods, others are opposed to the idea both in principle and on possible health grounds. Pesticides, while necessary to keep crops free of insect infestation, can also contribute to a range of diseases. On the other hand, if someone were starving and these foods would actually increase his or her life expectancy, then the issue becomes more complicated. Is it better to forgo production of genetically modified foods or spraying crops with pesticides and live to age thirty or engage in both practices and live to age forty?

The 2009 H1N1 crisis generated considerable fear of a global pandemic—even though far more people died that year from regular flu. The spread of disease within and across borders can pose an immediate threat to those people who are exposed, and containment can be very difficult. The Spanish flu epidemic of 1918 and 1919, for example, killed 50 million people worldwide. By 2004, tuberculosis infected about 8.7 million people; the disease killed 1.7 million in 2009. Left unchecked, tuberculosis could infect an estimated 1 billion people by 2024, with 35 million people dying due to contact with these contagious airborne bacteria.[51] Malaria, a parasitic disease carried by mosquitoes, kills an average of 1 million people every year, seven hundred thousand of whom are children.[52] Influenza, a highly contagious viral infection, causes outbreaks every year, resulting in between 3 and 5 million cases of severe illness and between 250,000 and 500,000 deaths annually.[53] In 2004, the World Health Organization warned that avian flu could prompt an international pandemic, killing an estimated 7 million people.[54]

Each year, millions of people die from preventable, curable, and treatable diseases. Most of these deaths occur in regions of the world with other weaknesses, including a lack of vaccines and basic sanitation. Over 3 million people die each year from water-related diseases, and 1 billion people do not have sustained access to safe drinking water.[55] The United Nations estimates that nearly 10 million children under the age of five die every year from preventable diseases such as diarrhea, measles, and acute respiratory infections.[56] An increase in the availability of just vitamin A and zinc would prevent an estimated 684,000 deaths among children every year. One of the greatest preventable threats to human security is self-inflicted: 6 million people around the world died in 2009 alone as a result of smoking cigarettes, and as smoking laws became tougher in the developed world, many companies aggressively targeted advertising toward children in the underdeveloped areas of the planet. By 2030, as many as 10 million people per year will die from smoking-related disease, with most of those deaths occurring in the developing world. [57]

Some disease outbreaks are localized but so severe that they strike widespread fear. Ebola hemorrhagic fever, for example, is spread by direct contact with the blood, secretions, organs, or other body fluids of infected people. Infection is thought to have spread to humans from gorillas or chimpanzees in Africa. Mourners burying Ebola victims and health workers are frequently infected while handling the dead. The disease incubates for two to twenty-one days, and outbreaks spread rapidly. Someone stricken with Ebola will have sudden onset of fever, intense weakness, muscle pain, headache, and sore throat. These symptoms are followed by vomiting, diarrhea, rash, impaired kidney and liver function, and possibly internal and external bleeding. While considerable attention is given to this disease, the numbers it kills are minor compared to common viruses and bacterial infections. Ebola strikes primarily in central African rainforests; there were 1,850 cases with over 1,200 deaths between 1976 and 2008. [58]

Among infectious diseases, HIV/AIDS is the world's most serious human-security threat given its impact on those who suffer from the illness and the global consequences. Originally noticed in homosexual communities in the developed world in the 1980s, HIV/AIDS has spread across the globe as a consequence of sexual contact, infections of the blood supply, and drug use. HIV is the virus that is transmitted and ultimately causes AIDS, a breakdown of the immune system. Medical breakthroughs can halt or slow the spread of the disease in individuals. However, once AIDS develops, it is incurable. Between 1981 and 2010, some 25 million people worldwide died of AIDS, and by 2010, about 33 million were estimated to be living with HIV. In 2004, 50 percent of all people in the world with HIV were women, and fifteen- to twenty-four-year-olds represented almost 50 percent of all new HIV infections. In developing countries, only 12 percent of the people who would benefit from drug treatments received them. In low- and middle-income countries, only one in ten pregnant women was offered services to prevent mother-to-child HIV transmission. AIDS has wiped out entire families in some countries, leaving 12 million children orphaned in sub-Saharan Africa, where an average of eight thousand people died from AIDS every day by the turn of the century. [59] In 2010, this average had declined to fifty-four hundred per day. In 2004, an estimated 15 million children worldwide had been orphaned by the AIDS epidemic. This number was expected to rise to 18.4 million by 2010. [60] Even with the best of medical care, death from AIDS is gruesome, painful, and prolonged. In countries lacking adequate medical facilities, the situation is worse. For example, in Cambodia, only one in five of the twenty-five thousand AIDS patients near death receives basic care, with most victims tragically left to rot.[61]

In April 2000, the United States formally identified the disease as a security problem, noting that the spread of AIDS can weaken foreign governments, contribute to ethnic conflict, and undermine efforts to expand international trade. According to the U.S. National Intelligence Council, "At least some of the hardest-hit countries, initially in sub-Saharan Africa and later in other regions, will face a demographic catastrophe" by 2020. The United States further stated that dramatic declines in life expectancy were a strong risk factor for "revolutionary wars, ethnic wars, genocides, and disruptive regime transitions" in the developing world and that the social consequences of AIDS have "a particularly strong correlation with the likelihood of state failure in partial democracies."[62] This concern has been especially high in Africa, where an estimated 22.5 million people lived with HIV in the sub-Saharan region in 2010.

Sub-Saharan Africa is home to about 10 percent of the world's population and about two-thirds of all people living with HIV. In 2003, 3 million people were estimated to have been infected, and 2.2 million died—which equaled 75 percent of the 3 million global AIDS deaths that year. In some African countries, such as Swaziland, 35 percent of the population was infected with HIV.[63] African countries are further hindered by a stark decline in life expectancy across the continent as a direct result of AIDS. In seven countries—Zimbabwe, Swaziland, Lesotho, Zambia, Malawi, Central African Republic, and Mozambique—average life expectancy is less than forty years.[64] Between 2001 and 2003, there was a global rise in AIDS orphans from 11.5 to 15 million, with 80 percent of these children living in sub-Saharan Africa. In Botswana, which has a population of only 1.5 million, 10 to 15 percent of all children were orphans, and 37.4 percent of all pregnant women were HIV-positive by the end of 2003.[65]

While Africa entered the twenty-first century in the midst of a full-blown AIDS crisis, other regions of the world also confront pending catastrophe if the disease is left unchecked. In Asia, there have been dramatic increases in HIV infection in China, Indonesia, and Vietnam. By 2004, some 7.4 million people in Asia and Southwest Asia were living with HIV, including an estimated 5.1 million in India alone. In Eastern Europe and Central Asia, 1.3 million people were living with HIV, with more than 80 percent under age thirty. Latin America had about 1.6 million living with HIV, and the Caribbean had about 430,000. Haiti had the highest percentage of people infected outside Africa (5.6 percent). In the United States, there were about 950,000 people living with HIV; Western Europe had about 580,000. China, Russia, and India were on the verge of having catastrophic HIV/AIDS conditions by 2025. According to one projection, a mild epidemic in China would produce 32 million new HIV cases, and a severe epidemic would produce 100 million. In India the same conditions would produce 30 million new cases of HIV in a mild epidemic and 140 million in a severe epidemic. In Russia, a mild epidemic would result in 4 million infected, and a severe epidemic would generate 19 million. Among these three countries, a mild epidemic would project a combined total of 43 million AIDS deaths, and a severe epidemic would produce a total of 155 million dead by 2025. Even a mild epidemic in Russia would lead to a level of economic output lower in 2025 than in 2000. For India, a mild epidemic would depress predicted economic growth by about two-fifths. For China, a mild epidemic would cut anticipated economic growth by about 50 percent.[66]

HIV/AIDS also impacts the military dimension of security. Average infection rates for soldiers around the world are significantly higher than for the same age groups in the civilian population. By 2002, the average HIV infection rate for African militaries was about 30 percent. In some states, more than two-thirds of the military were infected. The disease is present in 75 percent of the military in Malawi and in 80 percent of the military in Zimbabwe. In Africa, AIDS was the primary cause of death in many armies. This was true even for a state like Congo, which experienced frequent and severe military conflicts during the 1990s and, by 2011, had seen over 5.4 million people killed in direct war and subsequent fighting.[67] In the Rwandan genocide, between two and five hundred thousand women were raped in a matter of weeks, risking increased spread of the disease; in some cases, this outcome was seen as a purposeful tool of war. The weakening of militaries can place severe strains on state abilities to defend against external attack or to maintain domestic order. The disease also reaches deep into some of the most central functions provided by the most productive members of society. In Africa, 10 percent of all teachers were expected to have died from AIDS by 2005. In some countries, as many as 25 to 50 percent of health-care workers will likely die from the disease.[68] While HIV/AIDS is not likely to be the sole cause of failed states, it is a major factor compounding already existing weaknesses.

The networks of global security also provide new mechanisms through which disease spreads. A person who falls ill with a viral or bacterial infection in one area can travel by plane to another part of the world and infect people while in transit and on arrival. This scenario occurred during the global spread of a new virus that causes SARS, an upper-respiratory infection related to the common cold and similar to pneumonia, in 2002 and 2003. SARS has no known treatment, and while many victims survive, it is often fatal. SARS spread because of poor public health services and a lack of public transparency and accountability in China. In February 2003, a doctor who had become infected in China traveled to Hong Kong, where he unknowingly infected a dozen people, some of whom then traveled to Vietnam, Singapore, and Toronto, where the disease spread farther. Health-care workers treating the unknown illness also became ill and took the disease home, spreading it to their families.[69] By May 2003, the total number of SARS cases had reached eight thousand worldwide, and over eight hundred had died.

The SARS pandemic was relatively limited compared to the risks to human security that other diseases present. However, its spread caught public health officials off guard and illustrated the potential dangers lurking in the networks of globalization. For example, terrorist groups could use a small amount of a naturally occurring disease to create panic in multiple locations at the same time. Any use of disease as a weapon of mass destruction would require complex and highly expensive weaponization procedures beyond the likely capabilities of terrorist groups. Viruses, bacteria, fungi, parasitic organisms, and toxins that are by-products of living organisms can all have very danger-ous effects on a human population.[70] While each of these have been devel-oped or considered as warfare agents, to date no case of large-scale biological warfare has been confirmed in history.[71] A terrorist might, however, be more interested in spreading fear than doing actual damage with the disease. Thus, biological agents could be used in limited conditions to create psychological results—as when anthrax was mailed to victims in the United States in fall 2001. Perhaps more dangerous is the risk of major outbreaks of new versions of disease like influenza, as the H1N1 outbreak demonstrated. The U.S. Cen-ters for Disease Control estimates that a "medium-level epidemic" of a much more dangerous avian flu would kill 207,000, hospitalize 734,000, and sicken one-third of the American population. Such an outbreak would cost the U.S. economy $166 billion in direct medical expenses. On the other hand, avian flu would still have to evolve to a point where it spread from human to human; currently, it does not, except in very limited and very close exposure cases.

The Human Costs of War

The use of military force can have a major impact on human security. War often includes the purposeful or accidental targeting of civilians and related critical civilian infrastructure, such as hospitals or electric power grids. War includes the use of weapons, which do not discriminate between soldiers and civilians. Weapons of war can also have lasting environmental consequences. The World Health Organization showed that in 1998 alone, there were some 588,000 war deaths and 736,000 homicides worldwide.[72] Overall, the costs of war in Africa were, by 2011, equivalent to about fifteen years worth of devel-opment aid, stripping hundreds of billions of dollars from economic growth and humanitarian causes. War and violence cause various threats to human security that result from the immediate effect of combat on individuals, the social effects of war, and the effects of war on the environment.

The Impact of War on Individuals

Historically, most wars were fought primarily by soldiers. Over time, the world has agreed to legal restrictions on who and what is targeted in war. Nevertheless, in modern warfare, these constraints are regularly violated—with a range of consequences. During the twentieth century, the extent of damage to civilian life grew extensively, so that by the end of the century, over 80 percent of casualties in conflicts were civilian. During World War I, parts of the battlefield of Verdun were so wasted by artillery shells that even weeds still will not grow in some spots. A generation of French peasants was emptied from the French countryside at Verdun.[73] Devastation associated with war has included the destruction of priceless property, art, and other irreplaceable aspects of culture. The most severe example of ruinous violence, the dropping of nuclear bombs on Japan at Hiroshima and Nagasaki, showed the immediate and horrific consequences war can have for a civilian population. Other human costs include the opportunity costs of planning for war. Money spent on weapons and training for war is money not spent on education, roads, hospitals, and other improvements to the human condition.

Small arms such as handguns, mortars, submachine guns, grenades, and landmines have a unique impact on civilian populations. Small arms account for 90 percent of all civilian casualties and kill tens, if not hundreds, of thousands of people every year. Small arms in private hands are often leftovers from military conflicts or remnants of military stockpiles. These weapons kill an additional two hundred thousand people every year. In Brazil, the United States, and South Africa, guns are a leading cause of death among young men. Worldwide, an estimated 2 million children were killed by small arms between 1990 and 2003, and an estimated 1.5 million are wounded by small arms every year.[74] Over 600 million small arms and light weapons are in global circulation. Of forty-nine major conflicts during the 1990s, forty-seven were waged with small arms as the weapon of choice.[75] The United Nations reports that "small arms and light weapons destabilize regions; spark, fuel and prolong conflicts; obstruct relief programs; undermine peace initiatives; exacerbate human rights abuses; hamper development; and foster a 'culture of violence.'"[76] West Africa is especially affected by the relationship between small arms and persistent violence. Nigerian customs services reported that in 2002 they confiscated $30 million worth of small arms and ammunition over a six-month period. In November 2003, some 170,000 rounds of ammunition were seized. By May

2004, Nigeria had seized 112,000 illegal firearms.[77] According to Human Rights Watch, these weapons were used in the massacre of several hundred people in May 2004.[78] In the Delta State area of Nigeria, militia groups have used automatic and semiautomatic rifles, along with fishing spears and cutlasses, to kill hundreds of people, displace thousands more, and destroy property.

Cluster bombs and landmines, which do not discriminate between soldiers and civilians, have a uniquely negative impact on civilian society. Cluster bombs are small explosives dropped over a large dispersal area and targeted against troop concentrations. These weapons can miss their targets and hit civilians, or they can fail to detonate and sit on the ground unexploded. Unexploded cluster munitions were a serious problem in Kosovo, Afghanistan, and Iraq. Often, they are discovered by children, who see them as toys and touch them, then are maimed or killed when they explode. In Afghanistan, their use was especially problematic because they resembled ready-to-eat meals that the U.S. military was dropping from the air as part of its humanitarian mission. Landmines have a similarly negative impact on civilians both during and after conflicts. They are left, often in unmarked areas, in fields where people congregate or children play. Even wars ostensibly fought for just causes can have negative human costs. At the most general level, war itself diverts resources from other human security needs. For example, within a week, the U.S.-led attacks on Libyan government forces in March 2011 had cost up to $1 billion. While there is no question this saved people in Libya from brutal attacks, the moral dilemma was that there was no clear end to that war, and one could make the case that $1 billion spent elsewhere in Africa—for instance, in the Sudan or as part of the United Nations Population Fund—might have been far more effective in terms of the number of lives saved.

In September 2003, U.S. President George Bush called the war in Iraq "one of the swiftest and most humane military campaigns in history."[79] By 2011, however, violence continued to disrupt the country, and in the absence of fifty thousand U.S. troops, chaos may ensue in the years to come. During the initial three weeks of major hostilities, thousands of Iraqi civilians were inadvertently killed by U.S. forces. A significant cause of these civilian casualties was persistent violation of the rules of war by Saddam Hussein's military leadership. These violations included the use of human shields, abuse of the Red Cross and Red Crescent emblems, use of antipersonnel landmines, location of military objects in protected areas (mosques, hospitals, and cultural landmarks), and failure to take adequate precautions to protect civilians from military activity. Some Iraqi military also wore civilian clothes, creating confusion about who was a combatant and who was a noncombatant.

The United States also contributed to civilian casualties in Iraq with the widespread use of cluster bombs. The United States reported that it used

10,782 cluster munitions, which would contain at least 1.8 million submunitions. Both the United States and the United Kingdom regularly used these weapons to attack Iraqi positions in civilian residential neighborhoods. An average failure rate of 5 percent would have left about ninety thousand dud bombs sitting on the ground in Iraq following the invasion. Among the civilian casualties of the invasion of Iraq, more than 400 civilians are known to have died in Al-Nasiriyah, including at least 72 women and 169 children; more than 700 additional women and children were injured. Baghdad had high casualties from ground fire—with perhaps as many as seventeen hundred civilians killed and eight thousand wounded there. In Al-Hilla, U.S. ground-launched cluster munitions caused 90 percent of all civilian casualties.[80]

The postwar American occupation of Iraq created significant human-security challenges. During the occupation, an insurgency movement attacked American soldiers, international aid workers, and Iraqis. By 2005, insurgents were estimated to have killed twelve thousand Iraqi civilians and security forces.[81] By 2010, even though the major insurgency was not as active, civilians were regularly killed in large explosions in Iraq. An independent British study described the Iraq War as a public "health disaster." After the war, previously well-controlled diseases reemerged in Iraq, including diarrhea, acute respiratory infections, and typhoid, while more children were underweight or malnourished in 2005 than in 2000. After the war, the quality of health services had declined due to chronic underfunding, poor physical infrastructure, mismanagement of supplies, and staff shortages.[82] Another study by UNICEF showed that malnutrition among children aged six months to five years grew from 4 percent before the U.S. invasion to 7.7 percent in the first two years afterward.[83] Still, most of the Iraqi deaths resulted from Iraqi-on-Iraqi violence. In December 2006 alone, sectarian violence led to the deaths of thirty-eight hundred civilians.

The Social Effects of War

War can have long-term effects on societies. For example, many modern warriors are neither modern nor warriors—they are children. There are on average as many as three hundred thousand children around the world serving either voluntarily or involuntarily in militaries or private militias. Children under the age of eighteen fought in Sierra Leone, Liberia, Congo, Sudan, Sri Lanka, Afghanistan, and Myanmar in the 1980s and 1990s. In Sierra Leone's civil war, children fight for both sides. Often rebels will attack a village and abduct the surviving children, many of whom have already witnessed the horror of their parents' murder. They are then taken to special camps, where they are trained and prepared to fight on behalf of their captors. Those few who escape often sign up to fight with a pro-government militia force. Children and small arms mix together in these conflicts, as a child with a light weapon can move quickly and close to an enemy. Children are also seen as less costly and easier to influence than adults. Indeed, many children are sent into battle high on drugs provided by adult officers or paramilitary elders. In Myanmar, children are used not only in combat but also in slave labor camps, carrying army supplies to soldiers and working involuntarily on government construction projects used by the military.[84] Police video taken in the July 2010 riots in Belfast, Northern Ireland, showed that most of the perpetrators among Catholics were youths—some as young as eight. Nearly 50 percent of the 3.6 million people killed in war between 1990 and 2004 worldwide were children.[85]

Testimonials of child warriors and refugees recorded by the British Broadcasting Corporation illustrate the severe impact of war on children. Zaw Tun, a Burmese veteran at age fifteen, says, "An army recruitment unit arrived at my village and demanded two new recruits. Those who could not pay 3,000 kyats had to join the army." Charles, a twelve-year-old Rwandan refugee, says, "I was so afraid of dying. But my friends warned me if the rebel commanders detected any fear in me they would kill me. So I had to pretend to be brave." Asif, a twelve-year-old Afghan refugee, says, "When I get older, I will organize a gang and seek my father's revenge." Htay, an ex-Burmese army soldier, says, "I joined the army when I was young [at fifteen] without thinking much. I admired soldiers, their guns and crisp, neat uniforms. I just wanted to fight the way they did in the movies and so I joined the army." Charlie, a ten-year-old Sudanese refugee, says, "Two hundred gone, we pray that war in our country will stop quickly. We also pray for their souls to rest in peace." Christopher, twelve, from Uganda says, "I just want to go home and be with my family."[86]

In some conflicts, children are seen as legitimate military targets. A Rwandan radio station broadcasted in 1994 the statement that "to kill the big rats, you have to kill the little rats." During that conflict, three hundred thousand children were killed. For a five-year-old child in the former Yugoslavia in 1991, the odds are very high that for the next five years, life was defined by the physical and visual horrors of war and the psychological fear they generated—if not the actual violence. A child growing up in Iraq during the 1980s and 1990s would have known nearly constant war, including the Iran-Iraq conflict, the Iraq invasion of Kuwait and subsequent 1991 Gulf War, American and British air strikes and sanctions, and then the 2003 American invasion and subsequent occupation and insurgency. UNICEF estimates that between 1993 and 2000, 2 million children worldwide were killed in war, 4 to 5 million were disabled, 12 million were left homeless, more than 1 million were orphaned or separated from their parents, and 10 million were psychologically traumatized.[87] Meanwhile, children were used as fighters in at least twenty-two conflicts between 2001 and 2004. Even the United States sent sixty-two children aged seventeen into combat in Iraq and Afghanistan.[88] On average, by 2010, three children per day were being killed in the ongoing war in Afghanistan. In the United States, military recruiters can be found frequently at family-oriented events, with video game demonstrations made to appeal to young children.

While most child soldiers are young boys, girls are also inducted into military life. Girl soldiers are vulnerable to rape, sexual slavery, and abuse both by captors and by the militias or militaries that recruit them—though the same is true for boys as well. A fourteen-year-old girl soldier abducted from Kitgum in Uganda by the Lord's Resistance Army (LRA) said, "We were distributed to men and I was given to a man who had just killed his woman. . . . I was not given a gun, but I helped in the abductions and grabbing of food from villagers. . . . Girls who refused to become LRA wives were killed in front of us to serve as a warning to the rest of us." Another girl gave birth on open ground to a daughter from one of her LRA abductors: "I picked up a gun and strapped the baby on my back and continued to fight the government forces."[89] Even in the advanced militaries in the United States and Britain, female soldiers periodically experience sexual harassment or discrimination. Crimes including rape often occur but are not reported due to victims' fear of losing promotion opportunities.

Women have increasingly become targets of fighting and are highly vulnerable to sexual violence in war. As one study shows, "In certain villages bordering conflict young girls have admitted that armed men come in at night—these girls are used as sex workers—they are not allowed to protest—they are not allowed to lock their doors and the whole community tolerates this because these armed men protect the community—so it is a trade-off."[90] In Sudan, police officers sent to restore order in the Darfur region were found by the United Nations to have systematically sexually exploited refugee women. For example, women refugees were promised safety when hunting for firewood in exchange for sexual favors.[91] Vulnerabilities for women vary from direct violence to socioeconomic disruption as they are traditionally left behind during major conflicts to manage day-to-day routines; however, they can emerge widowed and without support after a war.

War can have an enduring psychological impact long after the conflict ends. Post-traumatic stress disorder, associated with depression and anxiety, is common among those exposed to combat, either as participants or spectators. By 2010, the suicide rate among American soldiers who had served in Iraq and Afghanistan had reached crisis levels in the armed forces. As one of five psychiatrists in the city of Quetta during the Afghan war in 2003 said of the social victims in war-torn societies, "They are depressed and anxious, they are irritable, have lost their appetite. There is a real feeling of loss—loss of body, loss of money, loss of friends and family." The doctor added, "Their psychological trauma is deep. Their basic needs have been ignored. They feel insecure, have no stability, and are suffering the effects of war, deficiency in food."[92] While the actual number of individuals permanently disabled psychologically by war might be small, exposure to war among the young creates a particular risk of long-term psychological damage. Human Rights Watch reported that in Chechnya "there was no water, electricity or food: only constant explosions. In the refugee camps in Ingushetia, many children suffered extreme cold throughout the winter and start to cry when the warplanes fly over on their bombing missions." As the report's author summarizes,

> In one hospital, I met a five-year-old girl, the only survivor in her family, thrashing around in her bed from the shrapnel wounds which had become infected with gangrene. In the next room was a wounded father, who recounted to me how his younger daughter had died in his arms from an exploding bomb.... [As the reporter was leaving he received a letter from a child saying, "]All these wars fell hard on my studies. The school year started very well. I was attending school, and was fond of music and fond of English. But one day the war crossed it all out. We became refugees in Ingushetia. I am missing my school year.... Peter, when you are in America, please ask all children to write letters to [Vladimir] Putin to stop the war in Chechnya and not to kill civilians, especially children. During the first war, I spent 20 days in the cellar with my parents. In fact, it is not as romantic as it appears to be in the action movies. Our house was hit by a bomb."[93]

Addressing such long-term psychological needs in postconflict situations can thus form a crucial component of attaining long-term peace and reconciliation. For many societies, it is hard to invest in peace if the perpetrators of wartime abuses against civilians remain at large. War crimes tribunals have served to rectify this problem by visiting justice on those who commit atrocities in warfare. However, even then the psychological scars of war can linger for generations, making postconflict rebuilding a very difficult task.

The Impact of War on the Environment

War can significantly damage the environment and lead to near- and long-term complications for the natural world and its inhabitants. Even in peacetime, military presence, planning, and exercising can impact the environment. In the United States, for example, the war on terrorism and the invasion of Iraq prompted the military to seek new exemptions from environmental restrictions around some of its bases. Deemed necessary by military planners, these exemptions would also place endangered species at further risk, allow toxic rocket fuel not to be cleaned up, permit ocean testing that jeopardized marine mammals, and provide exemptions from clean-air laws and hazardous waste regulations. These requests were made despite a report from the U.S. General Accounting Office claiming that environmental rules did not impair military readiness. The head of the U.S. Environmental Protection Agency told Congress that no evidence existed of "a training mission anywhere in the country that is being held up or not taking place because of environmental protection regulation."[94]

The relationship between war-fighting capabilities and the environment presents four central challenges.[95] First, the production and testing of nuclear weapons is a significant environmental problem. The release of radioactivity during production and testing threatens general public health when people are exposed. During the twentieth century, nuclear weapons were tested 423 times above ground and 1,400 times under ground. These tests led to the release of radionuclides estimated to be at 16 to 18 million curies of strontium-90; 25 to 29 curies of cesium-137; 400,000 curies of plutonium-329; and, in atmospheric tests, 10 million curies of carbon-14. There is some scientific dispute about the impact of tests. However, the U.S. government has awarded compensation to three thousand current and former employees adversely affected.

A second major environmental challenge from war stems from bombardment from air or sea. The advent of airpower in World War II allowed for the large-scale bombing of civilian populations. During conventional bombing of Tokyo in 1945, between one and two hundred thousand people were killed. Between 1943 and 1945, the Allied bombing of seventy German cities led to between five and eight hundred thousand deaths. The destruction of forests, farms, and irrigation networks resulted in some 50 million refugees at the end of World War II. In Japan, severe food shortages followed the end of the war due to the failure of the 1945 rice harvest, causing significant malnutrition and hunger. Landmines represent a third major environmental consequence of war, with 70 to 100 million active mines worldwide by 2000. In the years since World War II, 400 million landmines have been deployed worldwide. The fear of landmines accelerates environmental damage: denied access to abundant natural resources and arable land, populations are forced to move into marginal and fragile environments to avoid minefields, and this migration speeds depletion of biodiversity. Also, landmine explosions disrupt soil and water processes.[96]

The purposeful destruction of the environment has also been a tool of modern warfare. During World War II, dikes and dams were sabotaged and destroyed. In the Vietnam War, defoliants were used to clear forests. From 1965 to 1971, the United States sprayed 3,640 kilometers of cropland with herbicides to deny the enemy sources of food and cover.[97] Contemporary conflicts, including those in Central Africa, Mozambique, Sudan, and Afghanistan, have contributed to deforestation, encroached on vulnerable ecosystems and national parks, and caused water pollution, sanitation degradation, air pollution, and loss of endangered species.[98] Klaus Toepfer, executive director of the United Nations Environment Program (UNEP), writes, "Warring factions and displaced civilian populations can take a heavy toll on natural resources. . . . Decades of civil war in Angola have left its national parks and reserves with only 10 percent of the original wildlife. . . . Sri Lanka's civil war has led to the felling of an estimated five million trees, robbing farmers of income." Toepfer notes that greed over the environment has fueled conflict as "some individuals and groups can make a fortune under the cloak of an ideologically motivated war. . . . It is estimated that UNITA rebels in Angola made over $4 billion from diamonds between 1992 and 2001. . . . The Khmer Rouge was, by the mid-1990s, making up to $240 million a year from exploiting Cambodia's forests for profit."[99]

The 1991 Persian Gulf War illustrates the danger to the environment of a purposeful act of war. Saddam Hussein ordered that 789 oil wells be set on fire in Kuwait as Iraqi forces retreated. By burning the oil fields, Hussein hoped to cripple the Kuwaiti economy and punish coalition forces that had ousted Iraq. Possibly these fires were set to make marching on to Baghdad more difficult for coalition troops. By March 1991, 6 million barrels of oil were burning per day. A massive cloud of fire, smoke, and soot rose high into the air, covering a one-thousand-mile radius around the Persian Gulf. While the fires were put out and postconflict studies showed the immediate damage was not as great as initially feared, lasting damage was done. Approximately 500 million tons of carbon were released into the atmosphere, and an estimated 250 million gallons of oil were pumped into the Persian Gulf—roughly twenty times the amount spilled by the *Exxon Valdez* in Alaska in 1989. The end result was severe damage to biodiversity and the coastline of Saudi Arabia.[100] Large pools of oil were left behind in Kuwait, including a half-mile-long and twenty-five-foot-deep oil reservoir—nine times bigger than the *Exxon Valdez* spill. As one report showed, "Some 6 million to 8 million barrels of oil dumped into the Indian Ocean created oil slicks that coated the shoreline. . . . Bird Life International, a global partnership of non-governmental conservation organizations, estimates the layers of thick, black goop killed 35,000 wintering birds and tens of thousands of wading birds."[101] Also during the Gulf War, the movement of Iraqi and American troops altered up to 90 percent of the Kuwaiti desert surface. Unexploded bombs left in the sand killed herds of wild camels and other animals.

During the 2003 Iraq War, UNEP noted that burning oil wells in southern Iraq and oil-filled trenches and fires in Baghdad further exacerbated the environmental consequences of war for that country. According to UNEP, "The black smoke that we see on television and in satellite pictures contains dangerous chemicals that can cause immediate harm to human beings—particularly children and people with respiratory problems—and pollute the region's natural ecosystems."[102] Nevertheless, the environmental impact of war in 2003 was less significant than in 1992—especially given a concern that Iraq might release water from dams and flood valleys, then blame the action on the United States. There was also concern that Iraq might again set oil fields ablaze and sabotage oil platforms and pipelines. In the 2003 war, the U.S. military placed a high value on rapid movement toward protecting oil fields. Meanwhile, large ammunition dumps went unprotected—providing a source of weapons for the emerging insurgency. UNEP indicated by spring 2005 that it would be almost impossible to improve Iraq's environmental situation because of the declining security situation there. UNEP officials noted that key weapons storage facilities had been looted after the U.S. invasion, including a facility south of Baghdad where five thousand barrels of chemicals were "spilled, burned, or stolen."[103]

The use of particular materials that advance military technology can also have a lingering environmental or health impact. Depleted uranium has been a significant source of concern in this context. Depleted uranium is used to harden conventional shells, such as those used for artillery. After the conflict in Bosnia-Herzegovina, a UNEP postconflict environmental assessment discovered that NATO's depleted-uranium shells left traces of uranium in soil samples. Contamination was widespread, but not at levels significant enough to cause safety concerns. However, during the war, the use of depleted uranium had also contaminated local drinking water. The UNEP study identified four key lessons about how depleted-uranium impacts the environment. First, ground contamination occurs at depleted-uranium impact points at low levels and is highly localized. Second, shells buried near the ground surface corrode rapidly and will disappear completely in twenty-five to thirty-five years. Third, where groundwater is contaminated, alternative water sources must be found, and regular sampling and measurements should continue for an extended period. Fourth, contamination of the air occurs due to wind or human action.[104] While the UNEP study showed a relatively minimal impact from the depleted uranium, there remains dispute over the material's use. A number of NATO peacekeeping troops in areas where depleted uranium was found suffered from diseases, including cancers, that would not likely have developed otherwise.

Afghanistan illustrates the extensive long-term environmental costs of war—in this case, resulting from more than two decades of conflict. UNEP's

Postconflict Assessment Unit found that the pressures of warfare, civil disorder, lack of governance, and drought dramatically impacted natural and human resources. War in Afghanistan had a major impact on usable water, which is essential to agricultural productivity in this arid land. UNEP found that many of the country's wetlands were completely dry and no longer supported wildlife populations. Similar declines have occurred in forestry areas, leading to loss of fuel wood and construction materials needed for cooking, shelter, and overall survival. Loss of forests and vegetation, combined with excessive grazing and dryland cultivation, has led to soil erosion from wind and rain. In the Badghis and Takhar regions, there remain almost no trees. In 1977, these areas had been, respectively, 55 and 37 percent forested. The value of the land is declining and driving people from rural to urban areas. This population migration has placed pressure on the weak post-Taliban Afghan government, which struggles to meet its citizens' most basic human needs while also building a democracy. Within the cities, there are no proper landfills or proper means of ensuring against groundwater contamination or toxic air pollution. Safe drinking water in urban areas reaches only 12 percent of the people. Kabul's water system is losing up to 60 percent of its supply because of leaks and illegal use. In the city of Herat, dumpsites were found in dry riverbeds upstream from the city. At the first sustained rain, they would likely wash down into the city. UNEP also shows that the natural wildlife heritage of the country is under threat. Flamingos have not bred in Afghanistan for four years, and the last Siberian crane was seen in 1986.[105] Also, after the United States overthrew the Taliban regime, Afghanistan resumed its role as the world's primary exporter of opium—providing 87 percent of global supply. Opium trade accounted for $2.8 billion and contributed 60 percent of Afghanistan's gross domestic product—an increase of 64 percent between 2003 and 2004. An average farmer could earn ten times more growing opium instead of wheat.[106] And yet, in 2010 the discovery of large deposits of lithium in Afghanistan appeared to provide a resource justification for the war there in that stability could lead to economic gain in the future as lithium is a major component in computer batteries. The Pentagon estimated that Afghanistan had as much as $1 trillion in as-yet untapped mineral deposits.

Summary

Human security is a somewhat controversial paradigm as it risks an overly broad application such that virtually everything can become a security issue. Nevertheless, the human-security agenda has made a major contribution to the study of global security by refocusing the traditional emphasis on the security of the nation-state onto that of individuals or groups. The substantive focus on the human-security agenda provides an important basis for addressing both research and policy aspects of some of the most important challenges to international peace and stability in the global security dynamic of the twenty-first century. The study of human security also paves the way for a new assessment of the issues of environmental and energy security.

Suggested Reading

Diamond, Jared. *Guns, Germs, and Steel: The Fates of Human Societies*. New York: W. W. Norton, 1999.

Donnelly, Jack. *Universal Human Rights: In Theory and Practice*. 3rd ed. Ithaca, NY: Cornell University Press, 2006.

Farmer, Paul. *Partner to the Poor: A Paul Farmer Reader*. Berkeley: University of California Press, 2010.

Garrett, Laurie. *Betrayal of Trust: The Collapse of Global Public Health*. New York: Hyperion, 2001.

Hampson, Fen Olser, Jean Daudelin, John B. Hay, Holly Reid, and Todd Martin. *Madness in the Multitude: Human Security and World Disorder*. Oxford: Oxford University Press, 2001.

Human Security Centre. *Human Security Report: 2005*. Oxford: Oxford University Press, 2006.

Huntington, Samuel. *The Third Wave: Democratization in the Late Twentieth Century*. Norman: University of Oklahoma Press, 1993.

Kaldor, Mary. *Human Security*. Cambridge, UK: Polity Press, 2007.

MacFarlane, S. Neil, and Yuen Foong Khong. *Human Security and the UN: A Critical History*. Bloomington: Indiana University Press, 2006.

McDonald, Brian, Richard Anthony Matthew, and Kenneth R. Rutherford, eds. *Landmines and Human Security: International Politics and War's Hidden Legacy*. New York: State University of New York Press, 2004.

One of three wind turbines at F. E. Warren Air Force Base, Wyoming. They face the wind coming across the high plains and push against the clouds in the distance, which later dropped a few inches of snow on the base and surrounding city of Cheyenne on April 6, 2010. Source: U.S. Air Force photo/Lance Cheung.

9

The Environment and Energy Security

$\mathbf{T}$HE GLOBAL ENVIRONMENT AND THE DEMAND for natural resources, particularly energy, are two of the most significant security challenges of the twenty-first century. The relationship between the environment and energy as security issues challenges many preexisting concepts about both power and peace. The very definition of security and the determination of what is to be secured are open to question when the environment and energy are placed in the security context. Environmental conditions can have a major impact on economic development, shaping security needs and requirements. Similarly, energy consumption and access to resources can have major security implications. Environmental and energy security also goes beyond the impact of the environment on humans. Security also applies to the safety and well-being of the environment. Increasingly, national security, technology, new forms of conflict, and human security are all linked to global environmental and energy trends. Some of the most significant twenty-first-century threats and opportunities for positive outcomes lie in the area of the environment and energy. This chapter surveys major conceptual approaches to environmental and energy security. It then examines specific environmental threats that have global and regional security implications.

What Is Environmental Security?

If the environment is not adequately maintained for human life, humanity will have to adapt or face severe hardship. Even those countries that currently have considerable wealth and resources are not immune to environmental challenges. As the Soviet Union discovered at the Chernobyl Nuclear Power Plant in 1986 and the United States learned with the British Petroleum oil platform explosion and spill in 2010, societies whose ambition to exploit resources for energy consumption runs ahead of their capacity can experience serious crises. Environmental threats are not amenable to traditional security responses, and the meaning and role of power and peace are rendered, at best, ambiguous by environmental security questions. Military power has little utility in resolving environmental security problems. Conversely, some threats, such as global warming, have the potential to damage the world's environment on par with a nuclear war. Local environmental problems can spill over state borders and exacerbate existing security challenges, such as refugee crises, urban development, and disease. Acting alone to achieve national security is generally not a functional means of managing environmental challenges—and can even make them worse. Managing environmental security problems thus places a high demand on international governmental and private-sector cooperation. Yet, other more immediate perceptions of traditional security threats often subsume such cooperation on long-range environmental challenges. Furthermore, new dilemmas emerge, for example, in that modern societies need energy, but energy consumption contributes to new threats, like climate change. The primary alternative energy source available is nuclear; yet, as Japan experienced in 2011, nuclear energy can be highly dangerous. Not moving forward with nuclear plants could, however, increase the dangers of climate change. Even major wind farms create geothermal energy that goes up into and can warm the atmosphere. Ironically, the advancement of modern industrial society, which is built on the exploitation of oil, has improved human security around the world, but now, that same basis of consumption threatens to contribute to new challenges to the human population as supplies run short, accidents damage the environment, and carbon emissions warm the atmosphere. The result is a gathering storm of both natural and human-caused environmental catastrophes that risks going unchecked by major world powers that seem to not wish to make near-term sacrifices in favor of long-term gains.

The Environment As a Source of Conflict

There are various ways to conceptualize environmental security. Richard A. Matthew defines environmental security as a clear and distinct concept applicable to the entire world at the highest levels of generalization. He defines environmental security as (1) a condition in which environmental goods—such as water, air, energy, and fisheries—are exploited at a sustainable rate; (2) a condition in which fair and reliable access to environmental goods is universal; and (3) a condition in which institutions are competent to address inevitable crises and manage the likely conflicts associated with different forms of scarcity and degradation.[1] Thomas Homer-Dixon asserts that it is necessary to separate the line of inquiry between the social effects of environmental change and examination of the kinds of conflicts most likely to result from such effects.[2] Homer-Dixon provides a set of variables to consider in assessing environmental security. The impact of human activity on the environment within an ecological area is treated as a function of two main variables: (1) the product of total population and its physical activity per capita, and (2) the vulnerability of an ecosystem to those human activities. Activity is also a function of available physical resources and ideational factors. This social and psychological context is immensely broad and complex: it includes patterns of land and wealth distribution; family and community structures; the economic and legal incentives to consume and produce goods (including the system of property rights and markets); perceptions of the probability of long-run political and economic stability; beliefs of people in government, industry, and academe about the patterns of trade and interaction with other societies; the distribution of coercive power within and among nations; the form and effectiveness of institutions of governance; and metaphysical beliefs about the relationship between humans and nature.[3]

Environmental change can cause scarcity conflicts in which states or groups of people compete over resources such as river water, fish, and agriculturally productive land. Group-identity conflicts can occur when various ethnic groups are intermixed as a result of some sort of dislocation caused by environmental problems. Also, relative-deprivation conflict can occur within, and spill over from, societies when domestic conflicts emerge between social groups. Groups that do not have political or economic power might reach a threshold of human insecurity to the point where they will engage violently against those who have power and wealth. Alternatively, those who do have power and wealth might fight to keep their relative status as a response to a decline in environmental conditions.[4] People who are deprived of natural resources and military capabilities might find it structurally impossible to challenge an existing status quo. Consequently, the developed world might ultimately find an interest in not addressing environmental challenges on a global basis.[5] However, Homer-Dixon cautions that "the North would surely be unwise to rely on impoverishment and disorder in the South for its security."[6]

Homer-Dixon and Jessica Blitt demonstrate that, under some conditions, scarcity can lead to conflict. They frame the question of environmental security by focusing on scarcity and noting the existence of several types.

Supply-induced scarcity results directly from a degradation or depletion of environmental resources. Demand-induced scarcity results from population growth or increase in consumption of a resource. Structural scarcity results from an unequal social distribution of a resource.[7] Each of these scarcities can be exacerbated by the inability of markets to adjust to new challenges, by social friction, or by the availability of capital to meet new challenges generated by environmental complexities. By surveying Chiapas (Mexico), Gaza, South Africa, Pakistan, and Rwanda, Homer-Dixon and Blitt demonstrate a correlation between poor countries and environmental scarcity contributing to conflict. Their study found that environmental scarcity is caused by degradation and depletion of renewable resources, increased demand for these resources, and/or their unequal distribution. These three sources of scarcity often interact and reinforce one another. Environmental scarcity can also encourage powerful groups to capture valuable environmental resources and prompt marginal groups to migrate to ecologically sensitive areas. These two processes—called resource capture and ecological marginalization—in turn reinforce environmental scarcity and raise the potential for social instability.[8]

Water is an area of potential conflict that has received increasing attention for its security implications. For example, Peter H. Gleick measures the conditions under which states might be vulnerable to water-related conflict.[9] He identifies threats to security as "resource and environmental problems that reduce the quality of life and result in increased competition and tensions among sub-national or national groups."[10] In the case of water, such threats include several sources. First, water resources can be a direct military and political objective in conflict. In cases where access to water is an important measure of economic or political strength, ensuring access to it can be a justification for war. Conditions affecting whether water is likely to become a strategic objective include the degree of scarcity, the extent to which the water supply is shared by more than one region or state, the relative power of the basin states, and the ease of access to alternative freshwater sources. Second, water resource systems can be both targets and tools of war. Gleick notes the targeting of water supplies in AD 689 when Assyria destroyed a city by attacking water supply canals. In the twentieth century, hydroelectric dams were bombed during World War II. Iran bombed hydropower stations during its war with Iraq in the 1980s. In the 1990s, Iraq destroyed much of Kuwait's hydropower when it invaded there. Iraq suffered its own water supply and sanitation problems in the aftermath of America's bombing campaign to expel it from Kuwait. Meanwhile, Saddam Hussein reportedly had water supplies poisoned and drained in southern Iraq to punish a revolt against his leadership.

Some countries could reach an absolute limit on the type and extent of development due to a lack of access to freshwater. Such limits depend on the absolute availability of water, the population needing to be supplied, and the level of development desired, as measured by the need for water and the efficiency with which it is used.[11] Gleick points to a variety of other water-related conflicts that have secondary security consequences, such as water development, irrigation, hydroelectric projects, and flood control. Water-management issues can lead to large population displacements and do significant damage to ecosystems with related secondary effects for populations. Gleick shows that water-resources vulnerability is a function of economic and political conditions, water availability, and the extent to which a source of water supply is shared and vulnerable to hydrologic conditions, which impacts total electrical supply.[12]

The Middle East provides an important example of the relationship between environmental scarcity and water conflict. Israel has a significant dependence on water located below the West Bank of the Jordan River. The Palestinian Arabs tend not to want to work on even small water projects in the region until larger issues driving the Arab-Israeli conflict are settled. Of the three main aquifer groups in the area, only one is located in Israel. Miriam Lowi notes that "from the outset of the Zionist movement's endeavors, unrestricted access to water resources was perceived as a non-negotiable prerequisite for the survival of a Jewish national home."[13] Lowi shows that the occupation of the West Bank by Israel "guarantees the state control over vital water supplies that originate in the West Bank but are consumed, for the most part, in Israel."[14] Between 1967 and 1993, no new Palestinian Arab individual or village received drilling permission. Israel's policy ensures that "only existing uses" of water are recognized, using the 1967–1968 years as the baseline for existing uses. Water allocations to Arab agriculture had, by 1993, remained at their 1968 levels, with only a slight margin for growth. Technology for deep drilling and rock drilling remained in Israeli control, and West Bank Arabs were not allowed to use water for farming after 4:00 p.m. While Israeli water projects were heavily financed by the Israeli government, the Arab population received no subsidy and paid as much as six times more for water than Israeli settlers in the West Bank.[15] Perception of power and control over resources can thus shape the context of negotiating peace. This constraint is important because, as Robert North has demonstrated, resource conflicts involve not only actual scarcity but also the political and psychological expectations about whether the supply will exist in the future and why it might not.[16]

An Evolving Environmental Security Paradigm

The protection of the environment has been a major international issue since 1972 when states met in Stockholm to build a process for shaping international environmental policy. The general international emphasis has been on sustainable development and the protection of sovereignty rights in terms of economic development and protection against transboundary environmental damage. With the end of the Cold War, the search for a new security agenda quickly encompassed environmental issues. A common interest was seen among environmentalists, who would welcome a new direction of governmental resources into environmental security and government bureaucracies, which would continue to justify their budgets. By the end of the 1990s, most states had factored at least some aspects of the environment into their foreign and security policies. The U.S. Central Intelligence Agency and Department of Defense have each, for example, identified climate change as a national security problem. A series of major international conferences, treaties, and national security policy statements signaled that environmental concerns were becoming priorities for nation-states. The new state-driven focus placed the environment within the traditional terms of national security. In this sense, the question was mainly how to sustain development in the context of diminishing resources. Critics eventually viewed such an approach as treating the security of the state as a means to defend a status quo rather than to adjust policies that lead to environmental damage.

The environment—measured in terms of the quantity and quality of resources—is clearly important to state interests. The idea that international environmental problems are threats to be managed enhances the role of the state as a barrier against international anarchy. In this context, Michel Frederick defines environmental security as representing "an absence of nonconventional threats against the environmental substratum essential to the well-being of [the state's] population and to the maintenance of its functional integrity."[17] Frederick identifies four key analytical components for measuring and assessing the core elements of environmental security. First, environmental security is placed within a state perspective. Such an approach recognizes the reality that the state remains the predominant actor in the international system and within international institutions. This context does not imply that the state will hide behind sovereignty to blindly destroy the environment. Rather, it offers a basis from which to organize coalitions of states that share common interests in managing environmental threats. Second, the natural environment can pose dangers that threaten the quality of life of a state's population or limit policy options for advancing the national interest. Third, damage—either natural or human generated—to the environment and ecosystems can pose an immediate threat to a state and its interests. Fourth, a state's social and economic well-being requires regular assessment of the degree of risk when faced with particular environmental problems.[18]

Contrasting with considerations of national interests in environmental security is the view that the environment must be secured against abuse by states or private actors. It is not the state that must be protected from the environment; rather the environment must be protected from abuses by states and private, commercial interests. Some activists have sought to expose this situation as one of exploitation by the few that damages the interests of the many. Mohandas K. Gandhi stressed living a simple life that required only what was necessary to live as part of nature. Gandhi possessed minimal clothing and material objects, and he recycled paper and other goods to make maximum use of them. Gandhi also focused his attention on how industrial agriculture served as a basis for exploitation. In an American context, John Muir described the dangers posed by people who would exploit the environment:

> In the settlement and civilization of our country, bread more than timber or beauty was wanted; and in the blindness of hunger, the early settlers, claiming Heaven as their guide, regarded God's trees as only a larger kind of pernicious weed, extremely hard to get rid of. Accordingly, with no eye to the future, these pious destroyers waged interminable forest wars; chips flew thick and fast; trees in their beauty fell crashing by millions, smashed to confusion, and the smoke of their burning has been rising to heaven [for] more than two hundred years. After the Atlantic coast from Maine to Georgia had been mostly cleared and scorched into melancholy ruins, the overflowing multitudes of bread and money seekers poured over the Alleghenies into the fertile middle West, spreading ruthless devastation ever wider and further over the rich valley of the Mississippi and the vast shadowy pine region about the Great Lakes. Thence still westward the invading horde of destroyers called settlers made its fiery way over the broad Rocky Mountains, felling and burning more fiercely than ever, until at last it has reached the wild side of the continent, and entered the last of the great aboriginal forests on the shores of the Pacific.[19]

Such universal perspectives consider the security of humankind and nature as one. As Muir wrote, "The universe would be incomplete without man; but it would also be incomplete without the smallest transmicroscopic creature that dwells beyond our conceitful eyes and knowledge." Muir wrote in 1896 that "the battle we have fought, and are still fighting, for the forests [of the Sierra] is a part of the eternal conflict between right and wrong, and we cannot expect to see the end of it."[20]

In 1962, Rachel Carson warned in her book *Silent Spring* of the impact of man-made chemicals on the environment and public health. She showed that scientific and technological specialization promoted a narrow look at progress without factoring for a more holistic scientific assessment. When this trend was combined with the dominance of industry and associated greed, humankind faced a danger.[21] By 1970, the environmental cause had become ingrained in American political activism with the advent of the first "Earth Day" held on April 22, 1970. Protection of the environment has also been at the core of research into the role of international institutions and global governance. Oran Young, for example, explains the demand that drives states toward multinational cooperation over environmental policy. He assesses the environment in the context of global commons in that the environment is of benefit to all humankind. In that context, a number of issues force a reconsideration of interests beyond those strictly defined by national borders. Shared natural resources are those natural ecological systems that either cross or form boundaries between two or more states. Transboundary externalities are those activities undertaken within a state that spread outside it with a potentially negative impact on other states. Finally, linked issues are those areas in which the effort to manage environmental problems creates new challenges. For example, economic development can be hindered in the near term by efforts to set standards for environmental protection.[22] Within this framework, Marc Levy has shown that it is possible to gain both a global and a local assessment of threats to the environment and solutions. Such a new awareness of the nature of environmental harm can establish the framework for cooperation on solving challenges.[23]

This trend has been affirmed by the creation of the United Nations Environment Program. Other major institutions, such as the World Bank, have come to factor environmental impact assessments into their loan programs for the developing world. However, it is equally probable that states will not think more holistically about their interests and emphasize short-term concerns. After the global economy crashed in 2008, the relative urgency of addressing long-term climate-change problems was narrowed for many states struggling with the immediate crisis of the day. In that case, nongovernmental organizations, international scientific communities, and transnational popular movements have played a role beyond nation-states in advancing information about threats to the environment and facilitating momentum in favor of environmental concerns. Movements like the Rainforest Action Network seek to advance transparency about state and business activity by informing the public through grassroots information campaigns. Activist groups such as Greenpeace have staged large public protests and engaged in civil disobedience—for example, by placing a flotilla of boats inside French nuclear test areas in the South Pacific. This publicity significantly raised the political costs of a French decision to test nuclear weapons. The Greenpeace ship *Rainbow Warrior* was targeted for violent attack in 1985 by French security forces seeking to punish Greenpeace and dissuade it from future protest activity. Fringe groups of environmental radicals have used ecosabotage and even violent ecoterrorism to advance their worldviews, raising an entirely different—and dangerously negative—element of environmental security.

Some conceptual approaches see environmental challenges as providing new incentives for human adaptation that will better both humanity and the environment. Julian Simon places the environment within the context of human ingenuity and the competitive forces of the market that create innovation. More people create more pressure for technological advancements, which allows for more progressive adaptation.[24] This approach acknowledges massive population growth but notes that, nevertheless, people are living (overall) in much more wealth and better conditions than ever before. While there are inequities in the distribution of that wealth, environmental pressures will, over time, produce adaptation for the better. For example, humankind has developed cleaner ways of generating power with nuclear energy. Modern societies are exploring solar and wind sources for clean energy. Innovative and positive adaptations are essential for addressing environmental issues and preventing them from becoming severe security challenges in the future. Some crises, however, might emerge too quickly for humans to adjust to them, while others might take so long to develop that humans might not recognize the relationship between current activity and long-term impact— as many critics of American plans to continue offshore drilling pointed out following the massive Gulf of Mexico oil spill in 2010. It is also possible that humankind has reached the limits of its capacity to further advance technological and economic adaptation for environmental protection.

Beyond Environmental Security

Comprehensive environmental security, some experts assert, can never be attained because of a fundamental disconnect between human needs or desires and the general welfare of the environment. If this is so, then the only way to achieve environmental security would be for humankind to undergo a paradigm shift in terms of its relationship to the environment. The environment is increasingly seen by the world's population and its governments as worth protecting. However, this interest often relates to maintaining and securing the existing level of economic and social well-being. So long as humanity sees the environment as something to manage, tame, or control as part of its own global hegemony among species, it will not attain true harmony or peace with nature. On the other hand, perhaps human dominance is the natural order and justified in its economic and social development, guided by survival of the fittest. After the Republican Party won control of the U.S. House in the 2010 midterm elections, a conservative party member who was competing to chair the committee responsible for oversight of energy issues declared that God had given people the Earth to exploit—and had also promised Noah that after he built his ark, there would be no more global destruction. So serious regulation, apparently, in this paradigm was not needed. More disconcerting to scientists has been a growing antiscience view among many Americans that explicitly denies evidence demonstrating the reality of many crises, like global climate change. Thus, in this context, some analytical frameworks seek to expose more fundamental power and cognitive dilemmas regarding the relationship between the environment and security.

Some critics of the concept of environmental security believe that equating the environment with security creates new conceptual and policy problems. The challenge, in this view, is to transcend the concept of security entirely. A critical analysis suggests that resolving environmental problems in a security context prohibits a comprehensive and inclusive approach necessary for resolving environmental problems. Simon Dalby, for example, critiques the application of security discourse to the environment[25] and questions what is being secured in relation to it. Dalby focuses analytical attention on the context in which society values something—and thus prioritizes that which must be secured. In that sense, for example, it would be the American congressman's belief in God that needed to be secured from the threat of science. To Dalby, violence and other forms of disruption affect trans-state politics by way of an emergent sphere of political activity linking human rights, environment, gender, and development issues. "Discussions of global security," writes Dalby, "are premised on the modern assumptions that the state is the provider of security, that legal systems uphold individual human rights, that the latter have been universalized to provide a benchmark for political conduct globally, and that—implicit to much of the conventional security discourse—modernity has to be extended to the poor and backward parts of the world for the greater benefit of all."[26]

Dalby cites as an example the marketing of SUVs in terms of their ability to enhance individual security. The Chevy Blazer was depicted in advertising as conquering natural environmental challenges only to emerge unscathed at a beach or a large suburban home. The slogan for the Blazer was "a little security in an insecure world."[27] However, he notes a "very powerful irony here in that the vehicle uses fossil fuels to propel itself and its passengers through storms, the frequency of which may be increased by the global climate changes brought on precisely by the use of fossil fuels. Big vehicles, specifically the popular sport utility vehicles like the Chevy Blazer, are fuel inefficient and, if buying trends at the turn of the century are maintained, will ensure that many states have little hope of meeting carbon dioxide emissions levels agreed to in international climate change agreements in the 1990s."[28]

Dalby observes, "Our quest for 'security' in modern economic production is currently undermining the conditions for terrestrial habitability. . . . This is the [environmental] security dilemma in its largest form."[29]

Jon Barnett similarly challenges the application of security discourse to the environment, advocating instead a "green theory" approach. Barnett bases his approach one three core assumptions. First, there is a suspicion that modern anthropogenic and utilitarian cosmology is responsible for environmental degradation as a consequence of human social development in the twentieth century. Second, there is a particular philosophy of space and scale built around the core notion of interconnectedness. Third, there is sensitivity toward the complexity and interdependence within and between social and ecological systems.[30] Barnett views the developed world's exploitative exercise of power as the general cause of environmental insecurity. This position of power was attained through patterns of trade, colonization, and resource extraction from the underdeveloped world. He notes that the wealthiest 20 percent of the world's population consumes 84 percent of all paper and 45 percent of all meat and fish; this group owns 87 percent of the world's vehicles and emits 53 percent of carbon dioxide. The underdeveloped world will feel the main negative security consequences of these activities on the part of the developed world.[31] Protection of this status quo is now seen as among the "environmental security" needs of the developed world. Thus, Barnett writes, "the processes that create environmental insecurity may be defended so that the relatively secure remain so."[32] Barnett promotes "ecological security," focusing on the "ecosystems and ecological processes that should be secured; the prima facie referent is therefore non-human."[33] Barnett concludes that a failure to move beyond "environmental security" perpetuates insecurity derived from a concept that "propagates the environmentally degrading security establishment; . . . talks in terms of, and prepares for, war; . . . defends the environmentally destructive modern way of life; and . . . ignores the needs and desires of most of the world's population."[34]

In a postmodern perspective, "securing" the environment requires policy actions placed within a larger social transformation. The "defense" against environmental insecurity would not, therefore, be defense of the nation-state. Rather, the solution would lie in the evolution toward a "global civil society." Ronnie Lipschutz develops an approach to global civil society in which agents act collectively through networks of knowledge and practice and work in opposition to some states and in concert with others.[35] Constitutive of a general change in social thinking about the environment are four major elements of global civil society: organizations or alliances that practice at the international or global level or across national borders; organizations that provide technical assistance to local groups engaged in resource restoration; individual groups that belong to national or transnational alliances; and groups and organizations "in touch" with their counterparts elsewhere around the world or simply sharing an ecological epistemology.[36] Such movements can serve as new transmitters of knowledge, information, and power, which can shed light on environmental problems and further raise consciousness of the need to make environmentally necessary adjustments. Importantly, such approaches emphasize information, education, and wisdom as the path to environmental security. Such movements can increasingly use the channels of globalization to proliferate their networks and shift the focus of power further beyond that traditionally held by governments.

Conceptualizing Energy Security

Energy is a highly strategic element of environmental security. Access to energy is central to modern life and to bettering the overall human condition in the world. State interests might mean that resource wars could be fought among great and small powers as nonrenewable energy sources become increasingly scarce. Also, the use of particular kinds of energy can have serious effects on human security. Energy security additionally raises the question, Security for whom? For example, as China and India pursue economic development, their combined 2.4 billion will consume increasing amounts of energy. This development will increase the standard of living for hundreds of millions of Chinese and Indians. However, growth will place pressure on already developed economies like the United States, Europe, and Japan. The significantly increased energy demands of China and India will impact availability in those states that have benefited from relatively inexpensive energy supplies. Alternatively, failure to adopt clean-energy and environmentally friendly policies in China and India could hinder their long-term growth prospects. Such an ebb and flow of energy power could be the major cause behind the rise and decline of great powers in the twenty-first century. Questions of who controls energy resources, where energy resources are allocated, and how energy use impacts both human and ecological systems are major determinants of global security.

Securing Energy Resources and Flows

The expansion of energy interdependence has been on the international security agenda since oil and gas shocks created a significant energy crisis in the United States during the 1970s. As the developed world took note of the vulnerability that energy interdependence creates, the future of energy moved to the forefront of national security policy. American president Jimmy Carter declared in April 1977 that energy supply shortages presented a problem unprecedented in history. Carter asserted, "With the exception of preventing war, this is the greatest challenge that our country will face during our lifetime. . . . The oil and gas that we rely on for 75 percent of our energy are simply running out."[37] Carter noted that it was necessary to promote "permanent renewable energy sources like solar power." Nevertheless, the world's reliance on oil, gas, coal, and nuclear energy has grown since the 1970s. New priorities focusing on protecting the flow of energy resources from the Persian Gulf and opening new areas of resource extraction have had a major impact on national security planning.

In the 1980s, energy policy was elevated to a primary national security issue in the United States. Donald J. Goldstein, from the U.S. Department of Defense, illustrated this trend when he noted that energy security had direct bearing on questions of territorial integrity, political independence, and the physical well-being of populations. Goldstein argued that treating energy as a unique security issue would help to frame strategy and organize governmental efforts for dealing with energy-induced political, economic, or geostrategic difficulties. By moving the question of energy into the security arena, "greater resources [could] also be brought to bear than exist in the economic area alone," and public opinion would be more readily mobilized for energy-related security engagement.[38] According to Goldstein, "Diverse questions such as the future of nuclear energy, energy-environmental trade-offs involving coal, natural gas import patterns, domestic stability in [less developed countries], and the development of oil resources in the [then] Soviet Union all become linked in a vast security affairs matrix."[39] Goldstein noted the dual-use potential in the development of nuclear energy for the development of nuclear weapons capabilities. He also noted the need to focus policy on the stability of governments that produced energy supplies. The flow and safety of pipelines and potential regional conflicts in areas with energy-production capabilities would likely shape the future security agenda. Goldstein concluded that "the energy crisis is not merely the moral equivalent of war, it is the extension of war by other means."[40]

Similarly, Howard Bucknell III stressed the uncertainty and lack of predictability that the demand-and-supply equation of oil placed on the needs of modern society. Energy insecurity thus results from strategic vulnerabilities of competition, such as that for control of oil in the Middle East among great powers. Bucknell used the oil embargoes imposed on the United States by energy-producing countries in 1973 and 1974 to show how serious the domestic dislocation was on American society. He concluded that the embargoes' effects, together with America's reaction to them, caused a 10 to

12 percent reduction in the immediate availability of liquid fuels, a rise in the price index of 5 percent, and the immediate unemployment of about five hundred thousand people in the United States.[41] Ultimately, the United States and its allies would face three significant choices: find new sources of oil and natural gas, produce more of their own resources, or find alternative energy sources. Getting beyond the existing framework has been difficult as entrenched interests make investment in new energy sources difficult to prioritize, particularly as demand increases create short-term profits for energy companies.

Energy dependence on strategic regions of the world forces states to place access to energy reserves, particularly oil and gas, at the high end of national security. In the late 1970s, the United States promised to support friendly oil-producing governments in the Persian Gulf and to secure the unfettered transit of oil. To make such an approach feasible, the United States created a rapid military deployment capability to project military power into the Persian Gulf. During the 1980s, the United States deployed power into the Persian Gulf to escort oil-bearing ships during the Iran-Iraq War. In 1990 and 1991, the planning was put to large-scale effect following Iraq's invasion of Kuwait. Defending Kuwait was important, but the larger concern was Saudi Arabia. Since the 1970s, Saudi Arabia has been the key swing state in oil production—setting the price of oil by controlling its flow. A strategic interdependence emerged as the United States would defend the Saudi government while the Saudis would provide relatively low-cost oil.

Various threats exist to the regular supply of energy—either from direct or asymmetric attack. First, transportation is a major vulnerability. Pipelines often flow across unstable areas, and ships pass through narrow lanes where they might be exposed to military or terrorist attack. Sabotage of shipping can lead to a halt in the flow of energy supplies and significantly raise the costs of energy transport. Writing in 1981, Bucknell forewarned of significant security risks to oil transit:

> To mention but a few opportunities available to those interested in the rapid demise of the existing Western order of things: the tankers could be attacked by submarine; the straits could be mined surreptitiously or openly; with properly organized support, a sabotage effort could be mounted in the Persian Gulf itself that could convert it into a sea of flames inextinguishable for perhaps a year. As an alternative the oil extracted from the Persian Gulf region could be rendered radioactive by covert chemical treatment and thus made useless at the ports of debarkation in Europe, Japan, and the United States. The forces of terrorism are abroad in our international society. To ignore them is dangerous. To employ them as surrogates may be a tempting possibility to some nation.[42]

Second, in extreme circumstances of strangulation or blackmail of the developed world's economies by oil-producing states, it might be necessary to intervene with force to gain access to oil. Third, during the twentieth century, definitions of national interest became equated with oil. For the United States, this relationship forced it to abandon principles in favor of interests as it has supported a number of oppressive governments in the Middle East that provided cheap oil.

Michael Klare has shown how access to energy supplies has come to dominate major power interests and affect military planning. Klare notes that "whereas weapons technology and alliance politics once dominated military affairs, American strategy now focuses on oil-field protection, the defense of maritime trade routes, and other aspects of resource security."[43] Klare sees the focus on energy security as reflecting a fundamental rethinking of how power and influence matter in international security after the Cold War. "Whereas, in the past, national power was thought to reside in the possession of a mighty arsenal and the maintenance of extended alliance systems, it is now associated with economic dynamism and the cultivation of technological innovation."[44] Klare identifies several kinds of insecurity that can emerge because of resource conflict. First, conflict can develop over the allocation of a particular source of supply that extends across international boundaries—such as a large river system or underground oil reserves. Second, contested claims to offshore areas that have significant resources can lead to conflict. Third, disputes can arise over access to bodies of water that are essential for the transportation of vital natural resources.[45]

The expansion of global energy requirements, supply and refinery shortages, and ownership conflicts are all likely to place new stresses on the stability of the international system. Klare uses the Persian Gulf to show that the presence of large reserves of oil increases the likelihood and intensity of interstate conflict. Writing before the U.S. invasion of Iraq in spring 2003, Klare noted three scenarios for oil-driven war in the Persian Gulf. First, a recurrence of the 1990 Iraqi drive on the oil fields of Kuwait and Saudi Arabia would have threatened the largest supply of oil in the region. Second, an effort by Iran to close off the Strait of Hormuz or otherwise constrain the flow of shipping from the Persian Gulf would likely prompt an American military intervention. Third, an internal revolt against the Saudi royal family might lead to major domestic instability.[46]

Some critics of the 2003 U.S. invasion of Iraq asserted that the war was guided mainly by an attempt to gain strategic dominance over Persian Gulf oil supplies. Such a strategic move would, in theory, give the United States a continued advantage in relative energy capabilities into the twenty-first century. This would be especially important to counter the influence of the rising demand for energy from China and India. Compelling as this theory might be, there was also reason for skepticism. First, the United States had a significant interest in ending the need to place its troops in Saudi Arabia to contain Iraq. By removing Saddam Hussein as a threat to regional stability, the United States could extricate itself from Saudi Arabia. The American presence in Saudi Arabia had, during the 1990s, become a particularly virulent propaganda tool for extremist fundamentalist Islamic movements. Second, the United States could have gained access to Iraqi oil at far lower cost than via an invasion. Washington simply could have cut a deal with Saddam Hussein that allowed the United Nations to lift sanctions. This would have let Iraqi oil reenter world markets without a war. Also, there are other major areas of the world with energy reserves besides the Middle East; if more fully developed, they could have provided alternatives to accessing Iraqi oil.

With massive proven and unproven reserves, the Caspian Sea region has looked to many observers like a future source of resource wars. There has been a significant amount of posturing over whether pipelines would flow west (a benefit to the United States and Europe); north (a benefit to Russia); east (a benefit to China and Japan); or south (a benefit to Iran). Any major power that could exert primacy in this region might be able to wield significant global power in the twenty-first century. Moreover, the Siberian area of Russia might look attractive for future oil and natural gas development if technology will permit access into the frozen ground that covers much of the resource supply there. The South China Sea, which also has significant energy reserves, also holds potential for conflict should China expand its naval capacity. Some extreme scenarios posit a future war between China and Russia over Siberia's natural gas and oil reserves. Meanwhile, parts of Africa and Latin America also offer potential for future energy development, depending on the degree of stability in states such as Nigeria and Venezuela. Finally, the seabed could prove to be an area of competition for energy resources should technology permit regular access to deep-sea drilling.

The more energy demands grow, the more vulnerable societies are to security challenges involving energy. The one-day loss of electric power around the northeastern United States in summer 2003 showed the seriousness of the energy-demand problem in modern society. Much of the eastern United States was merely inconvenienced without power for several days. However, the situation was potentially severe in Cleveland, Ohio, which could not start its water-purification capacities, as they were generated by electricity. A city area of over 1 million people faced the prospect of losing access to fresh drinking water. The electricity was restored in time to avoid such a crisis. However, the Ohio National Guard was on call to ration drinking water in affected areas. Energy security is a problem with multiple sources and vulnerabilities ranging from overuse to sabotage as populations expand and become more urban centered. Each kind of energy has its own unique vulnerabilities. Oil is especially vulnerable to transportation disruptions and attack, threats to imports and shipping capacity, infrastructure weakness, collaborative policies of the countries that produce oil (the Organization of Petroleum Exporting Countries, or OPEC), the use of oil as a policy leverage against states that need it, and rapid fluctuations in prices due to location-specific or broader structural crises.[47] Electricity is vulnerable to a variety of purposeful or demand-driven disruptions and reliability problems, weak infrastructure, risks associated with nuclear energy, and specific policies and pricing structures set by states that produce electricity. Natural gas also is vulnerable to disruptions, infrastructure problems, and state policies and pricing strategies affecting those who rely on the import of natural gas.[48] In 2008, Russia threatened to cut off gas flows to the Czech Republic as punishment for its signing on to a missile-defense plan with the United States. No doubt, the United States factored in the danger of the disruption of global oil supplies versus the dangers of an Iran with nuclear weapons in calculating whether it could, or should, attack Iranian nuclear facilities.

Economic Development and Energy Security

The use of energy can help to maximize state power and raise the standard of living among populations by contributing to economic development. However, as Jose Goldemberg notes, despite technological advances, modern energy supplies are not accessible to some 2 billion people around the world. Unreliable energy supplies are a hardship and an economic burden for a larger portion of the world's population. For those who access energy supplies, human health is threatened by pollution resulting from energy use at household, community, and regional levels. The environmental impacts of many energy-linked emissions—including suspended fine particles and precursors of acid deposition—also contribute to air pollution and degradation of ecosystems. Finally, emissions of anthropogenic greenhouse gases, mostly from the energy sector, are altering the atmosphere in ways that may already be having a discernible influence on the global climate system.[49] The status quo thus perpetuates a dilemma in that the more humans advance their material conditions, the more they risk creating energy-induced insecurity.

The demand for energy in China and India could have a serious global effect on energy supplies and transboundary environmental pollution. Forecasts show that between 2000 and 2020, China and India will increase their coal-fired power-generating capacity by at least 220 and 60 gigawatts, respectively.[50] In 2010, China was likely to pass Japan as the largest importer of coal in the world, and in 2019, Indian demand was likely to pass that of China. The rapid growth of China's economic productivity over a ten-year period, combined with the population needs of 1.2 billion people and socioeconomic shifts from agriculture livelihoods to urban industrial life, had already pushed China's energy capacity to maximum output by 2004. A shift by China to natural gas would benefit the environment. However, that would require major infrastructure changes and also increase pressure on natural gas capacity worldwide. China has instead relied on existing coal-fired power plants to meet severe shortages in electricity production.

By August 2004, China had a thirty-thousand-megawatt electricity shortage. The response was to build additional coal-fired power plants, which emit massive amounts of sulfur dioxide into the air, causing acid rain and respiratory illnesses. These coal plants account for 75 percent of China's power-production capacity. The Chinese government has recognized the scale of its problem, noting that acid rain fell annually on 250 cities in China and caused about $13 billion in economic losses every year. In 2003, some twenty-one tons of sulfur dioxide from coal emissions were discharged. This represented a 12 percent increase from 2002. An additional 6 million tons were expected to have been added to this annual emission by 2006.[51] The World Bank estimates that four hundred thousand people die every year from air-pollution-related illnesses in China (data that China sought to keep out of the public domain in World Bank reporting in 2007). The pollution effects have spread into South Korea and Japan, an estimated 40 percent of whose air pollution comes from China. On some days, 25 percent of air pollution in Los Angeles can also be traced to China. A senior Chinese environmental official concludes that by 2020, pollution levels in China could quadruple if energy consumption and automobile use are not moderated.[52] With this in mind, the Chinese government has launched a comprehensive program to reduce sulfur emissions, and by 2010 it was showing positive results at least on this particular environmental concern.

China's energy policy is, overall, environmentally damaging and economically inefficient. China uses 57 percent more energy than Indonesia to produce the same amount of economic output. As a percentage of relative economic output, China consumes 3 times more energy than South Korea, 3.5 times more than the United States, and 8 times more than Japan.[53] China does impose taxes on polluters and has made some efforts to curb pollution. However, its leadership appears convinced that China is not wealthy enough to run a clean-energy policy. In July 2004, China ordered emergency shipping of coal on its roads and waterways and began building ninety new coal-fired power plants. Meanwhile, large power cuts in cities were reported, street lights were switched off, and factories were ordered to stop production or switch to off-peak electricity-use hours.[54]

Beyond states, individual materialism and consumption are also causing increases in energy demand with significant human and environmental costs. For example, the use of SUV-type automobiles grew dramatically in the United States during the 1990s. The extreme version, the HUMMER, is highly inefficient—getting about fifteen miles per gallon of gas. As a result, everyone in the United States, even those who purposefully purchased more fuel-efficient automobiles, paid a higher price for gasoline. While practical and necessary in rough rural or mountain conditions, the SUV and the HUMMER largely became status symbols for urban drivers who had no functional need for such environmentally damaging automobiles. Purchases of these automobiles declined commensurate with rising gasoline prices in 2007, and consumer patterns indicated a preference for long-lasting and fuel-efficient cars. This long-term demand shift played a role in the collapse of General Motors in the United States, which had to be bailed out and restructured by the American government in 2009.

Environmental Dangers

A number of specific environmental issues create serious global security challenges. Some, like climate change, could have devastating effects. Other issues, including deforestation and land and water use, can have local impacts with broader regional consequences. Energy-resource scarcity and safety challenges can cause major instability within states, place large populations in danger, and risk proliferation of dual-use technology applicable for both civilian and military purposes. Consequently, environmental dangers can exacerbate tensions between states already facing traditional security dilemmas while seriously stressing the capacity of governments to meet the basic needs of their citizens.

Climate Change

There is broad agreement in the international scientific community that the Earth's temperature is elevating due to a combination of natural and human-caused activity. The burning of fossil fuel has significantly increased the amount of carbon dioxide emissions released into the atmosphere, which then traps heat and raises average air temperatures. Climate change also occurs naturally, but it is being accelerated by human activity. Human-caused contributions to climate change include such activities as driving cars, using power from coal-fueled electricity sources, home heating from natural gas and oil, and large industrial manufacturing and agricultural activity. Some political leaders argue that there is not enough evidence to support the conclusion that human behavior is the primary cause of global warming. However, scientific experts are in agreement on the facts the phenomenon—as evidenced by multiple peer-reviewed studies sponsored by the United Nations, national governments, and the private sector. The scientists who produced these findings were awarded the Nobel Peace Prize in 2007.

The United Nations has engaged more than twenty-five hundred of the world's top climate experts, economists, and risk analysts to study global warming. According to UN surveys, the trend is already a real and significant problem. Observed evidence of climate change includes an increase in global average surface temperature of about one degree Fahrenheit over the twentieth century, a decrease of snow cover and sea ice extent and the retreat of mountain glaciers in the latter half of the twentieth century, a rise in global average sea level and an increase in ocean water temperatures, a likely increase in average precipitation over the middle and high latitudes of the Northern Hemisphere and over tropical land areas, and increasing frequency of extreme precipitation events in some regions of the world. Physical and ecological changes already occurring include thawing of permafrost, lengthening of the growing season in middle and high latitudes, poleward and upward shifts of plant and animal ranges, the decline of some plant and animal species, earlier flowering of trees, earlier emergence of insects, and earlier egg laying in birds.[55]

Unchecked global warming over an extended period could pose one of the most serious threats to international security that humanity has ever experienced. Even a small rise of about two degrees in the Earth's temperature would have very significant consequences, including further melting of glaciers and polar ice caps, dramatic shifts in agricultural seasons, rain and floods in some areas, and desertification in others. The UN studies on global warming predict current trends will produce a rise in atmospheric temperature of between 2.5 and 10.4 degrees over the next one hundred years. This, it is estimated, will result in a rise in the sea level of between 3.5 and 34.6 inches, leading to coastal erosion, flooding during storms, and permanent inundation of seawater; severe stress on many forests, wetlands, alpine regions, and other natural ecosystems; greater threats to human health as mosquitoes and other disease-carrying insects and rodents spread sickness over larger geographical regions; and disruption of agriculture in some parts of the world due to increased temperature, water stress, and sea-level rise in low-lying areas such as Bangladesh or the Mississippi River Delta.[56] The Union of Concerned Scientists demonstrates that atmospheric warming in the twentieth century was greater than at any time in the past four to six hundred years and that seven of the ten warmest years in the twentieth century occurred in the 1990s. That was, however, outdone by the years between 2001 and 2010 (with 2005 being the warmest), and a steady 2.5 percent rise in Earth temperatures is predicted. In 2009, science was showing that sea waters were already rising much faster than previously anticipated. The Arctic ice pack had lost about 40 percent of its thickness during the past four decades, and the global sea level rose about three times faster over the past one hundred years than in the previous three millennia.[57] Mountain glaciers around the world have been receding at rates far beyond any normal pattern of ice melt. With about 75 percent of the world's freshwater stored in glacier ice, this shrinkage has a cumulative effect on river flows and long-term freshwater availability.[58]

Global warming presents a unique environmental security dilemma because the consequences of current human activity might not be felt for generations. More immediate worst-case scenarios of abrupt climate change do, however, exist. Sudden global climate changes could result from a shift in a major ocean current and associated winds combined with additional direct effects of ice melt. Such environmental shifts could bring about a climate-change crisis that emerged not over a century but over a decade. Current scientific knowledge does not have a baseline for establishing the threshold that would instigate abrupt climate change. How much change, for example, in the flow of ocean currents such as the Gulf Stream might trigger climatic change? The danger is that, once abrupt climate change occurs, it could be too late to make effective policy changes.

Donald Kennedy, editor in chief of the journal *Science*, asserts that "an environmental scientist concerned with the processes that drive environmental change can say something useful about security."[59] Kennedy describes life at the Ganges-Brahmaputr river delta in Bangladesh, which has low elevation and a very dense human population. Ongoing rising sea levels, combined with powerful storm surges caused by global warming, would cause the displacement of tens of millions of people in this region. Already, there has been considerable emigration from the delta to nearby India, which exacerbates tensions between native populations and immigrants in areas affected by extreme poverty and overpopulation. Kennedy also notes that a shift in the flow of warm water from the Gulf Stream in the Atlantic would have a major impact on the temperate climates of Europe. An injection of freshwater in the north would impact the salinity of the Atlantic and lead to a significant change in the water temperature or flow of the Gulf Stream. The end result would be a significant decline in fisheries, shortened seasons of agricultural productivity, and an increase in disease—all with associated economic dislocation in

Europe. More broadly, Kennedy notes that malaria and other diseases would spread widely around the world with the increase in numbers and vertical distribution of mosquitoes. A study by the United Nations University projects that by 2050, more than 2 billion people worldwide could be at risk of flood devastation. This number would be twice that projected to occur in a period of normal climate change. Just in the period between 1987 and 1997, flooding incurred some 228,000 deaths and $136 billion in economic losses.[60] Global warming also risks accelerating the hurricane cycle, which normally follows a ten-year period of relative calm, then increasingly violent storms, followed by additional calm. A typical Caribbean hurricane releases the same destructive power as one hundred thousand Hiroshima-type nuclear bombs.[61] Meanwhile, the European Environment Agency predicts that Europe is warming faster than the rest of the world and that cold winters could disappear there entirely by 2080. European temperatures are expected to rise between 3.6 and 11.3 degrees over the next hundred years.[62]

The U.S. Department of Defense takes global warming seriously enough to have commissioned a study by two climate-change experts, Peter Schwartz (former head of planning at Royal Dutch/Shell Group) and Doug Randall (of the Global Business Network). Schwartz and Randall stressed that they were thinking in worst-case terms to "push the boundaries of current research on climate change so we may better understand the potential implications on United States national security."[63] They also stressed that their scenario is plausible and would have immediate and profound national security implications. Schwartz and Randall accept as a given that significant global warming will occur during the twenty-first century. The changes that they predict could last from one hundred to one thousand years once they occur. The end result would be a "significant drop in the human carrying capacity of the Earth's environment."[64]

According to Schwartz and Randall, specific sources of conflict could include food shortages due to decreases in net global agricultural production; decreased availability and quality of freshwater in key regions due to shifted precipitation patterns, causing more frequent floods and droughts; and disrupted access to energy supplies due to extensive sea ice and storminess. The end result would be a new era of global competition between those with resources who seek to build virtual fortresses around their countries. Less fortunate nations would "initiate in struggles for access to food, clean water, or energy. . . . Unlikely alliances could be formed as defense priorities shift and the goal is resources for survival rather than religion, ideology, or national honor."[65] Specific areas of strategic crisis could include an America that turns inward, giving up much of the stability its global presence provides; a Europe that, hard hit by temperature change, confronts refugee influxes from Africa; and a seriously impacted China, given its population and food demand. Other areas in Asia, such as Bangladesh, could become nearly uninhabitable due to rising sea levels that contaminate inland water supplies. Russia would be particularly vulnerable as its political system increasingly weakened and nearby countries considered invading to gain access to its abundant and untapped natural resources.

The study speculates as follows: Picture Japan eyeing nearby Russian oil and gas reserves to power desalination plants and energy-intensive farming. Envision nuclear-armed Pakistan, India, and China skirmishing at their borders over refugees, access to shared rivers, and arable land. Imagine Spain and Portugal fighting over fishing rights.[66] The authors conclude that such a scenario would severely damage "the world's 'carrying capacity'—the natural resources, social organizations, and economic networks that support the population. . . . Technological progress and market forces, which have long helped boost Earth's carrying capacity, can do little to offset the crisis—it is too widespread and unfolds too fast." Eventually, "an ancient pattern re-emerges: the eruption of desperate, all-out wars over food, water, and energy supplies." War itself may "define human life."[67]

Treaties such as the Kyoto Protocol on global warming have sought only to slow the growth of carbon dioxide emissions over time, and Kyoto itself failed to gain the support of the United States and other major contributors to carbon emissions. In December 2009, a major summit on climate change in Copenhagen failed to achieve more than aspirational goals. To many states, curbing the increase in carbon dioxide emissions inevitably infringes on their right to maximize short-term gains from economic growth and development. Also, the need for transparency in reporting can expose state failures, something that China was especially concerned about at the 2009 Copenhagen meeting. These are not minor issues for underdeveloped states already suffering extreme challenges involving economic crises and human suffering. Meeting basic needs in the context of expanding populations in underdeveloped states means providing sanitation, health, employment, and the necessities of modern living. This requires the expenditure of energy in societies where clean-energy technology does not exist or is too expensive to put in place. Thus, the global warming security dilemma places near-term human security for large parts of the world's population in direct conflict with humanity's future. At the same time, much of the problem of global warming is caused by those who enjoy the good life available in modern society. The end result of these competing political and economic pressures is that, to date, major efforts to decrease the causal variables affecting global warming have been minimal.

Deforestation and Land Use

Humanity depends on forests and the land for survival, and the depletion of forests and the mismanagement of land create a variety of environmental challenges with security implications. Worldwide, some 1.6 billion people rely on forests for their livelihoods, and 12.4 million acres of tropical forests are destroyed every year.[68] People are directly impacted by deforestation, and the process is often a contributing factor to global warming when forests are burned to clear more farmland. The loss of forests simultaneously removes a major means by which carbon dioxide is eliminated from the atmosphere. The loss of forests can lead to desertification and soil erosion, which depletes vital minerals necessary for productive agriculture. The soil can spill out into rivers, creating silt and destroying fisheries. This soil runoff and depletion of usable land can lead to population movements away from traditional life-styles into urban environments, contributing to further population pressures in large cities. Deforestation and poor land management can strain states' capacity to meet the needs of their populations, leading to internal instability or conflict over resources.

The Food and Agricultural Organization (FAO) defines deforestation as the loss of tree cover to below 10 or 20 percent of crown coverage. FAO stud-ies show that most deforestation occurs in the developing world, which lost over 200 million acres between 1980 and the turn of the century.[69] While some deforestation occurs naturally through fires or other climatic events, the human impact on forests is severe. The primary driver behind deforesta-tion is economic demand. Wealthy people in developed countries use timber for wood materials in construction, while poor people in underdeveloped countries use timber provided by forests to meet basic needs, for fuel and heating, and for export. Importantly, much of the demand for logging done in underdeveloped countries comes from the developed world, and many developed countries have to import their lumber. Thus, lumber has become an important means of economic development and trade. While a country like Japan has a stable situation regarding its own forests, it achieves this by consuming 50 percent of all wood that is cut from rainforests. Ethiopia has gone from being 45 percent forested in 1900 to 2.5 percent forested at the turn of the twenty-first century. Haiti has gone from being mostly forested to a contemporary barren landscape.[70] Overall, 98 percent of Haiti's forests are gone, which leaves no topsoil to hold rains, leading to flooding and the destruction of vital food resources.[71] The security implications of deforesta-tion are summarized in a study for the U.S. Army: reduced carrying capacity of the land; fewer forests as a component of the carbon cycle, resulting in loss of carbon dioxide removal capacity; loss of biodiversity with all of its known and unknown implications; increased flooding and loss of soils, with resultant mud slides and waterway siltation; and declining economic benefits due to the loss of forests as a renewable resource.[72]

Of 8.7 billion acres of cropland, pastures, and forests worldwide, nearly 2 billion have been degraded over the past fifty years.[73] More than 250 million people and one-third of the Earth's land surface are impacted by resulting desertification.[74] The tropical rainforests of Latin America, especially Brazil, have received considerable focus since the 1980s when large-scale burning of the rainforests garnered significant international attention. Rainforest destruction from 1995 to 2000 averaged almost 2 million acres per year—the equivalent of seven football fields per minute and a significant increase since the early 1990s. This increase coincided with new plans by the Brazilian government to build expansive road networks, railroads, hydroelectric reservoirs, and power and gas lines in a project totaling $40 billion in infrastructure development that would infringe on the rainforests, which would cause even further deforestation.[75]

Despite the dangers posed by overdevelopment of the Amazon rainforest, Brazil has accelerated its exploitation. In 2003, some 9,169 square miles of rainforest disappeared, which was a 2 percent increase over the previous year. Near-term economic priorities are driven by Brazil's role as the world's second-largest producer of both soy and cattle. Between 1997 and 2003, beef exports increased by a factor of five, and soy production grew from 32 to 52 million tons between 2000 and 2003.[76] Yet, this too could create serious vulnerabilities, as in 2009 the world demand for soy dropped considerably, and major drought led to a bust in Brazil's production in this area. The dynamics of rainforest depletion have direct consequences for indigenous peoples. Some tribes in the rainforests have lived for centuries untouched by the developed world. They have now been exposed to new diseases. Some 6 to 9 million indigenous people were estimated to inhabit the Brazilian rainforest in 1500; in 1992 there were fewer than two hundred thousand.[77]

Mexico lost an average of 2.72 million acres of forests and jungles annually between 1993 and the turn of the century. This deforestation was twice as much as the Mexican government declared officially at the time. Areas including the Yucatan Peninsula, Tabasco, Veracruz, and Chiapas were all in critical danger as a result of deforestation, much of it due to an increase in farming and grazing land cleared by 10 to 15 million poor farmers with no other means of income.[78] Guillermo Montoya Gomez notes that "these people will starve if they don't cut down more trees, and a comprehensive solution will be complicated and costly."[79]

Some 50 percent of Southeast Asia's forests have been destroyed with an annual loss of 1 percent. Throughout East Asia, forest cover is depleting by 1.4 percent annually. Indonesia's 120 million hectares of forests are shrinking at a rate of 1.5 million hectares annually. Since 1985, as much as 30 percent of Indonesia's forest cover has disappeared. In Indonesia, how trees are felled also impacts surrounding forests and future growth. While only 3 percent of the trees are cut, logging operations in Indonesia generally damage some 49 percent of the trees in a forest area.[80] Indonesia's forests will be reduced by a total of 50 percent by 2030 at current rates of deforestation.[81]

Africa also faces serious deforestation challenges. Though it has 30 percent of the world's tropical forest growth, the continent faces a unique combination of poor governmental attention to the issue, creeping desertification, and destructive human activity. In sub-Saharan Africa, cut wood accounts for 52 percent of all energy sources.[82] Mali has been losing about four hundred thousand acres of tree cover every year due to growing demand for timber and fuel wood.[83] This small country of 12 million people uses 6 million tons of firewood per year—about 1.5 kilograms per day for every inhabitant of the largest city, Bamako.[84] In Kenya, the combination of population growth, droughts, poor land management, and increasing deforestation has led to accelerated desertification. Kenyan forests now cover only 2.8 percent of total land area.[85] Even without losing any more forests, Benin, Burundi, Cameroon, Côte d'Ivoire, Kenya, and Nigeria could lose more than a third of their primate species within the next several decades. However, this problem is likely to grow substantially worse as West Africa is expected to lose, by 2040, 70 percent of its remaining native forest. In East Africa the loss is expected to be as high as 95 percent.[86] In Africa, the primary cause of deforestation is direct human use of cut wood.

As the world warms and human activity destroys animal and plant habitats, entire ecosystems are placed at risk. Using computer models to estimate the movement of plants, mammals, birds, reptiles, frogs, butterflies, and other fauna in response to changes in ecosystems, scientists estimate that in the rich biodiversity regions of the world—about 20 percent of the Earth—some 15 to 37 percent of all species could be driven to extinction by 2050. The impact could eventually drive 1 million species into extinction—and affect billions of people who rely on complex ecological systems for their survival. The director of the United Nations Environment Program concludes, "If one million species become extinct, it is not just the plant and animal kingdoms and the beauty of the planet that will suffer. . . . Billions of people, especially in the developing world, will suffer too as they rely on nature for such essential goods and services as food, shelter, and medicines."[87]

Water Security

Humans and animals cannot live without water. The combination of water scarcity, degradation, and growing demand makes access to freshwater one of the most significant emerging security issues of the twenty-first century. By 2015, the United Nations predicts that 40 percent of the world's population will live in areas where one cannot safely drink the water. Already, 39 percent do not have basic sanitation, and 1 billion people have no access to clean water sources. Progress is being made in making drinking water and sanitation more accessible, but absent greater effort, population growth will eventually outstrip improvements. According to a study by the United Nations Children's Fund, some four thousand children die every day from illnesses caused by the lack of clean water.[88] While the world is covered with ocean water, it is salty and undrinkable. As ice caps melt due to global warming, more freshwater will likely accelerate climate change as ice melt mixes with warm ocean waters, thereby affecting the pace of global warming. Too much rain and the consequent flooding or too little rain and expanding desertification are becoming significant trends in heavily populated regions of the world. Agricultural demand currently accounts for 70 percent of all water use worldwide, while 22 percent of total water use is for industrial activity. People in rich countries use ten times more water than those in underdeveloped countries.[89] Meanwhile, waterways that cross national borders also render downstream or adjacent states vulnerable to the activity of upstream states. Water can cause conflict over control of water resources, serve as a military or political tool, become a target of terrorism, and play a major role in economic-development disputes and conflict resolution.[90]

The UN World Water Development Report illustrates the global scale of water-security challenges. By 2015, an additional 1 billion people will need access to both water supplies and sanitation.[91] In a country like Ethiopia, only 20 percent of the population has adequate access to clean water.[92] Entire freshwater ecosystems are affected by increased water use due to population and consumption growth. Infrastructure development, such as the construction of dams and levees, can alter river beds, produce sediment, and change water temperature, impacting water quantity and quality, floodplains, delta economies, and fisheries. Land conversion can eliminate major components of aquatic environments, impacting natural flood control and animal habitats. The overharvesting and exploitation of fisheries depletes living resources, negatively impacting food production as well as water supply in terms of both quantity and quality. Meanwhile, the release of pollutants into land, air, or water alters the chemistry and ecology of rivers, lakes, and wetlands, thereby damaging water supply and quality, habitats, and food production. More than 50 percent of the world's wetlands have been lost since 1900.[93] Every day, 2 million tons of human waste are disposed of in waterways. Even in the United States, 40 percent of water bodies assessed in 1998 were not fit for world distribution. In Asia, all rivers running through cities are badly polluted. On a global scale, 60 percent of the world's 227 largest rivers are severely fragmented by dams, diversions, and canals.[94] Rivers like the Nile are vitally important to survival in the desert areas of northeastern Africa; yet, the tributaries and main river are reaching an unsustainable point of overuse.

Water-related disasters that occur in nature or will be exacerbated by global climate change also pose a serious threat to populations. There were some twenty-two hundred water-related disasters between 1990 and 2001. These crises included floods (50 percent), waterborne disease outbreaks (28 percent), droughts (11 percent), landslides and avalanches (9 percent), and famines (2 percent). Most such disasters occur in Asia (29 percent) and North and South America (20 percent). In 1998 and 1999, a total of ninety thousand people died as a result of water-related natural disasters, costing $70 billion in 1999. Between 1991 and 2000, droughts accounted for 280,000 deaths. Between 1987 and 1997, some 228,000 lives were lost just in Asia from floods. From 1992 to 2001, developing countries accounted for 20 percent of all water-related disasters and over 50 percent of all disaster fatalities, and people in these countries were thirteen times more likely to die from such disasters than people in developed areas of the world.[95] In 2010, Pakistan was ravaged by floods that displaced millions of people. Even highly developed countries are not immune from such disasters, as the United States discovered when hurricanes Katrina, Rita, and Wilma hit in 2005.

A survey of "water hot spots" by the British Broadcasting Corporation shows the diverse impact of water issues around the world.[96] In Australia, power and irrigation have damaged the two largest rivers and reduced their flows to the sea by 75 percent while providing 40 percent of Australia's farms with water. In India, the sacred Ganges River suffers from depletion and pollution; it is also the source of political conflict between India and Bangladesh. Climate change is reducing the ice melt that feeds the Ganges, while deforestation has caused subsoil streams flowing into the river to dry up. India also controls the flow of water into Bangladesh via a hydroproject near the two countries' mutual border. India has periodically diverted the river toward Calcutta to stop its port from drying up during hot seasons. This upstream action helps Indian farmers but denies Bangladeshi farmers water. China suffers from flooding in its south and drought in its north. China has built a massive dam project on the Yangtze River (the Three Gorges Dam), the largest of its kind in the world. In its construction, 1 million people have been uprooted. In 1997, China's Yellow River ran dry for 226 days, and between 1991 and 1996, the water table beneath the North China Plain fell by an average of 1.5 meters per year. The freshwater supplied by the Mekong River plays a major role in China's policy of exerting control over the Tibetan plateau, where the river has its headwaters.

In Eurasia, the Aral Sea saw a drop in water level of sixteen meters between 1962 and 1993 as a result of water-redistribution programs to grow cotton by the Soviet Union. This area now has one of the highest infant-mortality rates in the world, and anemia and cancers caused by chemicals blowing off the dried seabed are common. Iraq has lost 90 percent of its wetlands in the southern part of the country. Some twenty thousand square kilometers of freshwater were drained by the government, leaving only salty, crusted earth behind. Turkey has sought to increase its existing water reserves and to boost its hydroelectric capabilities via a system of twenty-two dams on the Tigris and Euphrates rivers. The filling of these dams has occasionally stopped the flow of water to Iraq and Syria. Israel and its neighbors face the potential for significant competition over water resources. Both Israel and Jordan rely on the Jordan River, though Israel controls it and has cut supplies during times of scarcity. The Sea of Galilee's water levels have been declining, which could lead to increased salination of Israel's main reservoir. Israelis in the West Bank use four times as much water as their Palestinian neighbors. In 2002, Israel threatened military action in Lebanon when that country opened a new pumping station that took water from a tributary of the Jordan.

In Africa, Lake Chad was once a huge body of water on the borders of Chad, Niger, Nigeria, and Cameroon. However, it has shrunk in size by 95 percent since the mid-1960s. The region's climate has changed as monsoon rains that previously replenished the lake have been reduced. The region's 9 million farmers, fishermen, and herders now face water shortages, crop failures, livestock deaths, collapsed fisheries, soil salinity, and increasing poverty. The Nile River may pose the biggest single cause of water conflict in Africa in the coming decades. As population demands grow in Egypt, Ethiopia, and Sudan, competition for the Nile's waters will be intense. Egypt said in 1991 that it was ready to use force to protect its access to the river's flows, even though its tributaries run through nine different countries.

In the Western Hemisphere, Mexico City is sinking as the water underneath it is pumped out. Over the last five hundred years, the lakes around Mexico City have been drained and the surrounding forests chopped down. As the city grew in size, the water problem magnified. The city is now at serious risk of running out of clean water, while an estimated 40 percent of the water it does have is lost through leaky pipes that are more than one hundred years old. In North America, much of the freshwater in the United States is underground. One crucial source is the eight-hundred-mile Ogallala aquifer that stretches from Texas to South Dakota and supplies water to one-fifth of irrigated land in the United States. The aquifer has been cut off from its original natural sources and is thus being depleted at a rate of 12 billion cubic meters per year. This amounts to a total depletion of a volume equal to the annual flow of eighteen Colorado rivers. Some estimates conclude that the entire aquifer will be dry in as little as twenty-five years.

There is actually little historical evidence that water is a direct cause of war. Historically, water wars have not been strategically effective. In only seven cases have armies been mobilized or shots fired across international borders for reasons of water access. In these seven cases, disputes did not escalate into warfare.[97] Water conflicts can, however, exacerbate existing tensions. For example, in 2003, Russia built a dike that connected its coast with Tuzla Island in the Kerch Strait near Ukraine's Crimean Peninsula. Ukraine protested this move as intruding on its sovereignty over the island, which Russia said it did not recognize. Ukraine responded by deploying fifty troops to Tuzla and threatened to abandon agreements with Russia though no actual conflict broke out.[98] While it is true that such conflicts historically do not lead to war, never before has Earth witnessed the kinds of pressures on water supplies that it will confront in the twenty-first century. History, therefore, may not be a useful guide as the world addresses water issues in the decades to come. The ongoing exploitation of the Mekong River by China via new dams has raised substantial tensions between it and Vietnam, which relies on the flows into the Mekong Delta for its economic livelihood. This issue became especially acute in 2010 when severe drought compounded the diversion of the Mekong flows into Vietnam. Myanmar, Cambodia, Laos, and Thailand are also affected as the Mekong provides livelihoods for about 60 million people in Southeast Asia.

There are many transboundary basins in the world, including fifty-nine in Africa; fifty-eight in Asia; seventy-three in Europe; sixty-one in Latin America and the Caribbean; seventeen in North America; and one in Oceania. A total of 141 countries have territory within a transboundary basin, and 21 lie entirely within one. The UN World Water Development Report notes that, of 1,831 interactions over the last fifty years involving transboundary waterways, only 7 have involved violence (though 507 conflicts have occurred).[99] Nevertheless, new conditions can create new outcomes and, as William Mitsch notes, "We have had oil wars. . . . That's happened in our lifetime. . . . Water wars are possible."[100]

It is also, however, just as possible that states might see increasing incentives to cooperate and overcome differences to meet their water needs. The real threat relevant to water security might thus not be international conflict but rather the added burden on state capacity to meet citizens' basic needs. The major challenge posed by water-security dilemmas might involve instability within states, of which water supply issues might be a major component. With over sixty states facing water stress in the next twenty-five years, it would be a mistake to assume that future instability and conflict might not be affected by this condition.[101]

Energy Scarcity and Safety

By 2011, the price-per-barrel of oil averaged about $79, and gasoline prices in the United States had reached levels that consumers were long unaccustomed to paying. In 1999, one could find gasoline for as low as 79 cents per gallon; on average, by 2010, it cost $2.84. In some parts of America, in summer 2008, gasoline prices topped $4 a gallon; they rose again in early 2011. The immediate problem was not a lack of supply but rather growing demand relative to the ability to access or refine sufficient energy for industry, society, and transportation. Scarcity or supply disruptions of energy resources such as oil and natural gas place pressure on states to develop oil-containing areas, to burn less-clean sources of energy such as coal, or to seek energy alternatives. Two major security issues are impacted by these trends. First, states that depend on external energy suppliers are vulnerable. Control of energy flows, such as pipelines and shipping lanes, could therefore be a major source of future conflict. Second, the relative safety of energy use creates significant issues for states ranging from the impact on the environment of burning fossil fuels to challenges associated with the use of cleaner nuclear energy.

Energy scarcity will become a worldwide problem if demand continues to rise and sources of energy become fewer. The International Energy Agency (IEA) estimates that by 2020, global energy demand will have increased by 57 percent from levels in the late 1990s, with an average annual increase of 2 percent. Demand for both oil and natural gas is expected to increase substantially. The Energy Information Administration predicts the world demand for oil will total almost 118 million barrels per day in 2025.[102] Natural gas and coal demand is rising faster than that for oil. China and India account for two-thirds of the increased demand. World economic growth is expected to continue, and thus energy demand will grow exponentially. Some future projections were built around an assumption that oil and gas prices would remain stable and relatively low. However, the price of oil in 2005 was over twice the dollar amount initially projected by the IEA. Uncertainty has been introduced into global energy markets. As the price of energy goes up with increased demand, it is also possible that states will move toward fuel alternatives. The Energy Information Administration predicts that by 2025, natural gas will meet 24 percent of end-use energy requirements. However, if existing trends remain in place, geothermal and solar energy will provide less than 1 percent of the energy used for space and water heating.

The IEA estimates that the total investment requirement for energy-supply infrastructure worldwide between 2001 and 2030 will be $16 trillion. This expenditure would be necessary to expand supply capacity and to replace existing and future supply facilities that will be exhausted or become obsolete.[103] Electricity is seen as a particularly important area for future investment, costing about $10 trillion. Even in countries like the United States, electricity has become a major challenge as outdated electrical power grids have struggled to keep pace with the dramatically accelerated demand. In summer 2003, large areas of the eastern United States and Canada were blacked out when integrated power networks failed because tree limbs fell on some wires. The energy situation is far worse in the developing world, where China is expected to have to spend $2.3 trillion to meet its growing energy needs. Worldwide, most of the projected investments in energy infrastructure are needed just to maintain current levels of demand and do not account for growing future demand. According to the IEA, 51 percent of investment in energy will be needed to replace or maintain existing and future production capacity. The remaining 49 percent will be needed to meet the rising demand of natural gas at 2.4 percent annually, oil at 1.6 percent annually, coal at 1.4 percent annually, and electricity at 2.4 percent annually.[104] China, Russia, India, Indonesia, and Brazil will account for one-third of future global electricity investment.

States that factor environmental concerns into their energy policies could have an important positive impact on the worldwide demand for energy investment and extraction. If, however, the environmental costs of burning fossil fuels are not substantially addressed by governments, or if alternative energy sources are not fully utilized, then the overall costs of major climate change for the world's security could prove insurmountable. As populations grow and demand for the basic necessities of life increases, more energy will be needed. States that cannot afford substantial investments in clean-energy sources will likely continue to exploit resources, doing considerable environmental damage. The immediate demand for energy and its impact on populations in the underdeveloped world is often overlooked by societies seeking to secure access to cheap gasoline to power their automobiles. For example, the World Energy Outlook 2002 showed that at the turn of the century, 1.6 billion people had no access to electricity, and 2.4 billion depended on basic wood or dung sources for cooking and heating, which accelerates air pollution problems. Even with substantial investment in energy sources over the next thirty years, 1.4 billion people will still live day to day with no electricity.[105] This means they will have no electricity for making clean and drinkable water, no electricity for hospitals, and no electricity for schools. Currently, four out of five people without electricity live in rural areas of the developing world—primarily in sub-Saharan Africa and South and Southeast Asia. It is expected that, by 2030, large segments of this population will have moved into massive third-world megacities, creating enormous strains on current urban capacity to provide for basic energy needs, health and sanitation, education, and other social requisites for human development.

The growth of China's economy, coupled with the movement of agrarian peasants into cities and a new generation of wealth, is having an especially significant impact on global energy demand. As China emphasizes coal burning for energy, its contribution to global warming will rise. China can sustain its rapid economic growth by mining more coal. However, China will still face major oil shortages of 5.9 to 8.8 million barrels per day by 2015, according to the U.S. Department of Energy.[106] As urban environmental pressures mount, public attitudes in China are also likely to create pressures for cleaner energy sources combined with increasing demand in industry and transportation sectors of the Chinese economy. If China were to move rapidly toward a substitution strategy, moving away from coal and toward oil, combined with increasing use of petroleum fuel for automobiles, the impact on global energy prices could be significant. In a worst case, China's demand for energy could prompt new alliances over pipeline flows from the Middle East and Central Asia, purchases of energy-production facilities from Russia, or even military conflict in areas such as the South China Sea. At a minimum, China's growing energy demand will increase pressure for further energy exploration and likely raise prices for those countries whose economies are currently benefiting from low-cost energy supplies.

Nuclear Energy

Nuclear power is one of the cleanest and cheapest sources of energy—and potentially the most dangerous. Nuclear power plants generate 20 percent of the world's energy. Some countries, like France, rely on them for as much as 75 percent of their energy supply. Such plants release low levels of waste during normal operations, and emissions are strictly controlled by states around the world. In small amounts, radiation exposure is not harmful to human beings—though long-term exposure can have some genetic impact. Nuclear accidents have been rare. However, in circumstances where accidents have occurred, human exposure to radiation has had dangerous consequences. Humans can be exposed to radiation as a result of rain washing materials out of the air, external radiation directly emanating from a radioactive cloud, external doses from radioactive materials deposited on the ground, and internal exposure from eating and drinking radioactive materials in food and water.[107]

The International Atomic Energy Agency (IAEA) notes that most environmental impacts from radiation have resulted from nuclear weapons tests. These tests have propelled into the upper atmosphere a variety of radionuclides, including hydrogen-3 and plutonium-241, which then fall on the Earth's surface. Some five hundred aboveground nuclear explosions were conducted up until 1963, and a number of others were conducted in the 1980s and 1990s. The IAEA concludes that the global collective dose of radiation from weapon tests fallout is now about thirty thousand man sieverts annually.[108] Processing and storage of nuclear waste is also a serious problem. Even a wealthy country like the United States has not been able to determine effectively what to do with its nuclear waste or how to manage the environmental impact of weapons-manufacturing and -storage facilities. However, the most serious challenge is in the former Soviet Union, as we still do not entirely understand where the nuclear hot spots are. In 1957, a nuclear accident in Mayak released seventy to eighty tons of radioactive material into the air. Siberia's two main rivers, the Ob and the Yenisei, are radioactively contaminated. Once-privileged Russian nuclear scientists often go without pay; as such, some are available to the highest foreign bidder for employment. The Kola Peninsula has 29,040 fuel elements, nine reactor cores, and 21,067 cubic meters of solid-fuel nuclear waste.[109]

Russia has acute experience with the dangers of nuclear energy. In April 1986, something went very wrong at Chernobyl. While putting the poorly designed plant through a test, workers failed to communicate with each other. In the process they created a power surge that set off explosions in the nuclear core of one of the reactors. High levels of radiation were released over ten days and fell not only around the Soviet Union but also in northern and southern Europe, Canada, Japan, and the United States. In some areas near the reactor and in other local hot spots where radiation fell due to weather patterns, radioactive cesium will be present for three hundred years. The spread of radioactivity was stemmed by the brave efforts of emergency responders—thirty-one of whom died from direct exposure—who placed a cap on top of the burning reactor core.

More than one hundred thousand people within a thirty-mile radius of the accident site at Chernobyl were evacuated; they received significant radiation doses to their bodies and thyroid glands. So-called liquidators included six hundred thousand workers and military personnel who were involved both in emergency actions during the accident and in the subsequent cleanup, which lasted several years. About four hundred people received very high exposure to radiation during the accident itself. About 270,000 people continue to live in areas of the former Soviet Union that were contaminated with radiocesium and require protection measures. Outside the former Soviet Union, radioactive materials including iodine and cesium spread through the Northern Hemisphere. Health and agricultural impact outside the former Soviet Union has been minimal—although in certain areas of Scotland, radioactivity still required careful monitoring of livestock fifteen years later. Around the area of the accident, soil and agriculture continue to be affected by radioactivity. High rates of thyroid cancer and lingering psychological effects persist.

The problem at Chernobyl was never actually resolved as the fire in the reactor was capped but not permanently extinguished. The "sarcophagus" that encases the reactor was only meant as a temporary solution, and it is increasingly at risk for corrosion and leakage. Around the plant, there are eight hundred sites of buried equipment contaminated with radioactivity, all of which are sources of groundwater contamination. Some estimates suggest that as many as 3.5 million people, one-third of them children, have suffered illness as a result of this accident. Overall, the radiation leak was five hundred times greater than that released by the atomic bomb on Hiroshima at the end of World War II.[110] The level of radioactive contamination of the land is 23 percent in Belarus, 5 percent in Ukraine, and 1.5 percent of total land in Russia.[111]

According to the IAEA, the overall impact of Chernobyl was actually less serious than initially feared. While about eighteen hundred children developed thyroid cancer from overexposure to radioactive isotopes, this treatable disease is rarely fatal. However, this is also the largest group of cancers known to have occurred due to a single incident in history.[112] The IAEA concludes that "with this exception, there is no scientific evidence of increases in overall cancer incidence or mortality or in nonmalignant disorders that could be related to radiation exposure."[113] The IAEA further concludes that there is "no evidence of a major public health impact attributable to radiation exposure 14 years after the accident."[114] Yet, at the same time, at least eight thousand—and in some estimates as many as fifteen thousand—people died as a result of exposure to radiation over time.[115] Meanwhile, about 4.5 million people continue to receive government relief as a direct result of displacement due to the incident, which strains governments in Ukraine and Belarus.

Even in the highly advanced country of Japan, a major nuclear accident occurred in 1999 at a plant northeast of Tokyo. Worker error led to a major radiation leak, exposing 600 people to radiation and dislocating about 320,000. The United States experienced a nuclear accident at Three Mile Island in Pennsylvania in 1979. As of 2011, the United States has 103 aging plants in operation, conducts few inspections, and has been spending less money on maintenance—although in 2011 a review of the safety of American plants was commenced. The Davis-Besse plant near Cleveland, Ohio, was found to be operating with cracks in the infrastructure around the nuclear reactor core and has had to be shut down for extended periods. The U.S. Department of Energy recovers an average of three unwanted, high-risk radiological sources every week in the United States. One Russian national, who had a radiation dump discovered near his garage, illustrated the general international lack of awareness of the nature of the radiological challenge: "I'm from Moldova and I drink Moldovan wine. . . . It cleans everything. Radiation doesn't hurt me."[116]

Even small amounts of radioactive material used in medical laboratories or university research institutes can pose a threat if used with radioactive dispersal devices, which include "any device, including any weapon or equipment, other than a nuclear explosive device, specifically designed to employ radioactive material by disseminating it to cause destruction, damage, or injury by means of the radiation produced by the decay of such material."[117] The spread of radioactive isotopes in the environment could make an area of major economic activity uninhabitable for many decades or create extremely costly cleanup needs. The pure volume of radioactive material held by governments and in the private sector makes its control very hard to secure. Even a technologically advanced country like the United States has serious problems in this area. Between 1998 and 2003, there were an estimated thirteen hundred disappearances of radioactive materials in the United States. Most of this material was recovered, but in reality, the United States does not know how much low-grade radioactive material exists in private use on its territory. Some 114 American universities that possess radioactive plutonium-239 tried (unsuccessfully) to return it to the U.S. government, but the U.S. Department of Energy did not have enough storage space. In March 1998, a North Carolina hospital discovered that nineteen sealed sources of radiological material, including highly dispersible cesium-137, had gone missing from a locked safe. In March 1999, an industrial radiography camera with iridium-192 was stolen from a private Florida home, and two universities found that doors where this same material was stored had been left unlocked.[118]

Summary

The environment and energy are extraordinarily important challenges that have significantly expanded the debate over the meaning of security. The most significant threats will likely affect states' capacity to meet their peoples' basic needs, which risks the spread of instability within and among states. Skeptics about the role the environment historically plays in conflict have considerable evidence to support their conclusions. Moreover, it is just as possible that environmental and energy scarcities will produce cooperation rather than conflict. However, even best-case-scenario projections for future environmental and energy dynamics depict a future for Earth and its carrying capacity for which experience provides little guidance.

Suggested Reading

Dalby, Simon. *Environmental Security.* Minneapolis: University of Minnesota Press, 2002.

——. *Security and Environmental Change.* New York: Polity, 2009.

Degeest, Theresa Manley, and Dennis Clark Parages. *Ecological Security: An Evolutionary Perspective on Globalization.* Lanham, MD: Rowman & Littlefield, 2003.

Diehl, Paul F., and Nils Petter Gleditsch, eds. *Environmental Conflict.* Boulder, CO: Westview Press, 2000.

Gleick, Peter H. *The World's Water 2008–2009: The Biennial Report on Freshwater Resources.* Washington, DC: Island Press, 2009.

Haas, Peter M., Robert O. Keohane, and Marc Levy, eds. *Institutions for the Earth.* Cambridge, MA: MIT Press, 1993.

Homer-Dixon, Thomas. *Environment, Scarcity, and Violence.* Princeton, NJ: Princeton University Press, 2001.

Kalicki, Jan, and David L. Goldwyn, eds. *Energy and Security: Toward a New Foreign Policy Strategy.* Baltimore: Johns Hopkins University Press, 2005.

Klare, Michael. *Rising Powers, Shrinking Planet: The New Geopolitics of Energy.* New York: Holt Paperbacks, 2009.

Roberts, Paul. *The End of Oil: On the Edge of a Perilous New World.* New York: Houghton Mifflin, 2004.

Williams, Michael. *Deforesting the Earth: From Prehistory to Global Crisis.* Chicago: University of Chicago Press, 2002.

Classroom in Afghanistan, supplied by the U.S. military. The school provides secondary education to nearly one thousand students in the area, despite shattered windows and deteriorated wooden ceilings. Source: U.S. military photo by Sandra Arnold.

10

Meeting the Challenges of Power and Peace

M EETING THE CHALLENGES OF POWER AND PEACE surveyed in this book requires applying the full range of conceptual frameworks for thinking about global security and also for realizing the positive potential to build a better, more peaceful world. The traditions of realism, which focus on power, and the traditions of liberalism, which focus peace, each have prominent roles to play. The application and testing of conceptual frameworks helps distinguish between what will and will not work in organizing power in the pursuit of peace. The cases in this book show the extent to which security has become a global issue. Some of the threats confronting humanity are truly overwhelming. However, a careful examination of security challenges shows that the more we know about particular security threats, the better able we will be to avert or resolve them. This chapter reviews the relationship between evolving conceptual frameworks and global security. The conclusion stresses the role of education as an asset in moving the world toward a condition in which the pursuits of power and peace are one and the same. Finally, the chapter offers some suggestions for how people across society can play a proactive role in producing a positive global future.

Applying Global Security Concepts

This book demonstrates that it is no longer sufficient to think of "national security" or "international security"; rather the two are important subsets of global security. The cases herein illustrate how adaptation of the international system has come to reflect a globalization of security. In particular, power has far more manifestations than previous approaches to understanding security have taken into account. International security concepts, however, continue to provide a strong foundation for understanding these changes. Realists often criticize idealist schools as naïve about the inherent dangers in the international system. Meanwhile, idealists tend to criticize the realist schools as perpetuating self-fulfilling prophecies that preclude more positive outcomes of cooperation in favor of lasting peace. This book is neutral on the value of each general approach and instead offers the general conclusion that each worldview has an important role to play. Some frameworks do have greater applicability than others depending on the issue area. Testing conceptual frameworks with empirical evidence can lead to stronger theories and more effective policy. Of course, what defines a successful security outcome is highly contingent on who or what is being secured. Thus, students and practitioners have to make choices. These decisions will more likely increase security if existing assumptions are challenged with a range of conceptual choices.

The Quest for Power

The relative distribution of power in the international system remains the fundamental constant that defines global security. The meaning and application of power are changing as a result of globalization—but, as realists posit, power remains a central starting point to understanding global security. The globalization of security also confirms the realist focus on anarchy in the international system. The global diffusion of power makes international anarchy even more unpredictable and heightens the sense of uncertainty and speed that decision makers confront when shaping policies. The realist focus on the nation-state also remains valid—though with some significant qualifications. The state remains the primary barrier that delineates international and domestic politics and is a key line of defense against foreign threats. However, the nature of new threats increasingly challenges nation-states' capacity to meet security challenges with traditional tools of power. Furthermore, the economic dimension of security has been increasingly important, requiring a new perspective on the relationship between military spending and state power. Paradoxically, the state is simultaneously challenged and strengthened in the twenty-first century.

Realism appears to have its highest explanatory value when applied to relationships among the world's great powers. At the dawn of the twenty-first century, American political, economic, and military primacy framed the global security system, but questions about whether that primacy was in decline emerged. The distribution of power within the major regions of the world shows that American dominance confronts significant constraints. In particular, the nuclear capabilities of Russia and China constrain the exercise of American power. For example, in the 2008 war between Russia and Georgia, the United States might have wanted to support its West-leaning friends in Tbilisi, but the relative risks of confrontation with Russia limited what Washington could do. European dependence on Russian energy supplies also limited traditional alliance sentiment within NATO. While power fluctuates, direct war between the major countries of the world is highly unlikely, and deterrence appears further to help contain regional conflicts, including between India and Pakistan, China and Taiwan, and on the Korean Peninsula. Meanwhile, both defensive and offensive realism offer important frameworks for assessing the rationale for major state activity such as the 2003 U.S. invasion of Iraq. Also, realism has been adapted to account for the role that soft power can play in defining balancing strategies for nation-states and other international actors.

Realism also can provide an important framework for understanding sources of international cooperation. It might explain the structural realignment of an enlarged NATO after the Cold War but can also be used to test nonrealist assumptions about the effectiveness of the alliance absent a major threat like the Soviet Union. Even if not organized around state-to-state relationships, alliances can reflect approaches by countries to cooperate over how to best consolidate and organize power to achieve common national interests. Alliances can also include networks of relationships among nonstate actors such as popular movements and nongovernmental organizations. Basic elements of realism, of course, also explain the continued role that concert balance-of-power arrangements and strategic partnerships play among states in the international system. The overall role of classical deterrence has featured less prominently but, especially regarding nuclear weapons, does persist. Moreover, new concepts like dissuasion provide useful alternatives by raising the costs of aggression.

Realism can explain asymmetric tactics and the strategic rationale behind them. Terrorism, for example, is a tactic in the service of a broader strategic goal. One does not win wars by battling tactics—wars are won by defeating an enemy's objective. New approaches to understanding the strategic logic behind asymmetric threats can thus help to inform decision makers about how to overcome these barbaric tactics. Realist warnings about potential negative impacts of interdependence and possible clashes of civilizations resulting from globalization also show how these trends can lead to new forms of conflict. Realism has also focused on the key role of relative power, particularly the economic foundations of power. Additionally, realism allows for optimism regarding international cooperation. If states and the key actors in the system place a high value on cooperation and applying power toward peace, nothing inherent in realism precludes such outcomes. It, however, does provide a strong dose of skepticism from which to challenge other approaches toward the search for peace.

The Search for Peace

History reflects a continuing desire among people to live in peace. Of course, history is also written around devastating wars and conflicts that shatter such noble goals. There is no reason that the international system must always reflect anarchy, competition, conflict, and war. While idealist traditions embodied in such classic organs of collective security as the League of Nations faltered, modern applications are available to those who wish to begin their inquiries into global security with the proposition that peace is possible. The diffusion of power in the twenty-first century creates a more level playing field on which individuals who wish to prioritize peace can organize and unite across borders, influencing the agenda of global security. Modern idealism is perhaps more potent now than at any time in history—an ironic conclusion given the nature of the severe security challenges that confront humanity. Humankind has nevertheless shown considerable resilience, adaptability, and optimism. It is in humanity's interests to find mechanisms to resolve proliferating security challenges, and there is no reason that people across borders cannot marshal the networks of power in a search for peace.

There is no guarantee that efforts to promote peace in the international system will not, at the same time, be violent. For some, moral causes continue to justify war as a tool of international change, as was the case with Kosovo in 1999 (genocide and ethnic cleansing), the 2003 invasion of Iraq (to promote democracy), and the war in Afghanistan (women's and human rights). Military intervention in the name of idealism raises the dilemma of what is "moral" in the search for peace and who defines the values to be spread in the name of global security. Short of war and intervention, diplomacy and economic incentives can advance peaceful change. Global interdependence might even place a higher priority on such tools than the use of military power—as worked in South Africa, Libya, and indeed Iraq. Thus, the historical record shows that peaceful evolution toward state change, backed by positive incentives, can be an effective tool for managing even high-end security problems like nuclear proliferation. There is therefore no inherent reason why such approaches could not apply to countries like Iran and North Korea—though some such cases might also require the complementary threat of force.

Among the modern conceptual tools aiding the search for peace, neoliberal institutionalism has been dominant since the 1970s, especially after the Cold

War. The primary evidence to support neoliberal approaches to international security is the expanded role of international institutions that reflect cooperative security architectures. The role of the United Nations, NATO, and the European Union was seriously challenged by the crises in the Balkans, Rwanda, and Sudan. Afghanistan had proven an especially difficult challenge to NATO and the credibility of its claims to a serious twenty-first-century role in global security. Nonetheless, international institutions promoting cooperative security have proven they can play an important part in fostering transparency and information sharing, which can diminish the classical security dilemma. While not always adhered to, information sharing by institutions can help state decision makers to adjust policies to reflect new realities. The more states learn about the global impact of human and environmental security threats, for example, the more likely they may be to work together to find common solutions. The conditions of global security place a very high value on good information sharing—for example, involving international environmental threats or transnational diseases.

The globalization of economic interdependence also places importance on the role of commercial liberalism as a path to peace. The belief that trade stimulates cooperation is deeply embedded in the modern international system, and globalization accelerates these dynamics. The rapid pace at which the 2008 global financial crisis spread and deepened through 2010 clearly indicated that with such benefits also come risks. Similarly, the proliferation of technology can also work to enhance the lives of billions of people worldwide, while simultaneously creating new means of fighting wars or carrying out asymmetric attacks. Meanwhile, the lack of full access of countries in Africa and elsewhere to developed markets also serves to consolidate wealth and deepen structural economic divides.

Democracy is important for advancing the cause of human security as it requires governments to be transparent and effective in responding to citizens' needs. Strong evidence also shows that modern democracies are not inclined to fight with each other. Indeed, they are more likely to place a high value on trust because of their ability to negotiate in a climate of transparency. The democratic peace approach does, however, confront some dilemmas. First, it is not clear how this theory applies in an era of common asymmetric threats. The freedoms that democracy protects can be taken advantage of by nonstate actors, like terrorists, seeking to change democratic priorities. Second, as states respond to external and internal threats, like terrorism, there is a danger that democratic freedoms could be sacrificed in the name of security. Third, if the democratic peace theory is accurate, then the question arises as to whether war is an appropriate means of spreading the democratic peace. Fourth, some of the world's most brutal dictators emerged from constitutionally legitimate democratic processes. Finally, some countries use democratic processes to expand knowledge and help societies meet new security challenges, making it more difficult for states to plan effectively to adapt to new threats.

A number of new approaches to global security seek to expose structural and practical components of how power and peace might relate to each other. Constructivism offers social explanations for why and how states formulate the policies that they advocate and how state activity both shapes and is shaped by the international system. In this view, anarchy, states, and other cornerstones of the global security system are manifestations of a reality conditioned by common human experiences. This approach implies that there is considerable room in the world for the power of ideas to evolve the global security climate toward a greater peace. The evolution of a transnational civil society of activists and networks of professionals that reach beyond state borders also challenges the lead role of states and international institutions in agenda setting. Meanwhile, pacifists and peace movements provide a moral, and potentially highly effective, alternative to violence.

Postmodernism, feminism, and gender analysis provide dramatic conceptual challenges to thinking about global security. These approaches are important because they challenge the meaning and sources of power and security and seek to expose how social interactions reinforce these concepts. The postmodern framework provides an important perspective for understanding dramatic enhancements in technology and communications. From the feminist and gender perspectives, new ways of thinking about power relationships can expose inequalities and biases in both theories and policy making. Other, more revolutionary theories, such as Marxism, no longer hold the appeal they did for many people during the Cold War. However, the analysis of economic disparity as a source of conflict does illustrate an important reality of structural divergence of economic power in the world and within societies. Some of these approaches (especially postmodernism) are not very accessible in terms of their rhetoric or application to real-world scenarios. Nevertheless, they do offer important perspectives for framing major global security processes and outcomes. Significantly, these approaches challenge the scholar and the student to examine their existing assumptions and to look more creatively at the nature of the world and how it is perceived.

From Theory to Practice: Education

No one overarching policy response will neatly resolve the complexity of global security in the twenty-first century. Rather, the one common point from which all effective possible policy options are likely to originate is the nexus between education and security. Education is a vital public-policy issue that decision makers clearly understand as relevant to state capacity and relative position in the international system. There is, for example, a strong relationship between national educational capacity and underdevelopment in Africa, where only one in three students completes primary school, and major universities are in a state of crises. Consequently, there are more African scientists and engineers working in America than in Africa.[1] Worldwide, by 2005, an estimated 125 million children were not going to school every day. The United Nations estimated the economic situations of 1 billion children deny them their childhoods. Many such children are forced in to labor, slavery, and prostitution.[2] Meanwhile, the American higher education system has grown commensurately with its rise to global power status in the twentieth century. But by the turn of the twenty-first century, the percentage of American jobs requiring a PhD in science, engineering, or high technology that were filled by foreign workers had risen from 24 to 38 percent. Even after the 2008 economic crisis and associated high unemployment, the United States continued to import high-skilled talent. Meanwhile, American youth had fallen substantially behind many other countries in the world in terms of reading, math, and science skills.[3]

Education and Global Security

The relationship of educational trends and the mobilization of resources in advancing global security remains a largely unexamined area of inquiry, one avoided by much of the literature in the field and by the major journals. There is, however, a dilemma of correlation and measurement in terms of how education and security might be related. For example, while only 26 percent of American high school graduates at the turn of the century scored well enough on college entrance exams to pass an entry-level university science course, the United States is not hurting for advanced technology. Consequently, the number of trained scientists and engineers currently in the United States does not necessarily translate into either more or less security. At the same time, it is not unreasonable to conclude that another country that invests heavily in the same areas might also make substantial economic, technological, and military gains if core competitiveness is not sustained. Indeed, in terms of pure quantity of scientific papers published, China was likely to surpass the United States by 2013. While the quality of Chinese scientific research still lagged in 2011, the classic security dilemma has to be seen as relevant by adopting education as a measurement of relative or latent power.

China and India offer illustrative examples of how education has factored into contemporary power distributions. It would reflect a major quantitative

Table 10.1. New Measures of Power in the Twenty-first Century

Country	Income Inequality[a]	Unemployment Rate[b]	Level of Democracy[c]	Gallup Global Well-being Index[d]	Food Insecurity[e]	Life Expectancy at Birth	Student Performance (Math Scale)	Student Performance (Science Scale)	Defense $/GDP (%)	Defense $/Population
Australia	30.5	5.1	9.22	62		81.72	514	527	2.24	1,056
Canada	32.1	8.0	9.08	62	8	81.29	527	529	1.19	597
Norway	25.0	3.7	9.80	69		80.08	498	500	1.49	1,264
Netherlands	30.9	5.5	8.99	68		79.55	526	522	1.41	738
Germany	27.0	7.1	8.38	43	6	79.41	513	520	1.28	570
Austria	26.0	4.6	8.49	57		79.65	496	497	0.77	389
Switzerland	33.7	3.9	9.09	62	4	80.97	534	517	0.83	542
Denmark	29.0	4.2	9.52	82	3	78.47	503	499	1.94	344
Finland	29.5	7.9	9.19	75		79.13	541	554	1.33	693
Belgium	28.0	8.1	8.05	56		79.37	515	507	1.10	534
Malta	26.0	7.0	8.28	40		79.59			0.60	122
Japan	38.1	5.2	8.08	19	7	82.17	529	539	0.93	362
Sweden	23.0	8.3	9.50	68	5	80.97	494	495	1.30	736
Hong Kong	53.3	4.6	5.92	65	6	81.96	555	549	N/A	N/A
Iceland	28.0	8.6	9.65	47		80.79	507	496	0.27	153
New Zealand	36.2	6.5	9.26			80.48	519	532	1.39	420
Luxembourg	26.0	5.5	8.88	45		79.48	489	484	0.43	478
United Kingdom	34.0	7.9	8.16		9	79.92	492	514	2.28	998

Country	GINI[a]	[b]	Democracy Index[c]	% thriving[d]	food[e]	life exp.	PISA	PISA		military
Ireland	30.7	*8.6*	8.79	49	7	80.07	**487**	508	0.60	382
Singapore	**48.1**	<u>2.3</u>	**5.89**	**19**	2	<u>82.06</u>	<u>562</u>	<u>542</u>	4.20	1,663
Cyprus	29.0	6.0	**7.29**	45	10	**77.66**	<u>546</u>	<u>538</u>	2.16	503
Korea	31.4	<u>3.7</u>	8.11	28	**16**	78.81	**483**	**489**	2.60	500
Italy	32.0	8.4	7.83	39	**15**	<u>80.33</u>	497	498	1.34	532
France	32.7	9.5	7.77	35	9	81.09	493	500	2.35	1,049
Czech Republic	<u>26.0</u>	9.3	8.19	39		77.01	493	500	1.46	310
Slovenia	28.4	**10.6**	7.69	27	*11*	**77.12**	501	512	1.53	415
Taiwan		<u>5.2</u>	7.52	22		78.15			2.76	458
Slovakia	<u>26.0</u>	**12.5**	**7.35**	**21**		**75.62**	497	*490*	1.55	271
Israel	39.2	6.4	**7.48**	<u>62</u>	*15*	80.86	477	455	7.41	2,077
Spain	32.0	**20.0**	8.16	36	*14*	81.07	**483**	488	1.20	276
Greece	33.0	**12.0**	7.92	31	9	79.80	466	470	2.85	946
Portugal	**38.5**	**10.7**	8.02	**22**	10	78.38	**487**	493	1.53	349
United States	*45.0*	*9.0*	8.18	57	**16**	**78.24**	487	502	4.88	2,290

Sources: Adapted from Charles M. Blow, "Empire at the End of Decadence," *New York Times*, February 18, 2011, www.nytimes.com/2011/02/19/opinion/19blow.html?_r=1 (accessed April 5, 2011), with data from CIA, "The World Factbook"; U.S. unemployment rate from the Bureau of Labor Statistics; Economist Intelligence Unit, "Democracy Index 2010"; Gallup; UNICEF; Organization for Economic Cooperation and Development's Program for International Student Assessment; International Institute for Strategic Studies, *The Military Balance 2010.*

Key: Italicized = *worst*; bold = **worst of the worst**; underlined = <u>best</u>
[a] GINI Index: higher numbers represent more income inequality.
[b] Most recent estimates.
[c] Scale of one to ten.
[d] Percentage thriving, 2010.
[e] "Have there been times in the past 12 months where you did not have enough money to buy food that you or your family needed?": percentage answering yes.

advantage if China were (according to the National Academy of Sciences in the United States in 2005) to have gained in 2004 some 600,000 new engineers, India 350,000, and the United States only 70,000. Nonetheless, as Fareed Zakaria shows, discounting two- and three-year programs doing basic training would lower the Chinese number to about 200,000 engineering degrees per year and Indian engineering graduates to about 125,000 per year. Therefore, the United States would, per capita, train both more and better engineers than either China or India. Zakaria notes that while there are elite opportunities in both China and India for advanced training, the overall educational infrastructure for higher education in these countries is weak. The United States finds itself with a quantity and quality advantage in terms of educational capacity in spite of glaring weaknesses in its system. Just in the area of computer sciences, the United States graduates about one thousand PhDs per year, whereas thirty-five to fifty graduate from Indian universities annually.[4] Nevertheless, as China and India (and especially other English-speaking countries) develop their higher education capacities, they can lure talented students away from the United States, thereby raising its costs in adapting to twenty-first-century global security dynamics.

Understanding just how education affects global security is difficult to isolate in terms of analysis. Of course, education "matters," but this notion is contingent in both manner and degree. It can, for example, drive possibly incorrect assumptions such as "The lack of education fuels terrorism." Empirical study of the link between education and Palestinians shows precisely the opposite. Higher education and standard of living are positively associated with membership in Hamas and the Palestinian Islamic Jihad and with volunteering to become a suicide terrorist.[5] Indeed, for terrorists, increased education enhances capacity to carry out sophisticated high-profile attacks, as was the case among those who hijacked airplanes on September 11, 2001, in the United States. Furthermore, it is not clear that a strong educational program in one country translates into gains in the international system. Singapore and Finland both have very high performance results in education, but neither is rising to the level of a major actor globally or even regionally. North Korea has a highly rigid and noninnovative national education system, but it has built a high-tech nuclear weapons program and associated advanced missile technology. It is thus important to distinguish between structural educational systems and a country's ability to translate that educational capacity into influence and power in the world.

Education is nonetheless an important tool to foster long-term solutions to our many global security challenges. A more educated, younger adult population in the underdeveloped world might wait longer to have children, learn about the dangerous behavior that can spread HIV/AIDS, and develop the tools necessary to finding local solutions to local security problems. The underdeveloped world does, however, confront significant difficulties in providing the most basic levels of education. In India, for example, on any given day about 25 percent of teachers are absent from school. Daily teacher absenteeism is 27 percent in Uganda, 17 percent in Zambia, and 16 percent in Bangladesh. In a developed country like the United States, daily teacher absenteeism is 5 to 6 percent. The problem is especially challenging for a large country like India, which has 34 percent of the world's illiterate population. Facilities are among the reasons that many teachers in India do not go to work: over 50 percent have leaking roofs, 89 percent lack functional toilets, and 50 percent have no water supply. In addition to serving as classrooms, some schools are used as cattle sheds, police camps, teacher residences, or areas for drying cow-dung cakes.[6]

The problem of education in the underdeveloped world extends beyond investment in school infrastructure. Creating more educational opportunities for training—for example, in the areas of medicine and health care—can help countries to develop their own solutions to human-security challenges. There was, by 2005, an estimated 4-million-person shortage of health-care workers in the underdeveloped world, though not for lack of ability. There were more Malawian doctors working, very successfully, in Manchester, England, than were working in their homeland. Of six hundred doctors trained in Zambia, only fifty had stayed in the country. Uganda has only one nurse for every eleven thousand people; Haiti has only one per ten thousand. In Africa, in order even to begin to grapple with the HIV/AIDS crisis, 1 million new health-care workers are needed.[7] Educating people to provide such services and giving them incentives to apply those skills at home, in local communities, would constitute major investments in global security with low cost and high return. In 2004, the Global Campaign for Education advocated an action plan to assure access to primary school for every child in the world by 2015 with a projected cost of $8 billion annually. This would have been accomplished via coordinated debt relief to poor countries, increased aid for basic education changes in International Monetary Fund policies to protect education spending during economic crises, increased investment in education, and changes in national policies by developing countries.[8] While the United States was, by 2010, spending $708 billion per year on national defense, this rather miniscule investment was set aside—and after the 2010 congressional elections, the new leaders in the U.S. Congress were talking of cutting such foreign aid. As an illustration of the grey area of morality in decision making, consider the following. In March 2011, President Barack Obama made a compelling case that it was necessary to intervene with military power in Libya to prevent the slaughter of civilians by Libyan troops in the city of Benghazi. How many might have been killed in the absence of intervention was unknown, but some advocates offered an estimate of one hundred thousand. The slaughter was halted with airpower, at least for a time, and civilians were saved—at a cost of $1 billion in military power over an initial ten days. But one might ask, what about the 10 million children who die every year from preventable and curable diseases? What is the morality in that situation, which the world could remedy but does not? How many mosquito-treated bed nets could have been bought for the cost of ten days of war in Libya? Would such a humanitarian effort not have saved far more people? This is not to say that the people of Benghazi did not merit saving. It does, however, illustrate the immorality of an untenable situation for helpless children that the world seems satisfied to ignore on a daily basis.

Education and National Power

The United States has historically led the world in correlating education and national security. After World War II, the GI Bill provided educational benefits for decommissioned military servicemen and women. Within two years, veterans made up 49 percent of college admissions, and by 1956, about 7.8 of 16 million veterans had participated in the program. The impact was direct in terms of modernizing American society as, by the time this program had run its course, the United States had gained 450,000 engineers, 240,000 accountants, 238,000 teachers, 91,000 scientists, and 67,000 doctors.[9] After the Sputnik crisis of 1957, when the Soviet Union launched a rocket and satellite into space, seemingly taking the lead in Cold War technological competition, the United States responded with a second major investment in the National Defense Education Act (1958). Speaking to his senior staff, President Dwight D. Eisenhower reframed the challenge as an opportunity saying, "People are alarmed and thinking about science, and perhaps this alarm could be turned to a constructive result."[10] Eisenhower endorsed the premise that, as he said, "one of our greatest and most glaring deficiencies is the failure of us in this country to give high enough priority to scientific education and to the place of science in our national life. . . . What will be needed is not just engineers and scientists, but a people who will keep their heads and, in every field, leaders who can meet intricate human problems with wisdom and courage. In short, we will need not only Einsteins and Steinmetzes, but Washingtons and Emersons."[11] Following from the 1958 legislation, a new generation of Americans engaged in the study of math, science, and languages and facilitated the growth of advanced university programs in these areas. All levels, from elementary schools to PhD programs, benefited from a massive government investment in national educational infrastructure. Other programs, like the National Science Foundation, National Aeronautics and Space Administration, an Defense Advanced Research Projects Agency, were also by-products of this initiative.

With the end of the Cold War, some forward-leaning thinkers in the United States looked anew at the need for education and national security to advance the relative position of the country in the world. Though small, the National Security Education Program has served to refocus educational priorities on bringing talented new skill sets into the U.S. government. The program was initiated by Senator David Boren who, in describing testimony he received from early pioneers of the American intelligence community, noted, "They said the most important thing you can have is a group of highly intelligent people who are extremely well-educated, who understand the cultures and speak the languages, who can go into (other) countries and be advocates for the United States. . . . It's human talent that is the key to our national security."[12] Another major study, by former senators Gary Hart and Warren Rudman (the Hart-Rudman Commission) completed in 2001 concluded, "The key factor driving change in America's national security environment over the next 25 years will be the acceleration of scientific discovery and its technological applications, and the uneven human social and psychological capacity to harness them. . . . Synergistic developments in information technology, materials science, biotechnology, and nanotechnology will almost certainly transform human tools more dramatically and rapidly than at any time in human history." The study continued, "Second only to a weapon of mass destruction detonating in an American city, we can think of nothing more dangerous than a failure to manage properly science, technology and education for the common good over the next quarter century."[13] The commission's call for a government research-and-development budget of about $160 billion by 2010 was not implemented.

The terrorist attacks of September 11, 2001, could have been a wakeup call for reprioritization of American national security needs in terms of education—but it was not. The United States continued long after the attacks to sustain major deficits in languages—like Arabic, Farsi, and Pashto—vital to combating terrorism and such security challenges as nuclear proliferation. In 2003, the Department of Education noted that of the 1.8 million graduates of American colleges and universities, a total of 22 had completed advanced degrees in Arabic.[14] The intelligence community was in particularly serious trouble, reportedly at only 30 percent readiness in critical global languages. Years after the attacks on New York City and Washington, DC, the United States still had documents and intelligence intercepts waiting to be translated regarding previous and potential terrorist attacks. By 2006, when the United States was at the brink of failure in Iraq, it only had ten fluent Arabic speakers deployed at the U.S. Embassy there. Meanwhile, through 2010, a fluent Arabic speaker discovered potentially to be gay was going to be forced to leave the military under then existing law.

Education in Peace and Conflict

Education has also become a tool essential to peace building and even war fighting in the twenty-first century. Attaining peaceful reconciliation in postconflict situations can require major transformation of and investment in education. For example, Sudan's national education program has been dominated by Islamic identity and neglected the country's Christian population. This reflects much of the divide in that country between the dominant Arab government and Christian minorities. Most Sudanese textbooks that mention a religion reference Islam. There are frequent references to violence, warfare, and promotion of military skills as an essential component of citizenry.[15] A sixth-grade-level Arabic-language book tells students, "You know what excellent rewards Allah prepares for Muslims for fighting Kufar [non-Muslims]."[16] Any eventual lasting peace between the warring parties in Sudan would have to include a major rewriting of textbooks for reconciliation to begin. In another example, in the Northern Ireland peace process, educational integration between Protestants and Catholics was essential to building the peace but had not even begun over ten years after the initial peace was achieved.

Peacekeeping as well as new warfare tactics, like modern counterinsurgency campaigns, place a high priority on military capabilities that can integrate cultural, anthropological, and linguistic skills, as well as public opinion and demographic knowledge, most often found not in militaries but in the civilian and university sectors. In 2007, the U.S. Department of Defense began to expand a program called the Human Terrain System that placed anthropologists and other social scientists with each of the twenty-six American combat brigades in Iraq and Afghanistan. Human Terrain teams include military personnel paired with social scientists, linguists, and area-studies experts who receive weapons training and wear military uniforms and play a noncombat support role. These individuals operate in a command relationship similar to that of chaplains and do not actively collect intelligence or participate in lethal targeting. Troops praised this initiative as "brilliant" in helping them to better understand how their actions are perceived within the local cultures and traditions of their areas of operation.[17] Such perspectives are now integrated into U.S. military training. For example, at the U.S. Marine Corps Command and Staff College, mid-level officers now take a course titled "Culture and Interagency Operations"—part of a ten-month curriculum that consists of thirty-four case studies and language instruction in Arabic, French, Chinese, or Korean.[18] One participant in the Human Terrain System summarized the net effect: "One anthropologist can be much more effective than a B-2 bomber—not at winning a war, but creating a peace one Afghan at a time."[19] Field commanders estimate that these new operational concepts decreased lethal combat operations, in some cases by as much as 70 percent.[20] Still, the hazards of having civilians with limited or no military training working in dangerous war zones became clear in spring 2008 when a political science graduate student working with combat troops in Afghanistan was killed by a roadside bomb.

In June 2008, the Defense Department formalized a new program named Minerva, after the Roman goddess of wisdom and warriors. For decades, some social scientists had resisted the idea of involving their expertise in military operations. Some scholars believed that it was inappropriate to allow military interests to guide social science research, especially in areas like anthropology, which requires embedded fieldwork guided by trust established with indigenous peoples. Historical experiences in Vietnam and Latin America fueled concerns among anthropologists. At the same time, however, academics have often criticized military operations for their lack of sensitivity to important local traditions and customs. Many in the military had viewed social scientists as critical of the military and not understanding operational requirements. By 2008 the program had begun to award $50 million in grants over five years to involve evolutionary psychologists, demographers, sociologists, historians, and anthropologists in security research. Grants were intended to prioritize translating original documents, studying changes in the Chinese army, explaining the resurgence of the Taliban in Afghanistan, and creating computational models to explain why groups and states make what are seen in the West as "irrational" decisions.[21] Yet, while anthropological (and other social science) skills are essential to successful modern military operations, skepticism has grown in academe. As one scholar writes, "Is it ethical for anthropologists to participate in combat support or counterinsurgency on the battlefield? To collect intelligence? To design propaganda?"[22] The concern among anthropologists is that, to do fieldwork, they must be able to integrate discretely with local cultures, and any perception of them as associated with the military or intelligence gathering could damage the trust essential to building community ties in the field—thereby corrupting the quality of vital research.

The role of education in major military operations has been made evident in both Iraq and Afghanistan. Iraq had substantial educational infrastructure dating to the 1960s. Yet, after the 2003 U.S.-led invasion, hundreds of professors and scientists were killed, thousands were forced into exile, and others operated under intimidation and coercion by insurgents and tribal militias. In one twelve-month period in 2006 and 2007, 78 professors were assassinated;

one estimate showed that 550 professors had been killed.[23] In some regions of Iraq, it was difficult, if not even impossible, to hold class. By 2006, on average only 30 percent of Iraqi students actually attended classes.[24] The initial postinvasion investment in education was almost irrelevant. In 2003, the Iraqi Ministry of Higher Education and Scientific Research estimated that it needed an immediate infusion of $1.2 billion. However, an international donors' conference in October 2003 offered zero funds for education in Iraq. A year later, the U.S. Congress appropriated $87 billion for Iraq's reconstruction, of which the provisional authority in Iraq sought $120 million for Iraqi higher education. Of that amount, however, Iraq only received $8 million. In 2004 and 2005, the entire national Iraqi spending on higher education was $225 million, 65 percent of which went to wages.[25]

Education was essential to any hope for immediate and long-term stability in Afghanistan. It was especially vital for countering the Taliban legacy of using schools to propagate radical Islam and barring women from education. Advances in education in Afghanistan were regularly cited by American officials as evidence of successful national rebuilding. According to the U.S. Department of State, in 1993, forty-five thousand children went to school in Afghanistan, of whom only 19 percent were girls. By late 2007, there were 6 million children in Afghan schools, 40 percent of whom were girls, and the percentage of women teachers had almost doubled from 15 to 29 percent between 1993 and 2008.[26] Despite these improvements, the average salary for a teacher was about $40 per month. Education success stories have also become targets of threats and violence from insurgents throughout Afghanistan. In 2005 and 2006, for example, there were seventeen assassinations of teachers and education officials and over two hundred attacks on teachers, students, and schools. Threatening "night letters" were often sent to teachers to frighten them out of cooperating with foreign troops. One illustrative letter warned, "Respected Afghans: Do not send your girls to school," or the Taliban would "conduct their robust military operations in broad daylight."[27] While overall numbers of students enrolled in Afghan schools had gone up since 2001, in some key areas of Taliban strength, such as Kandahar and Helmand provinces, over two hundred schools had to be shut down or were destroyed by insurgents.[28] The Taliban made clear they saw schools as legitimate targets because, as a spokesman said in March 2006, the "government has given teachers in primary and middle schools the task to openly deliver political lectures against the resistance put up by those who seek independence. . . . The use of the curriculum as a mouthpiece of the state will provoke the people against it. . . . If schools are turned into centers of violence, the government is to blame for it."[29] Meanwhile, Afghan president Hamid Karzai warned that many local Islamic schools were responsible for "exploiting poor, uneducated, desperate young children, motivating them into killing themselves, motivating them into attacking other people."[30]

Education also provides us with important information for making vital appraisals of the world and our place in it. This is especially important to the extent that fear can drive people to make quick, and often bad, assessments that actually do more damage in the long term. Just on the issue of terrorism, for example, Audrey Kurth Cronin has shown that the threat of terrorism is real and dangerous, and the globalization of technology serves to dramatically heighten its effects in frightening ways. But she also shows that terrorism ends. It can end when leaders of movements are killed or captured. It can end when groups enter into political processes and abandon their tactics. Terrorism can end when groups think they have accomplished their goals or lose public support. Terrorists can be defeated with brute force as well as by local societies that turn on them. The key point is that terrorism is not, nor need it be, a permanent state of affairs or an enduring factor in people's lives.[31]

What Can You Do?

It is all too easy to feel overwhelmed by the scope and complexity of global security challenges—and to forget that they are also opportunities for leadership. Moreover, today, the world exists in a greater state of general peace than it has ever attained. The potential to consolidate and expand this state is very real and within the grasp of a new generation of young people well schooled in the nature of global security. Every single global citizen has a role to play at school, at work, in the community, with elected leaders, and elsewhere in the world to make change happen. Individuals can choose how to frame the issues, and taking three basic steps can make an enormous difference in aligning the quests for power and peace as one.

First, as this chapter demonstrates, education has an essential role to play in addressing the range of global security challenges. There is, however, an all-too-common tendency to confuse being smart and wise with being educated. Some of the very smartest people never complete higher education. As a case in point, although most Afghan soldiers being trained by the United States in 2011 were illiterate, they are, by and large, highly intelligent and very creative people with a tremendous oral tradition of communication and a deep love of poetry. Still, having advanced skills is also a vital asset to individual and state power in terms of both competitiveness and generating solutions to challenges. This requires not only the serious, intensive focus that can come with math, science, and engineering skills but the broader perspective gained from creative engagement with the arts, literature, and history. Regrettably, even among the most developed countries in the world, education systems are very stratified. Moreover, a lack of enough jobs for the well educated people forces emigration and brain drain, thereby denying societies vital human capital.

Second, people need the required information to place threats in context. Despite all of the danger that this book takes into account, it is important to recall that the world is generally a very safe place for far more people than ever before—with more freedom, more advancements in human security, and less likelihood of a great power war. More countries are giving up than attaining nuclear weapons. Terrorism is an issue, but its impact has more to do with fear than actual risk. The most significant challenge is most likely the ongoing reliance on nonrenewable energy, declining access to freshwater supplies, and associated effects of climate change. Citizens have to know for themselves how to prioritize, because all too often the media does not help. Television news programs have been caught up in a twenty-four-hour news cycle that rewards whoever can defend the more extreme position. Look at the Web page of a local television news station on any given day, and the odds are high that most of its reports will be negative: "If it bleeds, it leads." Those who do good deeds, who write songs or poems for peace, are not celebrated or even recognized. And yet, every year on New Year's Eve, New Yorkers gather together just before midnight, and the city that suffered the largest terrorist attack in history commences the countdown by singing along to John Lennon's "Imagine."

Context is needed so that people have the ability to place facts in an accurate framework and thereby make well-informed assessments about global security trends. For example, Glenn Beck, a right-wing American commentator on FOX News, said on a radio program in late 2010 that at least 10 percent of all Muslims were acting as terrorists. He did no fact-checking, and millions of people heard this statement. Fareed Zakaria, an actual expert with a television program on CNN, asked terrorism analyst Peter Bergen whether Beck's assessment was accurate. Bergen said it was off by one thousand percent! Indeed, had Glenn Beck been correct, there would be 157 million terrorists setting out to destroy America. Beck had openly wondered why the mainstream media was not reporting this. Zakaria concluded that one reason probably had to do with the fact that what Beck was saying to his millions of listeners was "total nonsense—a figure made up by Glenn Beck with absolutely no basis in fact." Yet, Beck was one of the most influential people in America—a household name.

Third, individual citizens have the power to lead and to bring about positive change. Of course, some famous people have done this; for instance, Bill Gates, Ted Turner, and others like them have given billions of dollars to global health initiatives. Human rights campaigners—from Bishop Desmond Tutu to Aung San Suu Kyi—make a difference. Economist Jeffrey Sachs has devoted much of his career to the goal of ending poverty in Africa. Jody Williams won the Nobel Peace Prize in 1997 for her role in getting the world to embrace an international treaty to ban antipersonnel landmines. But alongside these people are thousands, indeed millions, who do what they can to make an immediate difference in people's lives on a regular basis but without fanfare. From those working in governments and international organizations to leading engineers and scientists looking for the next major breakthrough—all play a major role in promoting the use of power on the path to peace. Today, many young people are not waiting for a formal job—they are just taking the lead in forming microfinance programs and women's and education initiatives. Making a difference in the world does not happen on a lark; tireless years of hard work, preparation, study, engagement, language training, reading, fund-raising, and traveling are essential. But so are having balance and setting priorities so that people can see engagement as a marathon and not a sprint. That said, one does not have to wait. Consider just one example: visit a website called www.nothingbutnets.net, where, for the cost of a new music download or a nice cup of coffee, you can send a mosquito-treated bed net that will protect a child in Africa from fatal disease. By hitting a button on your computer, you can save a life.

Conclusion

The good news is that all of the global security challenges covered in this book have solutions. It is not really an issue of—as Barack Obama's campaign slogan stated in 2008—"Yes, we can," but rather, "Will we?" Perhaps being fortunate enough to live in relatively secure conditions creates a special obligation to heed the call of international or national public service. Be it as a member of the military or as a diplomat, intelligence analyst, Peace Corps worker, researcher, academic, journalist, customs worker, security guard, policeman, teacher, or politician, public and community service is the essential place to begin to make a contribution to increasing global security. International and nongovernmental organizations, universities, research institutes, science labs, and community groups, as well as individual doctors, nurses, information systems mangers, and linguists—even just one person with a computer or pen and paper—all of these have the power to engage. The globalization of security provides extraordinary opportunities for every individual to prove to those who would use the networks of power for evil that they will be outdone by someone advancing the search for peace.

Suggested Reading

Abrams, Irwin, and Jimmy Carter. *The Words of Peace: Selections from the Speeches of the Winners of the Nobel Peace Prize.* New York: Newmarket Press, 2008.

Cronin, Audrey Kurth. *How Terrorism Ends.* Princeton, NJ: Princeton University Press, 2009.

Fick, Nathaniel. *One Bullet Away.* Boston: Houghton Mifflin, 2005.

Havel, Vaclav. *Open Letters: Selected Writings, 1965–1990.* New York: Vintage Press, 1992.

Homer-Dixon, Thomas. *The Upside of Down: Catastrophe, Creativity, and the Renewal of Civilization.* Washington, DC: Island Press, 2008.

Krakauer, Jon. *Where Men Win Glory: The Odyssey of Pat Tillman.* Norwell, MA: Anchor Press, 2010.

Mortenson, Greg. *Stones into Schools: Promoting Peace with Education in Afghanistan and Pakistan.* New York: Penguin, 2010.

Power, Samantha. *Sergio: One Man's Fight to Save the World.* New York: Penguin, 2010.

Sachs, Jeffrey. *The End of Poverty: Economic Possibilities for Our Time.* New York: Penguin, 2006.

Williams, Jody, et al. *Banning Landmines: Disarmament, Citizen Diplomacy, and Human Security.* Lanham, MD: Rowman & Littlefield, 2008.

Notes

Chapter 1: The Dynamics of Global Security

1. These concepts were initially developed by Robert O. Keohane and Joseph S. Nye, *Power and Interdependence*, 3rd ed. (New York: Longman, 2001).

2. Joseph Stiglitz, *Globalization and Its Discontents* (New York: Norton, 2003), 1–10.

3. Arnold Wolfers, "National Security As an Ambiguous Symbol," *Political Science Quarterly* 67 (1952): 483.

4. Lester Brown, "Redefining National Security," Worldwatch Paper 14 (Washington, DC, 1977).

5. Barry Buzan, *People, States, and Fear: An Agenda for International Security Studies in the Post–Cold War Era*, 2nd ed. (New York: Lynne Rienner, 1991).

6. Graham Allison, "The Impact of Globalization on National and International Security," in *Governance in a Globalizing World*, ed. Joseph S. Nye and John D. Donahue (Washington, DC: Brookings Institute, 2000), 80–83.

7. Hans J. Morgenthau, *Politics among Nations*, 5th rev. ed. (New York: Knopf, 1978).

8. David A. Baldwin, "The Concept of Security," *Review of International Studies* 23, no. 1 (January 1997): 23.

9. Stanley Hoffmann, "The Clash of Globalizations," *Foreign Affairs* 81, no. 3 (July–August 2003): 106–7.

10. John Pomfret, "China Ponders New Rules of 'Unrestricted War,'" *Washington Post*, August 8, 1999.

11. Pomfret, "China Ponders New Rules."

12. Sean Kay, "NATO, the Kosovo War, and Neoliberal Theory," *Contemporary Security Policy* 25, no. 2 (August 2004): 252–78.

13. Edward N. Luttwak, "Power Relations in the New Economy," *Survival* 44, no. 2 (summer 2002): 10.

14. Bob Woodward, *Obama's Wars* (New York: Simon and Schuster, 2010), 307.

15. Robert A. Pape, "Empire Falls," *The National Interest*, January 22, 2009, www .nationalinterest.org/PrinterFriendly.aspx?id=20484 (accessed March 12, 2011).

16. See Robert Gilpin, *War and Change in World Politics* (Cambridge: Cambridge University Press, 1981).

17. Krishna Guha, "Paulson Claims Russia Tried to Foment Fannie-Freddie Crisis," *Financial Times*, January 29, 2010, www.ft.com/cms/s/0/ffd950c4-0d0a-11df -a2dc-00144feabdc0.html?nclick_check=1 (accessed March 12, 2011).

18. "China Accuses US of Arrogance over Taiwan Deal," *BBC News*, February 1, 2010, http://news.bbc.co.uk/2/hi/americas/8490537.stm (accessed March 12, 2011).

19. These issues are elaborated in Joseph S. Nye, *The Paradox of American Power: Why the World's Only Superpower Can't Go It Alone* (Oxford: Oxford University Press, 2002).

20. For further discussion, see Clyde Prestowitz, *Three Billion New Capitalists: The Great Shift of Wealth and Power to the East* (New York: Basic Books, 2005).

21. Fareed Zakaria, *The Post-American World* (New York: W. W. Norton, 2009), 17.

22. Dalia Dassa Kaye and Frederic M. Wehrey, "A Nuclear Iran: The Reactions of Neighbors," *Survival* 49, no. 2 (summer 2007): 114.

23. Ernst B. Haas, *When Knowledge Is Power: Three Models of Change in International Organizations* (Berkeley: University of California Press, 1991).

24. PEW Research Center for the People and the Press, *Global Attitudes Project* (Washington, DC: Pew Publications, 2002), 63.

25. PEW Research Center for the People and the Press, *Global Attitudes Project* (Washington, DC: Pew Publications, 2010).

26. Don Lee, "Global Cachet Comes with Chinese Deal for IBM Unit," *Los Angeles Times*, December 9, 2004.

Chapter 2: The Quest for Power

1. This summary is derived from John J. Mearsheimer, "The False Promise of International Institutions," *International Security* 19, no. 3 (winter 1994–1995): 5–49; and Charles W. Kegley Jr., ed., *Controversies in International Relations Theory: Realism and the Neoliberal Challenge* (New York: St. Martin's Press, 1995).

2. From Niccolò Machiavelli, *The Prince and the Discourses* (New York: Random House, 1940).

3. These quotes come from Thomas Hobbes, *Leviathan*, introduction by Richard S. Peters (New York: Macmillan, 1962).

4. Hans J. Morgenthau, *Politics among Nations, Brief Edition* (New York: McGraw-Hill, 1992).

5. George F. Kennan, *American Diplomacy, 1900–1950* (Chicago: University of Chicago Press, 1951).

6. Henry Kissinger, *A World Restored*, new ed. (London: Weidenfeld and Nicholson History, 2000).

7. Kenneth N. Waltz, *Theory of International Politics* (Reading, MA: Addison-Wesley, 1979).

8. Robert Gilpin, *War and Change in World Politics* (Cambridge: Cambridge University Press, 1983).

9. Robert J. Art, "To What Ends Military Power?" *International Security* 4, no. 4 (spring 1980): 3–14.

10. John Herz, *The Nation-State and the Crisis of World Politics* (New York: David McKay, 1976), 157.

11. Robert Jervis, "Cooperation under the Security Dilemma," *World Politics* 30, no. 2 (January 1978): 186–214.

12. Jervis, "Cooperation under the Security Dilemma," 190.

13. Stephen Van Evera, "Offense, Defense, and the Causes of War," *International Security* 22, no. 4 (spring 1998): 5–43.

14. Van Evera, "Offense, Defense," 43.

15. Thom Shanker and Nicholas Kulish, "Russia Lashes Out on Missile Deal," *New York Times*, August 15, 2008.

16. Ole R. Holsti, "Crisis Decision Making," in *Diplomacy: New Approaches in History, Theory and Policy*, ed. Paul Gorden Lauren (New York: Free Press, 1979).

17. Alexander George, "Coercive Diplomacy," in *The Use of Force: Military Power and International Politics*, ed. Robert J. Art and Kenneth N. Waltz, 6th ed. (Lanham, MD: Rowman & Littlefield, 2004), 70–76.

18. Barton Gellman, "The Path to Crisis: How the United States and Its Allies Went to War," *Washington Post*, April 18, 1999.

19. Mark Heinrich, "Is Kosovo Intervention More Bark Than Bite?" Reuters, August 7, 1998.

20. William Drozdiak, "Analysis: New Challenges Facing 50-Year-Old NATO," *Washington Post*, March 24, 1999.

21. Jim Hoagland, "Kosovos to Come," *Washington Post*, June 27, 1999.

22. John J. Mearsheimer, *The Tragedy of Great Power Politics* (New York: W. W. Norton, 2001), 29–54.

23. Mearsheimer, *Tragedy*, 141–47.

24. Mearsheimer, *Tragedy*, 227.

25. Stephen Walt, *The Origins of Alliances* (Ithaca, NY: Cornell University Press, 1987).

26. Randall L. Schweller, "Bandwagoning for Profit: Bringing the Revisionist State Back In," *International Security* 19, no. 1 (summer 1994): 72–107.

27. Gordon A. Craig and Alexander L. George, *Force and Statecraft: Diplomatic Problems of Our Time*, 2nd ed. (Oxford: Oxford University Press, 1990), 179.

28. Craig and George, *Force and Statecraft*, 179.

29. See John J. Mearsheimer, *Conventional Deterrence* (Ithaca, NY: Cornell University Press, 1985).

30. Robert Jervis, "The Utility of Nuclear Deterrence," *International Security* 13, no. 2 (fall 1988): 80–90.

31. John J. Mearsheimer, "Back to the Future: Instability in Europe after the Cold War," *International Security* 15, no. 1 (summer 1990): 35–50.

32. See Graham T. Allison and Philip Zelikow, *Essence of Decision: Explaining the Cuban Missile Crisis,* 2nd ed. (New York: Longman, 1999).

33. "Treaty of Westphalia," Avalon Project of Yale Law School, November 2004, http://avalon.law.yale.edu/17th_century/westphal.asp (accessed March 12, 2011).

34. Mancur Olson and Richard Zeckkauser, "An Economic Theory of Alliances," *The Review of Economics and Statistics* 47, no. 3 (August 1966): 266–79; Mancur Olson, *The Logic of Collective Action: Public Goods and the Theory of Groups* (Cambridge, MA: Harvard University Press, 1965).

35. These figures on European and American defense expenditures as a percentage of GNP were compiled from the International Institute for Strategic Studies, *The Military Balance* (London: Brassey's, 1960–1998).

36. Leonard Sullivan Jr. and Jack LeCuyer, *Comprehensive Security and Western Prosperity* (Washington, DC: Atlantic Council of the United States, 1988), 48.

37. See Robert Jervis, "Security Regimes," in *International Regimes*, ed. Stephen D. Krasner (Ithaca, NY: Cornell University Press, 1983), 173–94; and Paul Schroeder, "The Transformation of Political Thinking in the International System," in *Coping with Complexity in the International System*, ed. Jack Snyder and Robert Jervis (Boulder, CO: Westview Press, 1993), 47–70.

38. Charles K. Webster, *The Foreign Policy of Castlereagh, 1815–1822: Britain and the European Alliance*, 2nd ed. (London: G. Bell, 1934), 2.

39. Waltz, *Theory of International Politics*, 208–9.

40. Lisa Martin, "The Rational State Choice of Multilateralism," in *Multilateralism Matters: The Theory and Praxis of an Institutional Form*, ed. John Gerard Ruggie (New York: Columbia University Press, 1993), 91–121.

41. Christopher Layne, "From Preponderance to Offshore Balancing: America's Future Grand Strategy," *International Security* 22, no. 1 (summer 1997): 86–124.

42. Michael Mastanduno, "A Realist View: Three Images of the Coming International Order," in *International Order and the Future of World Politics*, ed. T. V. Paul and John A. Hall (Cambridge: Cambridge University Press, 1999), 23.

43. Mastanduno, "A Realist View," 28–36.

44. Mearsheimer, "Back to the Future," 35–50.

45. John J. Mearsheimer, "The False Promise of International Institutions," in *The Perils of Anarchy: Contemporary Realism and International Security*, ed. Michael E. Brown, Sean M. Lynn-Jones, and Steven E. Miller (Cambridge, MA: MIT Press, 1995), 337.

46. Kenneth N. Waltz, "The Emerging Structure of International Politics," *International Security* 18, no. 2 (fall 1993): 44–79.

47. Christopher Layne, "The Unipolar Illusion: Why New Great Powers Will Rise," *International Security* 17, no. 4 (spring 1993): 5–51.

48. Peter Liberman, "The Spoils of Conquest," *International Security* 18, no. 2 (fall 1993): 125–54.

49. Kenneth N. Waltz, "The Anarchic Structure of World Politics," in *International Politics: Enduring Concepts and Contemporary Issues*, ed. Robert J. Art and Robert Jervis, 5th ed. (New York: Longman, 2000), 61.

50. Waltz, "Anarchic Structure," 62.

51. Kenneth N. Waltz, "Globalization and Governance," *PS: Political Science and Politics* 32, no. 4 (December 2001): 693–700.

52. Mearsheimer, *Tragedy*, 372.

53. Randall L. Schweller, "Realism and the Present Great Power System: Growth and Positional Conflict over Scarce Resources," in *Unipolar Politics: Realism and State Strategies after the Cold War*, ed. Ethan B. Kapstein and Michael Mastanduno (New York: Columbia University Press, 1999), 28–68.

54. "Theory and International Politics: Conversation with Kenneth N. Waltz," Institute of International Studies, University of California, Berkeley, February 2003, http://globetrotter.berkeley.edu/people3/Waltz/waltz-con0.html (accessed March 12, 2011).

55. Charles Krauthammer, "The Unipolar Moment," *Foreign Affairs: America and the World* 70, no. 1(1990–1991): 23–33.

56. Charles Krauthammer, "The Unipolar Moment Revisited," *The National Interest* 70 (winter 2002–2003): 13.

57. Krauthammer, "Unipolar Moment Revisited," 14.

58. Michael Mastanduno, "Preserving the Unipolar Moment: Realist Theories and U.S. Grand Strategy after the Cold War," *International Security* 21, no. 4 (spring 1997): 49–88.

59. Stephen Brooks and William Wolforth, "American Primacy in Perspective," *Foreign Affairs* 81, no. 4 (July–August 2002): 20–33.

60. John Gerard Ruggie, "The Past As Prologue? Interests, Identity, and American Foreign Policy," *International Security* 21, no. 4 (spring 1997): 89–125.

61. Samuel P. Huntington, "Why International Primacy Matters," *International Security* 17, no. 4 (spring 1993): 68–83.

62. Samuel P. Huntington, "The Lonely Superpower," *Foreign Affairs* 78, no. 2 (March–April 1999): 41.

63. Huntington, "Lonely Superpower," 45.

64. Stephen Walt, "Living with the 800 lb. Gorilla: Global Responses to American Power" (Lyman Lecture, Ohio Wesleyan University, April 2004).

65. Joseph S. Nye, *The Paradox of American Power: Why the World's Only Superpower Can't Go It Alone* (Oxford: Oxford University Press, 2002), 8–9.

66. Nye, *Paradox of American Power*, 10–11.

67. Robert A. Pape, "Preventing 'Soft Balancing' against the United States" (draft, fall 2004, presented as "Soft Balancing: How States Pursue Security in a Unipolar World," paper prepared for the annual meeting of the American Political Science Association, Chicago, IL, September 2–5, 2004); also see Robert A. Pape, "Soft Balancing against the United States," *International Security* 30, no. 1 (summer 2005): 7–45.

68. Pape, "Preventing 'Soft Balancing.'"

69. Pape, "Preventing 'Soft Balancing.'"

70. Rajan Menon, "The End of Alliances," *World Policy Journal* 20, no. 2 (summer 2003): 1–20.

71. Bruno Tertrais, "The Changing Nature of Military Alliances," *The Washington Quarterly* 27, no. 2 (spring 2004): 145–50.

72. Richard L. Kugler, "Dissuasion As a Strategic Concept," *Strategic Forum* 196 (December 2002): 1–8.

73. Kugler, "Dissuasion," 4.

74. Sean Kay, "What Is a Strategic Partnership?" *Problems of Post-Communism* 47, no. 3 (May–June 2000): 15–24.

75. Robert A. Pape, "The Strategic Logic of Suicide Terrorism," *American Political Science Review* 97, no. 3 (August 2003): 344.

76. Pape, "Strategic Logic," 345.

77. Pape, "Strategic Logic," 347.

78. Chaim Kaufmann, "Possible and Impossible Solutions to Ethnic Civil Wars," *International Security* 20, no. 4 (spring 1996): 136–75.

79. Alastair Iain Johnston, "Realism(s) and Chinese Security Policy in the Post–Cold War Period," in *Unipolar Politics: Realism and State Strategies after the Cold War*, ed. Michael Mastanduno and Ethan Kapstein (New York: Columbia University Press, 1999), 261–318.

80. Johnston, "Realism(s) and Chinese Security Policy," 289.

81. Johnston, "Realism(s) and Chinese Security Policy," 290.

82. Samuel P. Huntington, "Clash of Civilizations," *Foreign Affairs* 72, no. 3 (summer 1993): 22–49.

83. Richard N. Rosecrance, *The Rise of the Trading State: Commerce and Conquest in the Modern World* (New York: Basic Books, 1986); Richard N. Rosecrance, *The Rise of the Virtual State: Wealth and Power in the Coming Century* (New York: Basic Books, 1999).

84. Barry Buzan, *People, States, and Fear*, 2nd ed. (New York: Lynne Rienner, 1991), 244–46.

85. Ethan B. Kapstein, *The Political Economy of National Security: A Global Perspective* (New York: McGraw-Hill, 1992), 80.

86. Robert Gilpin, *Global Political Economy: Understanding the International Economic Order* (Princeton, NJ: Princeton University Press, 2001), 302.

87. Gilpin, *Global Political Economy*, 304.

88. Mearsheimer, "The False Promise of International Institutions," 347.

89. Gilpin, *Global Political Economy*, 16.

90. Dale C. Copeland, "Economic Interdependence and War: A Theory of Trade Expectations," *International Security* 20, no. 4 (spring 1996): 5–41.

91. Charles L. Glaser, "Realists As Optimists," *International Security* 19, no. 3 (winter 1994–1995): 50–90.

92. E. H. Carr, *The Twenty Years' Crisis: 1919–1939* (New York: St. Martin's, 1939).

Chapter 3: The Search for Peace

1. Michael Doyle, "Kant, Liberal Legacies, and Foreign Affairs, Part 2," *Philosophy and Public Affairs* 12, no. 4 (fall 1983): 205.

2. Doyle, "Kant, Liberal Legacies," 206.

3. Seyom Brown, "World Interests and the Changing Dimensions of Security," in *World Security: Challenges for a New Century*, ed. Michael Klare and Yogesh Chandrani, 3rd ed. (New York: St. Martin's Press, 1998), 1–17.

4. Brown, "World Interests," 11–14.

5. Stephen Krasner, "The Accomplishments of International Political Economy," in *International Theory: Positivism and Beyond*, ed. Steve Smith, Ken Booth, and Marysia Zalewski (Cambridge: Cambridge University Press, 1996), 108–27.

6. Andrew Moravcsik, "Taking Preferences Seriously: A Positive Liberal Theory of International Politics," *International Organization* 51, no. 4 (autumn 1997): 513–53.

7. Robert O. Keohane, *Power and Governance in a Partially Globalized World* (New York: Routledge, 2002), 44–63.

8. Keohane, *Power and Governance*, 54–55.

9. Francis Fukuyama, "The End of History?" *The National Interest* 15 (summer 1989): 3–18.

10. Francis Fukuyama, "Second Thoughts: The Last Man in a Bottle," *The National Interest* 56 (summer 1999): 16–33.

11. Robert O. Keohane and Joseph S. Nye, *Power and Interdependence*, 3rd ed. (New York: Longman, 2001), 7.

12. Robert Powell, "Absolute and Relative Gains in International Relations Theory," in *Neorealism and Neoliberalism: The Contemporary Debate*, ed. David Baldwin (New York: Columbia University Press, 1993), 213.

13. Keohane, *Power and Governance*, 54.

14. See Lisa L. Martin and Beth A. Simmons, eds., *International Institutions* (Cambridge: MIT Press, 2001).

15. Robert O. Keohane and Joseph S. Nye, introduction to *After the Cold War: International Institutions and State Strategies in Europe, 1989–1991*, ed. Robert O. Keohane, Joseph S. Nye, and Stanley Hoffmann (Cambridge, MA: Harvard University Press, 1994), 2–3.

16. Robert Axelrod and Robert O. Keohane, "Achieving Cooperation under Anarchy: Strategies and Institutions," in Baldwin, *Neorealism and Neoliberalism*, 94.

17. Charles A. Kupchan, "The Case for Collective Security," in *Collective Security after the Cold War*, ed. George W. Downs (Ann Arbor: University of Michigan Press, 1994), 50–51.

18. Keohane, *Power and Governance*, 1.

19. Judith Goldstein and Robert O. Keohane, "Ideas and Foreign Policy: An Analytical Framework," in *Ideas and Foreign Policy: Beliefs, Institutions, and Political Change*, ed. Judith Goldstein and Robert O. Keohane (Ithaca, NY: Cornell University Press, 1993), 13.

20. Keohane, *Power and Governance*, 75.

21. Keohane, *Power and Governance*, 59.

22. Katja Weber, "Hierarchy Amidst Anarchy: A Transaction Costs Approach to International Security Cooperation," *International Studies Quarterly* 41, no. 2 (June 1997): 334.

23. Kenneth W. Abbott and Duncan Snidal, "Why States Act through Formal International Organizations," *Journal of Conflict Resolution* 42, no. 1 (February 1998): 3–32.

24. See Lisa L. Martin, "Interests, Power, and Multilateralism," *International Organization* 46, no. 4 (1992): 765–92.

25. Robert O. Keohane, *After Hegemony: Cooperation and Discord in the World Political Economy* (Princeton, NJ: Princeton University Press, 1984), 101.

26. Celeste Wallander, "Institutional Assets and Adaptability: NATO after the Cold War," *International Organization* 54, no. 4 (autumn 2000): 709.

27. Janne E. Nolan et al., "The Concept of Cooperative Security," in *Global Engagement: Cooperation and Security in the 21st Century*, ed. Janne E. Nolan (Washington, DC: Brookings, 1994), 4–5.

28. Nolan, "Concept of Cooperative Security," 10.

29. Antonia Handler Chayes and Abram Chayes, "Regime Architecture: Elements and Principles," in *Global Engagement: Cooperation and Security in the 21st Century*, ed. Janne E. Nolan (Washington, DC: Brookings, 1994), 65–130.

30. Allen Sens, "From Collective Defense to Cooperative Security?" in *NATO after Fifty Years*, ed. S. Victor Papacosma, Sean Kay, and Mark Rubin (New York: Scholarly Resources, 2001), 169–70.

31. Robert Gilpin, *The Political Economy of International Relations* (Princeton, NJ: Princeton University Press, 1987), 263–305.

32. Robert G. Gilpin, *Global Political Economy: Understanding the International Economic Order* (Princeton, NJ: Princeton University Press, 2001), 278.

33. "Multinational Corporations," International Labor Organization, Bureau for Worker's Activities, www.itcilo.it/english/actrav/telearn/global/ilo/multinat/multinat .htm (accessed March 12, 2011).

34. Karen Mingst, *Essentials of International Relations*, 2nd ed. (New York: W. W. Norton, 2003), 209–12.

35. Emmanuel Kant, *Perpetual Peace*. Excerpted in Richard K. Betts, ed., *Conflict after the Cold War: Arguments on Causes of War and Peace*, 2nd ed. (New York: Longman, 2002), 103.

36. John M. Owen, "How Liberalism Produces Democratic Peace," *International Security* 19, no. 2 (fall 1994): 87–125.

37. For a full critique, see Christopher Layne, "Kant or Cant: The Myth of the Democratic Peace," *International Security* 19, no. 2 (fall 1994): 5–49.

38. Charles Lipson, *Reliable Partners: How Democracies Have Made a Separate Peace* (Princeton, NJ: Princeton University Press, 2003), 4; see 77–111 for his full argument.

39. Lipson, *Reliable Partners*, 14.

40. Karl Deutsch et al., *Political Community in the North Atlantic Area* (Princeton, NJ: Princeton University Press, 1957), 5–6.

41. Deutsch et al., *Political Community*, 203.

42. Stephen Weber, "Does NATO Have a Future?" in *The Future of European Security*, ed. Beverly Crawford (Berkeley: Center for German and European Studies, University of California, 1992), 369–72.

43. Secretary of State Madeleine K. Albright, statement before the Senate Foreign Relations Committee, Washington, DC, October 7, 1997.

44. Emanuel Adler, *European Union: A Pluralistic Security Community* (Berkeley: University of California Press, 1991).

45. Deutsch et al., *Political Community*, 3.

46. Ronald L. Jepperson, Alexander Wendt, and Peter J. Katzenstein, "Norms, Identity, and Culture in National Security," in *The Culture of National Security: Norms and Identity in World Politics*, ed. Peter Katzenstein (New York: Columbia University Press, 1996), 34.

47. Jepperson, Wendt, and Katzenstein, "Norms, Identity, and Culture," 40.

48. Alexander Wendt, "Anarchy Is What States Make of It: The Social Construction of Power Politics," *International Organization* 46, no. 2 (spring 1992): 397.

49. Alexander Wendt, "The State As a Person in International Theory," *Review of International Studies* 30, no. 2 (2004): 289–316.

50. Alexander Wendt and Raymond Duvall, "Sovereignty and the UFO," *Political Theory* 36, no. 4 (2008): 607–33.

51. Hedley Bull, *The Anarchical Society: A Study of Order in World Politics*, 3rd ed. (New York: Palgrave, 2002).

52. Jessica T. Mathews, "Power Shift," *Foreign Affairs* 76, no. 1 (January–February 1997): 50.

53. Mathews, "Power Shift," 50–66.

54. Mathews, "Power Shift," 50–66.

55. Ernst B. Haas, *When Knowledge Is Power: Three Models of Change in International Organizations* (Berkeley: University of California Press, 1990).

56. Peter Haas, "Introduction: Epistemic Communities and International Policy Coordination," *International Organization* 46, no. 1 (1992): 1–35.

57. Jennifer Mitzen, "Toward a Visible Hand: The International Public Sphere in Theory and Practice" (PhD diss., University of Chicago, 2001).

58. Steven R. Ratner, "International Law: The Trials of Global Norms," *Foreign Policy* 110 (spring 1998): 67.

59. Ratner, "International Law," 72–77.

60. Robert O. Keohane et al., "The Concept of Legalization" *International Organization* 54, no. 3 (summer 2000): 401–19.

61. Kenneth W. Abbott and Duncan Snidal, "Hard and Soft Law in International Governance," in *International Law: Classic and Contemporary Readings*, ed. Charlotte Ku and Paul F. Diehl (Boulder, CO: Lynne Rienner, 2003), 51–79.

62. Ben Lowe, *Imagining Peace: A History of Early English Pacifist Ideas* (University Park: Pennsylvania State University Press, 1997).

63. David P. Barsh and Charles P. Webel, *Peace and Conflict Studies* (London: Sage, 2002), 50.

64. Joan V. Bondurant, *Conquest of Violence: The Gandhian Philosophy of Conflict* (Princeton, NJ: Princeton University Press, 1958).

65. Mary King, *Mahatma Gandhi and Martin Luther King Jr.: The Power of Nonviolent Action* (Paris: UNESCO Publishing, 1999), 272.

66. King, *Mahatma Gandhi*, 272.

67. Gen. Lee Butler, USAF (Ret.), "National Press Club Remarks," Washington, DC, December 4, 1996. Available at www.pbs.org/wgbh/amex/bomb/filmmore/reference/primary/leebutler.html (accessed March 12, 2011).

68. Henry Kissinger et al., "Toward a Nuclear-Free World," *Wall Street Journal*, January 15, 2007. Available at www.hoover.org/publications/hoover-digest/article/6109 (accessed March 12, 2011).

69. Paul R. Viotti and Mark V. Kauppi, *International Relations Theory: Realism, Pluralism, Globalism, and Beyond*, 3rd ed. (Boston: Allyn and Bacon, 1999), 18–21; and Pauline Marie Rosenau, *Post-Modernism and Social Sciences* (Princeton, NJ: Princeton University Press, 1992).

70. I am grateful to Kemi George for advancing this analogy.

71. Richard K. Ashley, "The Poverty of Neorealism," in *Neorealism and Its Critics*, ed. Robert O. Keohane (New York: Columbia University Press, 1986), 270.

72. William E. Connolly, "Identity and Difference in Global Politics," in *International/Intertextual Relations: Postmodern Readings of World Politics*, ed. James Der Derian and Michael J. Shapiro (Lexington, MA: Lexington Books, 1989), 323–26.

73. Ole Waever, "Securitization and Desecuritization," in *On Security*, ed. Ronnie Lipschutz (New York: Columbia University Press, 1995), 46–86.

74. David Campbell, *Writing Security: United States Foreign Policy and the Politics of Identity* (Minneapolis: University of Minnesota Press, 1992), 19–20.

75. Christine Sylvester, *Feminist Theory and International Relations in a Postmodern Era* (Cambridge: Cambridge University Press, 1994).

76. J. Ann Tickner, "A Critique of Morgenthau's Principles of Political Realism," in *Gender in International Relations*, ed. Rebecca Grant and Kathleen Newland (Bloomington: Indiana University Press, 1991), 17–29.

77. Tickner, "Critique of Morgenthau's Principles," 17–29.

78. See Joshua Goldstein, *War and Gender: How Gender Shapes the War System and Vice-Versa* (Cambridge: Cambridge University Press, 2003); and Joshua Goldstein, *International Relations*, 6th ed. (New York: Longman, 2004).

79. Thomas Homer-Dixon, *The Upside of Down, Catastrophe, Creativity, and the Renewal of Civilization* (Washington, DC: Island Press, 2006), 187.

80. Dwight D. Eisenhower, "Chance for Peace Speech" (address to the American Society of Newspaper Editors, April 16, 1953). Available at www.eisenhower memorial.org/speeches/19530416 Chance for Peace.htm (accessed March 12, 2011).

Chapter 4: Great Powers and Grand Strategy

1. International Institute for Strategic Studies (IISS), *The Military Balance: 2009–2010* (Oxford: Oxford University Press, 2005), 31–34.

2. David S. Cloud, "Navy to Expand Fleet with New Enemies in Mind," *New York Times*, December 5, 2005.

3. Craig Whitlock, "Obama 2011 Budget Request: Defense Department," *Washington Post*, February 1, 2010.

4. Linda J. Bilmes and Joseph Stiglitz, "The Iraq War Will Cost Us $3 Trillion and Much More," *Washington Post*, March 9, 2008.

5. Kori Schake, "Stop Spending So Much on Defense," ForeignPolicy.com, January 20, 2010, http://shadow.foreignpolicy.com/posts/2010/01/20/stop_spending _so_much_on_Defense (accessed March 12, 2011).

6. "U.S. Seen As Less Important, China As More Powerful," Pew Research Center, December 3, 2009, http://pewresearch.org/pubs/1428/america-seen-less -important-china-more-powerful-isolationist-sentiment-surges (accessed March 12, 2011).

7. "QDR Report: Draft As of December 3, 2009," POLITICO, December 3, 2009, www.politico.com/blogs/laurarozen/0110/QDR_draft_leaks.html (accessed March 12, 2011). The official version is published at www.defense.gov/QDR (accessed March 12, 2011).

8. "Ambassador Eikenberry's Cables on U.S. Strategy in Afghanistan," *New York Times*, January 26, 2010.

9. Text of Strategic Offensive Reductions Treaty, WhiteHouse.gov, April 8, 2010, www.whitehouse.gov (accessed fall 2010).

10. IISS, *Strategic Survey 2003–2004: An Evaluation and Forecast of World Affairs* (Oxford: Oxford University Press, 2003), 20–21.

11. Walter Pincus, "Defense Panel Faults Nuclear Plans," *Washington Post*, March 28, 2004.

12. Richard Sokolsky, "Demystifying the US Nuclear Posture Review," *Survival* 44, no. 3 (autumn 2002): 138.

13. David S. Cloud, "Pentagon Studies Pre-Emptive Nuclear Strikes," *New York Times*, September 11, 2005.

14. Christopher Bluth, "Russian Military Forces: Ambitions, Capabilities, and Constraints," in *Security Dilemmas in Russia and Eurasia*, ed. Roy Allison and Christopher Bluth (London: Royal Institute of International Affairs, 1998), 69.

15. "Russian Army Off-Duty Deaths Rise," *BBC News*, November 17, 2004, http:// news.bbc.co.uk/2/hi/europe/4020193.stm (accessed March 12, 2011).

16. Hans-Henning Schroder, "The Russian Army in Politics," in *Security Dilemmas in Russia and Eurasia*, ed. Roy Allison and Christopher Bluth (London: Royal Institute of International Affairs, 1998), 53.

17. Meg Clothier, "Iran and Russia Sign $1 bln Defense Deal: Reports," Reuters, December 2, 2005.

18. IISS, *Strategic Survey 2003–2004*, 121.

19. IISS, *Strategic Survey 2003–2004*, 121.

20. IISS, *The Military Balance: 2009–2010*, 222–34.

21. IISS, *The Military Balance: 2009–2010*, 222–34.

22. IISS, *The Military Balance: 2009–2010*, 222–34.

23. Dmitri Trenin, "Central Asia's Stability and Russia's Security," *PONARS* 168 (November 2000).

24. Matthew Bunn, "The Threat in Russia and the Newly Independent States," October 28, 2002, www.nunnturner.org/e_research/cnwm/threat/russia.asp (accessed fall 2004).

25. William Webster, *Russian Organized Crime* (Washington, DC: Center for International and Strategic Studies, 1997 and 2000).

26. Webster, *Russian Organized Crime,* available from www.csis.org (accessed fall 1998 and summer 2000).

27. "Radioactive Sources: Facts and Figures," International Atomic Energy Agency, June 2002.

28. Bunn, "The Threat in Russia."

29. David Holley, "Russia Seeks Safety in Nuclear Arms," *Los Angeles Times,* December 6, 2004.

30. Bunn, "The Threat in Russia."

31. Bunn, "The Threat in Russia."

32. Bunn, "The Threat in Russia."

33. Bruce G. Blair, "US Nuclear Posture and Alert Status Report Post Sept. 11," Center for Defense Information, January 28, 2002, www.cdi.org/nuclear/post911.cfm (accessed March 12, 2011).

34. Lachlan Forrow et al., "Accidental Nuclear War," *New England Journal of Medicine* 338, no. 18 (1998): 1328–29.

35. James Brooke, "The Asian Battle for Russia's Oil and Gas," *New York Times,* January 3, 2004.

36. "How Poor Is China?" *The Economist,* October 12, 1996, 35–36.

37. FY04 Report to Congress on PRC Military Power, *Annual Report on the Military Power of the People's Republic of China* (Washington, DC: U.S. Department of Defense, 2004).

38. Jane Perlez, "Across Asia, Beijing's Star Is in Ascendance," *Washington Post,* August 28, 2004.

39. James Miles, "Chinese Nationalism, US Policy and Asian Security," *Survival* 42, no. 4 (winter 2000–2001): 51.

40. Miles, "Chinese Nationalism," 53.

41. Audra Ang, "China Boosts Military Spending in Budget," Associated Press, March 6, 2004.

42. IISS, *The Military Balance: 2009–2010,* 398–404.

43. IISS, *The Military Balance: 2009–2010,* 398–404. Also see Edward Wong, "Chinese Military Seeks to Extend Its Naval Power," *New York Times,* April 23, 2010.

44. John J. Lumpkin, "China Launches New Class of Nuclear Sub," Associated Press, December 4, 2004.

45. Jason D. Ellis and Todd M. Koca, "China Rising: New Challenges to the U.S. Security Posture," *Strategic Forum* 175 (October 2000): 1.

46. Ralph Jennings, "Taiwan Says China Has 1,500 Missiles Aimed at Island," Reuters, February 13, 2009.

47. Ellis and Koca, "China Rising," 2.

48. David Shambaugh, "China's Military Views the World: Ambivalent Security," *International Security* 24, no. 3 (winter 1999–2000): 58.

49. FY04 Report to Congress, *Annual Report,* 58–60.

50. Denny Roy, "China's Reaction to American Predominance," *Survival* 45, no. 3 (autumn 2003): 62.

51. Ellis and Koca, "China Rising," 2.

52. Roy, "China's Reaction," 69.

53. Peter S. Goodman, "1,500-Mile Oil Pipeline Fading Fast for China," *Washington Post*, April 5, 2004.

54. Miles, "Chinese Nationalism," 59.

55. Quoted in FY04 Report to Congress, *Annual Report.*

56. David S. Yost, "The NATO Capabilities Gap and the European Union," *Survival* 42, no. 4 (winter 2000–2001): 101.

57. "European Defense 'Deal' Reached," *BBC News*, November 28, 2003, http://news.bbc.co.uk/2/hi/europe/3247826.stm (accessed March 12, 2011).

58. Charles Grant, "Big Three Join Forces on Defense," Center for European Reform, March 2004, www.cer.org.uk/pdf/grant_esharp_march04.pdf (accessed March 12, 2011).

59. Daniel Keohane, "EU on the Offensive about Defense," Center for European Reform, July 22–28, 2004, www.cer.org.uk/articles/keohane_europeanvoice_jul04.html (accessed March 12, 2011).

60. Kori N. Schake, "Do European Union Defense Initiatives Threaten NATO?" *Strategic Forum* 184 (August 2001): 6.

61. Bastian Giegerich and William Wallace, "Not Such a Soft Power: The External Deployment of European Forces," *Survival* 46, no. 2 (summer 2004): 164–68.

62. IISS, *The Military Balance: 2009–2010*, 129–34.

63. IISS, *The Military Balance: 2009–2010*, 134–37.

64. IISS, *The Military Balance: 2009–2010*, 134–37.

65. IISS, *The Military Balance: 2009–2010*, 129–34.

Chapter 5: Regional Flash Points

1. International Institute for Strategic Studies (IISS), *The Military Balance: 2009–2010* (Oxford: Oxford University Press, 2005), 367–70.

2. IISS, *The Military Balance: 2009–2010*, 359–64.

3. Details on nuclear capabilities come from Michael Quinlan, "How Robust Is India-Pakistan Deterrence?" *Survival* 42, no. 4 (winter 2000–2001): 145.

4. Quinlan, "How Robust Is India-Pakistan Deterrence?" 147.

5. These war games were reported and summarized by Thomas E. Ricks, "India-Pakistan Nuclear Rivalry," *Wall Street Journal*, June 24, 1998.

6. IISS, *Strategic Survey 2003–2004: An Evaluation and Forecast of World Affairs* (Oxford: Oxford University Press, 2004), 233.

7. Alexander Evans, "India, Pakistan, and the Prospect of War," *Current History* 100, no. 645 (April 2002): 160–65.

8. IISS, *Strategic Survey 2003–2004*, 233–35.

9. "The Consequences of Nuclear Conflict between India and Pakistan," Natural Resources Defense Council, www.nrdc.org/nuclear/southasia.asp (accessed March 12, 2011).

10. "The Global Threat," Nuclear Threat Initiative, www.nti.org/e_research/cnwm/threat/global.asp (accessed summer 2004).

11. "North Korea Country Profile," *BBC News*, February 11, 2011, http://news.bbc.co.uk/2/hi/country_profiles/1131421.stm (accessed March 12, 2011).

12. Gen. Thomas A. Schwartz, Commander, UNC/CFC/USFK, testimony before the Senate Armed Services Committee, March 5, 2002.

13. U.S. Department of Defense, *2000 Report to Congress: Military Situation on the Korean Peninsula* (Washington, DC: U.S. Department of Defense, 2000), 4.

14. Jonathan Pollack and Chung Min Lee, *Preparing for Korean Unification: Scenarios and Implications* (Santa Monica, CA: RAND Corporation, 1999), 67–68.

15. IISS, *The Military Balance: 2009–2010*, 411–13.

16. IISS, *The Military Balance: 2009–2010*, 413–16.

17. U.S. Department of Defense, *2000 Report to Congress*, 2.

18. Barton Gellman, "Pentagon War Scenario Spotlights Russia," *Washington Post*, February 20, 1992.

19. Bernard Trainor, "Worst Case Scenario: Suppose North Korea Starts a War," *Boston Globe*, May 24, 1997.

20. U.S. Department of Defense, *2000 Report to Congress*, 5.

21. U.S. Department of Defense, *2000 Report to Congress*, 6.

22. Donald MacIntyre, "Kim's War Machine," *Time Asia* 161, no. 7 (February 24, 2003).

23. Andrew Demaria, "North Korea: The Cost of Conflict," CNN, January 21, 2003, http://edition.cnn.com/2003/WORLD/asiapcf/east/01/21/nkorea.war (accessed March 12, 2011).

24. Hans M. Kristensen, "Preemptive Posturing," *Bulletin of the Atomic Scientists* 58, no. 5 (September–October 2002): 54–59.

25. IISS, *North Korea's Weapons Programmes: A Net Assessment* (Oxford: Oxford University Press, 2004).

26. Bruce B. Auster and Kevin Whitelaw, "Pentagon Comes Up with a Provocative Plan to Face Down North Korea," *U.S. News & World Report*, July 21, 2003, 21.

27. Richard C. Bush, Sharon Yanagi, and Kevin Scott, eds., *Brookings Northeast Asia Survey: 2003–2004* (Washington, DC: Brookings, 2003), ix.

28. Phillip C. Saunders and Daniel A. Pinkston, "Seeing North Korea Clearly," *Survival* 45, no. 3 (autumn 2003): 79–102.

29. Chris Rahman, "Defending Taiwan, and Why It Matters," *Naval War College Review* 54, no. 4 (autumn 2001): 71–74.

30. IISS, *The Military Balance: 2009–2010*, 427–29.

31. Thom Shanker, "U.S. Says China Is Stepping Up Short-Range Missile Production," *New York Times*, July 31, 2003.

32. Tim Luard, "Military Balance Goes against Taiwan," *BBC News*, March 9, 2004, http://news.bbc.co.uk/2/hi/asia-pacific/3545361.stm (accessed March 12, 2011).

33. Benjamin Kang Lim, "Taiwan Sees Military Balance Tipping to China by Next Year," Reuters, January 11, 2003.

34. Ching Cheong, "China-Taiwan War Unlikely before 2010, Says US Report," *Straits Times*, June 7, 2004; and U.S. Department of Defense, *2004 Report to Congress*.

35. Richard L. Russell, "What if . . . 'China Attacks Taiwan!'" *Parameters* 31, no. 3 (autumn 2001): 76–91.

36. Wendell Minnick, "The Year to Fear for Taiwan: 2006," *Asia Times*, April 10, 2004.

37. Michael O'Hanlon, "Can China Conquer Taiwan?" *International Security* 25, no. 2 (fall 2000): 51–86.

38. "Taiwan Stages War Games As Report Shows China Would Win in Six Days," AFP, August 12, 2004.

39. "Taiwan Could Fend Off China Attack for 2 Weeks," Reuters, August 12, 2004.

40. John M. Glionna, "China, U.S. Each Hold Major War Exercises," *Los Angeles Times*, July 20, 2004.

41. Michael D. Swaine, "Deterring Conflict in the Taiwan Strait: The Successes and Failures of Taiwan's Defense Reform and Modernization Program," *Carnegie Papers* 46 (July 2004).

42. Randall Schriver, deputy assistant secretary of state for East Asian and Pacific affairs, remarks to U.S.-Taiwan Business Council Defense Industry Conference, San Antonio, Texas, February 14, 2003.

43. Russell, "What if . . . 'China Attacks Taiwan!'" 76–91.

44. Chris Hogg, "Storm across the Taiwan Strait," *BBC News*, June 22, 2004, http://news.bbc.co.uk/2/hi/asia-pacific/3825927.stm (accessed March 12, 2011).

45. "Taiwan Needs Nuclear Deterrent," *Taiwan Times*, August 13, 2004.

46. David Albright and Corey Gay, "Taiwan: Nuclear Nightmare Averted," *Bulletin of the Atomic Scientists* 54, no. 1 (January–February 1998): 54–61.

47. Swaine, "Deterring Conflict in the Taiwan Strait," 21.

48. "Poll: Taiwanese Do Not Expect War with China Soon," Associated Press, July 22, 2004.

49. Republic of China Ministry of National Defense, *2002 National Defense Report, Republic of China* (Taipei, Taiwan: Ministry of National Defense, 2002).

50. See Graham E. Fuller, "Islamists in the Arab World: The Dance around Democracy," *Carnegie Papers* 49 (September 2004): 1–15.

51. IISS, *The Military Balance: 2009–2010*, 31–34.

52. IISS, *The Military Balance: 2009–2010*, 251–53.

53. Judith Yaphe, "Turbulent Transition in Iraq: Can It Succeed?" *Strategic Forum* 208 (June 2004): 5.

54. Nadia Abou El-Magd, "Insurgency Slowing Iraq Reconstruction," Associated Press, October 13, 2004.

55. Vali Nasr, "Regional Implications of Shi'a Revival in Iraq," *Washington Quarterly* 27, no. 3 (summer 2004): 7–24.

56. Yaphe, "Turbulent Transition in Iraq," 2.

57. Michael E. O'Hanlon and Adriana Lins de Albuquerque, "Iraq—by the Numbers," *Los Angeles Times*, September 3, 2004, and U.S. Department of Defense, *2000 Report to Congress*.

58. IISS, *The Military Balance: 2009–2010*, 251–53.

59. Institute for National Strategic Studies, *Strategic Assessment 1997* (Washington, DC: National Defense University Press, 1997), 83.

60. *Yas-e Now,* June 22, 2003. Referenced by Patrick Clawson, "Reading the Popular Mood in Iran," *PolicyWatch* 770, Washington Institute for Near East Policy, July 7, 2003.

61. Anoushiravan Ehteshami, "Iran-Iraq Relations after Saddam," *Washington Quarterly* 25, no. 4 (autumn 2003): 124–25.

62. See Anthony Cordesman, "Iranian Weapons of Mass Destruction: The Broader Context," Center for Strategic and International Studies, December 5, 2008, www.csis .org/media/csis/pubs/081208_irannucstratcon.pdf (accessed March 12, 2011).

63. "Iran Profile," Nuclear Threat Reduction Initiative, October 2010, www.nti .org/e_research/profiles/Iran/Missile/index.html (accessed March 12, 2011).

64. IISS, *The Military Balance: 2003–2004* (Oxford: Oxford University Press, 2004), 102–3.

65. Ze'ev Schiff, "New Iranian Missiles Put Europe in Firing Range," *Haaretz,* April 27, 2007, www.haaretz.com/hasen/pages/ShArt.jhtml?itemNo=709937 (accessed March 12, 2011).

66. IISS, *The Military Balance: 2004–2005,* 126–27; and IISS, *The Military Balance: 2009–2010,* 251–53.

67. Gal Luft, "All Quiet on the Eastern Front? Israel's National Security Doctrine after the Fall of Saddam," *Analysis Paper* 2 (March 2004): 15.

68. Jeffrey White, "Iranian Nuclear Weapons, Part III: How Might Iran Retaliate?" *PolicyWatch* 762 (May 29, 2003): 1–3.

69. White, "Iranian Nuclear Weapons," 1–3.

70. Shahram Chubin and Robert S. Litwak, "Debating Iran's Nuclear Aspirations," *Washington Quarterly* 26, no. 4 (autumn 2003): 99–114.

71. J. E. Peterson, *Saudi Arabia and the Illusion of Security,* Adelphi Papers 348 (London: Routledge, 2002).

72. G. Gregory Gause III and Jill Crystal, "The Arab Gulf: Will Autocracy Define the Social Contract in 2015?" in *The Middle East in 2015: The Impact of Regional Trends on U.S. Strategic Planning,* ed. Judith Yaphe (Washington, DC: National Defense University, 2002), 175.

73. Michael Knights, "Saudi Arabia Faces Long-Term Insecurity," *Jane's Intelligence Review* (July 2004): 20–22.

74. Sean Kay, "Geopolitical Constraints and Institutional Innovation: The Dynamics of Multilateralism in Eurasia," in *Limiting Institutions?: The Challenge of Eurasian Security Governance,* ed. James Sperling, Sean Kay, and S. Victor Papacosma (Manchester, UK: Manchester University Press, 2003), 125–43.

75. Richard Sokolsky and Tanya Charlick-Paley, *NATO and Caspian Security: A Mission Too Far?* (Santa Monica, CA: RAND Corporation, 1999), 13–21.

76. "Strategic Policy toward CIS Published," Foreign Broadcast Information Service Daily Report: Central Asia SOV-95, September 28, 1995, 19–20.

77. IISS, *Strategic Survey 2000–2001* (Oxford: Oxford University Press, 2001), 19–20.

78. "Strategic Policy toward CIS Published," 19–20.

79. Stephen J. Blank, *Energy, Economics, and Security in Central Asia: Russia and Its Rivals* (Carlisle Barracks, PA: U.S. Army War College, 1995).

80. IISS, *The Military Balance: 2009–2010*, 222–34.

81. Dmitri Trenin, "Central Asia's Stability and Russia's Security," PONARS Policy Memo 168, November 2000, http://csis.org/files/media/csis/pubs/pm_0168.pdf (accessed March 12, 2011).

82. Douglas Frantz, "Russia's New Reach: Gas Pipeline to Turkey," *New York Times* (June 6, 2001).

83. Haroutiun Khachatrian, "Creation of Rapid Deployment Force Marks Potential Watershed in Collective Security Development," *Eurasia Insight* (July 2, 2001).

84. "The GUUAM Group: History and Principles: Briefing Paper," GUUAM, November 2000, www.guuam.org/general/browse.html (accessed spring 2001).

85. Uzbekistan joined in 1999, at which time the name was formally expanded from GUAM to GUUAM.

86. Anatol Lieven, "GUUAM: What Is It, and What Is It For?" *Eurasian Insight* (December 18, 2000).

87. "Joint Statement by the Heads of State of the Republic of Kazakhstan, the People's Republic of China, the Kyrgyz Republic, the Russian Federation, the Republic of Tajikistan, and the Republic of Uzbekistan."

88. "Central Asia Bloc United Against Missile Shield," CNN, June 15, 2001.

89. Philip P. Pan, "China Links bin Laden to Separatists," *Washington Post*, January 22, 2002.

Chapter 6: Technology and the Business of Security

1. Abe Singer and Scott Rowell, "Information Warfare: An Old Operational Concept with New Implications," *Strategic Forum* 99 (December 1996): 1–3.

2. Theodor W. Galdi, "Revolution in Military Affairs?" CRS Report for Congress, Congressional Research Service, 95-1170-F, December 11, 1995.

3. "Historical Examples of RMAs," Center for Strategic and Budgetary Assessments, www.csbaonline.org/2Strategic_Studies/1Revolution-in-Military_Affairs/REvolution-Military_Affairs.htm (accessed summer 2004).

4. Robert S. Bolia, "Over-Reliance on Technology in Warfare: The Yom Kippur War As a Case Study," *Parameters* 34, no. 2 (summer 2004): 46–56.

5. Bob Drogin, "Spy Work in Iraq Riddled by Failures," *Los Angeles Times*, June 17, 2004.

6. "At-a-Glance: Butler Report," *BBC News*, July 14, 2004, http://news.bbc.co.uk/2/hi/uk_news/politics/3892809.stm (accessed March 12, 2011).

7. Joseph Cirincione, Jessica T. Mathews, and George Perkovich, *WMD in Iraq: Evidence and Implications* (Washington, DC: Carnegie Endowment for International Peace, 2004).

8. Douglas Jehl and Eric Schmitt, "Errors Are Seen in Early Attacks on Iraqi Leaders," *New York Times*, June 13, 2004.

9. David Talbot, "How Technology Failed in Iraq," *Technology Review*, October 31, 2004.

10. Mark Hanna, "Task Force XXI: The Army's Digital Experiment," *Strategic Forum* 119 (July 1997): 2.

11. Hanna, "Task Force XXI," 2.

12. Thomas K. Adams, "The Real Military Revolution," *Parameters* 30, no. 3 (autumn 2000): 54–55.

13. Caroline Drees, "US Military Taps Bugs and Weeds in War on Terror," Reuters, November 24, 2004.

14. Robert E. Armstrong and Jerry B. Warner, "Biology and the Battlefield," *Defense Horizons* 25 (April 2003): 1–8.

15. John L. Peterson and Dennis M. Egan, "Small Security: Nanotechnology and Future Defense," *Defense Horizons* 8 (March 2002): 1–2.

16. "Nano-Needle Operates on Cell," *BBC News*, December 15, 2004, http://news.bbc.co.uk/2/hi/science/nature/4078125.stm (accessed March 12, 2011).

17. Petersen and Egan, "Small Security," 2–3.

18. Robert O'Harrow Jr., "Tiny Sensors That Can Track Anything," *Washington Post*, September 24, 2004.

19. "Marines Aided by Robotic Airplane in Iraq," Associated Press, November 29, 2004.

20. Douglas Pasternak, "Wonder Weapons," *U.S. News & World Report*, July 7, 1997.

21. Curt Anderson, "Government Says Terrorists May Use Lasers," Associated Press, December 9, 2004.

22. Graham T. Allison and Paul X. Kelley, *Nonlethal Weapons and Capabilities* (New York: Council on Foreign Relations, 2004).

23. William M. Arkin, "The Pentagon's Secret Scream: Sonic Devices Are Being Deployed," *Los Angeles Times*, March 10, 2004.

24. William M. Arkin, "Pulling Punches," *Los Angeles Times*, January 4, 2004.

25. Barbara Starr, "Bunker Busters May Grow to 30,000 Pounds," CNN, July 21, 2004, http://articles.cnn.com/2004-07-20/us/big.bomb_1_massive-ordnance-air-blast-penetrating-bomb-targets-deep-underground?_s=PM:US (accessed March 12, 2011).

26. Bob Woodward, *Bush at War* (New York: Simon and Schuster, 2002).

27. Michael E. O'Hanlon, "Beware the 'RMA'nia!'" (paper presented at the National Defense University, Washington, DC, September 9, 1998).

28. Katherine Pfleger Shrader, "Spy Imagery Agency Watching Inside U.S.," Associated Press, September 27, 2004.

29. "Tiananmen: A Picture That Cost a Life," *BBC News*, June 4, 2004, http://news.bbc.co.uk/2/hi/asia-pacific/3777257.stm (accessed March 12, 2011).

30. Daniel B. Wood, "Radio ID Tags Proliferate, Stirring Privacy Debate," *Christian Science Monitor*, December 15, 2004.

31. Michael A. Wertheimer, "Crippling Innovation—and Intelligence," *Washington Post*, July 21, 2004.

32. Ben Charny, "World Net Population Nears 300 Million," ZDNet, October 13, 2000, www.zdnet.com.au/world-net-population-nears-300-million-120105670.htm (accessed March 12, 2011).

33. Nua Internet Surveys at www.nua.ie/surveys (accessed December 2005).

34. Available at www.nua.com/surveys/?f=VS&art_idz905358417&rel=true (accessed December 2, 2005).

35. Dan Kuehl, "Defining Information Power," *Strategic Forum* 115 (June 1997): 5.

36. Martin Libicki, "Information Dominance," *Strategic Forum* 132 (November 1997): 4.

37. Libicki, "Information Dominance," 4.

38. Bob Nonow, "Global Networks: Emerging Constraints on Strategy," *Defense Horizons* 43 (July 2004): 1–4.

39. Singer and Rowell, "Information Warfare," 4.

40. Richard E. Hayes and Gary Wheatley, "Information Warfare and Deterrence," *Strategic Forum* 87 (October 1996): 5.

41. "Net Security Threats Growing Fast," *BBC News*, September 20, 2004, http://news.bbc.co.uk/2/hi/technology/3666978.stm (accessed March 12, 2011).

42. Jacques S. Gansler, "Protecting Cyberspace," in *Transforming America's Military*, ed. Hans Binnendijk (Washington, DC: National Defense University, 2002), 336.

43. John S. Foster Jr. et al., "Report of the Commission to Assess the Threat to the United States from Electromagnetic Pulse (EMP) Attack," EMP Commission, April 2008, www.empcommission.org/docs/A2473-EMP_Commission-7MB.pdf (accessed March 12, 2011).

44. Foster et al., "Report of the Commission."

45. Jon B. Alterman, "The Information Revolution and the Middle East," in *The Future Security Environment in the Middle East*, ed. Nora Bensahel and Daniel L. Byman (Santa Monica, CA: RAND Corporation, 2004), 227–51.

46. Mark Mazzetti, "PR Meets Psy-Ops in War on Terror," *Los Angeles Times*, December 1, 2004.

47. Thom Shanker and Eric Schmitt, "Pentagon Weighs Use of Deception in a Broad Arena," *New York Times*, December 13, 2004.

48. Jim Wolf, "U.S. Eyes Space As Possible Battleground," Reuters, January 19, 2004.

49. See Lawrence M. Krause, *The Physics of Star Trek* (St. Helens, OR: Perennial, 1996); and Lawrence M. Krause, *Beyond Star Trek* (St. Helens, OR: Perennial, 1998).

50. James Clay Moltz, "Reigning in the Space Cowboys," *Bulletin of the Atomic Scientists* 59, no. 1 (January–February 2003): 6–8.

51. "The Historical Context: Some Scientific, Commercial and Military Uses of Space," Eisenhower Institute, www.eisenhowerinstitute.org/programs/global partnerships (accessed fall 2004).

52. Peter L. Hayes, "Current and Future Military Use of Space," in UN Institute for Disarmament Research, *Outer Space and Global Security* (New York: United Nations, 2003), 21–27.

53. Clay Moltz, "Future Space Security," Nuclear Threat Reduction Initiative, June 2002, www.nti.org/e_research/e3_13b.html (accessed March 12, 2011).

54. "Bush Plans for Shutdown of GPS Network during Crisis," Associated Press, December 16, 2004.

55. MAB, "On the Role of Outer Space in Confronting Aggressive Threats," Eisenhower Institute, Washington, DC, October 2002.

56. Bob Preston et al., *Space Weapons: Earth Wars* (Santa Monica, CA: RAND Corporation, 2002), 23–36.

57. Marc Lallanilla, "Space: The Final Battlefield? U.S. Military Takes First Step towards Weapons in Space," *ABC News*, March 30, 2004, http://abcnews.go.com/Technology/story?id=99558&page=1 (accessed March 12, 2011).

58. Moltz, "Future Space Security."

59. Michael Krepon, "Lost in Space: The Misguided Drive toward Antisatellite Weapons," *Foreign Affairs* 80, no. 3 (May–June 2001): 2–8.

60. Peter Hays, *United States Military Space: Into the 21st Century*, INSS Occasional Papers 42 (Maxwell AFB, AL: Air University Press, 2002): 101.

61. Lt. Col. Peter Hays, "Space Arms Control and Regulation: Opportunities and Challenges" (paper presented at the George Washington University, Space Policy Institute, Washington, DC, June 10, 2002).

62. Jeffrey Richelson, *The Wizards of Langley: Inside the CIA's Directorate of Science and Technology* (Boulder, CO: Westview Press, 2002).

63. Hays, *United States Military Space*, 98–99.

64. Krepon, "Lost in Space," 2–8.

65. "United States: Military Programs," Monterey Institute of International Affairs, cns.miis.edu/research/space/us/mil.htm (accessed fall 2004).

66. U.S. Space Command, "Vision for 2020," Federation of American Scientists, February 1997, www.fas.org/spp/military/docops/usspac/visbook.pdf (accessed March 12, 2011).

67. U.S. Strategic Command, Public Affairs, Fact File, Offutt Air Force Base, Nebraska, March 2004.

68. Theresa Hitchens, "Weapons in Space: Silver Bullet or Russian Roulette?" (paper presented at the George Washington University Security Space Forum, Washington, DC, April 18, 2002), 1.

69. Sean Kay and Theresa Hitchens, "Bush Policy Would Start Arms Race in Space," *Cleveland Plain Dealer*, May 25, 2005.

70. John M. Logsdon, "A Vital National Interest?" *Space News*, August 12, 2002, 12.

71. Norimitsu Onishi, "Japan Support of Missile Shield Could Tilt Asia Power Balance," *New York Times*, April 3, 2004.

72. Onishi, "Japan Support for Missile Shield."

73. Preston, *Space Weapons: Earth Wars*, 91–98.

74. David Rohde, "India's Lofty Ambitions in Space Meet Earthly Realities," *New York Times*, January 24, 2004.

75. "Brazil's Military Programs," Monterey Institute, cns.miis.edu/research/space/brazil/mil.htm (accessed fall 2004).

76. "Russia's Military Programs," Monterey Institute, at cns.miis.edu/research/space/russia/mil.htm (accessed fall 2004).

77. "China Eyes 2017 Moon Landing," Reuters, November 4, 2005.

78. "China Plans Big Production of Small Satellites," Reuters, December 14, 2004.

79. "Report of the American Physical Society Study Group on Boost-Phase Intercept Systems for National Missile Defense: Scientific and Technical Issues," American Physical Society, July 15, 2003, www.aps.org/about/pressreleases/upload/BPI_Executive_Summary_and_Findings.pdf (accessed March 12, 2011).

80. Lt. Gen. Henry A. Obering III, "Online Exclusive, Response to 'Missile Defense Malfunction': Setting the Record Straight," Carnegie Council for Ethics in International Affairs, www.cceia.org/resources/journal/22_1/special_report/002.html (accessed March 12, 2011). Also see "Missile Defense Agency Fact Sheet," Missile Defense Agency, December 12, 2008, www.mda.mil/mdalink/pdf/testrecord.pdf (accessed March 12, 2011).

81. See Victoria Samson, "Flight Tests for Ground-Based Midcourse Defense (GMD) System," Center for Defense Information, www.cdi.org/pdfs/GMD%20IFT3.pdf (accessed March 12, 2011).

82. See Joseph Cirincione, "The Declining Ballistic Missile Threat," U.S. House of Representatives Committee on Oversight and Government Reform, March 5, 2008, http://nationalsecurity.oversight.house.gov/documents/20080305141211.pdf (accessed in fall 2008).

83. Lt. Gen. Henry A. Obering III, "Testimony before the House Oversight and Government Reform Committee, National Security and Foreign Affairs Subcommittee," U.S. House of Representatives Committee on Oversight and Government Reform, April 30, 2008, http://nationalsecurity.oversight.house.gov/documents/20080430170809.pdf (accessed in fall 2008).

84. Anthony Seaboyer and Oliver Thranert, "What Missile Proliferation Means for Europe," *Survival* 8, no. 2 (summer 2006): 86–87. Also see John Liang, "DOD Finds Cruise Missile Defense 'Gaps,'" Military.com, August 17, 2006, www.military.com/features/0,15240,110199,00.html (accessed March 12, 2011).

85. Philip Coyle and Victoria Samson, "Missile Defense Malfunction: Why the Proposed U.S. Missile Defenses in Europe Will Not Work," *Ethics and International Affairs* 22, no. 1 (spring 2008), www.cceia.org/resources/journal/22_1/special_report/001.html (accessed March 12, 2011).

86. See Scott D. Sagan and Kenneth N. Waltz, *The Spread of Nuclear Weapons: A Debate Renewed* (New York: W. W. Norton, 2002).

87. Peter D. Zimmerman and Charles D. Ferguson, "Sweeping the Skies," *Bulletin of the Atomic Scientists* 59, no. 6 (November–December 2003).

88. David Wright and Laura Grego, "Anti-Satellite Capabilities of Planned US Missile Defense Systems," *Disarmament Diplomacy* 68 (December 2002–January 2003).

89. Laura Grego, "A History of US and Soviet ASAT Programs," Union of Concerned Scientists, www.ucsusa.org/global_security/space_weapons/a-history-of-asat-programs.html (accessed fall 2004).

90. Theresa Hitchens, "USAF Transformation Flight Plan Highlights Space Weapons," Center for Defense Information, February 19, 2004, www.cdi.org/program/document.cfm?DocumentID=2080&StartRow=1$ (accessed March 12, 2011).

91. Thom Shanker, "Bad Economy Drives Down American Arms Sales," *New York Times*, September 12, 2010, A15.

92. Ruth Leger Sivard, *World Military and Social Expenditures: 1996* (Washington, DC: World Priorities, Inc., 1996), 18–19.

93. Rachel Stohl, "Forget WMD—It's Conventional Arms That Are Killing GIs and Iraqis," *Los Angeles Times*, July 19, 2004.

94. Dana Priest and Bradley Graham, "Missing Antiaircraft Missiles Alarm Aides," *Washington Post*, November 7, 2004.

95. "Infrared Countermeasures Systems," GlobalSecurity.org, www.global security.org/military/systems/aircraft/systems/ircm.htm (accessed March 12, 2011).

96. Martin C. Libicki, "Global Networks and Security: How Dark Is the Dark Side?" in *The Global Century: Globalization and National Security*, ed. Richard Kugler and Ellen Frost (Washington, DC: National Defense University Press, 2001), 809–24.

97. Department of Transportation, "An Assessment of the U.S. Marine Transportation System: A Report to Congress," National Transportation Library, September 1999, http://ntl.bts.gov/DOCS/report/mtsfinal.pdf (accessed March 12, 2011), 2.

98. Stephen J. Lukasik, Seymour E. Goodman, and David W. Longhurst, *Protecting Critical Infrastructures against Cyber-Attack*, Adelphi Paper 359 (London: IISS, 2003).

99. Phil Williams, "Organized Crime and Cybercrime: Synergies, Trends, and Responses," usinfo.state.gov/journals/itgic/0801/ijge/gj07.htm (accessed fall 2004).

100. Phil Williams, "Transnational Criminal Networks," in *Networks and Netwars: The Future of Terror, Crime, and Militancy*, ed. John Arquilla and David Ronfeldt (Santa Monica, CA: RAND Corporation, 2001), 61–97.

101. "Fighting Transnational Organized Crime," Tenth United Nations Congress on the Prevention of Crime and the Treatment of Offenders, Backgrounder 1, March 2000, www.un.org/events/10thcongress/2088f.htm (accessed March 12, 2011).

102. "Fighting Transnational Organized Crime."

103. Williams, "Transnational Criminal Networks," 61–97.

104. Graham Allison, *Nuclear Terrorism: The Ultimate Preventable Catastrophe* (New York: Times Books, 2004), 80–81.

105. William Webster, *Organized Crime in Russia* (Washington, DC: Center for International and Strategic Studies, 1997 and 2000).

106. Matthew Bunn, "The Global Threat," November 14, 2002, www.nunnturner.org/e_research/cnwm/threat/global.asp (accessed fall 2004).

107. Matthew Bunn, "The Threat in Russia and the Newly Independent States," October 28, 2002, www.nunnturner.org/e_research/cnwm/threat/russia.asp (accessed fall 2004).

108. Bunn, "Threat in Russia."

109. "Crime, Corruption and Terrorism Watch," Radio Free Europe/Radio Liberty, November 12, 2001.

110. U.S. General Accounting Office, *Nuclear Nonproliferation: U.S. Assistance Efforts to Help Other Countries Combat Nuclear Smuggling Need Strengthened Coordination and Planning*, GAO-02-426 (Washington, DC: General Accounting Office, May 2002), 24.

111. Todd Pitman, "Miners Drawn to Illegal Congo Uranium," Associated Press, March 31, 2004.

112. David E. Sanger and William J. Broad, "From Rogue Nuclear Programs, Web of Trails Leads to Pakistan," *New York Times*, January 4, 2004.

113. Sanger and Broad, "From Rogue Nuclear Programs."

114. Peter Slevin, "Pakistani Scientist Tied to Illicit Nuclear Supply Network," *Washington Post*, February 5, 2004.

115. Joby Warrick, "Libyan Nuclear Devices Missing," *Washington Post*, May 29, 2004.

116. Peter Slevin, John Lancaster, and Kamran Khan, "At Least 7 Nations Tied to Pakistani Nuclear Ring," *Washington Post*, February 8, 2004.

117. Slevin, "Pakistani Scientist Tied to Illicit Nuclear Supply Network."

118. Ellen Nakashima and Alan Sipress, "Insider Tells of Nuclear Deals, Cash," *Washington Post*, February 21, 2004.

119. Nakashima and Sipress, "Insider Tells of Nuclear Deals, Cash."

120. William J. Broad and David E. Sanger, "Warhead Blueprints Link Libya Project to Pakistan Figure," *New York Times*, February 4, 2004.

121. Joby Warrick and Peter Slevin, "Libyan Arms Designs Traced Back to China," *Washington Post*, February 15, 2004.

122. John Lancaster and Kamran Khan, "Musharraf Named in Nuclear Probe," *Washington Post*, February 3, 2004.

123. George Jahn, "Nuclear Black Market Is Small, Covert," Associated Press, February 2, 2004.

124. Nakashima and Sipress, "Insider Tells of Nuclear Deals, Cash."

125. Warrick and Slevin, "Libyan Arms Designs Traced Back to China."

126. Joel Brinkley and William J. Broad, "U.S. Lags in Recovering Fuel Suitable for Nuclear Arms," *New York Times*, March 7, 2004.

127. Peter W. Singer, *Corporate Warriors: The Rise of the Privatized Military Industry* (Ithaca, NY: Cornell University Press, 2004); and Lawrence W. Serewicz, "Globalization, Sovereignty and the Military Revolution: From Mercenaries to Private International Security Companies," *International Politics* 39 (March 2002): 75–89.

128. Al J. Venter, "Market Forces: How Hired Guns Succeeded Where the United Nations Failed," *Jane's International Defense Review*, March 1, 1998.

129. David Shearer, "Outsourcing War," *Foreign Policy* 112 (fall 1988): 68–81.

130. Herbert Howe, "Global Order and Security Privatization," *Strategic Forum* 140 (May 1998): 1–7.

131. "Outsourcing War," *Businessweek*, September 15, 2003.

132. David Lazarus, "Taking the War Private," *San Francisco Chronicle*, January 21, 2004.

133. Ian Traynor, "The Privatization of War," *Guardian*, December 30, 2003.

134. Traynor, "Privatization of War."

135. David Barstow et al., "Security Companies: Shadow Soldiers in Iraq," *New York Times*, April 19, 2004.

136. Andre Verloy and Daniel Politi, "Contracting Intelligence," Center for Public Integrity, July 28, 2004, www.publicintegrity.org/wow/report.aspx?aid=361 (accessed fall 2004).

137. Peter W. Singer, "The Contract the Military Needs to Break," *Washington Post*, September 12, 2004.

138. "Private Contractors," Center for Public Integrity, June 13, 2004, www .publicintegrity.org/wow/report.aspx?aid=328 (accessed fall 2004).

139. Singer, "The Contract the Military Needs to Break."

140. Barstow et al., "Security Companies."

141. Pamela Constable, "U.S. Men Guilty in Afghan Case," *Washington Post*, September 16, 2004.

142. Richard Haass, "Sanctioning Madness," *Foreign Affairs* 76, no. 6 (November–December 1997): 74–85.

143. Institute for National Strategic Studies, *Strategic Assessment: 1996* (Washington, DC: National Defense University Press, 1996), 56–60.

144. Robert A. Pape, "Why Economic Sanctions Do Not Work," *International Security* 22, no. 2 (fall 1997): 90–136.

145. Gary Clyde Hufbauer, "Sanctions-Happy USA," Policy Brief 98-4, Peterson Institute for International Economics, July 1998, www.iie.com/publications/pb/ pb.cfm?ResearchID=83 (accessed March 12, 2011).

146. Gary Clyde Hufbauer, Jeffrey J. Schott, and Kimberly Ann Elliott, *Economic Sanctions Reconsidered*, 2nd ed. (Washington, DC: Institute for International Economics, 1991).

147. Barbara Crossette, "Iraq Sanctions Kill Children, U.N. Reports," *New York Times*, December 1, 1995.

148. Barton Gellman, "Iraq's Arsenal Was Only on Paper," *Washington Post*, January 7, 2004.

149. Nicholas Kristof, "Our Man in Havana," *New York Times*, November 8, 2003.

150. David Baldwin, "Sanctions Have Gotten a Bum Rap," *Los Angeles Times*, August 18, 2004.

Chapter 7: Asymmetric Conflict

1. Ivan Arreguin-Toft, "How the Weak Win Wars: A Theory of Asymmetric Conflict," *International Security* 26, no. 1 (summer 2001): 100–5.

2. Roger W. Barnett, *Asymmetrical Warfare: Today's Challenge to US Military Power* (Dulles, VA: Brassey's Inc., 2003), 18.

3. Stephen J. Blank, *Rethinking Asymmetric Threats* (Carlisle Barracks, PA: U.S. Army War College, Strategic Studies Institute, 2003), 18.

4. Montgomery C. Meigs, "Unorthodox Thoughts about Asymmetric Warfare," *Parameters* 33, no. 2 (summer 2003): 4–18.

5. Blank, *Rethinking Asymmetric Threats*, 41.

6. Steven Metz, *Asymmetry and U.S. Military Strategy: Definition, Background, and Strategic Concepts* (Carlisle, PA: U.S. Army War College, 2001).

7. Metz, *Asymmetry and U.S. Military Strategy*, 5–12.

8. Kenneth F. McKenzie Jr., *Revenge of the Melians: Asymmetric Threats and the Next QDR*, McNair Paper 62 (Washington, DC: Institute for National Strategic Studies, November 2000).

9. Stasys Knezys and Romanas Sedlickas, *War in Chechnya* (College Station: Texas A&M Press, 1999), 105.

10. Shahram Chubin and Jerrold D. Green, *Terrorism and Asymmetric Conflict in Southwest Asia* (Santa Monica, CA: RAND Corporation, 2002).

11. See Michael E. Brown, ed., *Ethnic Conflict and International Security* (Princeton, NJ: Princeton University Press, 1997).

12. David A. Lake and Donald Rothchild, "Containing Fear: The Origins and Management of Ethnic Conflict," *International Security* 21, no. 2 (fall 1996): 41–75.

13. Barry Posen, "The Security Dilemma and Ethnic Conflict," in *Ethnic Conflict and International Security*, ed. Michael E. Brown (Princeton, NJ: Princeton University Press, 1993), 103–24.

14. Stuart J. Kaufman, "Spiraling to Ethnic War: Elites, Masses, and Moscow in Moldova's Civil War," *International Security* 21, no. 2 (fall 1996): 108–38.

15. Christine Wallach, "Policy Forum: Bosnia—after the Troops Leave," *Washington Quarterly* 19, no. 3 (summer 1996): 3–6.

16. Alan J. Kuperman, *The Limits of Humanitarian Intervention: Genocide in Rwanda* (Washington, DC: Brookings, 2001), 9–12.

17. Philip Gourevitch, *We Wish to Inform You That Tomorrow We Will Be Killed with Our Families: Stories from Rwanda* (New York: Farrar Straus and Giroux, 1998), 93.

18. FAX NO: MOST Immediate-Code, Cable-212, Subject "Request for Protection of Informant," BARIL/DPKO/UNATIONS, January 11, 1994.

19. Arthur J. Klinghoffer, *The International Dimension of Genocide in Rwanda* (New York: New York University Press, 1998), 112–13.

20. Gourevitch, *We Wish to Inform You*, 95.

21. "Interview: General Romeo Dallaire," Ghosts of Rwanda, *Frontline*, April 1, 2004, www.pbs.org/wgbh/pages/frontline/shows/ghosts/interviews/dallaire.html (accessed March 12, 2011).

22. U.S. Department of State, Bureau of Intelligence and Research Assessment, "Roots of Violence in Rwanda," April 29, 1994.

23. Klinghoffer, *International Dimension of Genocide in Rwanda*, 113.

24. Kuperman, *Limits of Humanitarian Intervention*, 38–42.

25. Gourevitch, *We Wish to Inform You*, 134–35.

26. Kuperman, *Limits of Humanitarian Intervention*, 14–16.

27. Shaharyar M. Khan, *The Shallow Graves of Rwanda* (New York: London, 2000), 17.

28. Audrey Kurth Cronin, "Behind the Curve: Globalization and International Terrorism," *International Security* 27, no. 3 (winter 2002–2003): 34.

29. Bruce Hoffman, *Inside Terrorism* (New York: Columbia University Press, 1998), 15.

30. C. J. M. Drake, "The Role of Ideology in Terrorists' Target Selection," *Terrorism and Political Violence* 10, no. 2 (summer 1998): 53–85.

31. James Der Derian, "The Terrorist Discourse: Signs, States, and Systems of Global Political Violence," in *World Security: Trends and Challenges at Century's End*, ed. Michael T. Klare and Daniel C. Thomas (New York: St. Martin's Press, 1991), 237–65.

32. Hoffman, *Inside Terrorism*, 43.

33. Ariel Merari, "Terrorism As a Strategy of Insurgency," *Terrorism and Political Violence* 5, no. 4 (winter 1993): 215.

34. John Mackinlay, *Globalization and Insurgency*, Adelphi Paper 352 (London: International Institute for Strategic Studies, November 2002), 17–27.

35. Joey Hanzich, "Dying for Independence: World Separatist Movements and Terrorism," *Harvard International Review* 25, no. 2 (summer 2003): 33.

36. Ted Robert Gurr, "Some Characteristics of Political Terrorism in the 1960s," in *The Politics of Terrorism*, ed. Michael Stohl, 3rd ed. (New York: Marcel Dekker, 1988).

37. John Mueller, *Overblown: How Politicians and the Terrorism Industry Inflate National Security Threats, and Why We Believe Them* (New York: Free Press, 2007), 13.

38. Phil Williams, "Eurasia and the Transnational Terrorist Threats to Atlantic Security," in *Limiting Institutions?: The Challenge of Eurasian Security Governance*, ed. James Sperling, Sean Kay, and S. Victor Papacosma (Manchester, UK: Manchester University Press, 2003), 69–85.

39. Hoffman, *Inside Terrorism*, 94.

40. Bruce Hoffman, "Viewpoint: Terrorism and WMD: Some Preliminary Hypotheses," *Non-Proliferation Review* (spring–summer 1997): 48.

41. Robert A. Pape, "The Strategic Logic of Suicide Terrorism," *American Political Science Review* 97, no. 3 (August 2003): 343–61.

42. Pape, "Strategic Logic," 343.

43. Cronin, "Behind the Curve," 41–42.

44. W. Seth Carus, "The Threat of Bioterrorism," *Strategic Forum* 127 (September 1997): 1–4.

45. Douglas Frantz et al., "The New Face of Al Qaeda: Al Qaeda Seen As Wider Threat," *Los Angeles Times*, September 26, 2004.

46. Raymond Bonner and Don van Natta Jr., "Regional Terrorist Groups Pose Growing Threat," *New York Times*, February 8, 2004.

47. Brian M. Jenkins, "The Organization Men: Anatomy of a Terrorist Attack," in *How Did This Happen? Terrorism and the New War*, ed. James F. Hoge Jr. and Gideon Rose (New York: Public Affairs, 2001), 4–5.

48. Paul R. Pillar, *Terrorism and U.S. Foreign Policy* (Washington, DC: Brookings Institution Press, 2001), 19.

49. "Overview of the Enemy," Staff Statement 15, 9/11 Commission, June 2004, http://govinfo.library.unt.edu/911/staff_statements/staff_statement_15.pdf (accessed March 12, 2011).

50. Frantz, "The New Face of Al Qaeda."

51. "Overview of the Enemy."

52. "Overview of the Enemy."

53. Steve Coll and Susan B. Glasser, "Jihadists Turn the Web into Base of Operations," *Washington Post*, August 7, 2005.

54. Douglas Frantz, Josh Meyer, and Richard B. Schmitt, "Cyberspace Gives Al Qaeda Refuge," *Los Angeles Times*, August 15, 2004.

55. Sarah el Deeb, "Extremists Using Web to Spread Terror," Associated Press, June 13, 2004.

56. Don van Natta Jr. and Desmond Butler, "How Tiny Swiss Cellphone Chips Helped Track Global Terror Web," *New York Times*, March 4, 2004.

57. van Natta and Butler, "How Tiny Swiss Cellphone Chips Helped."

58. Michael Isikoff and Mark Hosenball, "Terror Watch: Like Clockwork," *Newsweek*, August 25, 2004, www.newsweek.com/2004/08/24/terror-watch-like-clockwork.html (accessed March 12, 2011).

59. Ken Menkhaus, *Somalia: State Collapse and the Threat of Terrorism*, Adelphi Paper 364 (London: Routledge, 2004), 54–56.

60. Douglas Farah and Richard Shultz, "Al Qaeda's Growing Sanctuary," *Washington Post*, July 14, 2004, A19.

61. Stern, *Ultimate Terrorists*, 8–10.

62. Graham Alison, *Nuclear Terrorism* (New York: Times Books, 2004), 67, 83–86.

63. "What Is Ricin?" CNN, October 23, 2003, http://articles.cnn.com/2003-01-07/world/ricin.facts_1_ricin-poisoning-castor-beans-bulgarian-dissident-georgi-markov?_s=PM:WORLD (accessed March 12, 2011).

64. Stephen E. Flynn, "The Fragile State of Container Security" (testimony before the Senate Governmental Affairs Committee, March 20, 2003).

65. Brian Ross, "New Report Reveals Gaps in Port Safety," *ABC News*, October 13, 2004, http://abcnews.go.com/WNT/story?id=162480 (accessed March 12, 2011).

66. Edwin S. Lyman, "Chernobyl on the Hudson? The Health and Economic Impacts of a Terrorist Attack at the Indian Point Nuclear Plant," Union of Concerned Scientists, September 2004, www.ucsusa.org/nuclear_power/nuclear_power_risk/sabotage_and_attacks_on_reactors/impacts-of-a-terrorist-attack.html (accessed March 12, 2011).

67. Alison, *Nuclear Terrorism*, 7–8.

68. "What If a Dirty Bomb Hit London?" *BBC News*, February 14, 2003, http://news.bbc.co.uk/2/hi/uk_news/2708635.stm (accessed March 12, 2011).

69. Peter D. Zimmerman with Cheryl Loeb, "Dirty Bombs: The Threat Revisited," *Defense Horizons* 38 (January 2004): 1–11.

70. "World 'Failed' Bhopal Gas Victims," *BBC News*, November 29, 2004, http://news.bbc.co.uk/2/hi/south_asia/4050739.stm (accessed March 12, 2011).

71. Charles D. Ferguson and William C. Potter, *The Four Faces of Nuclear Terrorism* (Monterey, CA: Monterey Institute, 2004), 6.

72. Matthew Brzezinski, *Fortress America* (New York: Bantam Books, 2004), 8.

73. Sean Kay, "New Afghan War Assumptions Must Be Weighed before a Surge," *Cleveland Plain Dealer*, October 25, 2009. Also see Bob Woodward, *Obama's Wars* (New York: Simon and Schuster, 2010).

74. Scott Wilson and Sewell Chan, "As Insurgency Grew, So Did Prison Abuse," *Washington Post*, May 10, 2004.

75. Seymour M. Hersh, "The Gray Zone," *New Yorker*, May 15, 2004, 38.

76. Richard A. Serrano, "Details of Marines Mistreating Prisoners in Iraq Are Revealed," *Los Angeles Times*, December 15, 2004.

77. Neil A. Lewis, "Broad Use Cited of Harsh Tactics at Base in Cuba," *New York Times*, October 17, 2004.

78. Christopher Lee and Sara Kehaulani Goo, "U.S. VISIT Program to Add 27 Countries," *Washington Post*, April 3, 2004; and Eric Lichtblau and John Markoff, "U.S. Nearing Deal on Way to Track Foreign Visitors," *New York Times*, May 24, 2004.

79. "Concern over Biometric Passports," *BBC News*, March 30, 2004, http://news.bbc.co.uk/2/hi/technology/3582461.stm (accessed March 12, 2011).

Chapter 8: Human Security

1. Lloyd Axworthy, introduction to *Human Security and the New Diplomacy*, ed. Rob McRae and Don Hubert (Montreal: McGill-Queen's University Press, 2001), 3.

2. Axworthy, "Introduction," 3.

3. Anne Gearan, "U.S.: 14 Nations Not Stopping Trafficking," Associated Press, June 4, 2005.

4. "A Perspective on Human Security: Chairman's Summary" (presented at First Ministerial Meeting of the Human Security Network, Lysøen, Norway, May 20, 1999).

5. "The Index of Human Insecurity," *AVISO* 6 (January 2000): 1–2.

6. United Nations, *Human Development Report 2010—20th Anniversary* (United Nations: New York, 2010).

7. Roland Paris, "Human Security: Paradigm Shift or Hot Air?" *International Security* 26, no. 2 (2001): 67–102.

8. UN Development Programme, *Human Development Report* (New York: Oxford University Press, 1994).

9. Commission on Human Security, *Human Security Now* (New York: Communications Development, May 2003).

10. Sadako Ogata and Johan Cels, "Human Security—Protecting and Empowering the People," *Global Governance* 9, no. 3 (2003): 274.

11. Caroline Thomas, introduction to *Globalization, Human Security and the African Experience*, ed. Caroline Thomas and Peter Wilkin (Boulder, CO: Lynne Rienner, 1999), 3–4.

12. Fen Osler Hampson et al., *Madness in the Multitude: Human Security and World Disorder* (Oxford: Oxford University Press, 2001), 16–34.

13. Human Security Report Project, www.hsrgroup.org.

14. Thomas, "Introduction," 4.

15. "About Us," Human Rights Watch, www.hrw.org/about (accessed March 12, 2011).

16. Human Rights Watch, *2003 World Report* (New York: Human Rights Watch, 2003), xxi.

17. Jack Donnelly, *Universal Human Rights: In Theory and Practice*, 2nd ed. (Ithaca, NY: Cornell University Press, 2003), 23.

18. Donnelly, *Universal Human Rights*, 23.

19. Annual Human Rights Watch reports, from which this data is compiled, are available at www.hrw.org.

20. U.S. Census Bureau, "Global Population at a Glance: 2002 and Beyond," *International Population Reports* (March 2002): 1–4.

21. See Nazli Choucri and Robert C. North, "Population and (In)security: National Perspectives and Global Imperatives," in *Building a New Global Order: Emerging Trends in International Security*, ed. David Dewitt (Oxford: Oxford University Press, 1993), 229–56.

22. Choucri and North, "Population and (In)security," 229–56.

23. Jaroslav Tir and Paul F. Diehl, "Demographic Pressure and Interstate Conflict," in *Environmental Conflict*, ed. Paul F. Diehl and Nils Petter Gleditsch (Boulder, CO: Westview Press, 2001), 58–83.

24. Tir and Diehl, "Demographic Pressure," 58–83.

25. Jack A. Goldstone, "Demography, Environment, and Security," in *Environmental Conflict*, ed. Paul F. Diehl and Nils Petter Gleditsch (Boulder, CO: Westview Press, 2001), 84–108; and Charles B. Keeley, "Demographic Developments and Security," in *Grave New World: Security Challenges in the 21st Century*, ed. Michael E. Brown (Washington, DC: Georgetown University Press, 2003), 197–212.

26. Myron Weiner, "Security, Stability, and International Migration," *International Security* 17, no. 3 (winter 1992–1993): 91–126.

27. Weiner, "Security, Stability, and International Migration," 91–126.

28. "Country Profiles," UN Fund for Population Assistance, www.unfpa.org/public/countries (accessed March 12, 2011).

29. John I. Clarke, "The Growing Concentration of World Population from 1950 to 2050," in *Human Population Dynamics: Cross-Disciplinary Perspectives*, ed. Helen Macbeth and Paul Collinson (Cambridge: Cambridge University Press, 2002), 56–59.

30. This data and that in the following paragraph are from "State of World Population 2003," UN Fund for Population Assistance, www.unfpa.org/swp/2003/english/ch1 (accessed March 12, 2011).

31. The data in this and following paragraphs come from U.S. Census Bureau, *Global Population Profile 2002* (Washington, DC: U.S. Census Bureau, 2002).

32. Jon B. Alterman, "On the Brink? Middle East Demographic Challenges and Opportunities," Center for Strategic and International Studies, www.csis.org/media/csis/events/030403_wilton.pdf (accessed March 12, 2011).

33. Alterman, "On the Brink?"

34. "United Nations Report on World Population and Aging," United Nations Population Fund, 2002, www.unfpa.org (accessed summer 2004).

35. Alterman, "On the Brink?"

36. Alterman, "On the Brink?"

37. Samuel P. Huntington, "The Hispanic Challenge," *Foreign Policy* (March–April 2004); the text and the debate are at www.foreignpolicy.com/story/cms.php?story_id=2495 (accessed March 12, 2011).

38. Detail is available at www.unhcr.ch/cgi-bin/texis/vtx/home (accessed summer 2004).

39. UN High Commissioner for Refugees, *Refugees by Numbers* (New York: United Nations, 2003).

40. UN High Commissioner for Refugees, *Refugees by Numbers.*

41. Weiner, "Security, Stability, and International Migration," 91–126.

42. World Commission of Dams, www.worldwatch.org/features/vsow/2003/06/12 (accessed summer 2004).

43. UN High Commissioner for Refugees, *Refugees by Numbers.*

44. Office for the Coordination of Humanitarian Assistance, *No Refuge: The Challenge of Internal Displacement* (New York: United Nations Press, 2003), 1.

45. Office for the Coordination of Humanitarian Assistance, *No Refuge*, 4.

46. Office for the Coordination of Humanitarian Assistance, *No Refuge*, 4.

47. Office for the Coordination of Humanitarian Assistance, *No Refuge*, 64.

48. Erik Assadourian et al., *State of the World: 2004* (New York: Norton, 2004), 8–10.

49. "The State of Food Insecurity in the World: 2004," Food and Agriculture Organization, ftp://ftp.fao.org/docrep/fao/007/y5650e/y5650e00.pdf (accessed March 12, 2011).

50. C. Ford Runge and Benjamin Senauer, "A Removable Feast," *Foreign Affairs* 79, no. 3 (May–June 2000): 39–51.

51. Anthony Mitchell, "U.N.: HIV/AIDS Fuels Tuberculosis Crisis," Associated Press, September 21, 2004.

52. Donald G. McNeil Jr., "Malaria Vaccine Proves Effective," *New York Times*, October 14, 2004.

53. "Influenza," Fact Sheet 211, World Health Organization, March 2003, www.who.int/mediacentre/factsheets/2003/fs211/en (accessed March 12, 2011), 1.

54. "WHO Warns of Dire Flu Pandemic," CNN, November 25, 2004.

55. Margaret Wertheim, "Drying the Tears of Thirsty Nations," *Los Angeles Times*, September 12, 2004; and World Health Organization, *Safe Water, Better Health* (New York: United Nations, 2008).

56. Sadaqat Jan, "UNICEF Says 170M Malnourished Children," Associated Press, December 5, 2004.

57. "Smoking Killing Millions Globally," *BBC News*, November 24, 2004, http://news.bbc.co.uk/2/hi/health/4034597.stm (accessed March 12, 2011); and "Tobacco Deaths to Reach 10 Million a Year by 2030," Reuters, November 9, 2007.

58. "Ebola Hemorrhagic Fever," Fact Sheet 103 World Health Organization, December 2008, www.who.int/mediacentre/factsheets/fs103/en (accessed March 12, 2011), 1–5.

59. UNAIDS, *2004 Report on the Global AIDS Epidemic* (New York: United Nations, 2004), 3–4.

60. Patricia Reaney, "AIDS Robs 15 Million Children of Parents—UN Report," Reuters, July 13, 2004.

61. Jason Burke, "AIDS, the New Killer in the Fields," *Observer*, October 17, 2004.

62. Barton Gellman, "AIDS Declared Threat to U.S. Security," *Washington Post*, April 30, 2000.

63. UNAIDS, *2004 Report*, 7.

64. Celia W. Dugger, "Devastated by AIDS, Africa Sees Life Expectancy Plunge," *New York Times*, July 16, 2004.

65. "The State of the World's Children: 2005," UNICEF, December 2004, www.unicef.org/publications/index_24432.html (accessed March 12, 2011).

66. Nicholas Eberstadt, "The Future of AIDS," *Foreign Affairs* 81, no. 6 (November–December 2002): 34–38.

67. Peter W. Singer, "AIDS and International Security," *Survival* 44, no. 1 (spring 2002): 147–48.

68. Singer, "AIDS and International Security," 149.

69. Elizabeth M. Prescott, "SARS: A Warning," *Survival* 45, no. 3 (autumn 2003): 211–12.

70. Laurie Garrett, "The Next Pandemic?" *Foreign Affairs* 8, no. 4 (July–August 2005): 4.

71. Jessica Stern, *The Ultimate Terrorists* (Cambridge, MA: Harvard University Press, 2001), 22–23.

72. "Facts about Injuries," World Health Organization, 2000, www.who.int/violence_injury_prevention/publications/other_injury/en (accessed summer 2004).

73. Gail Russell Chaddock, "War's Legacy and the Human Condition," *Christian Science Monitor*, April 27, 2000.

74. "Background Sheet," Intergovernmental Action Network on Small Arms, www.iansa.org (accessed summer 2004).

75. "Background Sheet."

76. "Small Arms and Light Weapons," United Nations, disarmament.un.org:8080/cab/salw.html (accessed summer 2004).

77. This data comes from "Small Arms and Conflict in West Africa: Testimony of Lisa Misol, Human Rights Watch Researcher, before the Congressional Human Rights Caucus," Human Rights Watch, May 20, 2004.

78. "Small Arms and Conflict in West Africa."

79. George W. Bush, address to the nation, September 7, 2003. Available at www.pbs.org/newshour/bb/white_house/july-dec03/bush_iraq_speech.html (accessed March 12, 2011).

80. "Off Target: The Conduct of the War and Civilian Casualties in Iraq," Human Rights Watch, December 11, 2003, www.hrw.org/reports/2003/usa1203 (accessed March 12, 2011).

81. Ellen Knickmeyer, "Iraq Puts Civilian Toll at 12,000," *Washington Post*, June 3, 2005.

82. Patricia Reaney, "Iraq War Is a Public Health Disaster," Reuters, November 30, 2004.

83. Matt Moore, "Malnutrition Rising among Iraq's Children," Associated Press, November 22, 2004.

84. "Children of Conflict," BBC World Service, www.bbc.co.uk/worldservice/people/features/childrensrights/childrenofconflict (accessed March 12, 2011).

85. UNICEF, "State of the World's Children: 2005."

86. "Children of Conflict."

87. Anup Shah, "Children, Conflicts, and the Military," *Global Issues*, September 27, 2003, www.globalissues.org/geopolitics/children.asp (accessed March 12, 2011).

88. "New Drive against Child Soldiers," *BBC News*, November 17, 2004, http://news.bbc.co.uk/2/hi/africa/4019087.stm (accessed March 12, 2011).

89. "Child Solders: An Overview," Child Soldiers, 2007, www.child-soldiers.org/childsoldiers (accessed March 12, 2011).

90. Charlotte Lindsey for International Committee of the Red Cross, *Women Facing War: ICRC Study on the Impact of Armed Conflict on Women, Executive Summary*, October 17, 2001, www.unhcr.org/refworld/docid/46e943750.html (accessed March 12, 2011), 561–79.

91. "U.N.: Sudan Police Sexually Exploiting Darfur Women," Reuters, August 14, 2004.

92. Martin Parry, "Mounting Concern over Human Cost of War in Afghanistan," AFP, November 16, 2001.

93. "The War through My Eyes: Children's Drawings of Chechnya," Human Rights Watch, www.hrw.org/campaigns/russia/chechnya/children (accessed summer 2004).

94. "At War with the Environment," *San Francisco Chronicle*, April 3, 2003.

95. This summary is from Jennifer Leaning, "Environment and Health: Impact of War," *Canadian Medical Association* 163, no. 9 (October 2000): 1157–61.

96. Leaning, "Environment and Health," 1157–61.

97. Leaning, "Environment and Health," 1157–61.

98. Leaning, "Environment and Health," 1157–61.

99. Klaus Toepfer, "In Defense of the Environment, Putting Poverty to the Sword," United Nations Environment Program, www.unep.org/Documents.Multilingual/Default.asp?ArticleID=3810&DocumentID=288 (accessed March 12, 2011).

100. Trade and Environment Database (TED) at www.american.edu/ted/KUWAIT.HTM (accessed summer 2004).

101. Amanda Onion, "Battle Scars: Considering Possible Environmental Fallout from a New Gulf War," *ABC News*, March 5, 2003.

102. "Air Pollution from Baghdad Fires Poses Risks for Human Health and Environment Says UNEP," UNEP News Release 2003/18, March 3, 2003.

103. Khaled Yacoub Oweis, "Postwar Iraq Paying Heavy Environmental Price," Reuters, June 2, 2005.

104. UN Environment Program, *Bosnia and Herzegovina: A United Nations Environment Program Post-Conflict Environmental Assessment on Depleted Uranium* (New York: United Nations, 2003).

105. UN Environment Program, *Afghanistan: A United Nations Environmental Program Post-Conflict Environmental Assessment* (New York: United Nations, 2003).

106. "UN Warns of Afghan Drug State," *BBC News*, November 18, 2004, http://news.bbc.co.uk/2/hi/south_asia/4022197.stm (accessed March 12, 2011).

Chapter 9: The Environment and Energy Security

1. Richard A. Matthew, introduction to *Contested Grounds: Security and Conflict in the New Environmental Politics*, ed. Daniel Duedney and Richard A. Matthew (Albany, NY: State University of New York Press, 1999), 13.

2. Thomas Homer-Dixon, "Global Environmental Change and International Security," in *Building a New Global Order*, ed. David Dewitt et al. (Oxford: Oxford University Press, 1994), 185–228.

3. Homer-Dixon, "Global Environmental Change," 191.

4. Homer-Dixon, "Global Environmental Change," 214.

5. Richard Ullman, "Redefining Security," *International Security* 8, no. 1 (1983): 129–53.

6. Homer-Dixon, "Global Environmental Change," 216.

7. Thomas Homer-Dixon and Jessica Blitt, eds., *Ecoviolence: Links among Environment, Population, and Security* (Lanham, MD: Rowman & Littlefield, 1998), 6.

8. Homer-Dixon and Blitt, *Ecoviolence*, 223–28.

9. Peter H. Gleick, "Water and Conflict: Fresh Water Resources and International Security," *International Security* 18, no. 1 (summer 1993): 79–112.

10. Gleick, "Water and Conflict," 87.

11. Gleick, "Water and Conflict," 95.

12. Gleick, "Water and Conflict," 104.

13. Miriam R. Lowi, "Bridging the Divide: Transboundary Resource Disputes and the Case of West Bank Water," *International Security* 18, no. 1 (summer 1993): 113–15.

14. Lowi, "Bridging the Divide," 113–15.

15. Lowi, "Bridging the Divide," 113–38.

16. Robert C. North, "Toward a Framework for the Analysis of Scarcity and Conflict," *International Studies Quarterly* 21 (December 1977): 569–91.

17. Michel Frederick, "A Realist's Conceptual Definition of Environmental Security," in *Contested Grounds: Security and Conflict in the New Environmental Politics*, ed. Daniel Duedney and Richard A. Matthew (Albany, NY: State University of New York Press, 1999), 100.

18. Frederick, "A Realist's Conceptual Definition," 101–4.

19. Muir Papers, University of the Pacific, Stockton, California; also see Stephen R. Fox, *The American Conservation Movement: John Muir and His Legacy* (Madison: University of Wisconsin Press, 1986).

20. "Address on the Sierra Forest Reservation," *The Sierra Club Bulletin* 7 (1896): 276.

21. Rachel Carson, *Silent Spring* (Boston: Houghton Mifflin, 1962).

22. Oran R. Young, *International Governance* (Ithaca, NY: Cornell University Press, 1994), 19–26.

23. Marc Levy, "Is the Environment a National Security Issue?" *International Security* 20, no. 2 (1995): 35–62.

24. Julian Simon, *The Ultimate Resource* (Princeton, NJ: Princeton University Press, 1987).

25. Simon Dalby, *Environmental Security* (Minneapolis: University of Minnesota Press, 2002).

26. Dalby, *Environmental Security*, 157.

27. Dalby, *Environmental Security*, 167.

28. Dalby, *Environmental Security*, 167.

29. Dalby, *Environmental Security*, 172.

30. John Barnett, *The Meaning of Environmental Security* (London: Zed Books, 2001), 2–3.

31. Barnett, *Meaning of Environmental Security*, 14.

32. Barnett, *Meaning of Environmental Security*, 22.

33. Barnett, *Meaning of Environmental Security*, 108.

34. Barnett, *Meaning of Environmental Security*, 122.

35. Ronnie Lipschutz, *Global Civil Society and Global Environmental Governance: The Politics of Nature from Place to Planet* (Albany, NY: State University of New York Press, 1996).

36. Lipschutz, *Global Civil Society*, 51.

37. President Jimmy Carter, "Address to the Nation on Energy," April 18, 1977, http://millercenter.org/scripps/archive/speeches/detail/3398 (accessed March 12, 2011).

38. Donald J. Goldstein, "Energy As a Security Issue," in *Energy As a Security Issue*, ed. Donald J. Goldstein (Washington, DC: National Defense University Press, 1981), 7.

39. Goldstein, "Energy As a Security Issue," 16.

40. Goldstein, "Energy As a Security Issue," 19.

41. Howard Bucknell III, *Energy and the National Defense* (Lexington: University of Kentucky Press, 1981), 103.

42. Bucknell, *Energy and the National Defense*, 126.

43. Michael Klare, *Resource Wars* (New York: Metropolitan Books, 2001), 6.

44. Klare, *Resource Wars*, 7.

45. Klare, *Resource Wars*, 21–22.

46. Klare, *Resource Wars*, 69.

47. See "Energy Security: Oil Security Resources," Energy Information Administration, www.eia.doe.gov/emeu/security/Oil/index.html (accessed March 12, 2011).

48. See "Energy Security: Introduction," Energy Information Administration, www.eia.doe.gov/emeu/security/Oil/index.html (accessed March 12, 2011).

49. Jose Goldemberg, "Energy and Sustainable Development," in *Worlds Apart: Globalization and the Environment*, ed. James Gustave Speth (Washington, DC: Island Press, 2003), 57–58.

50. Martha Harris, "Energy and Security," in *Grave New World: Security Challenges in the 21st Century*, ed. Michael E. Brown (Washington, DC: Georgetown University Press, 2003), 167–68.

51. "Booming China's Acid Rain 'Out of Control,'" Reuters, November 30, 2004.

52. Jim Yardley, "China's Next Big Boom Could Be the Foul Air," *New York Times*, October 30, 2005, www.nytimes.com/2005/10/30/weekinreview/30yardley.html (accessed March 12, 2011).

53. "China's Dependence on Coal for Energy Causing Pollution at Home and Abroad," AFP, July 28, 2004.

54. Louisa Lim, "China Tackles Energy Shortages," *BBC News*, July 29, 2004, http://news.bbc.co.uk/2/hi/asia-pacific/3937113.stm (accessed March 12, 2011).

55. "Global Warming," Union of Concerned Scientists, www.ucsusa.org/global_warming (accessed March 12, 2011).

56. "Global Warming."

57. "Global Warming."

58. Ed Cropley, "Melting Glaciers Threaten World Water Supply," Reuters, November 17, 2004.

59. Donald Kennedy, comments at "Environmental Change and Conflict Liability" seminar held at Stanford University, Center for International Security and Cooperation, Stanford, California, May 2002.

60. Tim Radford, "Flood Risk to 2bn by 2050, Says Study," *Guardian*, June 14, 2004, www.guardian.co.uk/environment/2004/jun/14/environment.weather (accessed March 12, 2011).

61. Tim Radford, "Destructive Power of 100,000 A-bombs," *Guardian*, August 16, 2004, www.guardian.co.uk/environment/2004/aug/16/usnews.naturaldisasters (accessed March 12, 2011).

62. Anna Mudeva, "European Winters Could Disappear by 2080," Reuters, August 18, 2004.

63. As summarized by David Stipp, "Climate Change a National Security Threat," *Fortune*, January 26, 2004. The original study is at www.gbn.com (accessed December 2005).

64. Stipp, "Climate Change a National Security Threat."

65. Stipp, "Climate Change a National Security Threat."

66. Stipp, "Climate Change a National Security Threat."

67. The original reporting of this study was by Stipp, "Climate Change a National Security Threat."

68. "UN-Backed Congress Calls for New Global Political Commitment to Save Forests," UN News Center, September 29, 2003, www.un.org/apps/news/stor.asp?NewsID=8390&Cr=forest&Cr1= (accessed March 12, 2011).

69. "Deforestation: The Global Assault Continues," World Resources Institute, www.wri.org/publication/content/8368 (accessed March 12, 2011).

70. Col. W. Chris King, *Understanding International Environmental Security: A Strategic Military Perspective* (Atlanta, GA: Army Environmental Policy Institute, 2000), 51–52.

71. Amy Bracken, "Deforestation Exacerbates Haiti Floods," Associated Press, September 23, 2004.

72. King, *Understanding International Environmental Security*.

73. "Backgrounder," International Food Policy Research Institute, www.ifpri.org (accessed fall 2004).

74. Anthony Boadle, "U.N. Seeks Donors to Fight Loss of Fertile Soil," Reuters, August 27, 2003.

75. "Smithsonian Researchers Show Amazonian Deforestation Accelerating," *ScienceDaily*, January 15, 2002, www.sciencedaily.com/releases/2002/01/020115075118.htm (accessed March 12, 2011).

76. Andrew Downie, "Amazon Destruction Rising Fast," *Christian Science Monitor*, April 22, 2004.

77. Catherine Caufield, *In the Rainforest* (Chicago: University of Chicago Press, 1984).

78. Lisa J. Adams, "Mexico in Danger of Losing Forests," Associated Press, December 5, 2001.

79. Gretchen Peters, "No Quick Solution to Deforestation in Lush Chiapas," *Christian Science Monitor*, January 14, 2002.

80. Gerald Urquhart et al., "Tropical Deforestation," NASA Earth Observatory, www.earthobservatory.nasa.gov (accessed fall 2004).

81. Brad Glosserman, "ASIA: Environmental Security Risks," *Japan Times*, November 26, 2002.

82. Yvonne Agyei, "Deforestation in Sub-Saharan Africa," *African Technology Forum* 8, no. 1 (1998).

83. UN Office for the Coordination of Humanitarian Affairs, "Mali: Government Imposes Six-Month Ban on Tree Felling," IRIN, August 11, 2004, www.irinnews.org/report.aspx?reportid=50997 (accessed March 12, 2011).

84. UN Office for the Coordination of Humanitarian Affairs, "Mali: Government Imposes Six-Month Ban."

85. UN Office for the Coordination of Humanitarian Affairs, "Kenya: Desertification Threatening Millions, Government Warns," IRIN, July 2, 2002, www.reliefweb.int/rw/rwb.nsf/db900SID/ACOS-64BVKJ?OpenDocument (accessed March 12, 2011).

86. "Studies Suggest Extinctions Continue Long after Deforestation," CNN, October 12, 1999, http://articles.cnn.com/1999-10-12/nature/9910_12_extinction.enn_1_bird-species-primate-species-extinction?_s=PM:NATURE (accessed March 12, 2011).

87. Alex Kirby, "Climate Risk 'to Million Species,'" *BBC News*, January 7, 2004, http://news.bbc.co.uk/2/hi/science/nature/3375447.stm (accessed March 12, 2011).

88. UNICEF, August 2004, www.unicef.org (accessed fall 2004).

89. Alex Kirby, "Why World's Taps Are Running Dry," *BBC News*, http://news.bbc.co.uk/2/hi/science/nature/2943946.stm (accessed March 12, 2011).

90. Peter Gleick, "Water Conflict Chronology," Pacific Institute, August 2003, www.worldwater.org/conflict (accessed March 12, 2011).

91. "Facts and Figures," World Water Assessment Program, www.unesco.org/water/wwap/facts_figures (accessed March 12, 2011).

92. "State of the World's Children: 2005," UNICEF, www.unicef.org/sowc05/english/index.html (accessed March 12, 2011).

93. "Facts and Figures."

94. "Facts and Figures."

95. "Facts and Figures."

96. "World Water Crisis," *BBC News*, http://news.bbc.co.uk/hi/english/static/in_depth/world/2000/world_water_crisis/default.stm (accessed March 12, 2011).

97. "Water and Human Security," *AVISO* 3 (June 1999): 2.

98. International Institute for Strategic Studies, *Strategic Survey 2003–2004: An Evaluation and Forecast of World Affairs* (Oxford: Oxford University Press, 2004), 127.

99. "Facts and Figures."

100. Quoted in Patrick McLoughlin, "Scientists Say Risk of Water Wars Rising," Reuters, August 20, 2004.

101. Green Cross International, "National Sovereignty and International Watercourses," UNESCO WebWorld, March 2000, http://webworld.unesco.org/water/wwap/pccp/cd/pdf/background_documents/national_sovereignty%20_international_water courses_2000.pdf (accessed March 12, 2011).

102. Energy Information Administration (EIA), *Annual Energy Outlook 2004*, EIA, January 2004, www.eia.doe.gov/oiaf/archive/aeo04/pdf/0383%282004%29.pdf (accessed March 12, 2011).

103. International Energy Agency (IEA), *World Energy Outlook 2002*, IEA, November 2002, www.iea.org/textbase/nppdf/free/2000/weo2002.pdf (accessed March 12, 2011).

104. IEA, *World Energy Outlook 2002*.

105. IEA, *World Energy Outlook 2002*.

106. I. Iain McCreary et al., *China's Energy: A Forecast to 2015* (Los Alamos, NM: U.S. Department of Energy, Office of Energy Intelligence, 1999).

107. International Atomic Energy Agency (IAEA), *Radiation, People, and the Environment*, IAEA, February 2004, www.iaea.org/Publications/Booklets/RadPeopleEnv/index.html (accessed March 12, 2011).

108. IAEA, *Radiation, People, and the Environment*.

109. "Analysis: The Soviet Nuclear Legacy," *BBC News*, October 20, 1998, http://news.bbc.co.uk/2/hi/europe/197295.stm.

110. "Chernobyl's Grim Legacy," *BBC News*, April 26, 2000, http://news.bbc.co.uk/2/hi/europe/727426.stm (accessed March 12, 2011).

111. "Millions of Chernobyl Victims Still Suffering," *BBC News*, February 7, 2002, http://news.bbc.co.uk/2/hi/europe/1806181.stm (accessed March 12, 2011).

112. "Chernobyl's Cancer World Record," *BBC News*, http://news.bbc.co.uk/2/hi/health/1615299.stm (accessed March 12, 2011).

113. "Chernobyl 'Not So Deadly,'" *BBC News*, June 13, 2000, http://news.bbc.co.uk/2/hi/europe/789822.stm (accessed March 12, 2011).

114. "Chernobyl 'Not So Deadly.'"

115. "Millions of Chernobyl Victims Still Suffering."

116. C. J. Chivers, "Moscow's Nuclear Past Is Breeding Perils Today," *New York Times*, August 10, 2004.

117. James L. Ford, "Radiological Dispersal Devices: Assessing the Transnational Threat," *Strategic Forum* 136 (March 1998): 1–5.

118. John Soloman, "Radioactive Materials Missing in U.S.," Associated Press, November 11, 2003.

Chapter 10: Meeting the Challenges of Power and Peace

1. Commission for Africa, "Our Common Interest: Report of the Commission for Africa," allAfrica.com, March 2005, http://allafrica.com/sustainable/resources/view/00010595.pdf (accessed March 12, 2011).

2. Global Education Campaign, "The State of the World's Children: 2005," press release, www.unicef.org (accessed spring 2005).

3. William C. Symonds, "America's Failure in Science Education," Bloomberg Businessweek, March 16, 2004, www.businessweek.com/technology/content/mar2004/tc20040316_0601_tc166.htm (accessed March 12, 2011).

4. Fareed Zakaria, "The Future of American Power: How America Can Survive the Rise of the Rest," *Foreign Affairs*, 87, no. 3 (May–June 2008): 30–32.

5. Claude Berrebi, "Evidence about the Link between Education, Poverty and Terrorism among Palestinians," *Peace Economics, Peace Science and Public Policy* 13, no. 1 (2007).

6. Diana Coulter, "India's Troubling Truants: Teachers," *Christian Science Monitor*, December 20, 2004.

7. Joint Learning Institute, *Human Resources for Health: Overcoming the Crisis* (Cambridge, MA: Harvard University, 2004). Available at www.healthgap.org/camp/hcw_docs/JLi_Human_Resources_for_Health.pdf (accessed March 12, 2011).

8. "Global Campaign Will Put Every Child in School," press release, Global Campaign for Education, www.campaignforeducation.org (accessed fall 2004).

9. Milton Greenberg, "The GI Bill of Rights" April 3, 2008, www.america.gov/st/educ-english/2008/April/20080423213340eaifas0.8454951.html (accessed in fall 2010).

10. "Memorandum of Conversation Pres-Rabi-Berkner et al.," October 16, 1957, www.eisenhower.archives.gov/dl/Sputnik/Sputnikocuments.html (accessed fall 2010).

11. "Memorandum of Conversation Pres-Rabi-Berkner"; and Presidential Address, November 13, 1957, www.eisenhower.archives.gov/dl/Sputnik/Sputnikdocuments.html (accessed fall 2010).

12. "History of the NSEP," NSEP, http://nsep.gov/about/history (accessed March 12, 2011).

13. U.S. Commission on National Security/21st Century, "Roadmap for National Security: Imperative for Change" (draft final report), Federation of American Scientists, January 31, 2001, www.fas.org/irp/threat/nssg.pdf (accessed March 12, 2011).

14. Samuel G. Freedman, "On Education: After Sputnik It Was Russian; After 9/11 Should It Be Arabic?" *New York Times*, June 16, 2004.

15. Linda S. Bishai, "Sudanese Universities As Sites of Social Transformation," Special Report 203, U.S. Institute of Peace, February 2008, www.usip.org/publications/sudanese-universities-sites-social-transformation (accessed March 12, 2011), 8.

16. Bishai, "Sudanese Universities," 8.

17. David Rohde, "Army Enlists Anthropology in War Zones," *New York Times*, October 5, 2007.

18. Rye Barcott, "Marine Experiences and Anthropological Reflections," *Survival* 50, no. 3 (June–July 2008): 139.

19. "Human Terrain System Overview," HTS, http://humanterrainsystem.army.mil/overview.html (accessed fall 2010).

20. See http://humanterrainsystem.army.mil/impacts.html (accessed fall 2010).

21. Patricia Cohen, "Pentagon to Consult Academics on Security," *New York Times*, June 18, 2008.

22. Roberto J. Gonzalez, "Anthropology and the White Man's Burden," *Survival* 50, no. 3 (June–July 2008): 149.

23. Imad Harb, "Higher Education and the Future of Iraq," Special Report 195, U.S. Institute of Peace, January 2008, www.usip.org/publications/higher-education -and-future-iraq (accessed March 12, 2011), 2–5.

24. Harb, "Higher Education," 5.

25. Harb, "Higher Education," 7.

26. "Background Note: Afghanistan," U.S. Department of State, www.state.gov/r/ pa/ei/bgn/5380.html (accessed spring 2008).

28. "Lessons in Terror: Attacks on Education in Afghanistan," *Human Rights Watch* 18, no. 6C (July 2006).

29. Afghan Islamic Press Agency, March 25, 2006.

30. Nikola Krastev, "Afghanistan: Karzai Highlights Agenda Ahead of UN Address," *Radio Free Europe*, September 19, 2006, www.rferl.org/content/article/1071452 .html (accessed March 12, 2011).

31. Audrey Kurth Cronin, *How Terrorism Ends* (Princeton, NJ: Princeton University Press, 2009).

Index

About the Author

Sean Kay is professor of politics and government at Ohio Wesleyan University, where he is chair of the international studies program. He specializes in international security, globalization, international organization, and American foreign policy. Kay is a Mershon Associate at the Mershon Center for International Security Studies at Ohio State University and also a nonresident fellow in foreign and defense policy at the Eisenhower Institute in Washington, DC. He was previously a visiting assistant professor in the government department at Dartmouth College.

Kay received his PhD in international relations from the University of Massachusetts, Amherst. Before joining academe, he was a visiting research fellow at the U.S. Department of Defense's Institute for National Strategic Studies, where he also served as an adviser to the U.S. Department of State on NATO enlargement. He worked previously for the NATO Parliamentary Assembly in Brussels, Belgium.

Kay lectures frequently in the United States and abroad on global security trends and their strategic implications. He has authored numerous articles, book chapters, and opinion pieces in major newspapers on international security issues. His previous books include *NATO and the Future of European Security*, *Celtic Revival?: The Rise, Fall, and Renewal of Global Ireland*, and the coedited volumes *NATO after Fifty Years* and *Limiting Institutions?: The Challenge of Eurasian Security Governance.*